Justice And Mercy Have Met

Justice and Mercy Have Met

*Pope Francis and the Reform
of the Marriage Nullity Process*

KURT MARTENS, EDITOR

THE CATHOLIC UNIVERSITY OF AMERICA PRESS
WASHINGTON, DC

Copyright © 2017
The Catholic University of America Press
All rights reserved

The paper used in this publication meets the minimum requirements of American National Standards for Information Science—Permanence of Paper for Printed Library materials, ANSI Z39.48-1984.
∞

Cataloging-in-Publication Data available from the Library of Congress

ISBN 978-0-8132-2967-6

Contents

Foreword
ROBERT J. KASLYN, SJ   vii

Introduction
KURT MARTENS   1

A First Approach to the Reform of the Process
for the Declaration of Nullity of Marriage
FRANS DANEELS, O. PRAEM.   5

An Analysis of Pope Francis' 2015
Reform of the General Legislation Governing
Causes of Nullity of Marriage
WILLIAM L. DANIEL   27

Reflections on the Role of the Diocesan
Bishop Envisioned by *Mitis Iudex Dominus Iesus*
BERNARD A. HEBDA   65

Mitis Iudex Canons 1671–1682, 1688–1691: A Commentary
JOHN P. BEAL   87

The Abbreviated Matrimonial Process before
the Bishop in Cases of "Manifest Nullity" of Marriage
WILLIAM L. DANIEL   159

The Ordinary Process According to *Mitis Iudex*:
Challenges to Our "Comfort Zone"
JOHN P. BEAL   233

The Notion of Canonical Jurisprudence and its
Application to the Tribunal of the Roman Rota
and Causes of Nullity of Marriage
WILLIAM L. DANIEL   271

Applying Article 14 of *Mitis Iudex Dominus Iesus*
to the *Processus Brevior* in Light of the Church's Constant
and Common Jurisprudence on Nullity of Consent
RONNY E. JENKINS   305

Implementation of *Mitis Iudex Dominus Iesus*
in the Diocese of Springfield in Illinois
THOMAS JOHN PAPROCKI 341

Questions Regarding the Motu Proprio *Mitis Iudex Dominus Iesus*
ROCH PAGÉ 355

Letters Clarifying Some Unclear Points of the Motu Proprio
Mitis Iudex Dominus Iesus
PONTIFICAL COUNCIL FOR LEGISLATIVE TEXTS 367

ROBERT J. KASLYN, SJ*

Foreword

Pope Francis reformed the law in reference to the nullity of marriage for the Latin Church through his motu proprio *Mitis Iudex Dominus Iesus* and the law for the Eastern Churches through his motu proprio *Mitis et Misericors Iesus*; both texts were issued on August 15, 2015 and became effective December 8 of the same year. Such important reform of procedural law requires an understanding not only of the *mens legislatoris* in promulgating the new law but also practical guidance to the interpretation and application by diocesan tribunals. This text, incorporating articles that had first appeared in *The Jurist*, offers an important contribution to understanding the theory and the praxis underlying *Mitis Iudex Dominus Iesus* and thereby assisting in its implementation.

This collection of articles interprets the new procedural law from the perspective of canon 17 of the *Codex Iuris Canonici*. This canon specifies the means of legal interpretation: the proper meaning of words in their text and context, with recourse, if necessary, to parallel places, to the purpose and circumstances of the law, and to the *mens legislatoris*. Through this legal interpretation, the new procedural law may more readily be understood and implemented by diocesan tribunals.

For Pope Francis, the teleology underlying *Mitis Iudex Dominus Iesus* is of paramount importance for the law's application. In his 2015 address to the Roman Rota, Pope Francis stated, "I would therefore like to exhort you all to grow in and cultivate passion for the task of your ministry, which

---

* Dean and Associate Professor, School of Canon Law, The Catholic University of America, Washington, DC.

is to tend to the unity of jurisprudence in the Church. There is so much pastoral work for the good of so many couples, so many children, who are all too often victims in these matters! Here, too, there is a need for pastoral conversion of the ecclesiastical structures in order to offer the *opus iustitiae* to all those who turn to the Church to shed light on their respective conjugal situations."

Opus iustitiae is demonstrated by this volume. For many contributors, the articles arose from their own study of the new law and its remote and proximate origins as well as through specific advice to individuals and to tribunals on the theology, interpretation and application of that law. Other contributors offer insights from their own experience in implementing the law. This combination of theory and praxis—both essential to the interpretation of law—reflects the emphasis of the School of Canon Law and of its Faculty on service to the Church in the ministry of justice. This volume intends to interpret and elucidate the law so that Pope Francis' reform will become effective in the Church and thus justice may be served.

In conclusion, may this publication fulfill the intent of Pope Francis in his reform: "*Salutis ergo animarum studium, quae—hodie sicut heri—institutionum, legum, iuris supremus finis manet.*"

KURT MARTENS*

Introduction

With the promulgation of the motu proprio *Mitis iudex Dominus Iesus* for the Latin Church and the motu proprio *Mitis et misericors Iesus* for the Eastern Catholic Churches, Pope Francis has changed and sought to simplify the procedure for the declaration of nullity of marriages. The new legislation came into effect on December 8, 2015. For an academic journal such as *The Jurist* it is extremely important to ensure that commentary on such a significant development is published in due time, in order to be of assistance to the countless practitioners who must apply the new law. Legislative initiatives, it is fair to say, take little account of academic planning and publication plans, but they challenge them by inviting us to commission and compile new commentaries designed to assist with the implementation and the application of the new law. That is exactly what happened with the second issue of *The Jurist* for 2015 and the first issue of *The Jurist* for 2016.

Since not everyone has ready access to *The Jurist*, and to make these important contributions available to the largest possible readership, it was decided to produce a separate volume. As the editor of *The Jurist*, also of this separate volume, I am immensely grateful to Dr. Trevor Lipscombe, director of *The Catholic University of America Press*, for making this possible. A word of thanks goes to the Reverend Robert J. Kaslyn, SJ, Dean of the School of Canon Law, for his willingness to write a short Foreword to this volume.

* Ordinary Professor, School of Canon Law, The Catholic University of America, Washington, DC.

The contributions presented in this volume are, on the one hand, the contributions written specifically for *The Jurist*, and, on the other hand, contributions that resulted from the workshop, hosted on March 11 and 12, 2016, by the School of Canon Law of The Catholic University of America here in Washington, DC. The workshop, the revival of the traditional spring canonical workshop, was entitled *"Mitis Iudex*. A Nuts and Bolts Approach." The well-attended workshop was co-sponsored by the Committee on Canonical Affairs and Church Governance of the United States Conference of Catholic Bishops. I wholeheartedly thank all the contributors to the workshop for their enormous effort to get their contributions ready for publication in *The Jurist*. Likewise, my gratitude also goes to the other authors who prepared a study on *Mitis Iudex*. All these contributions are now collected in this volume.

This book begins with an article by His Excellency, Most Reverend Frans Daneels, O.Praem., now the Emeritus-Secretary of the Supreme Tribunal of the Apostolic Signatura. Archbishop Daneels offers some initial thoughts on the revised legislation and sets the tone for the rest of the book. In a second contribution, William L. Daniel looks at the general principles guiding the reform of Pope Francis, and offers a key to understanding the new legislation in a broader context.

After these two introductory pieces, His Excellency, Most Reverend Bernard A. Hebda, Archbishop of Saint Paul and Minneapolis, focuses on the role of the diocesan bishop in the revised procedures, and offers some personal reflections drawn from his own extensive experience. This contribution, like the two preceding ones, places the renewed legislation in the context of the papacy of Pope Francis, and shows how this new legislation fits within the broader themes of this pontificate.

The first contribution of John P. Beal is set up as a traditional commentary on the ordinary process, commenting on the revised legislation canon by canon, and offering valuable insights and guidance. William L. Daniel guides us through the brand new *processus brevior* with valuable assistance on how to deal with and apply this new process, at the same time pointing out certain difficulties and warning for potential dangers. Especially for this publication, William L. Daniel has added examples of decisions in the *processus brevior*. In a further contribution, John P. Beal focuses again on the ordinary process, but this time, the contribution is written not as a commentary on the successive canons, but as an overview of the various parts of the process, focusing on, first, the static part, and, second, the dynamic part of the ordinary process.

Jurisprudence is an important consideration in dealing with the revised procedural law. Therefore, William L. Daniel gives a detailed analysis of the notion of canonical jurisprudence and its application to the Tribunal of the Roman Rota and causes of nullity of marriages, while Ronny E. Jenkins focuses in his contribution on article 14 of the procedural norms and some jurisprudential issues.

Two shorter pieces complete our treatment of the new legislation: His Excellency, Most Reverend Thomas John Paprocki, Bishop of Springfield in Illinois, reflects on his own implementation of the revised legislation in his diocese and how he, as a diocesan bishop, will be involved in the procedures, while Roch Pagé offers some general reflections on the reform of the canonical matrimonial process and its consequences.

With the promulgation of the motu proprio *Mitis iudex Dominus Iesus* and the motu proprio *Mitis et misericors Iesus*, questions arose about the interpretation of certain changes and novelties. The Pontifical Council for Legislative Texts has now issued a number of letters clarifying a number of unclear points in the new legislation. The publication of these letters in this volume will provide valuable assistance to canon lawyers in applying the new legislation. I sincerely thank His Eminence, Francesco Cardinal Coccopalmerio, President of the Pontifical Council for Legislative Texts, His Excellency, Most Reverend Juan Ignacio Arrieta Ochoa de Chinchetru, Bishop-Secretary, and Monsignor Markus Graulich, S.D.B., Undersecretary, for approving the translation of the letters that were not originally in English and for allowing the publication of all the letters in *The Jurist* and subsequently in this volume.

FRANS DANEELS, O.PRAEM.*

A First Approach to the Reform of the Process for the Declaration of Nullity of Marriage**

1. Introduction

On August 15, 2015 Pope Francis put his signature to new norms reforming the process for the declaration of the nullity of a marriage. The motu proprio *Mitis Iudex Dominus Iesus* for the Latin Church and the distinct motu proprio for the Oriental Catholic Churches were made public on 8 September 2015 and came into force on December 8, 2015. The following exposition concerns only the motu proprio for the Latin Church, but the one for the Oriental Churches is very similar to it.

After a short preliminary part that concerns especially the state and activity of ecclesiastical tribunals in the world, there follows a brief presentation of the motu proprio, and in the third part I will consider more closely the intention behind the reform and some of its key points, comparing them with the Final Report of the Extraordinary General Assembly of the Synod of Bishops of 2014. It should be clear, however, that it is too early for an in-depth study of the matter. Hence I consider my exposition only a first approach.

---

* Archbishop-Secretary of the Supreme Tribunal of the Apostolic Signatura, Vatican City.
** Revised text of a lecture given on February 26, 2016 at the Katholieke Universiteit Leuven in Leuven.

2. Some Preliminary Considerations.

2.1. According to the last published *Statistical Yearbook of the Church* in 2013 a total of 41,721 cases of marriage nullity were brought to conclusion in the first instance by the ordinary process: 33,438 received an affirmative decision and 3,460 received a negative sentence, while the rest ended through renunciation or abatement. In second instance, 21,007 decrees confirming the affirmative decision of the first instance were issued, in addition to 7,471 affirmative and 1,106 negative sentences. Of the 33,438 affirmative sentences in the first instance, 16,550 were issued in North America, 8,483 in Europe, 3,210 in South America, 2,906 in Asia, 1,469 in Central America (including Mexico and the Antilles), 460 in Africa, and 360 in Oceania.

In comparison with 1993, there was a significant growth in the number of affirmative sentences in Asia (from 787 to 2,906) and South America (from 1,033 to 3,210), while even the relatively low number of sentences in Africa more than doubled (from 213 to 460). There was almost a doubling in Central America (from 762 to 1,469) and some growth in Europe (from 6,372 to 8,483). By contrast, there was an enormous reduction in North America (from 40,664 to 16,550) and Oceania (from 864 to 360). Such a reduction also occurred in Belgium (from 204 to 53) and in Great Britain (from 1,141 to 437), while in Italy there was a significant growth (from 1,172 to 2,157), without doubt the result of a serious effort to make ecclesiastical tribunals more accessible, also with respect to the cost of the process and obtaining canonical advice.[1]

2.2. The interpretation of the statistical data is not all that easy. However, based on these and more detailed data, and also through almost thirty years of experience in monitoring the status and activity of the tribunals throughout the entire Catholic Church, I can affirm the following:

— The total number of cases of nullity of marriage throughout the world indicates that this is not an insignificant phenomenon, nor a purely academic one, but rather a reality which must not be underestimated.
— In some parts of the world the faithful have very limited access, and often no access at all, to a process for adjudicating the nullity of their

---

1. Cf. *Statistical Yearbook of the Church 1993* (Vatican City: Libreria Editrice Vaticana, 1995) 403–405; *Statistical Yearbook of the Church 2013* (Vatican City: Libreria Editrice Vaticana, 2015) 438 and 443.

marriage. As an aside, a parish priest in South America recently told me that he often advises the faithful to present their case to the interdiocesan tribunal, but that they almost never do so, due to the distance of the tribunal and the cost of the process.

— In countries where ecclesiastical tribunals are functioning and accessible, there is a great difference in the number of cases of marriage nullity and of affirmative sentences. Some causes of this phenomenon may be, for instance, the stability or reduction of the number of canonical marriages, the closeness to or growing distance from Church structures, or the presence or absence of attention to the possibility of presenting a case to the tribunal as part of the pastoral outreach for so-called broken marriages.

2.3. The quality of the administration of justice is also very different from region to region, and sometimes even from tribunal to tribunal. There remain a number of tribunals of low quality, which, due to poor understanding and a lack of improvement in their praxis, continue with a rather superficial jurisprudence. Such tribunals seem to consider the process for the declaration of nullity of a marriage an easy way to give a new chance to those in broken marriages, as if the mere fact of a broken marriage were evidence of its invalidity. Surely, for a good number of broken marriages a serious investigation into whether they are invalid is appropriate, but I do not think that this is the case for the large majority of such marriages, unless we no longer take the marriage bond seriously. On the other hand, I strongly believe that many more marriages could rightly be declared invalid, if the faithful in every place had the actual possibility of availing themselves of the service of an ecclesiastical tribunal.

3. Brief Presentation of the Motu Proprio *Mitis Iudex Dominus Iesus*

3.1. Most likely with an eye to the *Instrumentum Laboris* for the Extraordinary General Assembly of the Synod of Bishops of 2014 (artt. 98–102), Pope Francis, on August 27, 2014,[2] constituted a Special Commission for studying the reform of the canonical marriage process. The President of the Commission was Monsignor Pio Vito Pinto, Dean of the Roman

---

2. Cf. "Per la riforma del processo matrimoniale canonico," *L'Osservatore Romano*, September 21, 2014, 1.

Rota. In May 2015 this Commission presented the result of its work. Pope Francis then consulted four other experts in the matter and on August 15, 2015 signed the reform of the process for the declaration of the nullity of marriage. In this way, even before the Ordinary General Assembly of the Synod of Bishops of 2015, he responded to the "need to make the procedure in cases of nullity more accessible and less time-consuming, and, if possible, at no expense," as expressed in its *Instrumentum laboris*, n. 114, which in fact took up n. 47 of the 2014 Final Report.[3] The reform is clearly an exercise of the personal and supreme jurisdiction of the Roman Pontiff, even if he sees it as a service rendered to his brother bishops in a spirit of collegiality.

3.2. In the introduction of the motu proprio, Pope Francis stresses the need to protect the unity of faith and discipline regarding marriage and his intention of not introducing provisions that favor nullity, but rather those that favor the speediness of the process, along with an appropriate simplicity. In fact, charity and mercy require the Church, as a mother, to make herself closer to her children who consider themselves separated. Pope Francis clearly has in mind that a declaration of marriage nullity can offer a solution to many more cases than those actually examined by Church tribunals.

3.3. The Supreme Pontiff mentions then "a few fundamental criteria . . . that have guided the work of reform." In my opinion, several of these fundamental criteria are not so much guidelines for the work of reform as they are its key points. Moreover, some of the fundamental criteria did not influence the new body of canons, but instead appear to be indications for the application of the new canons. The fundamental criteria can be summarized as follows: the abolition of the need of a double conforming sentence in favor of the nullity of marriage; the faculty of the bishop-moderator of a tribunal to commit cases to a single judge (with two assessors, insofar as possible); the bishop himself as judge, especially in the briefer process, which now, alongside the ordinary process and the documentary process, has been introduced as a third distinct form of matrimonial process; the emphasis on appealing to the metropolitan

---

3. Nn. 114 and 116 of the *Instrumentum laboris* quote nn. 47–48 of the Final Report of the Extraordinary Synod, adding in nn. 115 and 117 some comments.

see as the ordinary appellate tribunal; the proper task of conferences of bishops in providing help for implementing the reform of the matrimonial process—which also concerns expenses, seeing to it that, insofar as possible, cases are handled free of charge; the possibility, in any event, of an appeal to the Holy See; the issuing of a separate motu proprio for the Oriental Churches.

3.4. The motu proprio presents then a new redaction of canons 1671–1691 of the 1983 Code of Canon Law concerning the special process for the declaration of marriage nullity. This new legislation entered into force on December 8, 2015. Several canons, however, have not been changed, except perhaps in their numbering or in their becoming a paragraph within a canon.[4] The most important changes seem to be the following:

— The tribunal of the quasi-domicile of the petitioner is now also competent to hear the case, while the restrictions for the tribunal of the domicile of the petitioner or that of most of the proofs are abolished (can. 1672). Things now being so, it will be necessary to determine carefully whether an asserted quasi-domicile is in fact truly established and to take care to protect the respondent's right of defense. I remember well the reaction from Latin America years ago against a similar norm then in use in the United States of America.[5]
— A college of judges can be composed of a presiding clerical judge and now two lay judges (can. 1673 §3); the bishop-moderator of a tribunal of first instance can entrust cases to a single clerical judge, if possible with two assessors (can. 1673 §4). In both cases a prior intervention of the conference of bishops is no longer required.
— The judicial vicar, admitting the *libellus*, decides whether the case is to be treated with the ordinary process or with the briefer process (can. 1678 §§12).
— The norm concerning the possibility that a judicial confession and the declarations of the parties might constitute full proof (can. 1678 §1) is not only presented in a more positive way, but also omits the

---

4. Cf. Philippe Toxé, "La réforme des procès en nullité de mariage en Droit canonique latin," *Nova et vetera* 15 (2015) 377–396, see 378.

5. See, v.g., Zenon Grocholewski, *Documenta recentiora circa rem matrimonialem et processualem* (Rome: s.n., 1980) 2: 123–125 for a reply of the Apostolic Signatura of March 3, 1978 to a request of the "Asociación Mexicana de Canonistas" in this matter.

introductory clause of the former can. 1679: "Unless there are full proofs from elsewhere." This way of proving the nullity of a marriage is thus no longer only a subsidiary one, but may also be used when full proof could be obtained otherwise, notwithstanding, of course, the obligation to reach moral certainty for a declaration of nullity.

— The sentence that first declared the nullity of the marriage, once the time limits for appeal have lapsed, becomes executive (can. 1679).
— If the appeal after an ordinary process clearly appears merely dilatory, the collegial appeal tribunal is to confirm the sentence by decree (can. 1680).
— A briefer process before the bishop is introduced under certain conditions (cann. 1683–1687).

Since this new legislation about the special process for the declaration of the nullity of marriage (can. 1691 §3), with due respect for its proper nature, refers, as before, to the canons on trials in general and the ordinary contentious trial, the Instruction *Dignitas connubii*, though never mentioned in the motu proprio, continues to be in force, except for the articles of the aforementioned Instruction that explained canons of the former legislation, now modified and no longer present in the new norms,[6] and also those articles that do not conform with the procedural rules attached to the motu proprio. In the interpretation of *Dignitas connubii*, one should moreover take into account the fundamental criteria of the reform.

3.5. Pope Francis then states that the suppression of the need for a double conforming sentence will apply to affirmative sentences published starting from the day the motu proprio comes into force, that is, from December 8, 2015. Every affirmative sentence published from that day on, and not appealed in due time, became immediately executive. It should be noted that a sentence is not considered published until it has been published to all the parties, including the defender of the bond, according to the norm of law.

The Holy Father continues by saying that he is attaching[7] procedural rules for the proper and accurate implementation of the motu proprio, which must be observed diligently. After this statement follows the formula giving force to the motu proprio, a formula that in my opinion left

---

6. Cf. Toxé, 378–379.
7. One of the English versions of the *Motu proprio* I consulted says about those rules: "Attached and made part hereof [the *Motu proprio*]," but neither the Latin text nor the Italian contain "and made part hereof."

no doubt that any and whatsoever provision to the contrary, even "worthy of most special mention," was suppressed. Whether or not this formula refers also to the attached procedural rules has become a point of discussion among canon lawyers. At any rate, being administrative rules, although issued by the Supreme Pontiff himself, it must be supposed that they cannot modify the strictly legislative part of the motu proprio, the new body of cann. 1671–1691.

3.6. The twenty-one attached procedural rules do not intend to explain the whole process in its entirety, but to illustrate the main legislative innovations and, where appropriate, to complete it. I offer only a brief and incomplete survey:

— Artt. 1–5 of the attached procedural rules concern the pre-judicial or pastoral investigation. The Final Report of the Extraordinary General Assembly of the Synod of Bishops (in n. 49) called for "specially trained counsellors who would be able to offer free advice to the concerned parties on the validity of their marriage. This work could be done in an office or by qualified persons (cf. *DC*, art. 113, 1)." I welcome the fact that this previous investigation, already called for by art. 113 §1 of *Dignitas connubii*, is to be carried out outside the tribunal itself, thereby avoiding the incongruity that a tribunal would somehow pronounce upon the *fumus boni iuris* of a case before it is formally introduced. Much will depend on the implementation of this pre-judicial or pastoral consultation for the success of the reform of the process. This has to be, in the mind of Pope Francis, an important part of the pastoral care of broken marriages. The implementation of this pastoral approach will remain a serious challenge for diocesan bishops.
— The titles of competence being equivalent, nevertheless the principle of proximity between the judges and the parties is raised (art. 7 §1). Such proximity would indeed foster the speed of the process. There are, however, no procedural means to enforce said proximity.
— Cooperation between tribunals (cf. can. 1418) should ensure that parties and witnesses can participate in the process with a minimum of financial cost (art. 7 §2). I hope that individual dioceses will take to heart this duty of cooperation, because sometimes the lack of cooperation very seriously delays the instruction of a case.[8]

---

8. Some examples may illustrate this point: A judicial vicar in Argentina sent, together with the annual report for the year 2013 submitted to the Apostolic Signatura (prot. n. 2019

— That a bishop who is able to constitute a working tribunal with qualified ministers may withdraw from an interdiocesan tribunal (cf. art. 8 §2) is, at least for the Apostolic Signatura, nothing new.[9]
— Artt. 9–13 and 21 repeat, at least substantially, either canons still in force or the norms of *Dignitas connubii*; artt. 14–20, concerning the briefer process before the bishop, will be considered, as far as necessary, further on.

3.7. In *L'Osservatore Romano* of November 8, 2015 there appeared a rather peculiar note stating that the Holy Father had asked the Dean of the Roman Rota to explain the mind of the supreme legislator concerning the motu proprio, in order to offer definitive clarity. This was done in two points, the first being a repetition of art. 8 §2 of the procedural rules on the faculty of a diocesan bishop to withdraw from an interdiocesan tribunal of first instance; the second asserting, *inter alia*, the faculty of two or more metropolitan bishops to constitute even interdiocesan tribunals of second instance, an assertion that does not correspond to the competence of conferences of bishops according to can. 1439, which was confirmed in can. 1673 §6 of the motu proprio.

As this note, however, did not bring definitive clarity, Pope Francis then issued on December 7, 2015 a Rescript on the implementation and observance of the new law on the matrimonial process, stating that it abrogates or derogates any contrary law or norm, even if approved *in forma specifica*, citing as an example the document *Qua cura* of Pius XI for Italy. The greatest part of the Rescript, notwithstanding its inscription, does not deal with the new law, but rather gives norms for the Roma Rota. Although the question of the abrogation or derogation of *Qua cura* concerns only Italy, I must observe that the Italian regional tribunals were serving the faithful very well and that subsequent to the new legislation there is now significant confusion in several places, and indeed not only in Italy, because

---

SAT), copies of seven unanswered solicitations forwarded in the past two years to another judicial vicar for the interrogation of two witnesses presented by the petitioner; similarly, in a letter dated 16 December 2015, the judicial vicar of an Italian regional tribunal requested the intervention of the Apostolic Signatura, because, notwithstanding several solicitations, a diocesan judicial vicar, after two years, had not yet answered a request for the judicial interrogation of a witness presented by the respondent (prot. n. 51234/15 VT).

9. Except for Italy, where the motu proprio *Qua cura* of Pius XI excluded the competence of diocesan tribunals for cases of nullity of marriage.

some have thought (and maybe continue to think) that the regional tribunals were abolished by the new legislation, without having a new working structure to replace them.[10]

4. The Intention and Some Key Points of the Motu Proprio

Paying attention to the Final Report of the Extraordinary General Assembly of the Synod of Bishops of 2014, this third part of the exposition offers some commentary on the introduction of the motu proprio and several of the fundamental criteria.

4.1. No Administrative Process Is Introduced, Since a Judicial Process Offers the Best Guarantees for Discovering the Truth Concerning the Indissoluble Marriage Bond

In the Final Report (*Relatio Synodi*) of the Extraordinary General Assembly of 2014 (n. 48) we find the proposal "of establishing an administrative means under the jurisdiction of the diocesan bishop" for the declaration of nullity of marriage, with the remark that "[s]ome synod fathers, however, were opposed." Pope Francis states in the introduction of the motu proprio that he has issued it "following in the footsteps of our predecessors who wished cases of nullity to be handled in a judicial rather than an administrative way, not because the nature of the matter demands it, but rather due to the unparalleled need to safeguard the truth of the sacred bond: something ensured by the judicial order." Pope Francis stresses indeed the indissolubility of marriage and the necessity that Church discipline be in conformity with this truth of faith. He writes that the reform commission therefore had prepared a proposal "upholding and keeping in first place the indissolubility of marriage." The reform of the process for the declaration of marriage nullity thus aims to protect "the unity of faith and discipline regarding marriage, the cornerstone and origin of the Christian family." Hence, Pope Francis has no intention "to introduce . . . provisions that favor the nullity of marriage."

---

10. The document Tribunale Apostolico della Rota Romana, *Sussidio applicativo del Motu pr.* Mitis Dominus Iesus (Vatican City: January 2016), was sent by the Dean of the Roman Rota on January 26, 2016 to the diocesan bishops of Italy, telling them that "si è provveduto per Superiore disposizione ad approntare un *Sussidio applicativo*."

The process for the declaration of marriage remains, therefore, a judicial process, not because this necessarily has to be so, but because it is the most suitable way to reach a decision based on the truth of whether the marriage bond exists. The judicial process indeed offers the best guarantees for protecting the marriage bond. For this reason, the motu proprio does not comply with the wishes of several members of the Extraordinary General Assembly of the Synod of Bishops to introduce an administrative process.[11] It should be noted, however, that they were most probably referring to a simple administrative procedure before the diocesan bishop (along the lines of cann. 50–51, for example), in order to ascertain the truth about the marriage, and not to an administrative process in order to arrive at a decision *ex aequo et bono* about what is prudently opportune and desirable in the given circumstances, whether or not this conforms to the truth. Indeed, the Final Report tells us a few lines later, in the same n. 48, that "the synod fathers emphasized the primary character of ascertaining the truth about the validity of the marriage bond."

As I have already said, the goal of the reformed process remains the discovery of the truth concerning the marriage bond, insofar as this is humanly possible. The introduction to the December 7, 2015 Rescript,

---

11. Cf. Frans Daneels, "Observations on the Process for the Declaration of Nullity of Marriage," *Forum* 11 (2000) 467– 477, see 472–473: "The structure of the judicial process for the declaration of nullity of marriage is very logical and rather simple. There are, however, those who have suggested that the said process may some day in the future be able to be handled through the administrative process rather than judicial. [. . .] On the one hand, it does not seem that the process for the declaration of nullity of marriage must by its very nature be a judicial one [. . .] On the other hand [. . .] it would appear that the judicial process is normally much more suited to a process for the declaration of nullity. [. . .] In any case, any eventual—although in reality improbable—administrative procedure in such a weighty matter would have to be serious. It could not prescind from the definition of the object of the investigation [. . .], from the real possibility of guaranteeing to those directly involved in and affected by the case—that is, the spouses—of intervening in the procedure, from a reliable means of collecting the proofs and from the discussion of those proofs, from the critical evaluation of the proofs which have been gathered by the one who is to make the decision, and also from the required moral certainty which that person must have in order to declare the nullity of marriage. Everything considered, such a procedure would not be very different from the present judicial process. In order to avoid errors against the indissolubility of marriage, such a hypothetical procedure would also demand an adequate preparation on the part of those who would render a decision in individual cases." The abstract possibility of an administrative procedure for the declaration of marriage nullity (cf. cann. 50–51) surely did not imply that it could no longer refer only to a declarative decision on whether or not a valid marriage bond exists, but on the contrary to a decision according to what in the given circumstances would appear opportune and preferable. In fact, I stressed in the same article that neither the spouses nor the deciding authority have free disposition of the marriage bond.

however, seems to me somewhat ambiguous in this regard, when it states that the reformed process concerns "justice and mercy regarding the truth of the bond of those who have experienced matrimonial failure" and "the closeness of the Church to wounded families, desiring that the multitude of those who live the drama of marital failure are reached by the healing work of Christ through ecclesiastical structures." Mercy for broken marriages requires that, when appropriate, the real possibility of a marriage process be offered—to be conducted with great humanity and delicacy—but the precise meaning of the expression "mercy regarding the truth of the bond" remains unclear to me. The tone of the introductions of the motu proprio and of the Rescript seem somewhat different.

4.2. Speeding Up and Simplifying the Judicial Process

The introduction of the motu proprio informs us, nonetheless, that Pope Francis, aware of the need to offer the faithful in many regions the real possibility of obtaining a just decision in a reasonable amount of time and without excessive difficulty, and in accord with the Final Report of the Extraordinary General Assembly of 2014, has taken steps to speed up and to simplify the process. For the Holy Father "the speed of the processes, along with the appropriate simplicity" is important. He is aware that the faithful in many countries "are too often separated from the legal structures of the Church due to physical or moral distance." He clearly prefers an appropriately speedy judicial process that is possible everywhere, rather than maintaining a more perfect system that was, in many places, not possible. The fact that, in order to attain this goal, some guarantees for a just decision have fallen by the wayside has to be accepted as the consequence of this choice. The underlying idea seems to be this: better the risk of some wrong decisions than no (or few) decisions in certain regions.

4.3. The Suppression of the Requirement of a Double Conforming Affirmative Decision

A fundamental point of the reformed marriage process is the suppression of the requirement of a double conforming affirmative decision,[12] before someone is allowed to enter a "new" canonical marriage. This requirement

---

12. Cf. for this matter Joaquin Llobell, "Prospettive e possibili sviluppi della *Dignitas connubii*. Sull'abrogazione dell'obbligo della doppia sentenza conforme," *Periodica* 104 (2015) 237–284.

was introduced by Benedict XIV on November 3, 1741 with the Constitution *Dei miseratione* in order to avoid mistakes in a matter of such great importance, namely to protect the indissolubility of marriage against the shoddy jurisprudence of several tribunals. The Code of 1917 confirmed this rule.

However, on April 27, 1970, the Council for the Extraordinary Affairs of the Church approved the so-called "American Norms," by which the conference of bishops in the United States was granted the faculty to declare an affirmative first instance decision for the nullity of a marriage immediately executive.[13] This was supposed to have been for exceptional cases, in which, according to the defender of the bond and the ordinary, a second instance was manifestly superfluous. But, as happens, the exception became the general rule, and in fact several hundreds of thousands of dispensations from the second instance were granted, even though the jurisprudence under the "American Norms" was considered by many as rather lax. For Australia and Canada as well there was some faculty given in the same matter.[14]

On March 28, 1971, however, Paul VI confirmed with *Causas matrimoniales* the requirement of the double conforming sentence, but simplified the procedure, rendering it possible to confirm by decree an affirmative first instance sentence after a short procedure in the second instance. When this rule appeared in the drafts for the new Code, it elicited a strong reaction, especially from Anglo-Saxon countries,[15] but to no avail. In effect, after the codification of 1983, these countries had to reconstitute their appellate tribunals. Experience shows that, in those tribunals, the handling of cases in second instance was, even up to this day, often merely formalistic and very superficial.

A discussion on this matter began again, this time also in Europe, at the time of the drafting of *Dignitas connubii*. The second commission under the guidance of Cardinal Pompedda proposed a rather moderate exception to the obligation of the double conforming sentences,[16] but

---

13. Cf. Ignacio Gordon and Zenon Grocholewski, *Documenta recentiora circa rem matrimonialem et processualem* (Rome: s.n., 1977) 1: 242–256.

14. Cf. ibid., 259–260; Grocholewski, *Documenta recentiora*, 2: 126–132.

15. Cf. Pontificium Consilium de Legum Textibus Interpretandis, *Congregatio Plenaria Diebus 20–29 octobris 1981 habita* (Vatican City: Typis Polyglottis Vaticanis 1991) 98–127 and 230–278.

16. Pontificia Universitas Gregoriana, *Instructionis* Dignitas connubii *synopsis historica* (Rome: s.n., 2015), see 241 and 243 for art. 43 of the "Novissimum Schema": "§1. Ius novas

his schema was not accepted. As is well known, the Instruction could not change the 1983 Code.

According to the Final Report of the Extraordinary General Assembly of 2014, however, a great number of members insisted on "the dispensation of the requirement of second instance for conforming sentences." The first criterion of the motu proprio answers their desire: "First of all, it seemed that a double conforming decision in favor of the nullity of a marriage was no longer necessary to enable the parties to enter into a new canonical marriage. Rather, moral certainty on the part of the first judge in accord with the norm of law is sufficient."

As indicated, the requirement of the double conforming sentence had the goal of avoiding errors in a matter of such great importance. Honest judges know that, even in good faith, an error is possible, and they are encouraged when their judgments are confirmed in second instance. The fact that their judgment had to go before a further instance was also an inducement for them to fulfill their task and to write up the sentences with care.[17] As a consequence, their judgment could, in many cases, be confirmed by a decree after a short procedure in the second instance.[18] To conclude from this fact, as Professor Llobell does, that the obligatory second instance had become pure formalism in a great percentage of cases, seems to me an exaggeration.[19] I must admit, as I said before, that in a number of

---

nuptias contrahendi oritur ex duplici decisione conformi . . . ; §2. Normae, de qua in §1 superiore, ipso iure derogatur tantummodo si: 1° causa a tribunali collegiali definita sit; 2° iudicum collegium insuper votum favorabile exprimat; 3° nec partes aut defensor vinculi sese opponant; 4° accedit denique consensus Moderatoris tribunalis primae instantiae."

17. Gordon Read, "Pope Francis simplifies and speeds up the process for declaring marriages null," *Canon Law Society of Great Britain and Ireland Newsletter* 183 (September 2015) 8–10, although welcoming the "removal from the process of the mandatory appeal" (sic), observes nevertheless: "The downside is that there will be a lack of 'quality control' except in the small number of cases appealed by one of the parties." Roch Pagé, "Reflections of a Judicial Vicar of an Appeal Tribunal on the Proposed Reform of the Canonical Matrimonial Process," *The Jurist* 75 (2015) 59–69, was not in favor of the abolition of the mandatory double conforming sentence (cf. 64–65).

18. According to the *Statistical Yearbook 2013* in that year the tribunals treated 30,061 cases in second instance, issuing 28,478 affirmative decisions, 21,007 by decree and 7,471 by sentence. It has to be noticed that the affirmative sentences are referring not only to affirmative but also to reversed negative first instance sentences, just like eventual negative second instance sentences may refer to affirmative but also to negative first instance decisions.

19. Llobell, 281–282: "può essere molto efficace l'abrogazione dell'obbligo della doppia sentenza conforme perché in un'alta percentuale di casi è divenuta 'puro formalismo'."

tribunals this was indeed pure formalism,[20] but there has also been some significant improvement in recent years as the result of the patient work of the Apostolic Signatura. Moreover, the obligation of a double conforming affirmative sentence often contributed to avoiding a considerable number of mistakes in the remaining percentage of cases.[21] Experience indeed shows that in several places serious appellate tribunals often overturned rather weak first instance decisions that had been given in favor of the nullity of a marriage.

On the other hand, it must be said that the suppression of the double conforming affirmative sentence will have the effect that much of the second instance personnel will be freed up to accelerate the first instance processes and even to constitute first instance tribunals where these are still lacking. For this reason, I welcome the new rule, though with some hesitation.

Indeed, much will depend on the seriousness and professionalism of the first instance judges and especially on whether or not the defenders of the bond will take up their responsibility to appeal against unconvincing sentences. I regret to say that experience teaches that flawed jurisprudence in a tribunal often goes hand-in-hand with a shoddy defense of the bond.[22] Only time will tell if, and to what degree, the advantages of the suppression of the double conforming affirmative sentence might compensate for doing away with a guarantee that sought to foster sound jurisprudence,

---

20. In the archives of the Apostolic Signatura there are several examples of the whole acts of second instance consisting in one pre-stamped page, in which only the number of the case, the names of the spouses, some check marks by the defender of the bond and the signatures of the judges and notary and the date had to be filled out. The annual reports show also that many tribunals never admitted a case to ordinary examination; one U.S.A. interdiocesan tribunal of appeal, for instance, issued 2,622 decrees of confirmation and not a single sentence, while no case ended through renunciation or peremption, in the year 2000 (cf. prot. n. 1116 SAT); in 2015, another U.S.A. Tribunal with eight judges issued not only 254 affirmative sentences in the first instance, but moreover 1,018 decrees of confirmation and one affirmative sentence in the second instance (cf. prot. n. 1134 SAT). One cannot understand, even in good faith, how only eight judges with such a heavy case-load in first instance could seriously study as collegiate tribunal all those cases in second instance.

21. This can be seen, for instance, from the petitions for a *Commissio Pontificia* from Poland that arrived at the Apostolic Signatura in 2015, where, in at least fifty of those cases, the second instance issued a negative sentence after an affirmative first instance decision.

22. Pagé, 65, contends that under the so called "American Norms" "the role of the Defender of the Bond was reduced to some insignificant formality and if the Defender challenged the decision of the Tribunal, he often found himself *persona non grata*. Some tribunals would even go so far to substitute the Defender of the Bond following the sentence to prevent any appeals."

even when this guarantee was not taken seriously in many appellate tribunals.

4.4. The Diocesan Bishop as Judge

The Final Report of the 2014 Extraordinary General Assembly states in n. 49: "With respect to marriage cases, the streamlining of the procedure requested by many synod fathers, in addition to the preparation of a sufficient number of persons—clerics and lay people—primarily dedicated to this work will require increased responsibility of the diocesan bishop," while earlier, in n. 48, there was mention of "the jurisdiction of the diocesan bishop" with reference to the proposed possibility of administrative means. The third criterion for reforming the marriage nullity process ("The bishop himself as judge") goes much further:

> In order that a teaching of the Second Vatican Council regarding a certain area of great importance finally be put into practice, it has been decided to declare openly that the bishop himself, in the church over which he has been appointed shepherd and head, is by that very fact the judge of those faithful entrusted to his care. It is thus hoped that the bishop himself, be it of a large or small diocese, stand as a sign of the conversion of ecclesiastical structures, and that he does not delegate completely the duty of deciding marriage cases to the offices of his curia.

The Constitution *Lumen gentium* of the Second Vatican Council states indeed in n. 27 that the *sacra potestas* of a bishop includes his duty before the Lord to render judgment. And according to traditional canonical doctrine, can. 1419 §1 states that in each diocese the diocesan bishop is the judge in the first instance and may exercise his judicial power either personally or through others, primarily the judicial vicar (who does not act with delegated, but vicarious power).

The most important question, though, is not whether bishops are exercising judicial power personally, but whether they are seeing to the functioning of their tribunals: preparing qualified ministers, providing all the necessary means for their speedy operation, monitoring their activity, and not indulging any laxism whatsoever.[23] When Pope Francis gently warns

---

23. According to the second fundamental criterion, the constitution of a single judge in the first instance is "committed to the responsibility of the bishop, who in the pastoral exercise of his judicial power is to take care that no laxism whatsoever is indulged."

his brother bishops that they should "stand as a sign of the conversion of ecclesiastical structures," then, in my estimation, this warning should concern not so much the personal exercise of their judicial power, but rather it should concern those bishops who are not seeing to it that their faithful are served by a working and accessible judicial structure or, if there is a tribunal, are not caring for it. There is some danger of forgetting this fundamental concern by focusing on the personal exercise of judicial power by the bishops, all the more since this was always allowed, observing the rules of procedural law (cf. can. 1419 §1). However, it is often the case that diocesan bishops do not have adequate preparation for personally exercising their judicial power.

At any rate, Pope Francis links the conversion of ecclesiastical structures especially to the briefer process, in which the bishop is acting personally as judge.

4.5. The Briefer Process

The Final Report of the Extraordinary General Assembly of 2014 states in n. 48 that the synod fathers proposed also "a simple process to be used in cases where nullity is clearly evident." Pope Francis focuses on this matter explaining the fourth criterion for the reform:

> aside from expediting the ordinary process for the declaration for the declaration of nullity, a form of briefer process is designated—in addition to the current documentary procedure—to be applied in cases in which the alleged nullity of the marriage is supported by particularly clear arguments. It has not totally escaped us that a briefer process can endanger the principle of the indissolubility of marriage. For precisely this reason we have chosen that in such a procedure, the judge is to be the bishop himself, who, due to his pastoral office, is with Peter the greatest guarantor of Catholic unity in faith and discipline.

Although its celerity is modeled on the oral process (cf. cann. 1656–1670), the briefer process is quite distinct from it: the judicial vicar decides whether or not this process can be used; the instructor, and not a judge, collects the proofs in a single session; after that session the diocesan bishop, having consulted with the instructor and the assessor and having considered the observations of the defender of the bond and, if there are any, the defense briefs of the parties, is to issue the sentence, if moral certitude about the nullity of marriage is reached (cf. cann. 1685–1687). It is clear that such a process places a heavy burden on diocesan bishops, who have many other duties and often lack adequate preparation in canon law and experience in judging matrimonial cases, which as a rule are in no way easy to judge. It should also be noted that, even when the principle of proximity between the parties and the judge is, as far as possible, observed (cf. art. 19 of the Procedural Rules), this procedure makes no provision for any direct contact between the bishop judging the case and the parties involved.

On the other hand, the briefer process should be rather rare, due to the two essential conditions for this kind of process: one, the consent of both spouses is required; two, the case should not demand a more accurate inquiry or investigation, since the circumstances of facts and persons, with substantiating testimonies and records, must make the nullity of the marriage plainly evident from the outset (cf. can. 1683). That the consent of both spouses is required does not mean that this process introduces some kind of "annulment" of a marriage with the consent of both spouses, but that, as in the oral process, both have to agree to the abbreviation of their exercise of the right of defense in this procedure. If one of the spouses does not agree (explicitly or through lack of reply), it will be, moreover, very difficult for the nullity of the marriage to be clearly manifest from the outset. With regard to the second condition, however, some difficulty arises from art. 14 §1 of the procedural rules, which offers an open-ended list of circumstances of things and persons that could allow a case to be handled by the briefer process. In fact this list contains some grounds of nullity—the allegation of which by itself does not render the nullity of marriage manifest—and many circumstances, which—perhaps for some particular case—might not demand a more accurate investigation. This list, however, in no way offers clear-cut cases for the briefer process.[24]

24. The first example of this list: "the defect of faith which can generate simulation of consent or error that determines the will." Apart from the fact that in such cases the nullity of marriage is generally not at all evident from the outset, it is interesting to note that the Final Report of the Extraordinary Synod (n. 48) mentions that, "Among other proposals, the role with faith plays in persons who marry could be possibly be examined by ascertaining the validity of the Sacrament of Marriage, all the while maintaining that the marriage of two baptized Christians is always a sacrament." Pope Francis, however, was clear in his allocution to the Roman Rota of January 22, 2016, reminding that: "It must be clearly stated that the quality of faith is not an essential condition of matrimonial consent, which, according to perennial teaching, can be undermined only at the natural level (cfr. CIC, can. 1055 §1 and 2). In fact, the *habitus fidei* is infused at the moment of Baptism and continues to have its mysterious influence in the soul, even when faith is not developed and seems to be absent psychologically. It is not uncommon that couples ready to marry, urged toward true marriage by

Wise and experienced ecclesiastical judges may have encountered in their career some rare case in which the nullity of marriage was manifest from the very start: for instance, because authentic medical documents were attached to the *libellus*, proving the clinical institutionalization of one of the spouses before and after the celebration of the marriage due to a most severe psychological illness. However, such rare cases would have been decided rather quickly anyway by the ordinary process.

At any rate, the Final Report of the Extraordinary General Assembly of 2014 suggested the introduction of a simple process to be used in cases where nullity is clearly evident. Pope Francis introduced this briefer process, but, aware that it can endanger the principle of the indissolubility of marriage, stated that the judge then has to be the bishop himself, as guarantor of Catholic unity in faith and discipline.

4.6. Insofar as Possible Free of Charge

The Final Report of the Extraordinary General Assembly of the Synod of Bishops emphasized "the need to make the procedure in cases of nullity ..., if possible, at no expense" (n. 48). In this regard Pope Francis, in the sixth criterion for the reform, enjoins conferences of bishops that they "should ensure, to the best of their ability and with due regard for the just compensation of tribunal employees, that processes remain free of charge, and that the Church, showing herself a generous mother to the faithful, manifest, in a matter so intimately tied to the salvation of souls, the gratuitous love of Christ by which we have all been saved." The competence given in this regard to conferences of bishops does not seem in full harmony with the remaining prescript of can. 1649 about the proper responsibility of the bishop moderator (or the group of bishops for an interdiocesan tribunal) in this matter.

While the obligation of a just and fair remuneration of the ministers and staff of the tribunals is rightly affirmed, the principle of gratuity completely turns on its head the contrary statement of *Dignitas connubii*, art.

---

the *instinctus naturae*, should have a limited awareness of the fullness of God's project at the moment of the celebration, and only later, in the life of family, should discover all that God, Creator and Redeemer, has prepared for them. Shortcomings of formation in the faith and even error concerning unity, indissolubility and the sacramental dignity of marriage vitiate matrimonial consent only if they determine the will (cfr. CIC, can. 1099). For precisely this reason, errors regarding the sacramentality of matrimony must be very carefully evaluated" (my translation from the Italian original).

302: "The parties are bound to contribute to paying the judicial expenses according to their ability." The same Instruction nevertheless stressed the right of the poor to obtain full exemption from the judicial expenses and the right of those who are unable to pay the full expenses to obtain partial exemption (cf. art. 305 DC) and that the faithful never should be kept away from the ministry of the tribunal by excessive expenses (cf. art. 308 DC). It has happened, even recently, that the tribunal fee for an interdiocesan tribunal was four times the minimal monthly wage.[25] As a first reaction to the motu proprio, several dioceses, especially in the United States, dropped tribunal fees altogether, inviting the parties to offer a freewill contribution when the sentence is issued. It should be noted, however, that in the new body of canons (cann. 1671–1691) there is no mention of judicial expenses. In other words, this fundamental criterion for reform appears to be a point to be kept in mind when the bishops issue particular norms in this matter.

At any rate, that cases be free of charge insofar as possible will doubtless make the matrimonial processes more accessible for many of the faithful.

4.7. Proximity to the Parties

The Final Report of the Extraordinary General Assembly also emphasized "the need to make the procedure in cases of nullity more accessible" (art. 48). In the sixth criterion for reform, Pope Francis warns conferences of bishops to respect absolutely "the right of the bishops to organize judicial power in their own particular churches" and speaks of the "restoration of the proximity between the judges and the faithful." As I mentioned above, the procedural rules endorse the principle of proximity regarding the equivalent titles of competence of tribunals (art. 7 §1) and stress the task of a bishop without his own tribunal to see to—as soon as possible—the formation of tribunal ministers who can assist in setting up a tribunal, while bishops retain the right to withdraw from an interdiocesan tribunal

---

25. Cf. the letter of December 1, 2015 of a Brazilian diocesan bishop to the Apostolic Signatura (prot. n. 2106 SAT).

of first instance (art. 8).[26] And the fifth criterion for the reform states that it is 'appropriate that the appeal to the metropolitan see be restored".[27]

On the other hand, can. 1673 §2 of the motu proprio continues to acknowledge the faculty of the diocesan bishop to approach a nearby interdiocesan tribunal, and can. 1673 §3 presupposes the legitimacy of interdiocesan appellate tribunals.

It would seem that the motu proprio, in both the criteria and the procedural rules, takes into consideration those countries where interdiocesan tribunals are common and ignores those places where the system of diocesan tribunals and appeal to the metropolitan see is longstanding, and hence without any need of restoration.

I offer only two observations: first, the Apostolic Signatura, in order to ensure the proximity of the tribunals to the parties, has a longstanding practice of recommending that instructory sections be set up in each diocese of an interdiocesan tribunal of first instance, a possibility consequently mentioned in art. 23 §2 of *Dignitas connubii*; second, in many places the interdiocesan tribunals remain, at least for the moment, the most realistic way to offer the faithful the service of justice. There are indeed many dioceses, including many metropolitan sees, which do not have a working tribunal and are not able to constitute one in the near future, or even to constitute collegial tribunals for second instance cases.

It is thus up to individual bishops to see how, in the concrete circumstances of their dioceses, they can best promote the desired proximity to the parties.

5. Conclusion

I strongly welcome the fact that for the cases of marriage nullity no administrative process was introduced by the new motu proprio, and that the

---

26. An interesting example is that of South Korea: the system of interdiocesan tribunals was already given up years ago for a system of diocesan tribunals appealing to the metropolitan see, once the single dioceses were ready for this step: cf. the decree of the Apostolic Signatura of 23 January 2008, prot. nn. 3100-3117/08 SAT.

27. Notice reached the Apostolic Signatura of the suppression of some interdiocesan appellate tribunals and the restoration of the appeal to the metropolitan see, since the suppression of the need for a double conforming decision for the nullity of marriage the caseload in second instance will be much reduced and hence the metropolitan tribunal will be again able to handle cases in second instance.

process remains a judicial one, which offers the best guarantees for discovering the truth concerning the marriage bond and protecting its indissolubility. Even though there may be some perplexity concerning some points of the reform, it cannot be denied that it constitutes a stringent challenge for diocesan bishops to see to it that there be working structures nearby, allowing the faithful everywhere to approach an ecclesiastical tribunal when they have a doubt about the validity of their marriage and to obtain a decision according to the truth in good time, while not being kept away because of financial expense. It is also important to note that Pope Francis challenges the bishops to be guarantors of Catholic faith and discipline in their tribunals. Just as in the past, much will indeed depend on sound jurisprudence, which presupposes well prepared and properly qualified ministers of justice with the correct *sensus Ecclesiae*.

For many years it has been the pressing concern of the Apostolic Signatura that the faithful everywhere should have the real possibility of approaching a functioning ecclesiastical tribunal when there is a serious doubt about the validity of their marriage and to obtain a just decision in a reasonable time and without excessive expense—and for the poor, without any expense at all. Some progress has been made in resolving this problem, but even up to now not in a very significant way. As I have been working for almost thirty years to reach this goal and the end of my term of office is approaching, I can only express the hope that the reform of the marriage process will be successful.

Many bishops in the recent meetings of the Synod of Bishops criticized the existing matrimonial nullity process; Pope Francis is now challenging them to make his reform of the process work.

ABSTRACT

After a short preliminary part that concerns especially the state and activity of ecclesiastical tribunals in the world, the author offers a brief presentation of the motu proprio Mitis Iudex Dominus Iesus. *In the third part of the contribution, the author considers the intention behind the reform and some of its key points and compares these elements with the Final Report of the Extraordinary General Assembly of the Synod of Bishops of 2014. The author emphasizes that it is too early for an in-depth study of the matter and that the exposition is only a first approach. He strongly welcomes the fact that for the cases of marriage nullity no administrative process was introduced by the new motu proprio, and that the process remains a judicial one, which offers the best guarantees for discovering the truth concerning the marriage bond and protecting its indissolubility. The author concludes by stating that many bishops in the recent meetings of the Synod of Bishops criticized the existing matrimonial nullity process and that Pope Francis is now challenging them to make his reform of the process work.*

WILLIAM L. DANIEL*

An Analysis of Pope Francis' 2015 Reform of the General Legislation Governing Causes of Nullity of Marriage

On the Solemnity of the Assumption of the Blessed Virgin Mary in the year 2015, His Holiness Pope Francis issued two apostolic letters given motu proprio by which he reformed the legislation of the Latin and Eastern Churches governing the judicial process for treating causes of nullity of marriage. The issuance of these two documents, which had been expected within some proximity to the celebration of the fourteenth ordinary assembly of the synod of bishops, was announced on September 7, 2015, and the texts were revealed the next day, the Feast of the Nativity of the same Blessed Virgin. That pertaining to the Latin Church bears the *incipit "Mitis iudex Dominus Iesus,"*[1] the Lord Jesus, meek judge, and that pertaining to the Eastern Churches *"Mitis et misericors Iesus,"*[2] the meek and merciful Jesus.

    This exercise of supreme legislative authority in the Church is of monumental significance, both because it reforms an institute that has for centuries been the object of the legislative attention of the Roman Pontiff and, most especially, because it touches upon a matter that is fundamental to every society, including the ecclesial society: the dignity, stability

---

* Assistant Professor, School of Canon Law, The Catholic University of America, Washington, DC.
    1. Francis, motu proprio *Mitis iudex Dominus Iesus*, August 15, 2015 (Vatican City: Libreria Editrice Vaticana, 2015).
    2. Francis, motu proprio *Mitis et misericors Iesus*, August 15, 2015 (Vatican City: Libreria Editrice Vaticana, 2015).

and sanctity of marriage and the family. Indeed, it dictates the manner of administering justice in the tribunals of the Church in causes of nullity of marriage, which constitute the vast majority, if not the totality of causes handled in those tribunals. While the individual norms are most worthy of detailed analysis, including the manner of their correct application, it is of primary importance for the Church, and especially those engaged in the canonical science and judicial praxis, to reflect upon how these norms were prepared and what principles influence them.

Accordingly, in this study, some observations are made about the process of reform that resulted in the two motu proprios. Then, there is an effort to highlight some of the principles or themes that seemed to guide their redaction. These principles include some that are common to canonical legislators preceding Pope Francis and some that are somewhat unique to him. Finally, some critical remarks are offered about the reform, in an effort both to promote among ministers of justice the most just application of the norms as possible and to foster continued discussion about the institute of the marriage nullity process in view of an eventual future reform of these norms, should Pope Francis or one of his successors entertain this possibility. In carrying out these analyses, reference will usually be made to the norms governing the Latin Church, considering that they are substantially and for the most part textually the same as those governing the Eastern Churches.

I. Observations about the Work of the Reform

The matrimonial nullity process in its modern form has been prepared with great care, gradual development, and much consultation and debate. For example, the canons that would be promulgated under Title XX of Book IV of the 1917 Code, *De causis matrimonialibus*, were based on a *votum* presented in 1908 and several *schemata* examined between the years 1909 and 1917, with general consultations of the College of Cardinals, bishops and religious superiors.[3] The later revision of these canons occurred

---

3. Cf. Joaquín Llobell, Enrique De León and Jesús Navarrete, *Il libro "De processibus" nella codificazione del 1917. Studi e documenti. Vol. I: Cenni storici sulla codificazione "De iudiciis in genere," il processo contenzioso ordinario e sommario, il processo di nullità del matrimonio*, Monografie Giuridiche 15 (Milan: Giuffrè Editore, 1999) 193–228.

within a longer period of time, in the context of the whole revision of the *De processibus*. There was a lengthy period of study, drafting and consultation from 1968–1976, and the canons that would comprise Chapter I of Title I of Part III of Book VII of the Code of Canon Law, *De causis ad matrimonii nullitatem declarandam*, were given particular attention in 1978 and 1979. And some of its norms were under consideration even until 1983, the year of their promulgation.[4] The labors resulting in the publication of the instruction *Dignitas connubii* to be observed in treating causes of nullity of marriage in diocesan and interdiocesan tribunals was initiated by John Paul II on February 24, 1996[5] and was finally approved and published in 2005.[6]

The revision work resulting in the promulgation of the two motu proprios, however, had a very different character. In the first place it was done most quickly. On August 27, 2014, Pope Francis established a pontifical commission for the reform of the marriage nullity process, chaired by the Dean of the Roman Rota, Msgr. Pio Vito Pinto.[7] It is notable that the

---

4. For a brief account of this history, see Pio Vito Pinto, *I processi nel Codice di diritto canonico: Commento sistematico al Lib. VII* (Vatican City: Pontificia Università Urbaniana, Libreria Editrice Vaticana, 1993) 11–12, note 11. In broader strokes, see Francesco D'Ostilio, *La storia del nuovo Codice di diritto canonico. Revisione—Promulgazione—Presentazione*, Studi Giuridici 6 (Vatican City: Libreria Editrice Vaticana, 1983).

5. Cf. Frans Daneels, "Una introducción general a la Instrucción Dignitas connubii," in *Procesos de nulidad matrimonial. La Instrucción "Dignitas connubii." Actas del XXIV Curso de Actualización en Derecho Canónico de la Facultad de Derecho Canónico (Pamplona, 24–26 octubre de 2005)*, ed. Rafael Rodríguez-Ocaña and Joaquín Sedano (Pamplona: EUNSA, 2006) 22, no. 2.

6. Pontifical Council for Legislative Texts, instruction *Dignitas connubii*, January 25, 2005 (Vatican City: Libreria Editrice Vaticana, 2005), hereafter cited as *DC*. The preamble describes the Pope's constitution of an interdicasterial commission in 1996, the cooperative effort in preparing the drafts, the consultation of conferences of bishops, the interim examination of the Pope, additional consultations within the Roman Curia, and the redaction of the final draft by the Pontifical Council for Legislative Texts in accord with the pontifical mandate of February 4, 2003 (ibid. 14–15). Cf. Frans Daneels, "Storia della redazione della *Dignitas connubii*," *Periodica* 104 (2015) 171–208.

7. "Istituita dal Pontefice una commissione speciale di studio per la riforma del processo matrimoniale canonico," *L'Osservatore Romano. Daily Italian edition* 154/215 (September 21, 2014) 1: "Il 27 agosto 2014, Papa Francesco ha deciso l'istituzione di una commissione speciale di studio per la riforma del processo matrimoniale canonico. Lo ha reso noto sabato 20 settembre un comunicato della Sala stampa della Santa Sede, nel quale si specifica che la commissione sarà presieduta da sua eccellenza monsignor Pio Vito Pinto, decano del tribunale della Rota romana, e sarà composta dai seguenti membri: il cardinale Francesco Coccopalmerio, presidente del Pontificio Consiglio per i testi legislativi; l'arcivescovo Luis Francisco Ladaria Ferrer, gesuita, segretario della Congregazione per la dottrina della fede; il vescovo Dimitrios Salachas, esarca apostolico per i cattolici greci di rito bizantino; i monsignori Maurice Monier,

commission, which was to begin its work immediately (*"quanto prima"*), was not entrusted with examining whether such a reform might be necessary. The need for reform was presupposed by the pontifical mandate. Indeed, the commission's charge, as described in the just quoted communiqué from the Holy See, was "to prepare a proposal to reform the matrimonial process, seeking to simplify the procedure, rendering it more agile and safeguarding the principle of the indissolubility of marriage." The preamble to *Mitis iudex Dominus Iesus* described the commission as "working quickly" (*"Alacriter operans"*) after it had prepared some schema after a brief time (*"brevi tempore"*). Indeed, the reform of the process was completed in less than one year, when the Pope affixed his signature on August 15, 2015. Given the fact that the norms, *inter alia*, abolish an institute that has characterized the matrimonial nullity process for 274 years and create a new process under the personal responsibility of the diocesan or eparchial bishop, one might have expected a more gradual, more thoroughly investigative approach to such a reform. A task to be accomplished in such a short period would ordinarily be one that is both urgent and of a relatively simple character; but legislative history has long held the norms governing causes of nullity of marriage to be marked with gravity and just complexity.

In addition, this revision was carried out with relatively limited, if any, direct consultation. It is true that this matter was proposed to the Church at large in preparation for the third extraordinary general assembly of the synod of bishops on pastoral challenges to the family in the context of evangelization held in Rome on October 5–19, 2014. Conferences of bishops were invited to solicit responses to numerous questions facing the current state of marriage and the family, among which were the following: "Could a simplification of canonical practice in recognizing a declaration

---

Leo Xavier Michael Arokiaraj e Alejandro W. Bunge, prelati uditori del tribunale della Rota romana; padre Nikolaus Schöch, francescano, promotore di giustizia sostituto del Supremo tribunale della Segnatura apostolica; padre Konštanc Miroslav Adam, domenicano, rettore della Pontificia università San Tommaso d'Aquino (Angelicum); padre Jorge Horta Espinoza, francescano, decano della Facoltà di diritto canonico della Pontificia università Antonianum; e il professor Paolo Moneta, già docente di diritto canonico presso l'università di Pisa. I lavori della commissione speciale nominata dal Papa inizieranno quanto prima e avranno come scopo di preparare una proposta di riforma del processo matrimoniale, cercando di semplificarne la procedura, rendendola più snella e salvaguardando il principio di indissolubilità del matrimonio."

of nullity of the marriage bond provide a positive contribution to solving the problems of the persons involved? If yes, what form would it take?"[8] And a number of the revisions implemented do correspond with what was included in the *Instrumentum laboris* for the extraordinary assembly.[9]

Still, it was never clear what relationship (if any) existed between the deliberations of the synod and the work of the commission. Were the responses and discussions of the synod intended to influence or direct the reform? This seems unlikely, since 1) the commission was named about one and a half months prior to the first congregation of the synod, 2) the synod fathers themselves were divided about the need for a reform,[10] and 3) notwithstanding what was just said, the reform was issued prior to there being any deliberations about the reform by the fourteenth ordinary general assembly of the synod of bishops on the vocation and mission of the family in the Church and in the contemporary world (to be held in Rome on October 4–25, 2015), leaving the latter no opportunity to resolve disputed points and even itself to examine the reform proposed

---

8. Synod of Bishops—III Extraordinary General Assembly, *Pastoral Challenges to the Family in the Context of Evangelization—Preparatory Document* (Vatican City: 2013) at II.4.F.

9. In particular, we read in no. 100: "On the subject of simplifying the canonical process, many responses make the following requests: a simpler and faster canonical process; the granting of more authority to the local bishop; a greater number of laity as judges; and the reduction of financial fees attached to the process. In particular, some question whether two confirming sentences are necessary, at least when no appeal is made, and, in some cases, to leave the obligation to make an appeal to the discretion of the defender of the bond. Others also propose decentralizing the third instance. Responses from the world over call for a more pastoral approach in ecclesiastical courts which gives greater attention to the spiritual needs of the persons involved" (Synod of Bishops—III Extraordinary General Assembly, *Pastoral Challenges to the Family in the Context of Evangelization—"Instrumentum laboris"* (Vatican City: 2014)).

10. We read in no. 48 of the *Relatio Synodi*: "A great number of synod fathers emphasized the need to make the procedure in cases of nullity more accessible and less time-consuming, and, if possible, at no expense. They proposed, among others, the dispensation of the requirement of second instance for confirming sentences; the possibility of establishing an administrative means under the jurisdiction of the diocesan bishop; and a simple process to be used in cases where nullity is clearly evident. *Some synod fathers, however, were opposed to these proposals, because they felt that they would not guarantee a reliable judgment.* In all these cases, the synod fathers emphasized the primary character of ascertaining the truth about the validity of the marriage bond" (III Extraordinary General Assembly of the Synod of Bishops, *"Relatio Synodi." The Pastoral Challenges of the Family in the Context of Evangelization* (Vatican City: 2014) emphasis added).

by the commission.[11] Nevertheless, it is observed that disagreements remain among those consulted in preparation for the fourteenth ordinary assembly.[12]

Moreover, the two references to the above-mentioned extraordinary synod in *Mitis iudex Dominus Iesus* (one of which is repeated in *Mitis et misericors Iesus*)[13] give the impression not that the synod was influencing the reform but that it corroborated some of the concerns addressed by the reform. That is, the Pope offers norms that correspond with some of the entreaties of some of the synod fathers for means that would make the marriage nullity process more agile and approachable.

Another aspect of consultation that was not evident during the process of reform concerns the relationship of the above mentioned pontifical commission with a study group (*Coetus studiorum*) internal to the Pontifical Council for Legislative Texts, which it created under the pontificate of Pope Benedict XVI. That study group for some years had been deliberating upon a possible reform of some of the norms of the instruction *Dignitas connubii*. The devoted and extensive activities of that commission have also been recognized by repeated, if brief, reports of the Pontifical Council itself. We read in 2009 that a study group "consisting of experts residing in Rome [was] established so that, convening each month, [it]

---

11. In this regard, it is notable that, on October 6, 2014, one of the members of the commission, Prof. Paolo Moneta, offered his impression that the commission would finish its proposal prior to the 2015 synod of bishops, so that the proposal would be submitted to the synod for its opinion. He states: "Anche per quanto riguarda i nostri lavori, l'indicazione è di muoverci celermente, in modo che la nostra proposta di riforma sia pronta per essere sottoposta al parere del Sinodo ordinario dei vescovi che si svolgerà nell'ottobre del 2015" (cf. http://www.unipi.it/index.php/tutte-le-news/item/4906-giurista-dellateneo-nella-commissione-per-la-riforma-del-processo-matrimoniale-canonico).

12. We read in no. 115 of the *Instrumentum laboris*: "[. . .] Regarding expenses, some suggest that dioceses provide a continuing service of marriage counselling at no expense. On the question of second instance for confirming sentences, *a significant number* are in favour of eliminating it, yet leaving the possibility of appeal to the defender of the bond or either of the parties concerned. *On the contrary, no agreement exists on whether the diocesan bishop might assume responsibility for the procedure; some point out problem areas.* Nevertheless, *a significant number* agree on the possible use of the summary process in canon law in clear cases of nullity [. . .]" (Synod of Bishops—XIV Ordinary General Assembly, *The Vocation and Mission of the Family in the Church and the Contemporary World*—"*Instrumentum Laboris,*" June 23, 2015 [Vatican City: 2015] emphases added).

13. The first is in the sixth paragraph of the preamble, and the second is in the introduction to the *Ratio procedendi in causis ad matrimonii nullitatem declarandam* appended to both documents.

might investigate certain questions pertaining to," *inter alia*, "procedural law" (*ius processuale*).[14] Later that year and in 2010 and 2011, this work "of 6–7 experts" was said to be continuing without any interruption.[15] It was stated in 2012 and 2013 that they "perspired at [this work] with their whole heart and mind"[16] after being given an additional encouragement by Pope Benedict XVI to explore possible reforms of the code. After describing the significant progress on the *Schema canonum* for the revision of Book VI and the progress on the study of the interrelationship between the *CIC* and the *CCEO*, the report reads: "The path of labor of the study group on matrimonial procedural law (*ius processuale matrimoniale*) continues."[17] In 2013, its work was making great progress and doing so with elegance.[18]

The existence and activity of this study group was mentioned publicly by the President of the Pontifical Council for Legislative Texts, Cardinal Francesco Coccopalmerio, at a conference in January 2015 at the Pontifical Gregorian University.[19] According to Cardinal Coccopalmerio, this study group—again, initially approved by Benedict XVI—was approved by Pope Francis as one in some way parallel to the commission of reform that he had established on August 27, 2014. It is unknown to the general public of canonists, however, what collaboration was carried out between them, if any. Nor is there any indication that the extensive labors of the study group internal to the Pontifical Council were ever drawn upon by the pontifical commission for the reform.

Yet another aspect of consultation concerns the composition of the membership of the pontifical commission. It is notable that the world's top experts in matrimonial procedural law were not named to the commission. One thinks in particular of Archbishop Frans Daneels, O.Praem. (Secretary of the Supreme Tribunal of the Apostolic Signatura), Bishop

---

14. See *Communicationes* 41 (2009) 45 sub A.
15. See *Communicationes* 41 (2009) 271, 42 (2010) 283, 43 (2011) 323.
16. "Qui Coetus toto animo et mente insudaverunt . . . ." (*Communicationes* 44 [2012] 362, 45 [2013] 108, 312–313).
17. See *Communicationes* 44 (2012) 262–263.
18. *Communicationes* 45 (2013) 313:"Labor Coetus studiorum quoad ius processuale matrimonale quam maximis itineribus progreditur necnon belle se habet."
19. This is testified to by Msgr. Joaquín Llobell, a presenter and also a member of the aforementioned study group, in his "Prospettive e possibili sviluppi della *Dignitas connubii*. Sull'abrogazione dell'obbligo della doppia sentenza conforme," *Periodica* 104 (2015) 238, note 3. As one honored to have participated in that conference, I, too, can testify to this, since I myself sat beside the Cardinal on the panel when he discussed this matter.

Antoni Stankiewicz (Dean *emeritus* of the Tribunal of the Roman Rota), Msgr. Gianpaolo Montini, (Promoter of Justice of the same Supreme Tribunal and professor of procedural law at the Pontifical Gregorian University), Msgr. Joaquín Llobell (long-time Referendary of the same Supreme Tribunal and ordinary professor of procedural law at the Pontifical University of the Holy Cross), Prof. Carmen Peña García (professor of the Pontifical University Comillas in Madrid and Defender of the Bond and Promoter of Justice of the Metropolitan Tribunal in that city), Fr. Manuel Jesús Arroba Conde (likewise a Referendary and ordinary professor of procedural law at the Pontifical Lateran University), and Msgr. Grzegorz Erlebach (Judge of the Tribunal of the Roman Rota). Evidently, the selection of members for a pontifical commission is entirely left to the discretion of the Supreme Pontiff. It is simply noteworthy, and somewhat perplexing, why those just mentioned were not named when they are not merely *other* experts in procedural law of equal merit to those that were named but *the leading* experts of procedural law in the Church.

The above-quoted communiqué suggests that it was only that group of men on the commission that would be making the proposal for the revision of the general legislation of the Church. And the preamble to *Mitis iudex Dominus Iesus* largely indicates likewise. We read:

> Conscious of this matter, we decided to take up the reform of the process concerning the nullity of marriage, and, to this end, we assembled a Group of Men marked by learning in the law, pastoral prudence and forensic experience who, under the direction of the Most Excellent Dean of the Roman Rota, outlined a plan of reform, having certainly protected the principle of the indissolubility of the matrimonial bond. Working quickly, the Group in a brief time created an outline of such a new procedural law which, being submitted to weighty consideration, and with the help of other experts, is now placed in the present Letter."[20]

---

20. "Cuius rei conscii decrevimus reformationem processuum de matrimonii nullitate suscipere, huncque in finem Coetum congregavimus Virorum, iuris doctrina, pastorali prudentia et forensi usu insignium, qui, sub moderamine Exc.mi Rotae Romanae Decani, rationem reformationis delinearent, in tuto utique posito principio vinculi matrimonialis indissolubilitatis. Alacriter operans, brevi tempore Coetus huiusmodi novae legis processualis adumbrationem concepit, quae ponderatae considerationi subiecta, vel cum aliorum peritorum auxilio, nunc in praesentibus Litteris transfunditur" (§4).

It is unknown who these other experts are, but it seems apparent that the input from the extraordinary synod of bishops was only partially influential and that neither it nor the fourteenth ordinary assembly of the synod of bishops had any direct involvement in the proposal of the reform. This is regrettable from a collegial perspective. Nor does it seem that the study group of the Pontifical Council for Legislative Texts had any real involvement, and this is most regrettable from a technical perspective.

Regardless of these questions of legislative procedure, it is undeniable that this canonical legislation proceeds from the normative will of the supreme legislator. And while its suitability can and will be disputed by canonists and theologians, it shall have universal binding force unless and until he or his successor revokes it.

II. Guiding Principles of the Reform

Any legislative work operates on the basis of certain guiding principles, which in effect motivate the legislator to settle on the formulation of the particular norms issued. Such principles result in norms that are general and abstract, inasmuch as they are meant to apply to all cases and depend for their application on the will of the individual authority acting in the case. Here it is a question of the judge, upon whom the legislator depends for the realization of these principles in concrete cases and in the habitual judicial activity of the Church's tribunals. The chief guiding principles that seem to have motivated the reform enacted by Pope Francis are three: 1) the principle of the celerity of the process, 2) the principle of the protection of the indissolubility of marriage, and 3) the principle of proximity between the judge and the parties. This section describes each of these principles and explains how they have come to realization in the reformed norms.

A. The Principle of Celerity

Just after the coming into effect of the 1983 Code, in his January 26, 1984 discourse to the Tribunal of the Roman Rota, John Paul II underscored his aim of promoting the celerity of the marriage nullity process in the reform of the norms governing it. He identified the complaint about "the slowness and excessive length of trials" as one "which was not completely without foundation." Thus, "accepting a deeply felt need, without wishing to impair or in the slightest way to diminish the necessary guarantees offered by the course and formalities of tribunal procedure, [the new law] has sought to render the administration of justice more flexible and functional by simplifying procedures, speeding up formalities, shortening the time-limits, increasing the discretionary powers of the judge, etc." The realization of such legislative reforms, however, could unfortunately be hindered by defects in application by individual ministers of justice, for example, "by delaying tactics or by a lack of care in studying cases, by an attitude of inertia that is wary of entering the new track for moving ahead, by a lack of expertise in applying the procedures."[21]

This has likewise been a serious pastoral preoccupation of Pope Francis and is in fact *the* guiding principle of the reform just carried out. Indeed, this was explicitly stated in the above quoted Vatican communiqué, which said that the commission's charge was to find a way to render the process "more agile" (*più snella*). And Pope Francis himself, in a January 24, 2015 address to those participating in a conference at the Pontifical Gregorian University on the tenth anniversary of the publication of the instruction *Dignitas connubii*, proposed that knowledge and experience with that body of norms could lead to the discovery of ways for abbreviating the process. And he told the Church to expect "in the future further legislative interventions directed toward this purpose."[22] Likewise, in the preamble to the new canons (§6), he declares that he was in agreement with those bishops of the extraordinary synod who were requesting that trials be made more agile (*iudicia agiliora*). And, not intending to facilitate the declaration of nullity of marriage, he wished to foster the celerity and simplicity of the process, "lest, on account of a prolonged conclusion of the trial, the

---

21. See *Papal Allocutions to the Roman Rota, 1939–2011*, ed. William H. Woestman (Ottawa: Saint Paul University, 2011) 184 (hereafter cited as *Papal Allocutions*). He also exhorted the Rota (and all judges) to avoid judicial delays in his discourse of January 30, 1986 (ibid., 189–190, no. 6). This principle was stressed also by Paul VI in his discourses of January 11, 1965 and January 30, 1975 (ibid., 81, 130–131) and by Benedict XVI in his January 29, 2010 discourse (ibid., 307).

22. Francis, discourse to the Faculty of Canon Law of the Pontifical Gregorian University, January 24, 2015: *AAS* 106 (2015) 192–193: "La conoscenza e direi la consuetudine con questa Istruzione potrà anche in futuro aiutare i ministri dei tribunali ad abbreviare il percorso processuale, percepito dai coniugi spesso come lungo e faticoso. Non sono state finora esplorate tutte le risorse che questa Istruzione mette a disposizione per un processo celere, privo di ogni formalismo fine a se stesso; né si possono escludere per il futuro ulteriori interventi legislativi volti al medesimo scopo."

shadows of doubt at last crush the hearts of the faithful awaiting a declaration of their status."[23]

Assuredly, the pace and length of the judicial process concerning the alleged nullity of marriage is a just concern for the supreme legislator, as well as for those entrusted with vigilance over the correct administration of justice, for ministers of justice and for pastors of souls. For those who approach the tribunal accusing their marriage of nullity are in search of something that pertains to their state in life and indeed their eternal salvation. Many unfortunately have a divorce-oriented mentality, seeing the declaration of nullity of their marriage merely as a ratification of their decision to divorce or of their situation of being a divorced person. Seeing themselves as essentially un-married, they may not appreciate the fact that they are introducing a true contention into the ecclesial society, asking that their marriage bond, (presumably) formed before God and the community and binding them in conscience before him, be declared non-existent from the time of the wedding. This defect of understanding is exacerbated when such persons have proceeded to live with another as if they were legitimately married, even while being in reality bound to another. Other persons have a more accurate understanding and are either aware of their objective state of grave immorality in cases of a subsequent attempted marriage, or are waiting to attempt another marriage in hopes of avoiding such a state of immorality, or are purely seeking clarification of their status as they discern how to respond to the divine call to holiness. Whatever the case may be, since the question of the nullity of marriage touches so intimately upon the spiritual well-being and ecclesial status of persons, it is incumbent upon the Church to adjudicate the matter as swiftly as possible, without prejudice to justice (*quam primum, salva iustitia*) and the indispensable obligation to declare the objective truth to the faithful.

In the present Franciscan reform, this principle of celerity has taken concrete form especially in the following legislative novelties:

— The elimination of the consultations of the respondent by his or her judicial vicar prior to the tribunal of the petitioner's domicile

---

23. "Quibus optatis omnino consonantes, statuimus hisce Litteris dispositiones edere quibus non matrimoniorum nullitati, sed processuum celeritati faveatur non minus quam iustae simplicitati, ne, propter elongatam iudicii definitionem, fidelium sui status declarationem exspectantium dubii tenebrae diutine opprimant praecordia."

or the forum of the majority of the proofs declaring its competence (cf. c. 1672, 2°–3°), allowing those tribunals simply to proceed to the citation upon receipt of a *libellus*;
— The ability (*facultas*) of a diocesan or eparchial bishop lacking a tribunal to entrust a cause to a neighboring tribunal (c. 1673 §2), avoiding delays in constituting his own tribunal. Notwithstanding the fact that the petitioner had requested the ministry of the approached tribunal (cf. c. 1504, 1°), the bishop also need not consult the petitioner about this decision, which should foster a more expeditious transfer of the cause;
— The generalized faculty of the diocesan or eparchial bishop to entrust a cause to a single clerical judge under certain conditions (c. 1673 §4), allowing more judges personally and more swiftly to instruct causes and bring them to a decision, without spending time scheduling a session of the college, holding a judicial discussion, and obtaining the signatures of the judges who are often not present daily in the tribunal;
— The derogation of the requirement for a double conformity of sentences, in virtue of which the tribunal first declaring the nullity of marriage no longer transmits the cause *ex officio* to the superior tribunal for its decision of whether to confirm the sentence immediately or admit the cause to an ordinary examination (cf. c. 1679 and derogated c. 1682). Evidently, this eliminates the (in practice) minimum two month period which it may normally take a superior tribunal to hear its defender of the bond and the spouses and make the decision by a collegial decision. And it eliminates also the possibility for an unappealed affirmative decision to be reformed by the superior tribunal, which in turn removes the possibility for it to be appealed to the third level of jurisdiction, and so on;[24]
— The institution of the abbreviated process before the bishop (*processus matrimonialis brevior coram Episcopo*) has as its more pronounced

---

24. The principle of celerity could have been further applied in the case of an appeal after a first affirmative sentence. In the interest of such celerity, one might have expected the appellate tribunal—having established that the appeal was not merely a delay-tactic—to have the obligation first to decide whether to confirm the affirmative sentence or to admit it to an ordinary examination (cf. *vetus* c. 1682 §2), instead of demanding the ordinary contentious trial in second instance from the outset (see *novus* c. 1680 §§2–3).

aim the rapid declaration of nullity of marriages, when such nullity is considered to be manifestly evident (cf. cc. 1683–1687). For it could be carried out within a month's time if all involved act with the highest efficiency. More realistically, though, it could be completed in approximately 100 days: after the *libellus* is registered in the book of protocols and is admitted by decree, and after the judicial vicar establishes the formula of the doubt and appoints the officials, the instructor has up to thirty days to complete the session for gathering the proofs (c. 1685), the defender of the bond and the advocates have fifteen days to submit their argumentation (cf. c. 1686); then the bishop receives and examines the acts and has up to one month to publish the definitive sentence to the spouses and the defender of the bond (see c. 1610 §3; *Ratio procedendi*, art. 20 §2);

— The faculty of the superior tribunal to confirm immediately a sentence appealed merely as a delay tactic (c. 1680 §2) and of the appellate bishop to reject an appeal introduced for the same motive (c. 1687 §4) prevents the supposedly useless treatment of the matter at the second level of jurisdiction.

B. The Protection of the Indissolubility of Marriage

Another principle guiding the reform is the need for there to be some procedural protection of the indissolubility of marriage in the Church. As is stated in the preamble, Pope Francis sought to be in concert with his predecessors in providing for "the demand . . . of greatly protecting the truth of the sacred bond" (§7). And so the new legislation proposes again the ordinary contentious judicial process as the standard path for challenging the presumed validity of marriage, as well as an abbreviated process before the diocesan or eparchial bishop as an alternative, when the nullity of marriage is manifestly evident and both spouses consent to that process. As judicial processes, the judge in making his decision may not act out of a favorable sentiment in the name of charity or mercy; but he is bound to reach moral certitude about the alleged nullity of marriage prior to declaring it by definitive sentence (see *Ratio procedendi* art. 12).

The protection of marriage also motivated Pope Francis to confirm the important function of the defender of the bond, who institutionally represents and actualizes the Church's solicitude for the dignity of marriage.

Prior to issuing this legislation he had underscored the importance of the defender of the bond, mentioning, for example, his "duty to appeal, even to the Roman Rota, against a decision he considers injurious to the truth of the bond."[25] And the new legislation recapitulates a number of the defender of the bond's procedural rights, in particular: to be cited (c. 1676 §1), to be heard prior to the formulation of the doubt and the decision about whether the cause is to be treated via the ordinary process or the abbreviated process (c. 1676 §2), to be fully involved in the instruction of the cause in accord with his function (cf. c. 1677 §1), to appeal or propose a complaint of nullity against the sentence (cc. 1680 §1, 1689) or make a new proposition of the cause (cf. c. 1681); in the abbreviated process, to propose observations (c. 1686; see also cc. 1688, 1690) which are to be weighed by the bishop before he makes his decision (c. 1687 §1) and, since an affirmative decision is a definitive sentence, to appeal or propose a complaint of nullity against it (cf. cc. 1626 §1, 1628, 1687 §3).

C. The Principle of Proximity and Accessibility of the Process

As supreme shepherd of the Church on earth, Pope Francis' reform has also been motivated by zeal for the more personal care of the faithful who find themselves in need of the Church's ministry of justice. Should those who wish to approach the Church's tribunals encounter interpersonal or financial obstacles, the Church would fail to shine forth in the world as the mirror of justice. Accordingly, echoing the teaching of Benedict XVI,[26] he has insisted on what he calls the principle of proximity and has promoted greater accessibility of the marriage nullity process for the faithful.

Indeed, in the preamble to the new canons (§6), he declares that he was in agreement with those bishops of the extraordinary synod of October 2014 who were requesting that trials be made easier to access (*iudicia . . . faciliora accessu*). This was already a concern of his, as was made evident in his first two annual discourses to the Tribunal of the Roman Rota. In 2014, he already began to describe the principle of proximity between the judge and the parties in these terms: "As a result, superficial knowledge

---

25. See Francis, discourse to the Plenary Session of the Supreme Tribunal of the Apostolic Signatura, November 8, 2013: *AAS* 105 (2013) 1153. See also Francis, discourse to the Faculty of Canon Law of the Pontifical Gregorian University, January 24, 2015: *AAS* 106 (2015) 193.

26. Benedict XVI, discourse to the Roman Rota, January 28, 2006: *Papal Allocutions*, 292: "It is nonetheless a grave obligation to bring the Church's institutional action in her tribunals ever closer to the faithful."

of the situation of people awaiting [the judge's] judgment will not suffice; rather, he will feel the need to enter more deeply into the situation of the parties involved, studying in depth the documents and every element relevant to the judgment." And in this connection he emphasizes that the judge is a shepherd, whose service to the people of God is the administration of the justice which they await.[27] And in 2015 he revealed his aspiration that all matrimonial processes might be free of charge for the parties,[28] which aspiration he renews in the preamble (see "VI.—*Episcoporum Conferentiarum officium proprium*," §3). This would include the goal of there being little expense to parties and witnesses who give their testimony at their local tribunal (cf. *Ratio procedendi* art. 7 §2).

In regard to the principle of proximity, he declares that the charity and mercy of the Church compel some outreach to those who cannot approach the Church's judicial ministry "due to physical or moral distance" (preamble §5). He concretizes this concern in several norms complementary to the motu proprios proper, namely, in the *Ratio procedendi*. There he exhorts bishops and pastors of parishes to keep (or now place) separated and divorced members of the faithful within their pastoral solicitude (art. 1). In particular, there are to be structures on the diocesan/eparchial and parish levels for aiding those in doubt about their juridical condition or convinced of the nullity of their marriage, so that they may discern whether and how to initiate an ordinary or abbreviated marriage nullity process (cf. art. 2). Local ordinaries/hierarchs are in fact to appoint suitable persons to carry out this work, not excluding interdiocesan/intereparchial or (presumably) interecclesial cooperation (cf. art. 3). This pastoral effort may even result in assistance with the preparation of the *libellus* and the initial approaching of the competent tribunal (cf. artt. 4–5).

Within the dynamics of the process, it seems to be the *mens legislatoris* that the competent forum that best promotes the proximity of the judge with the parties is to be used (see artt. 7 §1, 19). The principle of prevention is not operative here, such that a competent tribunal that does not foster this proximity becomes incompetent (cf. c. 1415). This *mens* rather amounts to a deontological principle, obliging the judge in conscience to promote the proximity of the judge and the parties.

---

27. See Francis, discourse to the Tribunal of the Roman Rota, January 24, 2014: *AAS* 105 (2014) 89–90.
28. See Francis, discourse to the Tribunal of the Roman Rota, January 23, 2015: *AAS* 106 (2015) 185.

III. Critical Analysis of the Reform

Being a reform of norms that touch upon a matter of such grave importance in the Church, and one that was carried out so quickly and with minimal consultation, it should come as no surprise that it may be open to some scholarly critique. The critique of canonical legislation, when carried out in a spirit of religious respect and obedience, is meant to be a service to the legislator and the Church. For the norms issued by Pope Francis in this case, as with so much of the Church's legislation, are human in nature and are thus ever subject to reform. While the new norms are binding and must assuredly be observed, a critical analysis of them may reveal how they may best be observed in a spirit of continuity with the Church's sacred discipline and the teaching of her magisterium.

A. Prevalence of the *Favor celeritatis* over the *Favor matrimonii*

The whole matrimonial canonical system rests on the foundation of the *favor matrimonii*, that is, the orientation of the juridical order to protect the stability of marriage, from the preparation of spouses for a free and total act of love toward one another (*matrimonium in fieri*), to its fruitful liturgical celebration, to its realization in the conjugal life of the spouses and the building up of the Christian family (*matrimonium in facto esse*). When spouses confront difficulties in their common life leading even to their separation, the *favor matrimonii* does not cease. Rather, marriage continues to be protected and cherished, and the community abides in hope of the spouses' reconciliation, especially through their recourse to the grace that is offered them through their marriage. If the Church's judiciary is called upon to examine the alleged nullity of the marriage, the *favor matrimonii* is not compromised, since it is wholly in harmony with the *favor veritatis*. Thus, a just declaration of nullity of marriage does not injure the *favor matrimonii*, since the marriage bond *in casu* is examined in a serious manner by the competent authority of the Church and is deemed not ever to have existed. In the same way, a just negative decision defends the marriage and pronounces the perpetuity of the bond notwithstanding the choice of one or both spouses to dissolve their common life.[29]

---

29. On the *favor matrimonii* and the place of the marriage nullity process within the Church's sought after culture of indissolubility, see John Paul II's January 28, 2002 discourse to the Roman Rota in *Papal Allocutions*, 270, no. 7.

When a marriage is challenged before the Church's judiciary, it is carefully examined according to the procedural norms applicable in the case—as a rule, the norms governing the ordinary contentious process. In carrying out that process, the judge is bound by the principle of celerity to proceed as expeditiously as possible, considering that the spiritual good of the parties is at stake. The adage *quam primum, salva iustitia* (c. 1453) thus intersects with the *favor matrimonii* when applied to causes of nullity of marriage. For justice in such causes has a notably public dimension, inasmuch as the validity and dignity of marriage are a public good not merely within the private interests of the spouses and their family. The ecclesiastical judge, therefore, proceeds as expeditiously as possible without doing the least harm to the truth about marriage (*quam primum, salvo matrimonio*). Thus, the principle of the celerity of the process is always subordinate to the protection of the indissolubility of marriage through a judicial process instrumental for discovering the truth.

This is testified to, for example, in the motu proprio of Paul VI issued after the Second Vatican Ecumenical Council and during the process for the revision of the Latin Code, in which he highlighted the Church's constant solicitude for the protection of the sanctity of marriage and her concern that the spiritual state of the faithful not become more serious as a result of unduly delayed marriage nullity trials.[30] Also, in reflecting on that reform in his January 30, 1975 discourse to the Roman Rota, he observed that he was moved to enact the reform in order "to render the exercise of judicial power more flexible and thus more pastoral." He, however, reminded the Church of the primacy to be given to the *favor veritatis*, laying emphasis on the *salva iustitia* of the above quoted adage. He continues: "Flexibility and pastoral concern will not, of course, prejudice the standards of truth and justice, which must be scrupulously observed in

---

30. Paul VI, motu proprio *Causas matrimoniales*, March 28, 1971: *AAS* 63 (1971) 441, 442: "Causas matrimoniales peculiari semper cura sancta Mater Ecclesia prosecuta est, quae quidem per eas sanctitatem germanamque naturam sacri vinculi matrimonii nititur tueri. Ecclesiasticorum enim iudicum ministerium aperte ostendit—etsi modo sibi proprio—pastoralem caritatem Ecclesiae, quae probe novit, quantopere in iudiciis matrimonialibus animarum saluti consulatur. . . . Mater Ecclesia fore quidem confidit, ut studium, a novissimo Oecumenico Concilio in matrimonii spirituali bono pastoralique cura illustrandis atque promovendis collocatum, fructus suos gignat, etiam quod ad firmitatem matrimonialis vinculi attinet; verumtamen ipsa vitare simul, opportunis statutis normis, exoptat, ne nimia iudiciorum matrimonialium diuturnitas plurium filiorum suorum spiritualem statum reddat graviorem."

a trial," which standards are to be under the wise solicitude of the bishops.[31] Likewise, on January 28, 1978, in his final discourse to the Rota, he states directly that "expeditiousness (*celerità*) is certainly desirable and is constantly being asked of you. At the same time, however, it must always be subordinate and at the service of the primary goal, which is justice."[32]

This was reiterated somewhat emphatically by John Paul II in his final discourse to the Roman Rota, delivered on January 29, 2005:

> Lastly, the *preliminary investigation of the case* is an important stage in the search for the truth. The very reason for its existence is endangered and degenerates into pure formalism when the outcome of the proceedings is taken for granted. It is true that the entitlement to timely justice is also part of the concrete service to the truth and constitutes a personal right. Yet *false speed* to the detriment of the truth is even more seriously unjust.[33]

This was not the first time he addressed this theme. On February 26, 1983, in the context of discussing the demand of reaching moral certitude before declaring the nullity of marriage and the use of a correct jurisprudence, he stated this: "If it is true that the new Code clearly imposes the obligation of rapidly bringing all processes of first and second instance to completion ([*CIC*] c. 1453), this must not result in the detriment of justice and protection of the rights of all the parties to the cause and the community of which they are members."[34] Elsewhere, he declared that causes of nullity of marriage should "be completed with the seriousness and swiftness required by their very nature,"[35] and the judge should "give priority to the search for truth."[36]

We respectfully observe, however, that in this reform of Pope Francis the *favor matrimonii* seems to have been subordinated to the *favor celeritatis*. That is, the celerity of the process, which is valuable in itself as emphasized above (*vide supra* II.A.), has prevailed as a principle over the judicial protection of the indissolubility of marriage (which has been little emphasized by Pope Francis' magisterium, to date). In fact, given the real dynamics of

---

31. *Papal Allocutions*, 132.
32. *Papal Allocutions*, 145. He continues by teaching that the reforms he had instituted were always to respect the "essential finality" of the process, namely, after a "conscientious examination of cases . . . to pass judgments which are conform[ed] to objective truth and issued 'with God alone before our eyes'" (ibid., 146).
33. *Papal Allocutions*, 284, no. 6, emphasis in original.
34. *Papal Allocutions*, 179, no. 4.
35. January 17, 1998: *Papal Allocutions*, 247, no. 5.
36. January 21, 1999: *Papal Allocutions*, 249, no. 2.

judicial praxis in the Church, especially in North America, some of his legislative choices could in reality turn to the detriment of the indissolubility of marriage, if they are not implemented with the greatest care. This can be seen in particular in the institute of the abbreviated process before the bishop and the derogation of the requirement for a double conformity of sentences.

1. The Abbreviated Process before the Bishop (cc. 1683–1687)

As is plain to see from the papal teachings cited throughout this study, the consolidated teaching of the magisterium of the Church and the sacred discipline established by the Supreme Pontiffs has expressly emphasized with consistency the primacy of giving protection to the dignity and sanctity of marriage, lest the Church fail to proclaim its indissolubility, which has been so undermined throughout the West, especially through the liberal authorization of divorce in the secular juridical orders. Any reform of the procedural norms governing causes of nullity of marriage have boasted of promoting and preserving this ideal.

In addition, the administrative norms approved by the Roman Pontiffs in application of the norms of matrimonial procedural law have clearly emphasized the highest value of protecting the indissolubility of marriage. In this regard, we read the following in the preamble of the instruction *Provida Mater Ecclesia* issued in 1936:

> In order that the provident Mother Church may protect the dignity of marriage and look after the salvation of souls, she employs her continuous solicitude by Constitutions and Instructions, prescribing rules pertaining, among other things, to causes concerning the validity of marriage, lest what God has joined man may dare to separate or, on the other hand, declare as valid the same bond suffering from nullity.[37]

Likewise, the first words of the instruction *Dignitas connubii* issued in 2005 described its principal aim in these terms:

> The dignity of marriage, which between the baptized 'is an image and participation in the covenant of love of Christ and the Church' [*Gaudium et spes*

---

37. Sacred Congregation for the Discipline of the Sacraments, instruction *Provida Mater Ecclesia*, August 15, 1936: *AAS* 28 (1936) 313: "Provida Mater Ecclesia, ut matrimonii dignitatem tueretur, animarumque saluti consuleret, constantem adhibuit sollicitudinem sive Constitutionibus sive Instructionibus, regulas inter alia praescribens causas de matrimonii valore respicientes, ne, quod Deus coniunxit, homo separare auderet, vel ex adverso validum idem enuntiaret vinculum nullitate laborans."

48d], demands that the Church with the greatest pastoral solicitude promote marriage and the family founded in marriage, and protect and defend them with all the means available.[38]

It is with some surprise, therefore, that one reads in the present reform an acknowledgement that the new institute of the abbreviated process before the bishop could place the indissolubility of marriage in jeopardy. In the preamble, the supreme legislator states: "Nevertheless, it is not hidden from us how much the principle of matrimonial indissolubility could be at risk from the abbreviated trial"; and he proposes that having the bishop as the judge would constitute a safeguard in this matter.[39] Prior to the project of this reform, one could not have imagined such a risk being voluntarily taken (*motu proprio*) by the Supreme Pontiff, guardian of the Christian family on earth.

The admitted risk posed by the very institute of the abbreviated matrimonial process before the bishop may take several forms. In particular, one may note the risk of judicially examining the difficult question of the alleged nullity of matrimonial consent with too much haste and that of doing so with an unjustly broadened notion of the nullity of consent.

1) In regard to the speed of such a process, it should be clear to those personally engaged in the administration of justice that space and time are needed for a thorough instruction of a cause and a serene pondering of the law and the facts, so that one may arrive at a just judgment. As Paul VI eloquently taught in his last discourse to the Roman Rota on January 28, 1978: "To assure judges of the atmosphere they need for a calm, attentive, carefully thought out, complete, and indeed, exhaustive examination of the questions at issue, and also to assure the parties of a real opportunity to explain their own positions, canon law prescribes a course of action which is defined by careful norms," namely, the norms governing

---

38. "Dignitas connubii, quod inter baptizatos 'est imago et participatio foederis dilectionis Christi et Ecclesiae' postulat, ut Ecclesia matrimonium et familiam in coniugio fundatam, maxima sollicitudine pastorali promoveat atque omnibus quibus potest mediis protegat ac defendat."

39. "Nos tamen non latuit, in quantum discrimen ex breviato iudicio principium indissolubilitatis matrimonialis adduci possit; eum nimirum in finem voluimus ipsum Episcopum in tali processu iudicem constitui, qui in fide et disciplina unitati catholicae cum Petro ob suum pastoris munus quam qui maxime cavet" (preamble, "IV.—*Processus brevior*," §2). The Italian of the quoted text reads: "Non mi è tuttavia sfuggito quanto un giudizio abbreviato possa mettere a rischio il principio dell'indissolubilità del matrimonio."

the judicial process (*ius processuale*) which, he says, are "the fruit of tested experience."[40]

Moreover, there is a risk that the Church will only exacerbate the common cultural impression according to which the grave obligations arising from matrimonial consent may in practice be dismissed by a simple procedure. And this will make it all the more difficult for the Church to proclaim with credibility her teaching on the indissolubility of marriage. In this connection, in his January 24, 1981 discourse to the Roman Rota, John Paul II underlined his grave pastoral concern about the easy and swift declarations of nullity of marriage issued by some tribunals of the Church. Likely, some of the tribunals he had in mind were those of the United States of America, before which marriages were routinely declared null by a single judge with no judicial controls by the appellate tribunal. He explained that, like divorce, this problem may make the preparation of future spouses for a perpetual conjugal union to be much more difficult. He declared that

> the preparation for matrimony itself could be negatively influenced by declarations or judgments of matrimonial nullity if these would be *too easily obtained*. If among the evils of divorce exists the danger of making the celebration of matrimony less serious and demanding to the point that today among many young people it has lost its due consideration, we must also fear that judgments of declaration of matrimonial nullity, if they were to multiply as *easy and hasty pronouncements*, would add to the same existential and psychological perspective.[41]

There is a risk that this same impression may result from a routine or too frequent use of the new abbreviated process.

2) In regard to a broadened notion of nullity of marriage, the new process is predicated on the situation of the alleged nullity being based on "particularly evident arguments" (preamble, "IV.—*Processus brevior*," §1) or facts which "render nullity manifest" (c. 1683, 2°). One wonders if this could be applied in such a way as to bring to realization the following concern of John Paul II described in his January 29, 2004 discourse to the Roman Rota: "The tendency to instrumentally broaden the causes for nullity, losing sight of the bounds of objective truth, involves a structural

---

40. *Papal Allocutions*, 145.
41. *Papal Allocutions*, 167, no. 4, emphases added.

distortion of the entire process."[42] In other words, the ordinary process involves a moderated and steadily evolving dialectic that allows the judge and all the participants in the trial to penetrate the hidden reality of the internal consent of the will of the spouses at the time of the wedding. Now, however, in order to treat the matter more rapidly, it seems that the subtlety of the question is minimized, such that consent could be considered vitiated for lighter reasons or without full proof. The very list of examples proposed by the legislator in art. 14 §1 of the *Ratio procedendi*, while not establishing new *capita nullitatis*, gives one the impression that nullity can occur in a way heretofore unanticipated.

2. The Derogation of the Requirement of a Double Conformity of Sentences

The most profound modification internal to the ordinary contentious process for causes of nullity of marriage is the derogation of the requirement of a double conformity of sentences from the general legislation governing the marriage nullity process. We read in the new canon 1679 of the *CIC*: "A sentence which first declares the nullity of a marriage becomes executable, once the time limits ordered by canons 1630–1633 have passed"[43] (cf. *CCEO* new c. 1365). This is the most profound, because it eliminates a safeguard of the indissolubility of marriage that had been established by Pope Benedict XIV in 1741[44] and confirmed by solemn acts of several of his successors throughout the last one hundred years—namely, by Pius X and Benedict XV in canon 1986 of the 1917 code, by Pius XI in art. 212 §2 of the instruction *Provida Mater Ecclesia* approved by him,[45] by Paul VI in the revisions instituted in the early 1970s,[46] and by John Paul II in canon 1682 of the *CIC*, in canon 1368 of the *CCEO* and in art. 265 of the instruction *Dignitas connubii* approved by him.

---

42. *Papal Allocutions*, 280, no. 6.
43. "Can. 1679. Sententia, quae matrimonii nullitatem primum declaravit, elapsis terminis a cann. 1630–1633 ordinatis, fit exsecutiva."
44. See Benedict XIV, constitution *Dei miseratione*, November 3, 1741: in *Codicis iuris canonici fontes*, vol. 1, ed. Pietro Gasparri (Rome: Typis Polyglottis Vaticanis, 1926) 698, §8.
45. See Sacred Congregation for the Discipline of the Sacraments, *Provida Mater Ecclesia*, at 314 and 355.
46. See Paul VI, *Causas matrimoniales*, 444, no. VIII; Paul VI, motu proprio *Cum matrimonialium*, September 8, 1973: *AAS* 65 (1973) 579, no. VIII.

Now, it appears to be a statistical fact that throughout the world,[47] and most especially in the United States,[48] the appellate tribunals, to which causes were transmitted *ex officio* by a tribunal first declaring the nullity of marriage, have confirmed the affirmative sentence in a great majority of cases—whether immediately or after carrying out an ordinary contentious process. This may give one the impression that the requirement of a double conformity of sentences, and the just-cited, now derogated procedural institute has been superfluous and thus not necessary for protecting the indissolubility of marriage.

This conclusion, however, fails to consider the example of the Tribunal of the Roman Rota, whose jurisprudence is of the highest value in the canonical system of matrimonial nullity,[49] including its jurisprudence in the area of the confirmability of an affirmative sentence. That jurisprudence has consistently and authoritatively taught that an affirmative sentence cannot be legitimately confirmed by the superior tribunal unless the superior college of judges is itself morally certain of nullity of the marriage in the case. It is illegitimate to reduce its task to a superficial review of the case, giving favor not to the validity of the marriage but to the affirmative sentence.[50] Moreover, the example of the Roman Rota has demonstrated that affirmative sentences are often not suitable for immediate

47. See Llobell, "Prospettive e possibili sviluppi," 256–257; idem, "Verità del consenso e nullità del matrimonio: il processo dichiarativo di nulltià," in *Matrimonio e famiglia. La questione antropologica*, Subsidia Canonica 15 (Rome: EDUSC, 2015) 249–250.

48. See William L. Daniel, "Ongoing Difficulties in the Judicial Praxis of American Tribunals in Causes of the Nullity of Marriage," *The Jurist* 74 (2014) 256–257.

Statistics more recent than the ones cited there have been published as submitted voluntarily to the CLSA concerning the activity of American Tribunals during the year 2013. The responding appellate tribunals issued 7,235 decrees of confirmation, 1779 affirmative sentences, and 135 negative sentences; in other words, 98.5% of the marriages examined at the appellate level were considered to be invalid; and the presumed validity of only 1.5% of those marriages was vindicated. 32 of the 61 responding tribunals issued no negative decisions in second instance, never failing to confirm an affirmative sentence. See "U.S. Tribunal Statistics 2013," *CLSA Proceedings* 76 (2014) 451–452.

49. The directive, unifying value of the jurisprudence of the Roman Rota in the matter of the nullity of marriage has been one of the richest areas of canonical teaching in the pontifical magisterium. See especially Benedict XVI's 2008 discourse to the Roman Rota (*Papal Allocutions*, 298–301) and those of John Paul II from 1981 (ibid., 168, no. 5), 1983 (ibid., 178–179, nn. 4–5), 1984 (ibid., 184–185, nn. 6–7), 1986 (ibid., 189 and 190, nn. 5 and 7) and 1992 (ibid., 220–221, no. 4), among others.

50. On this jurisprudence, see Grzegorz Erlebach, "I motivi di rinvio ad esame ordinario nella giurisprudenza della Rota Romana," in *La procedura matrimoniale abbreviata*, Studi Giuridici 49 (Vatican City: Libreria Editrice Vaticana, 1998) 31–58, esp. 56–58. See also William

confirmation. Its own statistical reports reveal that it has admitted causes to an ordinary examination much more frequently than it has confirmed affirmative sentences. Here are its statistics in the matter from 2000 to 2012:

JUDICIAL YEAR[51]	Decrees of Confirmation	Decrees of Admission to Ordinary Examination
2012	12	48
2011	27	63
2010	27	61
2009	23	71
2008	12	69
2007	16	64
2006	17	43
2005	21	61
2004	30	53
2003	21	51
2002	15	35
2001	16	57
2000	14	54
Total	251 (25.6%)	730 (74.4%)

Notwithstanding the activity of local tribunals viewed at a glance nationally, this data reveals that in almost 75% of the causes presented to the Roman Rota, it does not confirm affirmative sentences. In other words—to state it somewhat provocatively—about 75% of the affirmative sentences transmitted to the Rota for possible immediate confirmation

---

L. Daniel, "Motives *in decernendo* for Admitting a Cause of Marriage Nullity to an Ordinary Examination," *Studia Canonica* 45 (2011) 67–120.

51. For these statistics, respectively, see *L'attività della Santa Sede nel 2012* (Vatican City: Libreria Editrice Vaticana, 2012) 664, *sub* 1.5 and 1.7; *L'attività della Santa Sede nel 2011* (Vatican City: Libreria Editrice Vaticana, 2011) 640, *sub* 1.5 and 1.7; *Quaderni dello Studio Rotale* 21 (2011) 60, *sub* 1.5 and 1.7; 20 (2010) 73, *sub* 1.5 and 1.7; 19 (2009) 55, *sub* 1.5 and 1.7; 18 (2008) 89, *sub* 1.5 and 1.7; 17 (2007) 115, *sub* 1.5 and 1.7; 16 (2006) 79, *sub* 1.5 and 1.7; 15 (2005) 60, *sub* V and VI; 14 (2004) 148, *sub* 5 a) and b); 13 (2003) 170 and 172, *sub* 6 a) and b); 12 (2002) 192, *sub* c)—aa) and bb); 11 (2001) 186, *sub* c)—1° and 2°.

unjustly declared the nullity of marriage, whether because of a defect of proofs or a lack of foundation for the claim of nullity. Therefore, the requirement of a double conformity of sentences was not a superfluous institute falling somehow outside of the rationality of the canonical order. Rather, it was one that was poorly implemented and which the Apostolic See had not yet been able to address effectively, given the little heed that seemed to be paid to the guidance of the Apostolic Signatura in its function of providing for the correct administration of justice and to the consistent and thoroughly sound example of the Roman Rota. If the derogation was based merely on the empirical information gathered from local tribunals, it would seem that the consistent experience of the aforementioned apostolic tribunals was not duly weighed. This thus constitutes an eloquent example of the minimal influence of the *favor matrimonii* in the work of the reform.

B. Spirit of Favor toward Those Introducing Contention into the Sacramental Order

In the context of encouraging regional initiatives to bring to realization the Pope's aspiration for a free marriage nullity process, the reform describes the Church in this context as "a generous mother to the faithful" who, "in a matter so strictly connected to the salvation of souls, reveals the free love of Christ by which we have all been saved."[52] Assuredly, those cases of truly impoverished persons or those with quite limited means who wish to challenge the validity of their marriage should not be left without some assistance, even total aid, for pursuing their cause, this being a fundamental right in the Church (cf. cc. 221 §1, 1674 §1, 1°).

At the same time, one wonders if this posture of charity is not somewhat overstated. It is indisputable that the Church's ministry should reflect that of her divine founder, who though rich in divine majesty took the form of a slave, lived a life of simple poverty, subjected himself to suffering and death, and freely offers to all divine mercy and life eternal. This particular ministry of the Church, though, while it is ever to be exercised

---

52. "Una cum iudicis proximitate curent pro posse Episcoporum Conferentiae, salva iusta et honesta tribunalium operatorum mercede, ut processuum gratuitati caveatur et Ecclesia, generosam matrem se ostendens fidelibus, in re tam arcte animarum saluti cohaerente manifestet Christi gratuitum amorem quo salvi omnes facti sumus" (preamble, "VI.—*Episcoporum Conferentiarum officium proprium,*" §3).

with a demeanor of charity and compassion, is in its essence a ministry of justice. Those who approach the tribunal challenging the validity of their marriage, even if they may have been unjustly abandoned through the sin of their spouse, are asking the Church to declare that a sacred bond, and often even a sacrament of the new covenant, does not in fact exist—that is, that what the community thinks and presumes is a marriage, and one which may have even given birth to new human persons, is not a marital bond and does not bind them, even before God. Actually, the *libellus* could be considered an unjust act if it stirs up the contention of marital nullity when one in reality harbors a divorce-oriented mentality and in effect wants the Church to dissolve the bond. It could therefore be asked whether a global exemption from judicial fees is just toward the ecclesial society.

Even more broadly, and perhaps with particular attention to those regions of the Church that have a smoothly functioning judiciary, one could question the merit of the accessibility of the process to the faithful when it is so frequently employed with this divorce-oriented mentality. For, it needs to be recalled that, while giving the faithful convenient access to the Church's judiciary is a requirement of justice, the fulfillment of which should be motivated also by charity and mercy, declarations of nullity of marriage are not something to be promoted in the Church. Quoting Pius XII, John Paul II emphasized in 1981 that "everyone knows that the Church is rather wary and disinclined to favor them."[53]

C. Legislative Suspicion against Judicial Appeals

One element that is somewhat unsettling to see in the revised norms, which, as procedural norms, are in the first place meant to direct and give expression to the protection and vindication of the rights of Christ's faithful,[54] is a tone of suspicion against the decision one may make to appeal a definitive sentence. The preamble expresses caution about there being any abuse of the right of appeal,[55] and this is received into the

---

53. *Papal Allocutions*, 168, no. 4.

54. This is observed in the very title of the *schema* of what would become Book VII of the Latin Code. See Pontifical Commission for the Revision of the Code of Canon law, *Schema canonum de modo procedendi pro tutela iurium seu de processibus*, November 3, 1976: *Communicationes* 41 (2009) 350–447

55. "... cauto tamen in eiusdem appellationis disciplina ut quilibet cohibeatur iuris abusus, neque quid salus animarum detrimentum capiat" (preamble, "VII.—*Appellatio ad Sedem Apostolicam*," §1).

revised canons themselves, which anticipate an appeal that is "merely dilatory" (*mere dilatoria*), or a delay-tactic (cc. 1680 §2, c. 1687 §4).

Now, it is true that the Church's judiciary has been prone to some paralysis due to obstructionist maneuvers carried out by parties, perhaps with the counsel of an advocate. This is most especially a concern when it is a matter of the multiplication of recourses within the trial, making it very difficult to proceed smoothly. For example, a respondent who within one trial makes recourses against the decrees of the *ponens* to the college of judges by which the formulation of the doubt is established, a witness is excluded, an expert is appointed, and an extension is denied is probably obstructing the steady course of a trial.[56] Or a defender of the bond who routinely makes complaints of nullity and new propositions of causes may be obstructionistic.

The appeal, however, is an ordinary remedy that directly and principally concerns the merits of the case, namely, the alleged nullity of marriage.[57] The one who exercises this ordinary right should be favored with the presumed will simply of wishing to vindicate his right to a second hearing in the matter by a competent appellate judge. This is especially true in the case of an affirmative sentence in a system that rests on the foundation of the *favor matrimonii*. Therefore, a respondent's appeal against an affirmative decision cannot be considered a mere delay tactic because he wants the marriage to be considered valid; it should be presumed that he wishes to exercise his right to vindicate the validity of his marriage. Otherwise, the tribunal may show itself to have fallen prey to the "anti-respondent syndrome" in virtue of which the respondent's involvement in or bewilderment about the process or his or her attempts to defend the validity of marriage are experienced as threatening to the tribunal and the supposedly pastoral aim of helping the petitioner enter a new marriage.[58] In fact, the appellate tribunal/bishop is under no obligation to ascertain the motives of the appellant. It should simply proceed to handle the appeal, unless it is evident that it is merely a delay tactic (e.g., the respondent knows the

---

56. On this problem, see John Paul II's January 22, 1996 discourse to the Roman Rota, in *Papal Allocutions*, 239, no. 4.

57. It should be noted that, in his celebrated January 26, 1989 discourse to the Roman Rota on the right of defense, John Paul II acknowledged the problem of "obstructionism" in the exercise of this right; but he laid much greater emphasis on the right of appeal. See *Papal Allocutions*, 204–208.

58. Cf. Tribunal of the Roman Rota, Decree *c.* Doran, *Litoris palmen.*, *Nullitatis matrimonii, Nullitatis sententiarum*, November 29, 1990: *RRDecr* 8: 194–195, no. 17.A.

petitioner has a hoped-for wedding scheduled for a couple weeks later and is appealing only to impede that event). It would be the burden of the one aggrieved by the appeal to reveal this to the appellate judge.

D. Relationship with the Instruction *Dignitas connubii*

Just as the work of the reform seemed entirely to discount the detailed examinations of the instruction *Dignitas connubii* on the part of the Pontifical Council for Legislative Texts during the period 2009–2015,[59] so the motu proprio governing the Latin Church seemed entirely to ignore the existence of the same instruction. While *Dignitas connubii* was not a reform of the marriage nullity process, it was a very large undertaking within the Roman Curia accomplished just ten years ago with the aid of those most expert in the Church's sacred discipline regulating the same process. Were there no insights from *Dignitas connubii* upon which to draw in the work of this reform? More practically, the same instruction has been the object of study of ministers of justice throughout the world, and there have been continued efforts up to now for its correct application; have these efforts been in vain?

These questions aside, the fact of the reform and the motu proprio's silence about the instruction *Dignitas connubii* may leave ministers of justice with questions about the status of the instruction and its relationship to the motu proprio. This is especially so in view of the simultaneous issuance of the *Ratio procedendi*. We treat here, therefore, the juridical nature of the *Ratio procedendi* and the status of the instruction *Dignitas connubii*.

1. The Juridical Nature of the *Ratio procedendi*

Subsequent to the text of the motu proprios, beneath Pope Francis' signature, there is a brief body of norms entitled *Ratio procedendi in causis ad matrimonii nullitatem declarandam* ("Manner of Proceeding in Causes for Declaring the Nullity of Marriage"). They are not part of the motu proprio but are attached to it. While the motu proprio is clearly a document containing general pontifical legislation, and in fact an emendation of the codes themselves, the *Ratio procedendi* does not alter the codes and is in no way to be inserted into them. This gives rise to the question of

---

59. *Vide supra* section I.

their juridical nature, which is important in order to appreciate the scope of their binding force.

After giving the text of the reformed canons of Chapter I of Title I of Part III of Book VII of the Latin Code and Article 1 of Chapter I of Title XXVI of the Eastern Code *De causis ad matrimonii nullitatem declarandam*, the motu proprios identify and briefly describe the *Ratio procedendi* in these words: "A *ratio procedendi* is connected to the present [Apostolic Letter], which we bring forth for the correct and accurate necessary application of the renewed law to be zealously observed for fostering the good of the faithful."[60] And article 6 of the *Ratio* itself says that "the present *Ratio* does not intend to explain in detail the substance of the whole process but above all to describe and, where necessary, to complete the principal innovations of the law."[61] These texts offer some indications as to the juridical nature of the *Ratio procedendi*.

In the first place, it is clear that the author of the *Ratio procedendi*—that is, the authority from which it emanates—is Pope Francis himself, the supreme legislator. For, not only is no other authority indicated (e.g., a dicastery of the Roman Curia), but he identifies himself in the first person plural as the one issuing it: "ratio procedendi, quam *duximus*." They are thus norms of the supreme legislator of the Church.

What is less clear is whether they are legislative norms or administrative norms. While the Supreme Pontiff is a legislator, the supremacy of this designation does not make him *merely* a legislator. Indeed, apart from being a legislator and in addition to being the supreme judge of the whole Catholic world,[62] he is also the supreme organ of public ecclesiastical administration.[63] Accordingly, he is assuredly competent to issue acts of the executive power of governance. Apart from singular administrative acts (cf. *CIC* c. 35; *CCEO* c. 1510), this power is what is exercised in issuing general administrative norms. Canonical doctrine distinguishes between three classes of such norms: general executory decrees, instructions, and

---

60. "Praesentibus adnectitur ratio procedendi, quam duximus ad rectam accuratamque renovatae legis applicationem necessariam, studiose ad fovendum bonum fidelium servanda."

61. "praesens ratio non intendit summam totius processus minute exponere, sed praecipuas legis innovationes potissimum illustrare et ubi oporteat complere."

62. Cf. *CIC* cc. 1405 §1, 1442; *CCEO* cc. 1059 §1, 1060 §1.

63. Cf. *CIC* cc. 135 §1, 331, 333 §1; *CCEO* cc. 43, 45 §1, 985 §1.

independent norms.[64] The first two have largely the same character but a diverse audience. They both aim to prescribe how the norm of law (*lex*) is to be observed, whether this is a matter of determining some procedure or other rules for implementing it, explaining its proper meaning, or urging its observance (cf. *CIC* cc. 31 §1, 34 §1).

General executory decrees have the same audience as the legislation they are implementing (*CIC* c. 32), namely, "a community capable of receiving the law" (*CIC* c. 29); for this reason, they are to be promulgated in the same way that the law was promulgated (cf. *CIC* c. 31 §2). Instructions, on the other hand, are not directed to the community at large but to the public administration itself or to those whose duty it is "to take care that the laws are executed," as an instrument of directing their execution of the law (*CIC* c. 34 §1).[65] General executory decrees and instructions may be issued by any of the active organs of public administration, that is, "those

---

64. On these categories, see, e.g., Eduardo Baura, "Il valore normativo dell'Istruzione *Dignitas connubii*," in *Il giudizio di nullità matrimoniale dopo l'Istruzione "Dignitas connubii,"* ed. Piero Antonio Bonnet and Carlo Gullo, Studia Giuridici 75 (Vatican City: Libreria Editrice Vaticana, 2007) 1: 185–211; idem, "L'attività normativa dell'amministrazione ecclesiastica," *Folia Canonica* 5 (2002) 59–84; Andrea Bettetini, "'Statuti' e 'regolamenti' nel Codice di diritto canonico," *Il diritto ecclesiastico* 105 (1994–I) 3–14; María José Ciáurriz Labiano, "Las disposiciones generales de la administración eclesiástica," in *Le Nouveau Code de Droit Canonique. V*^{e} *Congrès International de Droit Canonique, Ottawa, 1984. The New Code of Canon Law. 5*th *International Congress of Canon Law, Ottawa, 1984,* ed. Michel Thériault and Jean Thorn (Ottawa: Saint Paul University, 1986) 1: 213–230; John M. Huels, "A Theory of Juridical Documents Based on Canons 29–34," *Studia Canonica* 32 (1998) 337–370; Eduardo Labandeira, *Trattato di diritto amministrativo canonico* (Milan: Giuffrè Editore, 1994) 238–257; Jorge Miras, Javier Canosa, and Eduardo Baura, *Compendio di diritto amministrativo canonico,* Subsidia Canonica 4, 2nd ed. (Rome: Pontificia Università della Santa Croce, 2009) 89–120; Tomás Rincón-Pérez, "Actos normativos de carácter administrativo," in *La norma en el derecho canónico. Actas del III Congreso internacional de derecho canónico (Pamplona, 10–15 octubre de 1976)* (Pamplona: EUNSA, 1979) 1: 959–976.

Independent norms are those non-legislative binding rules that do not execute legislative norms but enjoy autonomy from them. They are issued by the public administration for providing order to a juridical person or some group of the faithful. They may also be issued by the legislator (*CIC* c. 94 §3) or even by the faithful (cf. *CIC* c. 299); but in these cases they have the character of laws and private norms, respectively, not administrative norms. Falling into this category are the statutes and rules of order (*ordines*) of canons 94–95 of the 1983 Code. Statutes define a juridical person's purpose, composition, direction, procedures and activities (cf. *CIC* c. 117; *CCEO* c. 922), while rules of order apply to gatherings of the faithful, such as a diocesan synod or a particular council.

65. Cf. Javier Otaduy, "El sentido de la ley canónica a la luz del Libro I del nuevo Código," in *La nueva codificación canónica. I. Temas fundamentales en el nuevo Código,* XVIII Semana española de derecho canónico (Salamanca: Universidad Pontificia de Salamanca, 1984) 72.

who enjoy executive power, within the limits of their competence" (*CIC* cc. 31 §1, 34 §1), obviously not excluding the Supreme Pontiff. In discerning the nature of a norm, it is necessary to look beyond the title of the document in which it is stated, into its internal character and substance. For, as even the legislator acknowledges, norms of a given nature may be found in documents bearing diverse titles (cf. *CIC* c. 33 §1).

What is immediately notable about the *Ratio procedendi* is its deliberate placement outside of the motu proprio proper. This exhibits an intentional distinction of it from the revised canons of the Latin and Eastern Codes. In other words, they are not the revised legislation, and this is immediately evident from their location. They could have been incorporated among the revised canons, considering especially the fact that they are divided in the same way, bearing the same titles or subsection names.

The function of the *Ratio* as stated by the legislator and as practically observed in the tone of its provisions suggests that it is not legislation but a body of administrative norms. For in the first place, the legislator identifies its purpose as aiding in "the correct and accurate necessary *application*" of the revised canons, as is substantially reiterated in art. 6 of the *Ratio*. This corresponds with the fundamental character of administrative norms, as just discussed. In addition, the tone of the norms is directive and applicative vis-à-vis the new canons, not firm, original constitutional rules. For example, artt. 1–5 and 7 §1 give direction for concretizing the principle of proximity; art. 14 gives a non-exhaustive (*"etc."*), non-binding (*"sinunt"*) list of examples of factual situations that could justify use of the abbreviated process (§1) and what kinds of proof may support a petition for such a process (§2). Another clue resides in how the *Ratio* makes frequent cross-reference back to the revised canons and other canons of the general legislation it means to apply (see artt. 7, 8 §2, 11 §1, 14 §1, 15, 17, 19, 21).

Thus, it can be maintained that the prescriptions of the *Ratio* have the character of supreme administrative norms. The import of this is that they may lack the stability of legislation, while the revised canons are presumed to have the marks of stability and therefore perpetuity. Also, administrative norms would not be presumed to have revocatory force in relation to any canons of the code, were that question to arise. What kind of administrative norms they are is of less importance, but this is discerned by attending to their audience. As in the case of *Dignitas connubii*, which is called an instruction while, in the opinion of noted doctrine, in fact being a body of general executory decrees,[66] it is likewise a body of general executory decrees since it is not only directed to those entrusted with executing procedural law in causes of nullity of marriage. It also governs the whole process and the rights of all the faithful acting within it. Its audience is the same as that of Book VII of the 1983 Code itself and Title XXVI of the Eastern Code: all the faithful and all non-Catholics who may be subject to the Church's judiciary.

2. The Status of the Instruction *Dignitas connubii*

The instruction *Dignitas connubii* was approved by Pope John Paul II on November 8, 2004 and was issued by the Pontifical Council for Legislative Texts on January 25, 2005. It is a body of general administrative norms guiding the correct application of the canons of the Latin Code (art. 1 §1) regulating the conduct of the marriage nullity process. As was observed above, nowhere in the motu proprio for the Latin Church is the instruction *Dignitas connubii* mentioned. Therefore, it is clearly not explicitly revoked (see cc. 33 §2, 34 §3). The general revocatory formula in it only brings to cessation those prior norms that are contrary to the reformed canons (*"contrariis quibusvis, etiam specialissima mentione dignis, non obstantibus"*); this does not amount to an implicit revocation of *Dignitas connubii*, which regulates the same matter as the motu proprio, though in greater detail. The specific revocatory formula used in the document is the following: "Having thoroughly considered all of these things, we decree and establish that Chapter I of Title I of Part III of Book VII of the Code of Canon Law, on causes for declaring the nullity of marriage (cc. 1671–1691), is from December 8, 2015 integrally substituted as follows: [thus follow the revised canons]."[67] In other words, what were revoked were canons 1671–1691 of the Latin Code.

---

66. Cf. Javier Otaduy, "El principio de jerarquía normativa y la Instrucción *Dignitas connubii*," in *Procesos de nulidad matrimonial*, 45–80. Similarly, with regard to the "Instruction" *Redemptionis Sacramentum* on certain practices to be observed and avoided concerning the Most Holy Eucharist, see John M. Huels, "New Eucharistic Discipline in the Instruction *Redemptionis Sacramentum* and the Need for a Reform of Canons 29–34," *Studies in Church Law* 2 (2006) 33–59.

67. "Quibus omnibus mature consideratis, decernimus ac statuimus Libri VII Codicis Iuris Canonici, Partis III, Tituli I, Caput I De causis ad matrimonii nullitatem declarandam

Now, the norms of the instruction *Dignitas connubii* are meant to give application to all the laws that govern trials concerning nullity of marriage. They would cease to be binding to the extent that the laws binding such trials are revoked (cf. c. 33 §1: *"cessante lege ad cuius executionem data sunt"*). However, one can observe in the new canons 1671–1691 many norms that are substantially and often textually the same as those in the revoked canons—in particular, old canons 1671–1672, 1674–1675, 1678, 1680–1681, 1684 §1, 1685–1691. Thus, the norm of the revoked canon remains in effect, leaving the applicative administrative norm intact. Moreover, the new canon 1691 §3, like the reordered canon 1691, establishes that norms other than the canons issued in this Chapter are to be observed in the manner of proceeding in causes of nullity of marriage, namely, the canons concerning trials in general (Book VII, Part I) and concerning the ordinary contentious trial (Book VII, Part II). Drawing on judicial praxis, apostolic jurisprudence, authentic interpretations of law, and the teaching of the ordinary pontifical magisterium,[68] the norms of the instruction *Dignitas connubii* explain the manner in which many of these just-mentioned canons are to be applied in causes of nullity of marriage, and thus they remain in force.

Here it is worthwhile to identify those articles of the instruction *Dignitas connubii* that have been implicitly revoked due to the cessation of the law for whose execution they were issued.

— *The new canon 1672* integrally reorders the matter of old canon 1673, and thus the norms of *DC* on the application of the latter are also revoked, namely, artt. 10 §1 and 13.
— *The new canon 1673* applies several canons of Part I of Book VII to causes of nullity of marriage. Since the revocatory formula of the motu proprio was limited to the replacement of the old canons 1671–1691 with the new canons 1671–1691, it happens that canons of the Latin Code are not revoked but only their application to causes of nullity of marriage change. In other words, norms of *Dignitas*

(cann. 1671–1691), inde a die VIII mensis Decembris anni MMXV, integre substitui prout sequitur:"

68. Cf. Joaquín Llobell, "The Juridical Nature of the Instruction *Dignitas connubii* and Reaction to It in the Church," in *Studies on the Instruction "Dignitas connubii." Proceedings of the Study Day Held at the Pontifical University of the Holy Cross, Rome, January 19, 2006*, ed. Patricia Dugan and Luis Navarro, Gratianus Series (Montréal: Wilson & Lafleur, 2006) 3–15.

connubii are revoked but not the canons of the code that they apply. Accordingly:

- ◊ §3 of the new canon 1673 revokes *DC* art. 43 §2, such that *for causes of nullity of marriage*, the use of lay judges does not require the permission of the conference of bishops, nor does the use of one require a situation of necessity. For the universal law now authorizes the judicial vicar to appoint two lay judges when constituting a college of judges. However, in all other kinds of causes (e.g., the separation of spouses, causes of rights, penal causes), in accord with the un-revoked canon 1421 §2, a lay judge may only be included in the college of judges if the conference of bishops has permitted this and there is a need to appoint one owing to the absence of clerical judges.
- ◊ Likewise, §4 of the new canon revokes *DC* art. 30 §3 but not canon 1425 §4. Thus, the permission of the conference of bishops, now granted by the supreme legislator, is not needed for entrusting causes to a single clerical judge, while it is still needed for other kinds of causes. Accordingly, were another kind of cause reserved to a college of three judges (c. 1425 §1) to be decided by a single clerical judge, lacking the permission of the conference, the definitive sentence would be remediably null due to an illegitimate number of judges (c. 1622, 1°).
- ◊ In the same vein, the appellate college of judges in causes of nullity of marriage may be composed of a cleric and two lay judges in virtue of §5 of the new canon; but in other kinds of causes only one lay judge may be appointed (when permitted by the conference of bishops) and only then when a cleric is not available.

— Also, *the new canon 1673 §§2 and 4 revokes DC art. 24 §1 and 69 §2*, such that the diocesan bishop need not approach the Apostolic Signatura for an extension of competence in order to entrust causes within his competence to a neighboring (*vicinius*) tribunal.

— *The new canon 1675 revokes canon 1676* and the rather pastorally rich *DC* art. 65, both of which were in place to have the judge share in the Church's defense of the stability of marriage and the family and the effort to help avoid litigation in the Church. No longer is he bound to strive for the spouses' reconciliation; he may simply verify the irreparable rupture of their relationship.

— *The new canon 1676* revokes canon 1677 as well as a number of norms or parts of norms of *DC*, namely, those prescribing: a) the immediate constitution of a tribunal by the judicial vicar and notification of the names of the judges to the spouses (art. 118),[69] b) the direction of the introductory phase of the process by the presiding judge or, as the case may be, the *ponens*,[70] c) the advisable hearing of the defender of the bond prior to the admission of the *libellus* (art. 119 §2), and d) the limitation of the formulation of the doubt to the alleged grounds of nullity, since now the manner of proceeding is also to be decreed (cf. art. 135 §1).

— *The new canon 1678 §§1–2* revokes old canon 1679 and *DC* artt. 180 and 202.

— *The new canons 1679–1680* revoke old canons 1682–1683 and *DC* artt. 264–265 and the related elements of artt. 290 and 301 §1.

— *The new canons 1683–1687* are entirely new and revoke no canons of the Code but only *DC* art. 22 §2, which encouraged the bishop, on the contrary, to avoid adjudicating causes of nullity of marriage himself.

Therefore, bearing in mind the nuances just stated, the articles of the instruction *Dignitas connubii* that have been revoked are the following: artt. 10 §1, 13, 22 §2, 24 §1, 30 §3, 43 §2, 46 §2, 7°–10°, 47 §2, 65, 69 §2, 118, 119, 126 §1, 127, 135 §1, 140, 1°–2°, 180, 202, 264–265 and some aspects of artt. 290 and 301 §1. All the others retain their force and must be observed outside of the legitimate use of the abbreviated process before the diocesan bishop.

Dignitas connubii was intended to be a normative source that could simplify the carrying out of a trial for ministers of justice, but it has now become a somewhat complicated document, given the fact of all these derogations. It would be most appropriate, therefore, for the competent dicastery of the Roman Curia to issue a revised, complete, carefully drafted body of administrative norms to be observed for treating causes

---

69. Nevertheless, the name of the defender of the bond, whose pre-citation appointment in the case is presupposed by the new c. 1676 §1, is to be transmitted to the spouses at the time of the citation (see *DC* art. 127 §4).

70. Cf. *DC* artt. 46 §2, 7°–10°, 47 §2, 119, 126 §1, 127, 135 §1, 140°–2°.

of nullity of marriage. Notwithstanding the urgency of this serious matter, such a document may best be issued after a period within which the Church can obtain some experience of these procedural novelties, perhaps giving rise to additional prudent provisions.

IV. Conclusion

Issuing legislation is a governmental activity that is subject to the prudent judgment of the competent legislator; and as human law, it is perfectible and thus, from a scientific perspective, subject to respectful critique by those qualified (cf. c. 218). The value of canonical legislation in particular is especially assessed with reference to the consistent magisterium of the Church pertaining to the object of the legislation, and this is the vantage point out of which the canonist must operate in matters that are not of a merely technico-juridical nature.

The reform of legislation, which by its nature bears the mark of perpetuity and stability, is a serious matter. Before it is opportunely initiated, there is first the question of whether there is a real need for *legislative* reform. For the practical problems that exist in a society and in the activity of those entrusted with power in it may often amount to a problem of *application*, whether this be administrative or judicial application. While the present reform has been effectively accomplished in virtue of Pope Francis' supreme legislative authority in the Church as Vicar of Christ on earth, one may respectfully question its suitability. This, of course, like most things, will be subject to the judgment of history.

One assessment that can be made at the present moment is that what was and is in need of reform is not procedural law but its concrete application by ministers of justice throughout the world. Each nation, each tribunal, has its own challenges in the correct application of procedural and matrimonial law, and it is doubtful that the just completed alteration of the general legislation—the fruit of the Church's time-tested experience—offers a real solution. It may have been more effective for Pope Francis to provide instruments for the more expeditious and effective vigilance over the correct administration of justice. The Supreme Tribunal of the Apostolic Signatura has steadily and carefully carried out this function in the Church for decades, but its small staff and limited resources have naturally affected its ability to transform the daily operations and jurisprudence of local tribunals. It knows what happens in tribunals, though; it knows, for example, that some tribunals have allowed the construction of obstacles for parties even to initiate a trial, that others lack the personnel or expertise to complete a trial in a just period of time, and that still others, while very efficient, frequently operate out of a divorce-oriented mentality. Canonical legislation and the ecclesial magisterium address all of these matters, but the practical solutions reside not in sources of such a general character but in the concrete and effective intervention of those who have the responsibility to provide suitably prepared ministers of justice and to exercise vigilance over their judicial activity.

This study has aimed to demonstrate that the reform of the canons governing causes of nullity of marriage in the Church has given expression to certain principles articulated more than once already by Pope Francis in the first two and a half years of his pontificate. Standing out among the concrete norms of the reform are the principle of the celerity of the marriage nullity process and the principle of proximity between the judge and the parties. The same norms, however, in notable contrast with previous legislation in the matter, seem to minimize the principle of the protection of the indissolubility of marriage, which has been stressed frequently and eloquently in the pre-Francis pontifical magisterium. This could pose a risk to the Church's actual protection of marriage. And it demands that ministers of justice both acknowledge that the reform places the *favor celeritatis* in a place of precedence over the *favor matrimonii*, and to resolve firmly ever to administer justice in a manner that clearly radiates the *favor veritatis*. For it is above all the truth declared with charity that redounds to the salvation of souls, which is always the supreme law of the Church.

ABSTRACT

Pope Francis' 2015 reform of the marriage nullity process is of monumental significance for the canonical system. For it not only alters some matrimonial procedural norms that have been in place for centuries, but it also touches on a matter that is of foundational importance to every human society, including and especially the Church—namely, the stability of marriage and the family. The reform, which was carried out rather quickly and with relatively minimal consultation, was based especially on the principle of the greater celerity of the process, as well as the principle of proximity between the judge and the parties and the principle of the protection of the indissolubility of marriage. However, the new norms arguably reveal, in tension with canonical tradition and the consistent teaching of the magisterium, a preference for the celerity of the process over the protection of the indissolubility of marriage. They also introduce some ambiguities about the instruction Dignitas connubii, *published just 10 years ago. This reform, while effective and undoubtedly binding, gives rise to new questions in the canonical science's ongoing reflection about the best instruments for examining the alleged nullity of marriage.*

BERNARD A. HEBDA*

Reflections on the Role of the Diocesan Bishop Envisioned by *Mitis Iudex Dominus Iesus*

In order to gain a proper understanding of *Mitis Iudex Dominus Iesus* it would be essential to place the document in its proper context.[1] That requires that we have to have a sense of the person of the legislator, of Pope Francis, and be able to see this legislative action in the overall context of his way of exercising the Petrine ministry.

I would presume that those of us who have been trained in homiletics or public speaking would have been encouraged to avoid ever going back to material that we have already used, especially with the same audience, lest we be seen as repeating ourselves. If that is true for a parish priest, how much more must it apply to the Bishop of Rome, the Successor of Saint Peter. A Pope would normally have an entire staff assisting him in the preparation of his discourses and one of their traditional tasks has been to ensure that a Holy Father would not repeat himself, or go back too often to the same analogy. Repetition on the part of a Holy Father would be seen as beneath his dignity. Obviously, Pope Francis did not get that memo! There is a great deal of seemingly intentional repetition in what he

---

* Archbishop of Saint Paul and Minneapolis, MN.
1. Francis, motu proprio *Mitis Iudex Dominus Iesus*, August 15, 2015 (Vatican City: Libreria Editrice Vaticana, 2015). Hereafter cited as MI. Many of these same reflections could be made of the apostolic letter motu proprio *Mitis et Misericors Iesus*, but this article will directly address only the legislation for the Latin Church. See Francis, motu proprio *Mitis et Misericors Iesus*, August 15, 2015 (Vatican City: Libreria Editrice Vaticana, 2015).

has offered to the Church and to the world at large in the three years since his election. This repetition, rather novel for a Pope, helps us identify certain emphases in his ministry that in turn give us a better understanding of *Mitis Iudex Dominus Iesus*.

The Pontificate of Pope Francis as Context for the Reform

We must first of all see the legislation in the specific context of this Extraordinary Jubilee of Mercy. I remember being in Saint Peter's Square on the Sunday after Pope Francis had been elected. And what did the new Pope speak about on that first public occasion? Mercy. He said: "[God] always has patience, patience with us, he understands us, he waits for us, he does not tire of forgiving us if we are able to return to him with a contrite heart."[2] He quoted Cardinal Kasper and his work on the subject.[3] Normally, popes only quote their predecessors—other popes—or individuals whose first name is preceded by "Saint." Accordingly, to be quoting a living theologian, even if a cardinal, was a little bit unusual. It should have given us an indication that this pope would be sometimes willing to go outside the normal bounds, especially when it comes to making a key point or emphasizing an important theme.

Secondly, we have to understand the legislation in the context of Pope Francis' emphasis on the importance of putting people before things or processes. One of the references to which Pope Francis has frequently returned[4] is a rabbinical explanation of the Tower of Babel that appears in

---

2. Francis, Angelus Address, March 17, 2013: *L'Osservatore Romano. Daily Italian Edition* 153/65 (March 18–19, 2013) 7: "Sempre ha pazienza, pazienza con noi, ci comprende, ci attende, non si stanca di perdonarci se sappiamo tornare a lui con il cuore contrito."

3. See Walter Cardinal Kasper, *Mercy. The Essence of the Gospel and the Key to Christian Life* (Mahwah, NJ: Paulist Press, 2014).

4. As the Pope indicated himself in his discourse at the Pentecost Vigil with the Ecclesial Movements in St. Peter's Square, May 18, 2013, he had referred to the story on three different occasions in three different contexts in the same week. Francis, Discourse at the Pentecost Vigil with the Ecclesial Movements, May 18, 2013: *L'Osservatore Romano. Daily Italian Edition* 153/115 (May 20–21, 2013) 5: "Vorrei raccontarvi una storia. L'ho fatto già due volte questa settimana, ma lo farò una terza volta con voi. E' la storia che racconta un midrash biblico di un Rabbino del secolo XII. Lui narra la storia della costruzione della Torre di Babele e dice che, per costruire la Torre di Babele, era necessario fare i mattoni. Che cosa significa questo? Andare, impastare il fango, portare la paglia, fare tutto . . . poi, al forno. E quando il mattone era fatto doveva essere portato su, per la costruzione della Torre di Babele. Un mattone era

medieval midrash and that offers an interesting insight into why the erection of the Tower would have been so problematic that God would have wanted to thwart any further construction: at a certain point the bricks came to have a greater value in the estimation of those building the tower than the workmen who carried those bricks. That was a difficulty at the time of the Tower of Babel, and it also remains a risk for us. Pope Francis calls for us to reverse that priority, to value each individual, no matter who they are or how far removed they are from the Church. That, I think, is why he speaks to us so often about the importance of going out to the peripheries as missionary disciples who give witness to the joy of the gospel. He has made it clear that he is not just speaking about those at the physical outskirts of our towns and cities, but also those who are in any way distanced from the life of the Church; those who feel unwanted, unloved, disenfranchised, or confused.

Pope Francis wants us to know that the persons in those categories are people in need who need to be treated as a priority. That emphasis on putting people first is, I would argue, one of the keys to understanding *Mitis Iudex*. It is consistent with his call for the Church to be a poor Church for the poor. He often goes back to the importance of the Church, and all of us in the Church, having a real concern for the poor, a love for the poor, a respect for the poor, even to the point of falling on our knees before them.[5]

---

un tesoro, per tutto il lavoro che ci voleva per farlo. Quando cadeva un mattone, era una tragedia nazionale e l'operaio colpevole era punito; era tanto prezioso un mattone che se cadeva era un dramma. Ma se cadeva un operaio, non succedeva niente, era un'altra cosa. Questo succede oggi: se gli investimenti nelle banche calano un po' . . . tragedia . . . come si fa? Ma se muoiono di fame le persone, se non hanno da mangiare, se non hanno salute, non fa niente! Questa è la nostra crisi di oggi! E la testimonianza di una Chiesa povera per i poveri va contro questa mentalità."

5. Cf. Francis, General Audience Address, June 3, 2015: *L'Osservatore Romano. Daily Italian Edition* 155/125 (June 4, 2015) 8: "Nonostante tutto questo, ci sono tante famiglie povere che con dignità cercano di condurre la loro vita quotidiana, spesso confidando apertamente nella benedizione di Dio. Questa lezione, però, non deve giustificare la nostra indifferenza, ma semmai aumentare la nostra vergogna per il fatto che ci sia tanta povertà! E' quasi un miracolo che, anche nella povertà, la famiglia continui a formarsi, e persino a conservare—come può—la speciale umanità dei suoi legami. Il fatto irrita quei pianificatori del benessere che considerano gli affetti, la generazione, i legami famigliari, come una variabile secondaria della qualità della vita. Non capiscono niente! Invece, noi dovremmo inginocchiarci davanti a queste famiglie, che sono una vera scuola di umanità che salva le società dalla barbarie."

When he speaks about desiring bishops and priests to be shepherds with the odor of the sheep,[6] he is asking us to know intimately and personally the great needs of our flock. He wants us to understand that clergy are not to be simply bureaucrats or "airport bishops,"[7] but shepherds. How often he uses the image of the Church as a Field Hospital as a means of encouraging us to be in the midst of the chaos of the world, in the midst of the mess, and then to accompany those we find there, who are in need on their journey, even when that means getting dirty ourselves.[8] If you want to understand *Mitis Iudex*, you have to understand Pope Francis's

---

6. Cf. Francis, Homily for the Mass of Chrism, March 28, 2013: *L'Osservatore Romano. Daily Italian Edition* 153/74 (March 29, 2013) 8: "Da qui deriva precisamente l'insoddisfazione di alcuni, che finiscono per essere tristi, preti tristi, e trasformati in una sorta di collezionisti di antichità oppure di novità, invece di essere pastori con 'l'odore delle pecore'–questo io vi chiedo: siate pastori con 'l'odore delle pecore', che si senta quello–; invece di essere pastori in mezzo al proprio gregge e pescatori di uomini. È vero che la cosiddetta crisi di identità sacerdotale ci minaccia tutti e si somma ad una crisi di civiltà; però, se sappiamo infrangere la sua onda, noi potremo prendere il largo nel nome del Signore e gettare le reti. È bene che la realtà stessa ci porti ad andare là dove ciò che siamo per grazia appare chiaramente come pura grazia, in questo mare del mondo attuale dove vale solo l'unzione–e non la funzione–, e risultano feconde le reti gettate unicamente nel nome di Colui del quale noi ci siamo fidati: Gesù."

7. Cf. Francis, Address to a Group of Recently Appointed Bishops Taking Part in a Course Organized by the Congregation for Bishops and by the Congregation for the Eastern Church, September 19, 2013: *L'Osservatore Romano. Daily Italian Edition* 153/215 (September 20, 2013) 8: "Mi riferisco alla stabilità, che ha due aspetti precisi: "rimanere" nella diocesi, e rimanere in "questa" diocesi, come ho detto, senza cercare cambi o promozioni. Non si può conoscere veramente come pastori il proprio gregge, camminare davanti, in mezzo e dietro ad esso, curarlo con l'insegnamento, l'amministrazione dei Sacramenti e la testimonianza di vita, se non si rimane in diocesi. In questo, Trento è attualissimo: residenza. Il nostro è un tempo in cui si può viaggiare, muoversi da un punto all'altro con facilità, un tempo in cui i rapporti sono veloci, l'epoca di internet. Ma l'antica legge della residenza non è passata di moda! E' necessaria per il buon governo pastorale. Certo c'è una sollecitudine per le altre Chiese e per quella universale che possono chiedere di assentarsi dalla diocesi, ma sia per lo stretto tempo necessario e non abitualmente. Vedete, la residenza non è richiesta solo per una buona organizzazione, non è un elemento funzionale; ha una radice teologica! Siete sposi della vostra comunità, legati profondamente ad essa! Vi chiedo, per favore, di rimanere in mezzo al vostro popolo. Rimanere, rimanere . . . Evitate lo scandalo di essere "Vescovi di aeroporto"! Siate Pastori accoglienti, in cammino con il vostro popolo, con affetto, con misericordia, con dolcezza del tratto e fermezza paterna, con umiltà e discrezione, capaci di guardare anche ai vostri limiti e di avere una dose di buon umorismo. Questa è una grazia che dobbiamo chiedere, noi Vescovi. Tutti noi dobbiamo chiedere questa grazia: Signore, dammi il senso dell'umorismo. Trovare la strada di ridere di se stessi, prima, e un po' delle cose. E rimanete con il vostro gregge!"

8. Cf. Francis, *The Name of God is Mercy. A Conversation with Andrea Tornielli*, trans. Oonagh Stransky (New York NY: Random House, 2016) 52–53.

sensitivity to the pain of our brothers and sisters and his desire that the Church offer them healing.

Finally, we have to see the legislation in the context of Pope Francis' emphasis on the importance of dialogue, of conversation. From a canonical perspective, when we are so interested in everything that he says about the notion of synodality, it really boils down to what he is saying about dialogue and its role in the Church; how it is that we come to recognize the Lord's presence in the Church, and discern his will in the midst of our relationships.

My suggestion to you is that we have to see *Mitis Iudex* in the context we have just traced. When Pope Francis looks at the world, at those who have for example gone through the trauma of a failed marriage, he sees brothers and sisters on the periphery. We all know, especially those of us who work in tribunals, of the reality of this. We know that so often these people have a sense of alienation, a sense of failure, perhaps even guilt or blame. Certainly they often feel wounded, not just by their former spouse but also by the Church, and at times by God. This is a reality, and we do not need a Pew Study to acknowledge that one of the major reasons why people distance themselves from practicing the faith has exactly to do with these issues. Pope Francis's own instincts, which were then supported by the voices of those gathered at the last two meetings of the Synod of Bishops, is that the Church needs to do more to address that pain. We need to do more to tend to the wounds of those who have suffered through a divorce or separation. We need to go into those situations, those Field Hospitals, and remind people of God's mercy. When we consider this situation, we can see how all of those recurring Bergoglian themes mentioned above are being woven together in this legislation.

The Tribunal: a Ward in the Field Hospital

With this in mind, I would venture to say that the tribunal is a privileged "ward" in the Field Hospital that Pope Francis describes. He wants to make sure that the Tribunal is a place where people come to know the meekness and gentleness of Jesus; where they can come to know his healing and mercy. Pope Francis' hope is that this would be true whether or not the final decision of the tribunal would be in favor of a declaration of nullity. No matter the outcome of the proceedings, the Church needs to be facilitating an experience that offers an encounter with Christ. The tribunal process should be an experience of a Church that openly desires to accompany those in need.

People often tell me that they are afraid to go to the hospital because they hear so many stories of people getting infections, such as MRSA, while hospitalized, and sometimes those infections are untreatable and can be fatal. We need to make sure that those who come to our tribunals never risk picking up a spiritual MRSA that could leave them more alienated from the Church than when they came to our chanceries. Instead, the tribunal needs to be a place of encounter with the Church and her bridegroom.

The *Ratio procedendi* attached to *Mitis Iudex* highlights that objective when it requires that the diocesan bishop, as pastor of the whole diocese, be part of what goes on in that ward, in his tribunal, maximizing the chance of the desired encounter with Christ.[9] Pope Francis reminds us that the bishops are not there to replace all the tribunal personnel, but rather to be in the midst of the "mess," and, certainly, as we will discuss, to be involved in the work of healing and to be an example in some distinctly concrete and practical ways.

The Principle of the Involvement of the Diocesan Bishop

Many of those who have analyzed and commented on the two new motu proprios have focused on the role of the diocesan bishop. Monsignor Carlos Morán Bustos, the Dean of the Spanish Rota, for example, reports that the diocesan bishop is mentioned thirty-five times in the motu proprio; the most common noun referenced.[10] I want now to look at that emphasis.

---

9. *Ratio procedendi in causis ad matrimonii nullitatem declarandem*, Art. 1: "Episcopus vi can. 383 §1 animo apostolico prosequi tenetur coniuges separatos vel divortio digressos, qui propter suam vitæ condicionem forte a praxi religionis defecerint. Ipse igitur cum parochis (cfr. can. 529 §1) sollicitudinem pastoralem comparticipatur erga hos christifideles in angustiis constitutos." For a discussion of the juridical nature of the *Ratio procedendi*, see William L. Daniel, "An Analysis of Pope Francis' 2015 Reform of the General Legislation Governing Causes of Nullity of Marriage," *The Jurist* 75 (2015) 429–466, especially 456ff, and this volume, 27–64, especially 54ff.

10. Carlos M. Móran Bustos, "El proceso "Brevior" ante el Obispo Diocesano," in *Procesos de nulidad matrimonial tras la reforma del papa Francisco*, ed. Maria Elena Olmos Ortega (Madrid: Editorial Dykinson, 2016) 131.

Let's begin by looking at what Pope Francis himself states in the introduction to the document about the role of the bishop:

> In order that a teaching of the Second Vatican Council regarding a certain area of great importance finally be put into practice, it has been decided **to declare openly** (emphasis added) that the bishop himself in the church over which he has been appointed shepherd and head, is by that very fact the judge of those faithful entrusted to his care. It is thus hoped that the bishop himself, be it of a large or small diocese, stand as a sign of the conversion of ecclesiastical structures, and that he does not delegate completely the duty of deciding marriage cases to the offices of his curia.[11]

For anyone with a canonical background, this "open declaration" that the bishop is a judge should not be shocking. It is not nearly as novel as the paragraph might seem to suggest. Every canonist knows that the Code already speaks directly about the obligations of the diocesan bishop in the context of his tribunal. What we have here, however, is a fresh and unequivocal restatement, with a hint of dramatic bravado, of a canonical principle that is already well established.[12]

---

11. MI III: "Ut sane Concilii Vaticani II in quodam magni ponderis ambitu documentum ad effectum tandem ducatur, decretum est palam proferri ipsum Episcopum in sua Ecclesia, cuius pastor et caput constituitur, eo ipso esse inter christifideles sibi commissos iudicem. Exoptatur ergo ut in magnis sicut in parvis diœcesibus ipse Episcopus signum offerat conversionis ecclesiasticarum structurarum, neque munus iudiciarium in re matrimoniali curiæ officiis prorsus delegatum relinquat. Idque speciatim valeat in processu breviori, qui ad dirimendos casus manifestioris nullitatis stabilitur."

12. This would not be the first time that the Holy Father, as a master of the art of communication, re-presents a standard principle of canon law in a way that draws new (and positive) attention. When Pope Francis announced that he would be sending these missionaries into the world during the Extraordinary Jubilee of Mercy, he did so without giving a precise description of what they were going to be doing, or what faculties they would be given. In fact, he said initially that they would be given the ability of being able to forgive the *sin* of abortion, something that was already available to them, without drawing any juridical distinction between sin and delict. That was enough to cause heart palpitations amongst many canonists. In any event, by using common, untechnical language to give new emphasis to something that was already part of our tradition (but not known or understood by persons other than priests and canonists) he managed to draw fresh eyes not only to the problem, but to the solutions offered by the Church to these complex and difficult situations. Anecdotally, his remarks seem to have achieved their purpose, provoking a wave of penitents eager to take advantage of a "new" opening, completely unaware that the Church had long been providing for that opportunity for healing.

I would suggest that we would best understand the Holy Father's "open declaration" in that same context. In order to "wake up" the bishop and open his eyes to something that is already part of canonical tradition (even if not of practice). Might it be that Pope Francis

Certainly the inclusion of a role for the diocesan bishop is not entirely new. Pope Francis was not legislating in a vacuum, nor writing on a clean slate, but rather building on a long and solid tradition that is both theologically and canonically sound. When we consider what the Church teaches about the identity of the diocesan bishop, whether that be in the documents of the Second Vatican Council, in the Catechism of the Catholic Church, or in the Code of Canon Law, we are left with a clear idea of what the diocesan bishop is expected to do.

For example, in *Lumen Gentium* we read that the episcopacy is one of the vehicles through which Christ continues to be present in the midst of those who believe, one of the ways in which he continues to shepherd his flock.[13] Reflecting his triple *munera*, the bishop is priest, prophet, and king; he is called to sanctify, teach and govern. Each of those areas of episcopal ministry has to be understood as concretizations of the bishop's call to a ministry of service. In *Christus Dominus* we read: "In exercising his office of father and pastor, a bishop should stand in the midst of his people as one who serves. Let him be a good shepherd who knows his sheep, and whose sheep know him."[14]

He does this by accompanying them in their joys and struggles alike, always leading them toward the fullness of truth found uniquely in Christ. The pastors' sacred power, we read in the *Directory for the Pastoral Ministry of Bishops*, is to be used "exclusively for the spiritual development of their flock in truth and holiness, keeping in mind that he who is greater should become as the lesser, and he who is the leader as the servant (cf. *Lk* 22:26–27)."[15]

---

is simply accentuating the point because of his keen awareness that not every reader of the motu proprio will be a bishop with canonical qualifications?

13. Cf. Vatican II, *Lumen gentium* 18, November 21, 1964: *AAS* 57 (1965) 21–22. Hereafter cited as LG.

14. Vatican II, decree *Christus Dominus* 16, October 28, 1965: *AAS* 58 (1966) 680–681: "In exercendo suo munere patris ac pastoris, sint Episcopi in medio suorum sicut qui ministrant, boni pastores qui cognoscunt suas oves quosque et ipsæ cognoscunt, veri patres qui spiritu dilectionis et sollicitudinis erga omnes præstant, quorumque auctoritati divinitus quidem collatæ omnes grato animo sese subiciunt. Integram sui gregis familiam ita congregent atque efforment ut omnes, officiorum suorum conscii, in communione caritatis vivant et operentur." Hereafter cited as CD.

15. Congregation for Bishops, Directory for the Pastoral Ministry of Bishops *Apostolorum Successores*, February 22, 2004 (Vatican City: Libreria Editrice Vaticana, 2004) n. 158: "In forza di ciò, i Vescovi 'reggono le Chiese particolari loro affidate, come vicari e legati di Cristo, col consiglio, la persuasione, l'esempio, ma anche con l'autorità e la sacra potestà, della quale

Our theological and canonical tradition confirms that one aspect of the bishop's role as humble shepherd and servant is his role as judge. Canon 1419 §1, for example, specifies: "In each diocese and for all cases not expressly excepted by law, the judge of first instance is the diocesan bishop, who can exercise judicial power personally or through others."[16] Yet we know from our experience that it is rare to find a diocesan bishop making use of that prerogative, often for very good pastoral reasons. In fact, in the Instruction *Dignitas Connubii* we read that: "[In] each diocese the judge of first instance for causes of nullity of marriage not expressly excepted by law is the diocesan bishop, who can exercise judicial power personally or through others, in accordance with the law (cf. c. 1419 §1) . . . **Nonetheless, it is expedient that, unless special causes demand it, he not do this personally.**"[17] (emphasis added)

While some cynics might think that this suggestion arises from the lack of canonical competence on the part of the average bishop, I would suggest that the reason is principally pastoral: the conflict that potentially arises from judging the validity of a particular marriage could often make it difficult for the bishop to pastor the persons involved. Especially in a highly contentious proceeding, if the diocesan bishop is judging and is seen to be favoring one view or position over another, he could easily be misunderstood as in fact favoring one party over the other. The work of

---

però non si servono se non per edificare il proprio gregge nella verità e nella santità, ricordandosi che chi è più grande si deve fare come il più piccolo, e chi è il capo, come colui che serve'." Hereafter cited as AS.

16. *Codex Iuris Canonici auctoritate Ioannis Pauli PP. II promulgatus* (Vatican City: Libreria Editrice Vaticana, 1983) c. 1419 §1: "In unaquaque diœcesi et pro omnibus causis iure expresse non exceptis, iudex primæ instantiæ est Episcopus diœcesanus, qui iudicialem potestatem exercere potest per se ipse vel per alios, secundum canones qui sequuntur." English translation from *Code of Canon Law, Latin-English Edition: New English Translation* (Washington DC: CLSA, 1998). All subsequent English translations of canons from this code will be taken from this source unless otherwise indicated.

17. Pontifical Council for Legislative Texts, *Diginitas connubii. Instructio servanda a tribunalibus diœcesanis et interdiœcesanis in pertractandis causis nullitatis matrimonii*, January 25, 2005 (Vatican City: Libreria Editrice Vaticana, 2005) Art. 22 §§1–2: "§1. In unaquaque diœcesi iudex primæ instantiæ pro causis nullitatis matrimonii iure expresse non exceptis est Episcopus diœcesanus, qui iudicialem potestatem exercere potest per se ipse vel per alios, ad normam iuris (cf. c. 1419, § 1). §2. Expedit tamen, nisi speciales causæ id exigant, ne ipse id per se faciat." Hereafter cited as DC. English translation from Klaus Lüdicke and Ronny E. Jenkins, *Dignitas connubii: Norms and Commentary* (Washington DC: CLSA, 2006). All subsequent English translations of this document will be taken from this source unless otherwise indicated.

healing would be extremely difficult if the bishop's perceived actions have in any way alienated one of the parties.

I would suggest that there are also some very practical considerations that would suggest that the diocesan bishop not be routinely involved in judging. First amongst these is the question of time. There are many things that the Church today demands of a diocesan bishop, and the process of judging, and judging well, consumes both the judge's time and energy. Given that reality, does the Church really want the diocesan bishop to be engaged in this work, over and above other important tasks? To ask this question is not to undermine the importance of judging, but rather to emphasize it. If there are other important things that a diocesan bishop is obliged to do, can he really give the necessary time and attention to the task of judging?

All in all, where there exists the possibility of having some other qualified person carry out the work of judging, it would seem to make good pastoral and practical sense for the bishop to avail himself regularly of that option.[18] But in those instances and parts of the world where the diocesan bishop does not have anybody else to judge, and where he is therefore bound to do that work, it would be important for him to step up and engage in the task before him.

With this in mind, we can see that Pope Francis in *Mitis Iudex* is calling attention to two complementary dimensions of the episcopacy: the bishop as servant and the bishop as judge. While the thought of taking on additional responsibilities in the tribunal process may frighten many bishops, Pope Francis has emphasized and contextualized the involvement, speaking of it as both a "sacred right and duty" of the diocesan bishop "before the Lord himself to ensure that judgment can be enacted toward those entrusted to his care," whether indirectly through tribunal staff, or even directly as the diocesan bishop and pastor. Once again, its "people before processes."

While *Mitis Iudex* is by no means novel in its insistence that the bishop has a role to play in his tribunal, what is novel is what Pope Francis has to say about the extent to which that role can be delegated to others. While the motu proprio makes it clear that the bishop can fulfill his obligation *in part* through his tribunal staff, there is a somewhat jarring statement in the

---

18. Cf. DC Art. 22.

introduction to the document where Pope Francis expresses his desire that the bishop "not completely delegate his responsibility to others." While canonists will be debating exactly what that means, it is already clear that one of the ways in which Pope Francis has guaranteed the involvement of the diocesan bishop is through the institution of the *processus brevior*, which is uniquely tied to the diocesan bishop.

The *Processus Brevior* and the Diocesan Bishop

The new *processus brevior* attributes to the diocesan bishop a very direct and intimate role in judging cases qualifying for this process. The new can. 1687 §1 specifies that the diocesan bishop is to do four things: 1) consult with the instructor and the assessor; 2) consider the observations of the defender of the bond; 3) consider, if there are any, the defense briefs of the parties; 4) issue the sentence if moral certitude about the nullity of marriage is reached (otherwise, he is to refer the case to the ordinary method).[19] It is seemed to be premised on a fifth and primary responsibility, reviewing the acts that the bishop has received.

This role in the *processus brevior*, I must admit, seems to be one of the aspects of *Mitis Iudex* that has caused the most anxiety on the part of my brother bishops. There seems to be some apprehension concerning how difficult it will be for the bishop to arrive at moral certitude in individual cases and how time-consuming it will be to review the observations and briefs. Some of that anxiety seems to dissipate when the bishop is reminded that he makes decisions of equal importance and equivalent difficulty every day and has already been involved in Privilege of the Faith cases.

Anxiety aside, the *processus brevior* is nonetheless a very real way in which the diocesan bishop as pastor, but also as servant and judge, is being called to be involved in this important ministry in the life of the Church. Wherever and whenever this process is used, the diocesan bishop's role

---

19. Can. 1687 §1: "After he has received the acts, the diocesan bishop, having consulted with the instructor and the assessor, and having considered the observations of the defender of the bond and, if there are any, the defense briefs of the parties, is to issue the sentence if moral certitude about the nullity of marriage is reached. Otherwise, he refers the case to the ordinary method."

is going to be especially prominent. To emphasize this, the Holy Father writes: "We desire that the bishop himself be established as the judge in this process, who, due to his duty as pastor, has the greatest care for catholic unity with Peter in faith and discipline."[20] Certainly this *processus brevior* is a point of intersection between the judicial role of the diocesan bishop and his pastoral role.

Pope Francis, however, broadens the view of the pastoral function of the bishop when he explains that the bishops' role in the juridical process is tied particularly to the work and service of unity of all the bishops united with the Successor of Peter himself. The unity that bishops are called to promote is not only a unity of faith but also a unity of discipline. The bishop is not establishing his own discipline; he, in union with the Successor of Peter, is promoting the discipline of the universal Church.

In those exceptional cases qualifying for the *processus brevior*, the diocesan bishop is not simply being called upon to serve as judge but also as a pastor who, in union with the Successor of Peter, brings the light of Christ into the lives of those seeking the nullity at what could potentially be a very difficult time for them. His involvement in a pastoral way in the *processus brevior* is one of the ways in which Christ might be made known to those seeking a declaration of nullity.

The Diocesan Bishop and His Tribunal

As we have seen, Pope Francis has not so much opened a new approach in this legislation, other than with respect to the *processus brevior*, but rather has added a new emphasis on the role of the diocesan bishop in the process for the declaration of marriage nullity. This emphasis is significant. Through the legislation he has sought to bring the diocesan bishop physically into his tribunal, and to really remind the bishop that his role in the Tribunal has to be seen not as an option but as a sacred duty.

On a personal note, I must confess how rare it has been that I have visited the tribunal in the dioceses where I have served. Occasionally, the

---

20. MI IV: "Namque, ordinario processu matrimoniali expeditiore reddito, efficta est quædam processus brevioris species—præeter documentalem prout in præsentiarum vigentem—, in iis applicanda casibus in quibus accusata matrimonii nullitas pro se habet argumentorum peculiariter evidentium fulcimen."

staff or a disgruntled petitioner or respondent, or a report from the Signatura have brought something to my attention, but it has up to now never been my practice to set out proactively to familiarize myself with the specifics of the "what" and "how"—the nuts and bolts—of tribunal practice in "my" tribunal, contenting myself with maintaining the perspective that one receives from a relatively high altitude. For the most part, I have tried to stay out of the weeds so as not to interfere with the day-to-day workings of the tribunal. I suspect that this been the experience for many bishops.

I see *Mitis Iudex* as requiring somewhat of a change in that approach. By requiring the bishop to be directly involved at least in the *processus brevior*, Pope Francis is bringing the diocesan bishop face-to-face not only with his tribunal staff, but also with the realities met by those whose lives are so affected by the work that goes on in our tribunals. It brings the diocesan bishop into that ward of the Field Hospital where the wounds of those who are involved in marital breakdown cry out for care. The diocesan bishop will no longer be isolated from those matters and this, I really believe, will have in the long run a significant impact on the bishop's understanding of the importance of tribunal ministry, and of the ministry of *his* tribunal in particular.

As a result, I suspect we bishops will have a heightened sense of the urgency of effective tribunal ministry as we hear with our own ears, or read with our own eyes, the stories that tribunal staffs hear all the time.

In an address to those going through initial training for new bishops in September 2015, Pope Francis touched on this theme.[21] Although he was speaking about those who are, in general, alienated from the Church, and maybe even those have distanced themselves from the Church, he encouraged the newly ordained bishops to become actively involved in these peoples' lives. This now also applies to those who approach the marriage tribunal seeking clarity about their situation. The Holy Father told those new bishops that they need to walk with others as Christ did on the road to Emmaus, that they need to become seemingly "lost wayfarers" too, asking what happened in the "Jerusalem" of their life, and discreetly letting

---

21. Cf. Francis, Address to a Group of Recently Appointed Bishops Taking Part in a Course Organized by the Congregation for Bishops and by the Congregation for the Eastern Churches, September 19, 2013: *L'Osservatore Romano. Daily Italian Edition* 153/215 (September 20, 2013) 8.

the people pour out their heart to him.[22] Could this be a model for what might happen in the tribunal, too? The pope went on to say, "Do not be scandalized by their sorrows or their disappointment."[23]

How important it is that we bishops are willing to hear those things, to take them in, and to spend time with these people on their own "Emmaus road," their own rediscovery of the person of Christ. Here we have an opportunity to dispense words that reveal to them what they are still incapable of seeing, the potential good hidden by their disappointments. More than with words, too, we have an opportunity to warm their hearts by humble listening, and by showing a genuine interest in their circumstances and well-being, so that their eyes may be opened to see not just us, but Christ. I am convinced that this is going to be something really important not just for those whose eyes are opened on that road to "Emmaus," but also for the diocesan bishop, as he has that experience with the sheep of his flock.

I suspect that a firsthand experience of the situations of the faithful is also going to prompt the bishop to want to do more to help the tribunal. One of the things that I suggest will be a fruit of this is a greater sensitivity to the need to have adequate tribunal staff, and to make sure that such personnel are properly qualified and well prepared. As Archbishop Frans Daneels had emphasized when Secretary of the Apostolic Signatura, this must be a priority for a tribunal to run effectively and efficiently.[24]

So often, when we bishops have been trying to determine diocesan priorities, the well-functioning tribunal has suffered given that it is the proverbial squeaky wheel that usually gets the oil. By bringing the bishop into direct contact with the work of the marriage tribunal, *Mitis Iudex* may change some priorities. I suspect there is going to be more traction for requests for additional and better-trained personnel, personnel who are really capable of this ministry and have the appropriate canonical formation for this crucially important work.

More than that, though, the involvement of the bishop should also promote a better *pastoral* formation among tribunal staff, which is perhaps the key to the change in culture that Pope Francis seems to be desiring and

---

22. Ibid.
23. Ibid.
24. See Frans Daneels, "A First Approach to the Reform of the Process for the Declaration of Nullity of Marriage," *The Jurist* 76 (2016) 135, and this volume, 25.

effecting. Recall how often Pope Francis has spoken and written of the importance of accompanying those who are in need.

In theory, that should have already been a focus for bishops. The *Directory for the Pastoral Ministry of Bishops* tells us that the bishop needs to walk with his people, going ahead of them, and indicating the path to be traveled.[25] He does this first and foremost through his words and witness, but also with the authority he has received from Christ.

By bringing the bishop into his tribunal, *Mitis Iudex* allows the tribunal to benefit from the bishop's more generalized pastoral experience of accompaniment. It would be naïve to think that a bishop is going to be able to walk into his tribunal and have on day one an immediate pastoral impact on a seasoned tribunal staff somewhat set in its ways and practices. Yet my hope would be that the bishop's experience as a pastoral minister, and his participation in the Church's sanctifying office and teaching office, are all going to give him insights into the work that is already being undertaken in his tribunal. Then, as he comes to see a much broader reality through his involvement in the process, I suspect and hope that he will be in a position to bring a certain freshness to this work, and perhaps help those directly involved in the process on a daily basis to be renewed in their task.

For many of those working in tribunals, there can be a danger that such challenging and highly technical work could simply become routine. When the diocesan bishop, who presumably is going to be on his toes because of the newness of his engagement in the working of the tribunal, begins to view this ministry with a fresh set of eyes, there may be the opportunity for the bishop to assist the tribunal staff in developing a new or greater appreciation of the importance of their ministry, not just as functionaries of the diocese, but as Christians being called to accompany other Christians in their difficulties in a ministry that is certainly pastoral in its foundation.

---

25. Cf. AS 159: "Il Vescovo, guida del suo popolo. Il Vescovo è colui che deve camminare insieme al suo popolo ed andare avanti, indicando con la parola e con la testimonianza della vita, prima ancora che con l'autorità ricevuta da Cristo, il cammino da percorrere. Egli deve essere una guida spirituale coerente e coraggiosa, che, come Mosè, vede l'invisibile e non abbia titubanze ad andare contro corrente, quando il bene spirituale lo esige. Egli deve adoperarsi perché la sua parola e le sue iniziative siano bene accolte e non sia scalfita la sua autorità agli occhi della comunità diocesana, ma poi quello che deve maggiormente importare ad un Vescovo è il giudizio di Dio."

The Diocesan Bishop: Pastor and Guardian of Truth

Regardless of whether we are speaking of the technical involvement of the diocesan bishop in the *processus brevior* or in the general oversight of the ministry of his tribunal, the renewed engagement of the diocesan bishop required by *Mitis Iudex* is fundamentally pastoral because of its relationship with the truth. Given our conviction that Jesus Christ is the Truth, anything that we do to accompany our sisters and brothers to a greater appreciation of the truth of their situation, gives them the opportunity to see and encounter Jesus himself. This is always a profoundly pastoral act.

Writing in *The Jurist*, His Eminence Cardinal Burke speaks about how important it is that we do not misunderstand what it means to be pastoral in the tribunal setting.[26] It is not, he says, a question of sentimentality, even as we come to recognize the great pain that people are experiencing. Rather, if we truly seek to get to the heart of the matter, to the truth of their marital situation, we have a privileged opportunity to provide pastoral assistance to our petitioners (and to the extent that they participate, to the respondents as well).

When we hear the word "pastoral," especially in the context of tribunal ministry, we have to understand the term in relation to the truth, that is, in relation to the discovery of the truth about the marriage before us. Certainly, we have to be aware of the whole range of emotions and experiences that people so often bring into this difficult forum; but we are most appropriately "pastoral" when our efforts assist our brothers and sisters in the discovery of the truth. The pastoral element of tribunal work is about more than removing consequences of bad decisions or taking away pain, it needs to be centered always on walking with individuals in arriving at the objective truth of their situation or about themselves, even (perhaps, especially) when that is very difficult.

If we accept this understanding of the pastoral dimension of the diocesan bishop's engagement in the tribunal, we can also see how this new legislation also has the potential to increase the diocesan bishops' awareness of the importance of pastoral outreach to couples in trouble, whether they be couples still struggling to live together as husband and wife, or,

---

26. See Raymond Leo Cardinal Burke, "Canonical Questions Regarding the Proposed Pastoral Care of the Faithful Who Are Divorced and Have Attempted Marriage," *The Jurist* 75 (2010) 273–295, especially 279–281.

couples who have already separated, or couples who have already gone through a civil divorce. I would venture to presume that this involvement will also most probably lead to a renewed appreciation of the importance of premarital preparation and ministry to the newly married.

One of the things that I found in my own tribunal work early in my priesthood was that it provided a particularly helpful backdrop for preparing couples for marriage. It should not be surprising that the experiences shared day-in and day-out in our tribunals would give us insights into what we are doing well in preparing couples for marriage and where we are failing. By bringing the bishop directly into the tribunal process, and having him listen to the stories of people on the road to "Emmaus," *Mitis Iudex* can be expected to have a very positive impact at the diocesan level and in the establishment of pre-marriage preparation as an important priority as the Church strives to help people avoid the pain of a failed marriage, far before they come to the point of seeking the intervention of a tribunal.

In addition to creating circumstances that would favor the improvement of pre-marriage preparation, *Mitis Iudex* also calls for an improved pastoral response when a party first approaches the tribunal, prior to the initiation of any judicial action. Pope Francis stresses the importance of having people who are trained to work with couples at the time of the first contact, whether that take place in our parishes or at the tribunal itself One would imagine that the diocesan bishop should be directly involved in this, too, whether it be in appointing people to offer this pastoral service or by being involved in their formation. In theory, the bishop could even be directly involved in the work itself. Perhaps in larger dioceses he could even choose to establish a permanent office to provide this kind of outreach. Again, all of this emphasizes the spirit of apostolic zeal which Pope Francis seems to be so keen to promote, ensuring that bishops are directly attending to the needs of separated and divorced spouses, whether it be on an *ad hoc* basis, or through the establishment of stable administrative structures or offices.

Financial Concerns and Considerations

Another significant innovation introduced by *Mitis Iudex* of particular interest to the diocesan bishop would be the motu proprio's emphasis on eliminating cost as a factor that would prevent a party from seeking the assistance of a tribunal. This is going to be particularly challenging for the diocesan bishop, but perhaps also enlightening for him, given that Pope Francis seems to be really asking us to be able to offer this service, offer this ministry, without imposing an undue economic burden on those coming to seek our help.[27]

Those responsible for preparing diocesan budgets already know how difficult this can be: how can you continue to maintain a well-prepared staff if there is no income, or little income, coming into the tribunal, especially if we are foreseeing increased recourse to the tribunal? Many dioceses already feel a financial pinch from merely offering a partial subsidy to the tribunal—how can a struggling diocese be expected to provide a total subsidy?

A number of dioceses in the United States have already successfully responded to this call and eliminated fees in their tribunals, requiring the diocesan bishop to make adjustments in other areas of expenditure.[28] One would imagine, however, that as the average bishop becomes more familiar with the work of the tribunal, as he personally walks with more of his hurting brothers and sisters on the road to Emmaus, as he comes to recognize both the urgent need for healing and the extent to which financial considerations can be an obstacle to that healing, the easier it will be for him to justify the necessary adjustment in the diocesan budget. Even if he is not persuaded by those factors, the insistence of the Holy Father in this area should probably be sufficiently persuasive.

The Transformation in Approach Has Already Begun

I would like to conclude by sharing an example of how I have witnessed evidence of the fruit of Pope Francis's call for a new, more pastoral

---

27. Cf. MI VI: "Una cum iudicis proximitate curent pro posse Episcoporum Conferentiæ, salva iusta et honesta tribunalium operatorum mercede, ut processuum gratuitati caveatur et Ecclesia, generosam matrem se ostendens fidelibus, in re tam arcte animarum saluti cohærente manifestet Christi gratuitum amorem quo salvi omnes facti sumus."

28. The National Catholic Register noted that there seemed to be a trend in the Pope Francis pontificate to waive fees, even before *Mitis Iudex*: In an article by Peter Jesserer Smith on the Diocese of Pittsburgh's decision to waive all tribunal fees, *Honoring Year of Mercy, Pittsburgh Diocese Eliminates Annulment Fees*, April 2, 2015, the *National Catholic Register* noted that in 2014, the Dioceses of Rochester, N.Y., Cleveland, St. Petersburg, Fla., and Fort Wayne-South Bend, Ind., had all decided to eliminate the annulment fee and subsidize costs entirely from their operating budgets. http://www.ncregister.com/daily-news/honoring-year-of-mercy-pittsburgh-diocese-eliminates-annulment-fees/

approach, in the work of our tribunals. I recently received, for the first time ever, a letter from one of the Prelate Auditors of the Roman Rota, accompanying a negative decision, asking me to meet personally with the Petitioner and then to write back to the Rota with the assurance that a meeting had taken place. What did they want me to do? To explain to the person exactly what this judgment meant and to lay out for her what her options would be. They presumably were not asking me to do this because I had any kind of canonical background, but simply because I am the pastor of the local church. It was clear that they were concerned that the negative decision would have a negative impact upon the petitioner and they seemed to be concerned that I soften the blow. This was a "kinder, gentler" Roman Rota than many of us have experienced in the past. The request even came in a language other than Latin!

It was an interesting experience, as I indeed invited the person to visit and had an experience of the raw emotion that comes when a party receives a negative decision. The person had been waiting for three years, and at the end of that time, I think there was some expectation that if the bishop was calling, it was likely to be good news, yet instead it was a negative decision. Even though I had done tribunal work for many years, it was still challenging and enlightening for me to have to be explaining directly what are the options that are open to that person.

In this particular case, occurring just prior to the Rota receiving their new faculties at the end of last year which would have allowed them to decide on other grounds, I as diocesan bishop was concretely encouraged to suggest to the petitioner that she consider pursuing her case on other grounds. As I was asked to explain to the person that *perhaps* if they reintroduced the case on new grounds there might be a different decision, it was very clear to me that the Rotal judge truly cared about the petitioner.

I am not sure if the resulting encounter with the petitioner was helpful to her, or if I had helped her any more than my judicial vicar could have helped her, but I had a sense that the encounter did create a certain pastoral bond, and would have communicated to the petitioner that the Church cared, perhaps lessening the distance between her and the Church that had just given her a decision other than what she wanted. My involvement as a representative of the local Church would have communicated, I hope, that the Church wanted to be involved as she went forward, whether or not she pursued new grounds.

One point that I should raise concerning this particular experience, though, comes about because of the new circumstances of the *processus brevior.* In the course of my conversation with the petitioner and my explanation of the options before her, I began to wonder whether this would be a case for the *processus brevior*? It occurred to me that while I was meeting with her as her pastor, I might down the road have to be the judge of her case, in the event that she would decide to accept the Rota's suggestion and move forward on other grounds and in the event that my judicial vicar would determine that the *processus brevior* would be appropriate in this particular case.

There was a certain awkwardness in being both the pastor and the potential judge. While the relationship that I was building with the petitioner could foreseeably be strengthened by an eventual affirmative decision, a negative decision could be devastating. It made me wonder whether *Mitis Iudex* should have made some provision for exceptional delegation of the role given exclusively to the diocesan bishop in the *processus brevior.* It should not be surprising that there may be a need for some "tweaking" of the new legislation in response to such concrete but unforeseen circumstances encountered in the implementation of *Mitis Iudex.* It is clear that some of those circumstances are already being brought to the Roman tribunals and to the Pontifical Council for Legislative Texts.[29]

On the specific question of the potential delegation of the diocesan bishop in the *processus brevior*, I note that Professor William Daniel has already presented a strong argument in favor of that possibility. I hope that Professor Daniel's argument would be given serious consideration in Rome if and when the issue is considered.[30] While it seems clear that the norm does not presently give the diocesan bishop the option of delegation, it would seem to be worth considering whether there are some instances in which the present norm restricting the *processus brevior* to the diocesan bishop would effectively render it impossible for certain petitioners to have recourse to the *processus brevior*, simply because of the

---

29. The Pontifical Council for Legislative Texts has already issued a number of private "clarifications" concerning the motu proprios. They are available in English translation in *The Jurist* 75 (2015) 663–671 and *The Jurist* 76 (2016) 287–292, and in this volume, 367–380. Further clarifications are expected to be published on http://www.delegumtextibus.va/content/testilegislativi/it/risposte-particolari/procedure-per-la-dichiarazione-della-nullita-matrimoniale.html

30. See William L. Daniel, "The Abbreviated Matrimonial Process before the Bishop in Cases of 'Manifest Nullity' of Marriage," *The Jurist* 75 (2015) 539–591, especially 556–563, and in this volume, 159–232, especially 176–183.

particular diocesan bishop's prior or present personal connections to the parties or their families.

Conclusion

Pope Francis' *Mitis Iudex* can be expected to engage the diocesan bishop in a new way in his tribunal. The foreseen involvement can from one perspective be seen as clearly centered on a desire for a more efficient administration of justice but it should also be seen as a means by which the Legislator is attempting to mold structures in a way that both reflects and implements his teaching concerning the role of the Church and the role of the bishop. While our canonical tradition has long recognized the responsibility of the diocesan bishop for his tribunal, *Mitis Iudex* can be expected to make that involvement much more concrete, particularly as a result of the introduction of the *processus brevior*. It is hoped that canonists and bishops alike will monitor the impact that the legislation will have not only directly on the efficient resolution of individual cases and the molding of the tribunal into a vehicle for pastoral accompaniment, but also indirectly on ministry to the engaged, to couples and to those who are separated and divorced.

ABSTRACT

The author, himself a diocesan bishop, offers some reflections on the role of the diocesan bishop envisioned by the motu proprio Mitis Iudex Dominus Iesus. *In order to gain a proper understanding of* Mitis Iudex Dominus Iesus, *the author considers it essential to place the document in its proper context. For that to happen, it requires to have a sense of the legislator, that is, of Pope Francis, to be able to see this particular legislative action in the overall context of his way of exercising the Petrine ministry. There is a great deal of seemingly intentional repetition in what Pope Francis has offered to the Church and to the world at large in the three years since his election. This repetition helps us identify certain emphases in his ministry that in turn give us a better understanding of* Mitis Iudex Dominus Iesus.

JOHN P. BEAL*

Mitis Iudex Canons 1671–1682, 1688–1691: A Commentary

A. NEW BOOK VII, PART III, TITLE I, CHAPTER I, "CASES TO DECLARE THE NULLITY OF MARRIAGE" (CANN. 1671–1691)

ART 1. THE COMPETENT FORUM AND TRIBUNALS

Can. 1671 §1. Marriage cases of the baptized belong to the ecclesiastical judge by proper right.

This canon, which reproduces the original canon 1671 of the 1983 code and article 3 §1 of the instruction *Dignitas connubii* verbatim, asserts the Church's traditional claim to exclusive jurisdiction over the marriages of the baptized. Since, according to Catholic doctrine, "a valid matrimonial contract cannot exist between the baptized without it being by that fact a sacrament" (c. 1055 §2), it follows that the Church alone is competent to examine and decide whether sacramental marriages of the faithful are valid and, therefore, binding. The claim of exclusive jurisdiction extends not only to the marriages between two Catholics, but also to those of Catholics and baptized non-Catholics and of two baptized non-Catholics, since these marriages too are sacraments. Even though they are not considered to be sacraments, the marriages of baptized persons, whether Catholic or

---

* Ordinary Professor, School of Canon Law, The Catholic University of America, Washington, DC.

not, with non-baptized persons also fall within the exclusive competence of the Church.[1] Implicit in the Church's claim to exclusive jurisdiction over the marriages of the baptized is a flat refusal to recognize any authority of secular governments to regulate directly and by proper right marriages involving baptized persons, to judge their validity, or to rule on marital rights and obligations stemming from divine law. The Church denies that the secular state or any merely human power can dissolve a valid marriage, even marriages of the unbaptized. Thus, no divorce granted by a secular court is recognized by the Church as having any juridic effect whatsoever on a valid marital bond.

Divine law, both natural and positive, binds all people, whether Christian or not, and the Catholic Church claims to be the authoritative arbiter of this law. However, since 1983, it no longer holds baptized non-Catholics bound to merely ecclesiastical laws concerning marriage, that is, those laws enacted by the Catholic Church. Instead, it recognizes the competence of the authorities of non-Catholic churches and ecclesial communities to enact laws to govern marriage for their own subjects and even to judge the validity of their subjects' marriages as long as these judgments are consonant with divine law. More specifically, canons 780 §2, 1° and 781 of the Code of Canons of the Eastern Churches stipulate that marriages involving Eastern non-Catholics are to be judged by the laws of their own churches as well as by divine law. This provision of the Eastern code was extended to tribunals of the Latin Church by article 4 of the instruction *Dignitas connubii*.[2]

Eastern non-Catholic churches generally do not have processes for declaring marriages invalid. Instead, they have a process by which "the

---

1. See Joaquín Llobell, "The Competent Forum," in *Exegetical Commentary on the Code of Canon Law*, ed. Angel Marzoa, Jorge Miros, and Rafael Rodríguez Ocaña (Chicago: Midwest Theological Forum, 2004) 4/2: 1755–1759; Francisco J. Ramos and Delfina Moral Carvajal, *Diritto Processuale Canonico* (Rome: Angelicum University Press, 2013) 1: 85–91; Pio Vito Pinto, "Gli articoli preliminary (art. 1–7) della *Dignitas Connubii*," in *Il giudizio di nullità matrimoniale dopo l'istruzione "Dignitas connubii, Parte Seconda La parte static del processo*, ed. Piero Antonio Bonnet and Carlo Gullo, Studi Giuridici 76 (Vatican City: Libreria Editrice Vaticana, 2007) 20–23; Klaus Lüdicke and Ronny Jenkins, *Dignitas Connubii: Norms and Commentary* (Washington: CLSA, 2006) 18–19.

2. See, Pinto, "Gli articoli," 23; Lüdicke-Jenkins, 20–21; Urban Navarrete, "La giurisdizione delle chiese orientali non cattoliche sul matrimonio (c. 780 C.E.O), in *Il matrimonio nel Codice dei canoni delle Chiese orientale*, Studi giuridici 32 (Vatican City: Libreria Editrice Vaticana, 1994) 114–125.

matrimonial bond is dissolved through *oikonomia*, by a sentence or an administrative decree."[3] Therefore, when an Eastern non-Catholic who has received a decree of dissolution from his or her own church seeks to marry a Catholic, the case must be remitted to a Catholic tribunal of first instance for a process to determine the possible invalidity of the marriage. The decree of the Orthodox authority and any accompanying evidence could, of course, be admitted to the Catholic tribunal as documentary evidence in the marriage nullity process. Nevertheless, in the unusual case where an Eastern non-Catholic hierarch has issued a decree of nullity, a Catholic tribunal would have to examine this decree and the evidence on which it is based to determine whether it can be recognized by the Catholic Church as freeing the party to enter a new marriage. The Council for Legislative Texts suggests two ways of proceeding in such cases:

a) The Catholic appellate tribunal, after having considered the matter from the perspective mentioned above [i.e., ensuring that divine law was not violated in the process], must decide whether it is sufficient to confirm the sentence issued by the Orthodox authority by decree or, if necessary, admit the case to an ordinary examination in the second instance (cf. cann. 1682§2 CIC and 1368 §2 CCEO);

b) The judge of second instance, in the documentary process [in cases where the marriage is allegedly invalid because of an impediment or a defect in canonical form], must decide whether to confirm the sentence or to remand the case to the ordinary procedure; that is, to the tribunal of first instance (cf. cann. 1688 CIC and 1374 CCEO).[4]

A similar process would be followed in dealing with cases dealt with by the authorities of non-Catholic churches judged by the Catholic Church to be in a comparable ecclesial situation to the Eastern orthodox, e.g., the Polish National Church.

Western ecclesial communities stemming from the Reformation of the sixteenth century have generally rejected the sacramentality of marriage and, consequently, the Church's claim to jurisdiction over marriage.

---

3. Pontifical Council for Legislative Texts, "*Nota explicativa* quoad pondus canonicum divortii orthodoxi," *Communicationes* 44 (2012) 358. English Translation Pontifical Council for Legislative texts, "*Nota Explicativa* about the Canonical Significance of Divorced Orthodox," *The Jurist* 75 (2015) 254.

4. PCLT, "*Nota explicativa*, 359; ET, 256.

As a result, most of them have no marriage law of their own but defer to the authority of the state to regulate marriages and to deal with marital breakdowns and their consequences. Canons 780 §2, 2° of the Code of Canons of the Eastern Church and, for Latin tribunals, articles 2 §2, 2° and 4 §1, 1° of the instruction *Dignitas connubii*, stipulate that the marriage cases of baptized Catholics whose ecclesial communities have no proper marriage law are to be judged in accord with the law to which these ecclesial communities defer or which they use.[5] Thus, when a baptized non-Catholic whose marriage to another non-Catholic was declared invalid by a secular court seeks to marry a Catholic, the competent Catholic tribunal could follow a process similar to the one sketched by the Council for Legislative Texts for dealing with annulments granted by Orthodox authorities to determine if the civil annulment was at least consistent with divine law and based solidly on the facts of the matter.

Despite the Church claim to exclusive right over the marriage cases of the baptized, it does, however, recognize the competence of secular authorities to regulate the marriages of the non-baptized in the interest of the common good and to judge whether their marriages were valid or not, as long as the basis for a civil declaration of nullity was a matter of natural law or, if it was a matter of positive human law, e.g., *dolus* or fraud,[6] was at least not contrary to natural law. To make this determination when a non-baptized recipient of a civil annulment wishes to marry a Catholic, the tribunal should follow a process analogous to the one prescribed by the Council for Legislative Texts for cases involving annulments of Eastern non-Catholic churches.

---

§2. Cases regarding merely the civil effects of marriage belong to a civil magistrate, unless the particular law establishes that such cases, if carried out in an incidental or accessory manner, can be recognized by and determined by an ecclesiastical judge.

This canon renders verbatim the text of canon 1672 of the promulgated 1983 code and article 3 §3 of the instruction *Dignitas connubii*. Although the Church reserves to itself the sole right to judge the validity of the

---

5. See Navarrete, 122–123.
6. See Note, "Annulments for Fraud—New York's Answer to Reno?" *Columbia Law Review* 48 (1948) 900–920.

marriages of the baptized, it recognizes the authority of secular courts to deal with the merely civil effects of marital break down.[7] These civil effects include such matters as the distribution of property, child support, spousal support or alimony, custody of minor children, and child support and visitation. The mention of "particular law" (*ius particulare*) in the final clause of the canon is a reference to the fact that, in virtue of concordats or treaties between the Holy See and some nations, ecclesiastical tribunals may be empowered not only to judge the question of the validity of marriages but also to decide the civil issues that are accessory to the issue of marital nullity. Nations which recognize the civil effects of decisions of ecclesiastical tribunals include Columbia, Spain and Italy. In such cases, the secular law usually has some technical mechanism by which the state adopts or "makes its own" the decisions ecclesiastical courts.[8] In Italy, for example, decisions of ecclesiastical tribunals (including those outside Italy) must be certified as authentic by the Apostolic Signatura before they are given civil effects by the Italian courts. In other countries like Lebanon and other near Eastern countries, secular authorities simply defer to religious authorities in marital matters. Thus, the decisions of Church tribunals there have civil effects automatically.[9] Where ecclesiastical courts have the authority to determine the civil effects of declarations of nullity or decrees of separation, they treat the questions of nullity or separation as the principal issue and the question of civil effects as an incidental or accessory cases. (cc. 1587–1591)

The fact that the decisions of ecclesiastical tribunals do not have civil effects in North America should not blind these tribunals to the possibility that their decisions will be given civil effect elsewhere. Catholics who plan "destination weddings" in Rome after their prior union is declared invalid

---

7. Llobell, 4/2: 1760–1762; Ramos and Carvajal, 1: 91–94; Lüdicke-Jenkins, 19.
8. Llobell, 4/2: 1701.
9. Ibid. It is because of the deferral of the state to decisions of religious authorities in some countries with large concentrations of Eastern Catholics that canon 1358 of the CCEO and canon 1357, §2 of the apostolic letter *Mitis et misericos Iesus*, the companion to *Mitis Iudex* for the Eastern Catholic Churches, stipulate: "With due regard for *Personal Statutes* where they are in force, cases that principally concern the merely civil effects of marriage belong to the civil judge; if the case concerns the civil effects in an accidental and accessory manner, the ecclesiastical judge can also hear and decide them by proper authority." (Emphasis added) Victor Pospishil, *Eastern Catholic Church Law* (New York: Saint Maron Publications, 1996) 734 says that these personal statutes refer "to the nations in which the religious communities have jurisdiction also in the civil forum in matters of family law, such as what follows from marriage (alimony, etc.). This refers to many nations with an Islamic majority, especially in the Near East."

by tribunals in the United States will have to have the American tribunals' decisions given civil effect in Italy prior to the new wedding. Moreover, the relaxation of the norms on tribunal competence which will be discussed below make it likely that tribunals in the United States will be deciding cases involving petitioners now living in the United States or Canada but with former spouses living in their countries of origin where the state recognizes civil effects for decisions of ecclesiastical tribunals. Therefore, tribunals will have to be scrupulous about honoring the right of defense of respondents in such cases. Failure to do so may have costly and embarrassing consequences not only in the canonical sphere but in the secular sphere as well.

For example, in 2001, the European Court of Human Rights decided a case in which the plaintiff was a woman who had been the respondent in a case decided affirmatively by the Rota. When the decision became executory and in accord with the concordat between Italy and the Holy See, it was given civil effects in Italy by the appellate court in Florence. The woman subsequently petitioned the European Court with the claim that there had been serious violations of her right of defense in the proceeding before the Rota and that the Italian court had erred in giving civil effect to the ecclesiastical judgment.[10] The concordat between the Holy See and the Italian State requires that an Italian appellate court can give civil effects to an ecclesiastical decision only after ascertaining that "in the nullity proceedings the defense rights of the parties have been recognized in a manner compatible with the fundamental principles of Italian law."[11] The European Court found that serious violations of the woman's right of defense had indeed occurred during the ecclesiastical proceeding. Since the Holy See is not a signatory to the European Charter on Human Rights, the Court could not compel it to pay the woman damages. Instead, it was Italy, a signatory to the Charter, which was required to pay the plaintiff 10 million lire in damages and more than 18 million lire in court costs. The case is a cautionary reminder to ecclesiastical tribunals that procedural lapses can have consequences that are not only embarrassing but expensive.

---

10. European Court of Human Rights, Second Section, Case of Pellegrini v. Italy, application no. 30882/96, July 20, 2001. See Jean-Pail Costa, "The European Court of Human Rights and Its Recent Case Law," *Texas International Law Journal* 38 (2003) 464.

11. European Court of Human Rights, Case of Pellegrini v. Italy, I.32 (b).

Can. 1672. In cases regarding the nullity of marriage not reserved to the Apostolic See, the competencies are: 1° the tribunal of the place in which the marriage was celebrated; 2° the tribunal of the place in which either or both parties have a domicile or a quasi-domicile; 3° the tribunal of the place in which in fact most of the proofs must be collected.

This canon, which replaces canon 1673 of the promulgated version of the 1983 code, substantially alters the norms governing tribunal competence in marriage nullity cases.[12] Competence is the canonical term for the measure or amount of jurisdiction enjoyed by a tribunal. To say that a tribunal has "competence" to hear and decide a case is, to use the language of American law, to say that the court has jurisdiction over it. The new norm specifies which tribunals are competent to judge marriage cases which are not reserved to the Apostolic See. Although canon law does reserve some types of cases to the Holy See (c. 1405), very few of these reserved cases are likely to involve marriages.[13] The one reserved cases for which tribunals need to be alert are cases involving "those who hold the highest civil office of a state (*civitas*)." (c. 1405 §1, 1°) These cases would include marriage nullity cases involving the President of the United States or the governors of the several states while they hold office. For these cases all tribunals other than the Roman Pontiff himself or a tribunal delegated by him are absolutely incompetent. (c. 1406 §2)

The new canon 1672 simply reiterates the previous norm that tribunals are competent if they are the tribunals of the place where the marriage was celebrated (an adaption of the ancient notion of the forum of the place where the contract was entered) or the tribunals of the place where the respondent has a domicile or quasi-domicile or the tribunals of the place in which the majority of proofs are to be gathered. However, the new norm substantially expands the possibilities for tribunals to claim competence over cases where they are the places of their domicile or quasi-domicile

---

12. Llobell, 4/2: 1764–1765; Javier Ochoa, "I titoli di competenza," in *Il processo matrimoniale canonico*, ed. Piero Antonio Bonnet and Carlo Gullo, Studi Giuridici 29 (Vatican City: Libreria Editrice Vaticana, 1994) 145–181; Ramos and Carvajal, 1: 171–189; Lüdicke-Jenkins, 34–38.

13. Llobell, 4/2: 1764–1765.; Ochoa, 142–145; Ramos and Carvajal, 1: 169–171; Lüdicke-Jenkins, 27–29.

of the petitioner. The now abrogated canon 1673, 3° had limited the use of the forum of the petitioner as a basis of competence to situations where the tribunal was the place where the petitioner had a domicile and where both the petitioner and the respondent resided in the territory of the same episcopal conference. A person has a domicile in the place where they have taken up residence with the intention of remaining there permanently (*perpetuo*) unless called away or where they have actually lived for five complete years (c. 102 §1); a person acquires a quasi-domicile in the place or places where they have set up residence "with the intention of remaining there at least three months unless called away" or actually staying there three full months. (c. 102 §2) By expanding the forum of the petitioner to include the petitioner's quasi-domicile as well as his or her domicile, the new norm gives effect to the principle of proximity between the parties and the judge which permeated Pope Francis' reform of marriage nullity procedure (*Mitis Iudex, Ratio Procedendi*, art. 7 §1) and gives petitioners considerably greater freedom to approach a tribunal geographically close to where they are spending substantial parts of their lives and with which they can deal more directly. For example, graduate students may retain domiciles in the place where their parents live but acquire quasi-domiciles where they are enrolled. The new norm allows such graduate students to submit petitions to the tribunals of the dioceses where their universities are located and avoid the disruptions of their study schedules that would result if they had to go home every time they needed to offer their declarations, to review the acts after they are published, or to conduct other business with the tribunal. Similarly, petitioners whose domiciles are in regions with harsh winters and who habitually spend three or more months per year in warmer climes can present their marriage nullity cases to the dioceses in which the live as "snow birds."

Of greater practical significance is the fact that the new canon 1672, 2° no longer restricts the use of the forum of the petitioner as a basis for competence to situations where both parties to the marriage resided in the territory of the same episcopal conferences. This restriction posed a serious obstacle for North American tribunals approached for declarations of nullity by refugees and migrants whose marriages took place in and whose former spouses still lived in their countries of origin. Unless a fortuitous circumstance rendered them the tribunal where the majority of proofs had to be gathered (a circumstance that occurred with some frequency with petitioners from ethnic groups like the Vietnamese which sometimes fled their home countries in groups, often as villages, and settled near one another in this country), a tribunal which wanted to hear a case involving such a person could do so only if its competence was extended or prorogued by the Apostolic Signatura, a favor that was not granted routinely.

In the United States, the American Procedural Norms had introduced the forum of the residence of the petitioner without any qualification as a basis for tribunal competence.[14] This basis for competence was also granted by special norms for tribunals in Australia,[15] England and Wales,[16] and Canada[17] but not for the whole Latin Church until the promulgation of the 1983 code for the Latin Church. It only became available for tribunals of the Eastern Catholic Churches with the promulgation of the Code of Canons for Eastern Churches in 1990. Nevertheless, American use of this basis for competence prompted considerable grumbling about abuses, especially concerns that the right of defense of respondents residing outside the United States was dealt with cavalierly by American tribunals.[18] As a result, the territorial restriction on the use of the forum of the petitioner was added when this basis for competence was incorporated into canon 1673 of the 1983 code. Now that the territorial restriction has been removed, tribunals will have to be assiduous in facilitating the participation of respondents living in foreign countries in the nullity processes initiated by their former spouses in the countries where they now reside. Particular attention must be paid to communicating with respondents in foreign countries in a language they can readily understand and providing opportunities for them to offer their own declarations and for their witnesses, if any, to testify, in a format that accommodates their situations. When deal-

---

14. American Procedural Norms, Norm 7, Sacred Council for the Public Affairs of the Church, rescript, April 28, 1970, Prot. No. 3320/70, in *CLD* 7: 955.

15. Council for Public Affairs of the Church, rescript, November 1, 1974, in *Documenta recentiora circa rem matrimonialem et processualem*, ed. Ignatius Gordon and Zenon Grocholewski (Rome: Gregorian University Press, 1977) 259, n. 1456.

16. Apostolic Signatura, rescript, January 2, 1971, Prot. No. 945/70 VT, in *CLD* 7: 968.

17. Sacred Council for the Public Affairs of the Church, rescript, November 1, 1974, in *CLD* 7: 1170.

18. See Apostolic Signatura, "Litterae ad Praesidem Conferentiae Episcopalis Mexicanae, in *Documenta recentiora circa rem matrimonialem et processualem* (Rome: Gregorian University Press, 1980) 2: nn. 5456–5462 and Zenon Grocholewski, "Declaration of the Apostolic Signatura on the Competence of Ecclesiastical Tribunals in the United States of America," *Monitor Ecclesiasticus* 104 (1979) 142–159.

ing with the former spouses of relatively uneducated immigrants, tribunals cannot assume even a working knowledge of English or the ability of respondents and witnesses to offer their testimony in writing in response to printed questionnaires.

The former canon 1673 of the promulgated 1983 code required that, before a tribunal assumed competence over and accepted a case either as the forum of the domicile of the petitioner or as the forum where the majority of proofs are to be gathered, the judicial vicar approached by the petitioner was required to secure the consent of the judicial vicar of the respondent, a consent which could only be granted after this judicial vicar had heard any objections the respondent might have to the case's being heard in the forum chosen by the petitioner. These requirements of consultation and consent have been abrogated in the new canon 1672, 2° and 3°. The elimination of requirements of contacts with the respondents and their judicial vicars prior to accepting cases as the forum of the petitioner or of the majority of proofs will certainly simplify the marriage nullity process and shorten it at least marginally by removing one not terribly difficult or time-consuming formality. However, like most legal formalities, the requirement of consulting respondents about their possible objections to having their cases heard in a tribunal convenient for petitioners was intended to prevent the advantage to the petitioner of being able to deal with a nearby forum from unduly disadvantaging the respondent. With the disappearance of this formality, tribunals will have to take care that allowing a forum convenient for the petitioner does not have the inadvertent effect of riding roughshod over the rights of the respondent.

Can. 1673 §1. In each diocese, the judge in first instance for cases of nullity of marriage for which the law does not expressly make an exception is the diocesan bishop, who can exercise judicial power personally or through others according to the norm of law.

Although no comparable norm was included in the section of the 1983 code on "Marriage Process," the new canon 1673 §1 repeats article 22 §1 of the instruction *Dignitas connubii* and echoes canon 1419 §1 while giving it a particular application to marriage cases.[19] In virtue of office, the

19. On canon 1419, see Zenon Grocholewski, "The Judge", in *Exegetical Commentary*, 4/1:716–720; Piero Antonia Bonnet, "I tribunal nella loro diversità di grado e di specie," in

diocesan bishop enjoys legislative, executive and judicial power in accord with the norm of law. As a result, unlike other judges, the diocesan bishop does not need a degree in canon law to exercise judicial power. However, diocesan bishops often lack the time and expertise to deal with the messiness of marriage cases effectively and expeditiously. It was for this reason that the office of "the official" or *officialis*, now judicial vicar, was instituted.[20] Moreover, when cases before the tribunal are bitterly contested, a bishop who serves as judge rendering the decisions may compromise his ability to serve effectively as a pastor to both parties to the dispute. Consequently, canon law has traditionally encouraged diocesan bishops to exercise their judicial power through judicial vicars and judges they have appointed. Indeed, article 22 §2 of the instruction *Dignitas connubii* cautions that, although a diocesan bishop can exercise judicial power personally, "it is expedient that, unless special causes demand it, he not do this personally." However, in several places, *Mitis Iudex* encourages diocesan bishops to have a much more active role than has been usual in the recent past in the day-to-day operations of his tribunal and even calls on him to serve as the judge of record in cases that meet the criteria for the *processus brevior* sketched in canons 1683–1687. Moreover, in regions with scant trained personnel and resources, divorced members of the faithful may lack access to the sole ordinary method for resolving their status unless the bishop himself assumes personally the role of judge. Thus, repeating here what had been said earlier in the code about the role of the bishop as the chief judge of the diocese does not seems inappropriate.

Despite the emphasis of *Mitis Iudex* on the personal involvement of the diocesan bishop in the work of his tribunal, he is still required to appoint a judicial vicar with ordinary but vicarious judicial power who "constitutes one tribunal with the bishop." (c. 1420 §§1–2) In addition to his role as judge of cases coming before the tribunal, the judicial vicar also has administrative responsibilities to insure the smooth day-to-day operation of the tribunal. For example, the judicial vicar constitutes tribunals, that is, appoints judges and other court officials to adjudicate individual cases as they are presented. There are, however, some routine "housekeeping"

Il processo, 188–190; Ramos and Carvajal, 1: 212–219; Miguel Ortiz, "La potestà giudiziale in genere e i tribunali (art.22–32)," in *Il giudizio*, 2: 63–68; Lüdicke-Jenkins, 55–58.

20. See Jean-Georges Boeglin, "La préhistoire de la fonction d'Official et de l'Officialité," in *Tendances actuelles de la jurisprudence matrimoniale dans les tribunaux de l'Église: Approches comparés*, ed. Marc Aoun and Jeanne-Marie Tuffery-Andrieu (Bern: Peter Lang, 2012) 15–26 and Paul Fournier, *Les Officialités au moyen age* (Aalen: Scientia, 1984).

tasks that the law reserves to the diocesan bishop that could be usefully delegated to the judicial vicar. These include:

1) Entrusting marriage cases to a single clerical judge (c. 1425 §4; *Mitis Iudex*, c. 1673 §4);
2) Assigning cases to judges out of sequence or without following the established rotation (c. 1425 §3);
3) Allowing judges from other dioceses to gather evidence within the territory of the tribunal (c. 1469 §2);
4) Appointing notaries, auditors and assessors on a stable basis (cc. 483; 1428 §2; and 1673 §3);
5) Approving advocates to practice before the tribunal (c. 1488); and
6) Determining when the intervention in a case by the promoter of justice is necessary (c. 1431 §1).

Without compromising the bishop's oversight of the work of the tribunal, delegation of these rather mundane and frequently recurring tasks to the judicial vicar can prevent the needless delays in the process that can result when the tribunal must wait until the bishop is available to entertain and approve these requests. In places where the judicial vicar is not present in the tribunal office on a daily basis and his ordinary administrative functions have been delegated to the moderator of the tribunal chancery or "tribunal director," the diocesan bishop could also delegate these reserved functions to this moderator or director.

§2. The bishop is to establish a diocesan tribunal for his diocese to handle cases of nullity of marriage without prejudice to the faculty of the same bishop to approach another nearby diocesan or interdiocesan tribunal.

The main clause of this canon succinctly summarizes for marriage cases the norms of canons 1420–1422, 1428, 1430, 1432 and 483 concerning the various court officials diocesan bishops are to appoint to staff his tribunal.[21]

---

21. Zenon Grocholewski, "The Judge," in *Exegetical Commentary*, 4/1: 722–737; Id., "Auditors and Relators,' *Exegetical Commentary*, 4/1: 756–760; Carmelo de Diego-Lora, "The Promoter of Justice, the Defender of the Bond and the Notary," *Exegetical Commentary*, 4/1: 761–811; Bonnet, "I tribunal," 190–217; Ramos and Carvajal, 1: 219–236, 279–309; Claudia Izzi, "I ministri di giustizia in genere," in *Il giudizio*, 2: 103–130; Pasquale Silvestri, "I ministri di giustizia in specie: Il vicario giudiziale, I vicari giudiziali aggiunti e gli altri giudici," in *Il giudizio*, 2:

Consistent with the emphasis of *Mitis Iudex* on "the restoration of a proximity between the judges and the faithful," the new canon 1673 §2 reiterates the duty of the diocesan bishop to constitute a tribunal in his diocese with a staff adequate to deal with its case load in an expeditious manner. This obligation is underscored by article 8 §1 of the *Ratio procedendi* appended to the apostolic letter:

> In dioceses which lack their own tribunal, the Bishop is to take care that as soon as possible, persons are formed who are capable of zealously undertaking the work of constituting a tribunal for marriage cases. This is to be accomplished by permanent and ongoing courses promoted by dioceses and their groupings and the Apostolic See.

The apostolic letter recognizes, however, that some dioceses may not be able to establish effectively functioning tribunals, either temporarily or indefinitely. As a result, it offers diocesan bishops the alternative of availing themselves of the services of tribunals in near-by dioceses or becoming part of an interdiocesan tribunal so that at least some tribunal will be immediately available to the faithful. The law has long foreseen the possibility that some dioceses may have to use the tribunal of neighboring dioceses as its first instance tribunal when it is unable to establish a tribunal of its own. This option has often been employed temporarily when a diocese has recently been divided to create a new one and the new diocese needs time to develop the resources to render its own tribunal operational. It has also been used by tribunals suffering from a chronic dearth of qualified personnel. In these cases, the procedure to be followed for arranging a substitute for a diocesan tribunal has been for the diocesan bishop who could not establish his own tribunal to reach an agreement with a neighboring bishop to utilize the latter's tribunal and then to seek the prorogation of the competence of that tribunal from the Apostolic Signatura.[22] The new canon eliminates the requirement of prorogation of competence

---

131–156; Linda Ghisoni, "Il ministri di giustizia in specie: Uditori e Assessori," in *Il giudizio*, 2: 157–175; Vittorio Palestro, "Il difensore del vincolo ed il Promotore di Giustizia," in *Il giudizio*, 2: 177–190; Michael X. Leo Arokiaraj, "Il Moderatore della Cancellaria del Tribunale e gli altri notaio," *Il giudizio*, 2: 191–207; Lüdicke-Jenkins, 76–122.

22. *Dignitas connubii*, art. 24, §1. For example, the Apostolic Signatura has prorogued on a stable basis the competence of the tribunals of the Latin Church to hear marriage cases for which the tribunal of the Ukrainian Catholic Eparchy of Stamford would otherwise be competent. See Apostolic Signatura, decree, May 22, 1996, in *Roman Replies and CLSA Advisory Opinions 2006*, ed. Stephen Pedone and Lynn Jarrell (Washington: CLSA , 2006) 39–41.

by the Apostolic Signatura by giving diocesan bishops the faculty to make these arrangements with neighboring bishops on their own authority. The Apostolic Signatura should, of course, be informed of such an agreement by diocesan bishops.

Another option available to diocesan bishops who cannot establish marriage tribunals for their own dioceses is to join together with one or more neighboring bishops to establish a common first instance interdiocesan tribunal. Such interdiocesan tribunals of first instance have been established either at the initiative of the interested bishops or at the prodding of the Holy See in, among other places, Italy,[23] Canada,[24] and Scotland.[25] Although most of the existing interdiocesan tribunals of first instance were established by special decrees or later pursuant to norms issued by the Apostolic Signatura in 1970,[26] the establishment and governance of these interdiocesan tribunals are now regulated by canon 1423 of the code and articles 23 and 24 of the instruction *Dignitas connubii*. The establishment of these interdiocesan tribunals requires the unanimous consent of the participating bishops and the approval of the Apostolic Signatura. Since the addition of a new diocese to an already existing interdiocesan tribunal would constitute a significant innovation in the tribunal, it would seem that the approval of the Apostolic Signatura would be required for a bishop and his diocese to join an already established interdiocesan tribunal. Nevertheless, article 8 §2 of the *Ratio procedendi* empowers a bishop whose diocese has been participating in an interdiocesan tribunal of first instance to secede from it at his own initiative. Such a diocesan bishop need not secure the permission of the Apostolic Signatura to withdraw from an interdiocesan tribunal and establish his own diocesan tribunal, but he should notify the Signatura of his decision. Although explicit mention of the faculty of diocesan bishops to disengage from interdiocesan

---

23. Pius XI, motu proprio *Qua cura*, December 8, 1938: *AAS* 30 (1938) 410–413.

24. Congregation for the Discipline of the Sacraments, *decree* Excellentissimi Ordinarii, De ordinandi Tribunalibus ecclesiasticis ditionis Canadensis super causis nullitatis matrimonii decidendis," January 28, 1946: *AAS* 38 (1946) 218–284.

25. Episcopal Conference of Scotland, decree, May, 25, 1970, approved by Paul VI, July 3, 1970.

26. Apostolic Signatura, "Normae pro Tribunalibus interdiocecesanis, vel regionalibus aut interegionalibus," December 28, 1970: *AAS* 63 (1971) 486–492. Grocholewski, "The Judge," 740–741, notes: "Although the quoted *Normae* are no longer relevant inasmuch as the law (*REU*, art. 105) for their implementation is without force (cf. c. 33, §2), nevertheless, in the absence of new indications in this regard and taking into account canon 19, the existing practice should be substantially maintained, to such a degree as it does not contradict the new law."

tribunals of first instance of which their dioceses have been a part is not found in the previous law, the practice of the Apostolic Signatura has been to respect such decisions.[27] Despite these provisions for alternates to the diocesan tribunal, the expectation of *Mitis Iudex* clearly is that every diocese should have its own marriage tribunal and that diocese which currently lack tribunals or well-functioning tribunals will endeavor to bring themselves into compliance.

---

§3. Cases of nullity of marriage are reserved to a college of three judges. A judge who is a cleric must preside over the college, but the other judges may be laypersons.

Since the promulgation of the 1917 code, canon law has exhibited a strong preference for collegial decision making by a panel of at least three judges in marriage nullity cases and other cases of major import.[28] Like most legal systems, canon law presumes that three or more judges pondering the same law and evidence together are more likely to arrive at the correct judgment[29] than is a single judge operating in solitary splendor. This preference for collegial decision-making is repeated in new canon 1673 §3. To make it easier for tribunals to establish panels of three judges for marriage nullity case, Paul VI had authorized episcopal conferences to permit the appointment of lay men as judges and allowed the formation of a college with one lay judge and two clerics. When the norm of *Causas matrimoniales* was incorporated as canon 1421 §2 of the 1983 code, this allowance for lay judges was somewhat expanded to include lay people, both male and female, and for all types of cases within the scope of jurisdiction of ecclesiastical tribunals. Although the new norm does not change the requirement of canon 1421 §3 that the prior permission of the episcopal conference is required for a bishop to appoint lay people as judges, it does expand from one to two the number of lay people who can be used to constitute a college; the third members of the college must still be a cleric, that is, a deacon, presbyter or bishop. Although this expansion of the role of lay judges in marriage nullity cases compensates somewhat for the shortage of clergy trained and available for tribunal work, it does raise canonico-

---

27. Grocholewski, "The Judge," 740.
28. 1917 CIC, c. 1576, §1, 1°.
29. Paul VI, motu proprio *Causas matrimoniales*, V, §1, March 29, 1971: AAS 63 (1971) 443; CLD 7: 971.

theological questions about the connection between the power of governance which ecclesiastical judges enjoy and the power of orders which lay people, by definition, do not.[30]

---

§4. The bishop moderator, if a collegial tribunal cannot be constituted in the diocese or in a nearby tribunal chosen according to the norm of §2, is to entrust cases to a single clerical judge who, where possible, is to employ two assessors of upright life, experts in juridical or human sciences, approved by the bishop for this task; unless it is otherwise evident, the same single judge has competency for those things attributed to the college, the praeses, or the ponens.

In 1970, the American Procedural Norms had allowed the episcopal conference, with faculties to be granted by the Holy See, to allow tribunals to hear marriage cases with a single clerical judge.[31] A year later, in *Causas matrimoniales*, Paul VI opened an exception to the norm that marriage nullity cases were to be decided by colleges of at least three judges by allowing episcopal conferences to entrust marriages cases to a single clerical judges in individual cases and by permitting the conference to allow this faculty to be exercised on its behalf by a group of member bishops or an individual bishop designated by it.[32] Canon 1425 §4 simplified these post-conciliar exceptions by allowing the episcopal conference to permit diocesan bishops and bishop moderators of tribunals to entrust cases to single clerical judges "for as long as the impossibility [of establishing a collegiate tribunal] continues." The new canon 1673 §4 simplifies the appointment of single judges even further by removing the requirement that the diocesan bishop have the prior permission of the episcopal conference before appointing single judges for marriage cases. However, the new norm retains the restriction that it is the diocesan bishop or bishop moderator, and not the judicial vicar, who enjoys the faculty to entrust cases to a single judge. As was mentioned earlier, this quasi-administrative task is one that could be usefully delegated to the judicial vicar.

---

30. For an overview of the discussion of the possibility of lay people sharing in ecclesiastical power of governance, see John P. Beal, "The Exercise of Power of Governance by Lay People: State of the Question," *The Jurist* 55 (1995) 1–92, esp. 63–67.
31. American Procedural Norms, Norm 3, CLD 7: 952.
32. Paul VI, motu proprio *Causas matrimoniales*, V, §2: AAS 63 (1971) 443; CLD 7: 971.

The new canon 1673 §4 retains the recommendation of canon 1425 §4 that a single judge not proceed without seeking appropriate counsel. While canon 1425 recommends that a single judge use the services of an assessor and an auditor, the new canon 1673 like canon 1424 recommends the use of two assessors. Since the function of the auditor is to gather evidence under the supervision of the judge, a single judge might still want to designate an auditor from the pool approved by the diocesan bishop for service during the probative phase of the process. An assessor, on the other hand, is a person with expertise in human or juridic sciences, but not necessarily a degree in canon law, who advises the judge "on the proper direction of the case and the suitable evaluation of proofs"[33] but without any voice or vote in deciding the case. Thus, assessors assist the judge during the phase of decision. Assessors can be clerics or lay persons, male or female. However, unlike other mentions of assessors in the code and in the instruction *Dignitas connubii*, the new canon 1673 §3 stipulates that assessors are to be approved for this function by the diocesan bishop or bishop moderator. The judicial vicar or single judge can then draw from this pool of approved assessors for assistance on individual cases. This additional role for the diocesan bishop can be seen as another effort on the part of *Mitis Iudex* to emphasize the "hands-on" role it expects the diocesan bishop to play in his own diocesan tribunal and to underscore the responsibility of the bishop to insure that the introduction of streamlined procedures does not compromise the Church's witness to the indissolubility of marriage.

---

§5. The tribunal of second instance must always be collegiate for validity, according to the prescript of the preceding §3.

Although *Mitis Iudex* is rather generous in extending to diocesan bishops and bishop moderators the possibility of expediting marriage cases by the use of single judges at first instance, it retains the discipline of canon 1441 that requires a second instance tribunal to consist of at least three judges under pain of nullity of the sentence. Like a collegial tribunal at first instance, an appellate tribunal can now be composed of one clerical and two lay judges. The nullity of a sentence rendered by a tribunal of less than three judges is termed "remediable" or "curable" (c. 1622, 1°). Remediable

33. Zenon Grocholewski, "The Judge," *Exegetical Commentary*, 4/1: 744.

nullity must be challenged by the aggrieved party or the defender of the bond within three months of notice of the publication of the sentence. (c. 1623) If the invalid sentence is not challenged within that peremptory time frame, the nullity is healed or "sanated" by the passage of time.

---

§6. The tribunal of first instance appeals to the metropolitan tribunal of second instance without prejudice to the prescripts of cann. 1438–1439 and 1444.

This new canon implements the strong preference stated in the apostolic letter promulgating *Mitis Iudex* that "the appeal to the metropolitan be restored, especially because the function [of the Metropolitan] of being head of the ecclesiastical province stands firmly though the ages as a mark of synodality in the Church." In a metropolitan appellate system, the tribunal of the Metropolitan See is the ordinary appellate court for the tribunals of all its suffragan dioceses; appeals of cases decided by the Metropolitan Tribunal as a first instance court are sent to the tribunal or tribunals stably designated for this purpose with the approval of the Holy See. Provisions for stable appellate courts for metropolitan tribunals remain in place for cases decided according to the ordinary process laid out in *Mitis Iudex*; however, appeals against decisions rendered by the metropolitan personally pursuant to the *processus brevior* are now made to the senior suffragan see or the Roman Rota. (MI, c. 1687 §3).[34]

Despite the antiquity and simplicity of the metropolitan appellate system, it was displaced in many places because the volume of cases being forwarded to appellate tribunals for second instance process threatened to overwhelm the resources of some metropolitan tribunals. In the United States, the mandatory review of affirmative decisions was usually dispensed from 1970 to 1983 under the terms of the American Procedural Norms. As it became clear that the revised Code of Canon law would not continue this provision for dispensation from mandatory appeal, several interdiocesan tribunals were constituted by the interested diocesan bishops with the approval of the Holy See in accord with the Apostolic Signatura's 1970 *Normae* to replace metropolitan tribunals for marriage cases. Canon 1439 of the 1983 code and articles 25, 3°–4° and 26 of the instruction *Dignitas connubii* now govern the establishment and operation of these

---

34. See the commentary on this canon by William Daniel in *The Jurist* 75 (2015) 539–591 and in this volume.

interdiocesan appellate tribunals. In accord with canon 1439, authority to establish interdiocesan tribunals of second instance rests today not with the interested bishops but the episcopal conference which must still secure the approval of the Apostolic Signatura. (c. 1439) In the period following the promulgation of the 1983 code, several groupings of dioceses found both the Metropolitan and the interdiocesan appellate systems inadequate for their circumstances and, with the approval of the Apostolic Signatura, erected a hybrid appellate structure:

> For example, a number of first instance tribunals can be designated as the tribunals of appeal for one another: for example, Suffragan Tribunal A appeals to Suffragan Tribunal B, Suffragan Tribunal B appeals to Suffragan Tribunal C, Suffragan Tribunal C appeals to Metropolitan Tribunal D, and Metropolitan Tribunal D appeal to Suffragan Tribunal A. . . . It is also possible to vary this last structure by designating, for example, two smaller tribunals as the ordinary tribunal of appeal for one larger tribunal provided that the cases can be distributed in a stable and equitable manner.[35]

Mitis Iudex does nothing to alter the appellate arrangements—metropolitan, interdiocesan or hybrid—existing at the time of its promulgation.

Nevertheless, new canon 1679 eliminates the mandatory referral of all affirmative decisions in marriage nullity cases to an appellate court for a second instance process and provides for appeals of first instance decisions only by dissatisfied parties and defenders of the bond. Since it was precisely to manage the volume of these mandatory second instance processes that interdiocesan and hybrid appellate systems were created, the need for these alternate appellate structures will likely diminish as well once the norms of *Mitis Iudex* take effect. While existing alternatives to the metropolitan appellate system are acknowledged by *Mitis Iudex* and will continue to dictate the ordinary appellate courts for marriage cases until other arrangements are made, the diminished pressure to handle appellate cases in volume and with expedition should encourage provinces to revert to the Metropolitan Appellate system. However, *Mitis Iudex* does not allow groupings of bishops to dismantle their alternative appellate arrangement unilaterally. Changes in appellate structure will require the agreement of the bishops involved, especially the metropolitan whose tribunal will now bear the burden of handling appeals from all the suffragans, a

---

35. Raymond L. Burke, "The Distinction of Personnel in Hierarchically Related Tribunals," *Studia Canonica* 28 (1994) 97–98.

favorable vote of the episcopal conference and the approval of the Apostolic Signatura.

New canon 1673 §6 touches on a fundamental theological principle with eminently practical implications: "By reason of the primacy of the Roman Pontiff, any member of the faithful is free to bring or to introduce his or her own contentious penal case to the Holy See for adjudication in any grade of the trial and at any stage of the litigation." (c. 1417 §1) The new canon refers to this right of the faithful with its mention of canon 1444 which allows appellants, whether disgruntled parties or defenders of the bond, to appeal a decision of a first instance tribunal directly to the Roman Rota instead of to the ordinary appellate court of the tribunal which issued the sentence.

ART. 2. THE RIGHT TO CHALLENGE A MARRIAGE

Can. 1674 §1. The following are qualified to challenge a marriage: 1° the spouses; 2° the promoter of justice when nullity has already become public, if the convalidation of the marriage is not possible or expedient.

§2. A marriage which was not accused while both spouses were living cannot be accused after the death of either one or both of the spouses unless the question of validity is prejudicial to the resolution of another controversy either in the canonical forum or in the civil forum.

§3. If a spouse dies while the case is pending, however, can. 1518 is to be observed.

The new canon 1674 repeats verbatim canons 1674 and 1675 of the promulgated version of the 1983 code and articles 92–94 of the instruction *Dignitas connubii*.[36] The only change in the new canon is in the way the elements are enumerated, two distinct canons in the 1983 code, three distinct articles in the instruction, but only one canon with three paragraphs in *Mitis Iudex*. There is no reason to think that this merely organizational change has in any way altered the meaning of the canon.

In most cases, only the spouses themselves are considered to have sufficient personal interest in the issue of marriage nullity to have "standing" to

---

36. Rafael Rodriguez-Ocaña, "The Right to Challenge the Validity of Marriage," in *Exegetical Commentary*, 4/2:1776–1809; Frans Daneels, "Il diritto di impugnare il matrimonio," in *Il processo*, 393–403; Ilaria Zuanazzi, "Il diritto di introdurre l'azione o di partecipare al giudizio di nullità del matrimonio," in *Il giudizio*, 2/1: 249–295; Lüdicke-Jenkins, 167–171.

challenge it before an ecclesiastical tribunal. Under the regime of the 1917 code and the 1936 instruction *Provida Mater*, various classes of spouses were barred from the possibility of petitioning for declaration of nullity of their marriages. These groups included all non-Catholics, whether baptized or not, spouses responsible for the impediment or defect that allegedly invalidated their marriage, and certain excommunicates.[37] All of these restrictions on petitioning were swept away in the procedural reform legislation following the Second Vatican Council and were not incorporated into the 1983 code or the new legislation. Thus, any spouse without qualification can now petition a competent tribunal to examine the possible nullity of his or her marriage. However, the caution of article 3 §2 of the instruction *Dignitas connubii* remains in force: "[A]n ecclesiastical judge hears only those cases of nullity of marriages of non-Catholics, whether baptized or unbaptized, in which it is necessary to establish the free state of at least one party before the Catholic Church." In practice, this restriction means that Catholic tribunals should entertain cases involving two non-Catholics if one of the parties now wishes to marry a Catholic (or sometimes to become a Catholic) and this or her marital status needs to be clarified before this can take place. Otherwise, ecumenical courtesy suggests that the regulation of the marriages of two non-Catholics should be left to their authorities of their respective churches or ecclesial communities.

Although only the spouses are considered to have sufficient personal interest in the issue of the validity of their marriage to have standing to petition, marriage is not a purely personal or private matter. As a result, the law recognizes the right of the promoter of justice whose responsibility is "to provide for the public good" (c. 1430) to intervene to challenge a marriage under two conditions: 1) that the invalidity of the marriage has already been made public, and 2) it is impossible or inexpedient to convalidate the marriage. It has long been understood that such interventions by the promoter of justice should be truly extraordinary and are warranted only in cases where the failure of the Church to publicly declare the obvious nullity of a marriage is necessary to avert scandal.[38]

Since most spouses petition for declarations of nullity of their marriages solely so that they will be free to enter a new marriage in the Church or to have an existing civil union recognized by the Church, death

---

37. See John P. Beal, "Making Connections: Procedural Law and Substantive Justice," *The Jurist* 54 (1994) 118–120 and Rodriguez-Ocaña, 1777–1780, 1786–1787.

38. Rodriguez Ocaña, 1789–1791.

eliminates the prior marriage as an obstacle to a new one. Thus, there is rarely sufficient reason to pursue a declaration of nullity once one of the spouses dies. The law normally bars the introduction of a petition for nullity once one of the spouses is deceased. Nevertheless, canon 1674 §2 does allow the introduction of a petition even after the death of one or both spouses where resolution of an important matter hinges on the validity or invalidity of a deceased persons marriage. Such an issue may arise, for example, where the law governing succession to the throne of a kingdom or principality or intestate succession stipulates that only legitimate offspring are eligible heirs. For the same reason §3 allows a marriage nullity case which has already begun by the citation of the respondent to continue to a conclusion according to the norm of canon 1518. If the evidentiary phase of the process has not yet been concluded at the time of the death of one of the parties, it is suspended until resumed by the deceased's heir or another interested party; if the case has already reached the phase of discussion or decision at the time of the party's death, the judge is to consult the deceased's procurator or heir and, if this person wants the case to move forward, to proceed to a decision.

ART. 3. THE INTRODUCTION AND INSTRUCTION OF THE CASE

Can. 1675. The judge, before he accepts a case, must be informed that the marriage has irreparably failed, such that conjugal living cannot be restored.

Canon law has long seen adjudication as a last resort for the resolution of conflicts and has charged judges to seek non-litigious ways to bring controversies to a peaceful conclusion.[39] The new canon 1675 continues that tradition by encouraging judges to ascertain that a marriage is irretrievably broken before admitting it to the marriage nullity process. While the previous canon 1676 and article 65 of the instruction *Dignitas connubii* had charged judges to be actively engaged in pastoral efforts to reconcile couples where there seemed to be hope that such exertions might bear fruit, the new norm merely requires him or her to verify the irretrievable brokenness of the marriage before admitting a petition for declaring its

---

39. Antoni Stankiewicz, "The Office of Judge," in *Exegetical Commentary*, 1810–1811; Id., "I dovere del giudice," in *Il processo*, 304–308; Nikolaus, Schöch, "La disciplina da osservarsi nei tribunali (art. 65–91)," in *Il giudizio*, 2: 209–211; Lüdicke-Jenkins, 123–125.

nullity. This subtle change may reflect the expectation that, prior to the submission of a petition to the tribunal, the parties will have engaged in the pre-judicial or pastoral investigation sketched in articles 2–5 of the *Ratio procedendi* and that this preliminary process has already established that little hope for reconciliation remains. The change may also reflect an awareness that, because of the ready availability of divorce in many places and the absence of civil effects for decisions of ecclesiastical tribunals in most, spouses often do not even approach the Church's tribunals until well after hope for reconciliation with their now ex-spouses is exhausted.

Can. 1676 §1. After receiving the libellus, the judicial vicar, if he considers that it has some basis, admits it and, by a decree appended to the bottom of the libellus itself, is to order that a copy be communicated to the defender of the bond and, unless the libellus was signed by both parties, to the respondent, giving them a period of fifteen days to express their views on the petition.

§2. After the above-mentioned deadline has passed, and after the other party has been admonished to express his or her views if and insofar as necessary, and after the defender of the bond has been heard, the judicial vicar is to determine by his decree the formula of the doubt and is to decide whether the case is to be treated with the ordinary process or with the briefer process according to cann. 1683–1687. This decree is to be communicated immediately to the parties and the defender of the bond.

§5. The formula of doubt must determine by which ground or grounds the validity of the marriage is challenged.

This new canon represents a significant streamlining of the introductory phase of the contentious process for marriage nullity cases by concentrating responsibility for the several steps of this phase in the hands of the judicial vicar rather than in the hands of the single judge or *praeses* of the collegiate tribunal entrusted with the case. In the former canon 1677 §§1–2 and articles 114–137 of the instruction *Dignitas connubii* for marriage cases and in current canons 1505–1513 for non-matrimonial cases, the introductory phase of the contentious process unfolded in seven steps: 1) the submission of the *libellus* or petition; 2) the constitution of a tribunal consisting of a judge or judges, a defender of the bond, and a notary to hear the case by the judicial vicar; 3) the determination of competence by the single judge or *praeses*; 4) the admission or appointment of a procurator/advocate or guardian for the petitioner; 5) the acceptance or rejection of the petition by the single judge or *praeses*; 6) the citation of the respondent; and 7) the joining of the issues or setting the grounds on which the case will be decided by the single judge or *praeses* or *ponens* of the collegiate tribunal.[40] The judicial vicar was involved in only the second of these steps, the constitution of the tribunal, unless, of course, he assigned himself to serve as judge in the case.

The new canon vests responsibility for all of these tasks in the judicial vicar. After receiving the petition or *libellus*, he determines whether his tribunal is competent to adjudicate the case and whether the petition at least seems to have a basis in the law and facts. If so, the judicial vicar accepts the petition and cites the defender of the bond and the respondent by communicating to them copies of the petition to which he has attached a decree stipulating that they may offer observations on the petition within fifteen days. This citation of the respondent can, however, be omitted if he or she has cosigned the petition, a contingency not foreseen in the 1983 code. When citing the respondent and defender of the bond, the judicial vicar should suggest a possible "formulation of the doubt or doubts based on the *libellus* so that they may respond." (*Dignitas connubii*, art. 127 §2) Once the fifteen useful days for responding to the petition has elapsed, the judicial vicar is to set the ground or grounds of nullity on the basis of the information in the petition itself and any attached documentation and any responses to the citation.

Perhaps because it presumes that petitions will be drafted with the help of the pastoral agents designated by the diocesan bishop to conduct the pre-judicial or pastoral investigation in accord with articles 2–5 of the *Ratio Procedendi* attached to the apostolic letter and will contain all the elements necessary for acceptance by the judicial vicar, *Mitis Iudex* makes

---

40. Antoni Stankiewicz, "The Office of Judges," in *Exegetical Commentary*, 4/2: 1812–1816; Rodriguez Ocaña, "The Petition Introducing the Case," in *Exegetical Commentary*, 4/2: 1089–1135; Santiago Panizo Orallo, "The Summons and the Intimation of Judicial Acts," in *Exegetical Commentary*, 4/2: 1136–1150; Antoni Stankiewicz, "The Joinder of the Issues," in *Exegetical Commentary*, 4/2: 1151–1164; Luigi Mattioli, "La fase introduttoria del processo e la non comparsa della parte convenuto," in *Il processo*, 479–490; Rosario Colantonio, "La litis contestatio," in *Il Processo*, 491–538; Antonello Blaso, "Il libello introduttivo della causa (art. 114–125)," in *Il giudizio*, 3: 23–42; Massimo Del Pozzo, "La citazione," in *Il giudizio*, 3: 43–84; Giovanni Maragnoli, "La formula del dubbio (art. 135–137)," in *Il giudizio*, 3: 85–132; Lüdicke-Jenkins, 203–243.

no provision for recourses available to petitioners of their petitions are rejected. The code itself sets a rather low bar for accepting a petition. A libellus can be rejected only: 1) if the tribunal lacks competence 2) if the petitioner clearly lacks standing to initiate a case; 3) if one of the elements required by canon 1504, 1°–3° is missing from the petition; or 4) "If it is certainly clear from the [libellus] itself that the petition lacks any basis and that there is no possibility that any such basis will appear through the process." (c. 1505 §2; *Dignitas connubii*, art. 121 §1) These four circumstances remain the sole legitimate grounds for rejecting a libellus.

The code provides that a petitioner whose libellus is rejected can make recourse within ten (10) days of notice of the decree of rejection either to the college as a whole, if the petition was rejected by the *praeses*, or to the appellate tribunal (c. 1505 §4; *Dignitas connubii*, art. 124). Since in the introductory phase of the marriage nullity process as it has been revised by *Mitis Iudex* the judicial vicar is acting as a quasi-single judge when he accepts or rejects the petition, it would seem that recourses against rejection of petitions by the judicial vicar are to be made to the appellate court. Since appellate courts are to resolve these recourses *expeditissime* (c. 1505 §4; *Dignitas connubii*, art. 124 §1), there is no further recourse or appeal from its decision either by the petitioner or by the judge whose decree of rejection is overturned. (c. 1629, 5°; *Dignitas connubii*, art. 280 §1, 5°) If an appellate court sustains the judicial vicar's rejection of a petition, the case is closed; if it overturns the decree of rejection, the case is remanded to the first instance tribunal *a quo* for a first instance trial. (*Dignitas connubii*, art. 124 §2)[41] By rejecting the petition, the judicial vicar has shown himself inclined to believe the petition is without merit. Therefore, it might be appropriate for the petitioner whose petition is ordered accepted by the appellate court to recuse the judicial vicar and ask that a different judge or judges be constituted as a tribunal to hear the case. (cc. 1448–1451)

The apostolic letter *Mitis Iudex* is also silent about the rarely invoked provision of the code for the admission of a libellus by default. Canon 1506 and article 125 of the instruction *Dignitas connubii* stipulate:

> If within a month from the presentation of the *libellus* the judge has not issued a decree which accepts or rejects the libellus according to the norm of

---

41. For an opposing view, see Sean T. Doyle, "The *Libellus*: Rejection and Recourse," *The Jurist* 73 (2013) 371–438.

can. 1505, the interested party can insist that the judge fulfill his function. If the judge takes not action within ten days from the request, then the *libellus* is to be considered as accepted.

Since this provision of the law is intended to expedite the tribunal process by providing consequence for judicial "foot dragging," it would not seem that the apostolic letter had any intention of abrogating the norm.

The Instruction *Dignitas connubii* recommends consulting the defender of the bond prior to the acceptance of the petition (art. 119 §2) and calls for citation of both the respondent and the defender of the bond after the acceptance of the petition (art. 127 §1; CIC, c. 1508). New canon 1676 §1 also calls for citation of the defender of the bond. However, since no tribunal will yet have been constituted in the process limned by the new canon, it is not clear what defender is to be cited. It would seem that the judicial vicar should choose one of the defenders appointed for the tribunal on a stable basis by the diocesan bishop or bishop moderator and that this defender would continue to serve on the case for its duration, unless he or she is legitimately replaced in the course of the trial. (*Dignitas connubii*, art. 55)

According to canon 1508 §3 of the 1983 code and article 127 §3 of the instruction *Dignitas connubii*, a copy of the libellus is to be appended to the decree of citation and communicated with it to the respondent at the time of the first citation. For serious reasons, however, the code and the instruction permit deferral of the communication of the libellus to the respondent until after he or she has offered a declaration during the trial. Many North American tribunals have judged that concern for confidentiality in the tribunal process and fear that anger and recriminations will result from sharing their former spouses' accounts of their now failed marriages with respondents at the very outset of the process are always sufficiently grave causes for deferring the communication of the libellus to the respondent. Not rarely, the communication of the libellus with the decree of citation is simply omitted without any justifying decree. The new canon 1676 §1 no longer seems to provide the fig leaf of legitimacy for decisions to withhold the libellus from the respondent at the time of the initial citation. According to the new norm, it is no longer the libellus that is to be appended to the decree of citation, but the decree of citation that is to be appended to the bottom of the petition itself and both petition and appended decree of citation are to be communicated to the respondent. The new norm has no provision for deferring the communication of the libellus to the respondent. The absence of a clause offering an exception to the norm that the libellus be communicated to the respondent at the very outset of the process is a prod to tribunals to revisit the requirements for a libellus.

Canon 1504 and article 116 §1 of the instruction *Dignitas connubii* continue to specify the required content of the petition or libellus. It must:

> 1° express the tribunal before which the cause is to be introduced;
>
> 2° describe the object of the cause, that is, specify the marriage in question, present a petition for a declaration of nullity, and propose—although not necessarily in technical terms—the reason for petitioning, that is, the ground or grounds of nullity on which the marriage is being challenged;
>
> 3° indicate at least in a general way the facts and proofs on which the petitioner is relying in order to demonstrate what is being asserted;
>
> 4° be signed by the petitioner or his procurator, indicating also the day, month and year, as well as the place in which the petitioner or his advocate live, or declare they reside for the purpose of receiving acts;
>
> 5° indicate the domicile or quasi-domicile of the other spouse (cf. can. 1504).

The information the libellus must contain is rather limited. It consists of the names of and contact information for the parties, some basic information about the now failed marriage, and a brief description in non-technical language of the reasons why the marriage should be considered invalid and how that fact might be established. The necessary information can, in most cases, be summarized in one or two pages, especially if the petitioner has been assisted by one of the trained to conduct the preliminary investigation mentioned in articles 2–5 of the *Ratio procedendi* appended to *Mitis Iudex*. It is this compact statement of the issues that is the petition that must be communicated to the respondent with the citation. The lengthy and detailed "marital history" often submitted by petitioners with the libellus is not really part of the libellus itself but a supporting document. It is this supplementary document that is likely to evoke angry and often counterproductive responses from the respondent. However, it need not be communicated to the respondent at the outset of the process. In addition, although any documentary evidence, including copies of marriage certificates and divorce decrees, that will be proposed during the process should also be submitted with the libellus (*Dignitas connubii,* arts. 116 §2 and 117), these documents too are not part of the libellus itself and need not be communicated to the respondent at the time of the citation.

The citation of the respondent and the defender of the bond is to specify a time of fifteen (15) useful days within which they are to offer observations on the petition and the process it has initiated. When this period has elapsed, the judicial vicar is to issue a decree establishing the ground or grounds on which the case will be investigated and decided. The formulation of the doubt must specify not only the ground or grounds but also the party or parties whose consent was allegedly undermined by these grounds of nullity. This decree is to be communicated promptly to the parties and the defender of the bond. Canon 1513 §3 and article 135 §4 of the instruction *Dignitas connubii* allow those dissatisfied with the formulation of the grounds to make recourse to the single judge or college within ten days of notification of the decree joining the issues. One presumes that parties or defenders of the bond who believe the grounds have been wrongly specified can still make recourse but to the judicial vicar who joined the issues. (c. 1677 §4 and c. 1513 §3; Dignitas *connubii,* art. 135 §4) After hearing the parties, he can confirm the original decree of joinder or issue a new one. From this decree, there is no further recourse or appeal.

Once the doubt has been formulated, "it cannot validly be changed unless by a new decree, for a grave reason, at the request of a party, with the other party and the defender of the bond having been heard and their reasons considered." (*Dignitas connubii,* art. 136; c. 1514). The American Procedural Norms had authorized judges to add new grounds of nullity in the course of the trial *ex officio,*[42] but this norm was abrogated by the promulgation of the 1983 code. Despite the suggestion of some groups who offered *desiderata* to the pontifical commission charged with revising matrimonial procedure, the revised canon 1676 of the apostolic letter *Mitis Iudex* does not authorize the judge to change the ground unilaterally in the course of the process. Canonical commentators have differed sharply on the legitimacy of adding grounds or otherwise altering the decree joining the issues in the course of the trial. Some have insisted that, when a judge changes the grounds *ex officio* in the course of the trial not only is the decree changing the grounds invalid but the decision on the new ground is also irremediable null because the new ground or grounds were *ultra*

---

42. American Procedural Norms, Norm 11, *CLD* 7: 957.

petitum, i.e., not part of what was contained in the petition (c. 1620, 4°).[43] Others have insisted equally strongly that, as long as the parties and the defender of the bond have been consulted and offered an opportunity to raise objections, changing the grounds in the course of a marriage nullity case is within the legitimate discretion of the judge who, in cases affecting the public good like marriage cases, is empowered to act *ex officio* to "supply for the negligence of the parties . . . in lodging exceptions whenever [he or she] considers it necessary in order to avoid a gravely unjust judgment." (c. 1452 §§1–2; *Dignitas connubii*, art. 71 §§1–2)[44]

Changing the grounds in the course of the process usually becomes an issue when it becomes clear that the accumulating evidence does not support a decision on the ground or grounds established at the time of the joinder of the issues but some other ground. The law seems to presume that petitioners will be represented by well-trained advocates who are carefully following the progress of the case and who will, therefore, intervene to request a change in the grounds on behalf of their clients if they notice this situation. Unfortunately, in most parts of the world, and certainly in North America, petitioners are not represented by such knowledgeable and attentive advocates, and petitioners themselves are unlikely to have enough knowledge of canonical jurisprudence to be aware that their case is in jeopardy unless the grounds are changed. Those who hold that the judge cannot validly change the grounds *ex officio* suggest that, to avoid an unjust decision in these circumstances, the judge should inform the parties or their advocates of the problem or perhaps the promoter of justice and suggest that they petition for a change in the grounds.[45] While

---

43. See Ramos and Skoniecczny, 2/1: 135–140; Pio Vito Pinto, *Commento al Codice di Diritto Canonico*, 2nd ed. (Vatican City: Libreria Editrice Vaticana, 2001) 887–88; Michael Hilbert, "La contestazione della lite (can. 1513–1516, 1677)," *Forum* 4 (1993) 75; Maragnoli, in *Il giudizio*, 2/1: 125–130; Lüdicke-Jenkins, 241; Craig Cox, "The Contentious Trial," in *A New Commentary on the Code of Canon Law*, ed. John P. Beal, et al. (Mahwah: Paulist Press, 2000) 1770.

44. See Augustine Mendonça, "Change or Addition of Ground *Ex Officio*," in *Roman Replies and CLSA Advisory Opinions 2005*, ed. Stephen Pedone and James Donlon (Washington: CLSA, 2005) 99–104; Stankiewicz, "The Joinder of Issues," in *Exegetical Commentary*, 4/2: 1159–1160; Colantonio, in *Il Processo*, 535–536; Mario Pompedda, "Decision-Sentence in Marriage Trials: Of the Concept and Principles for Rendering an Ecclesial Sentence," *Quaderni del Studio Rotale* 5 (1990) 84; Luigi Chiappetta, *Il Codice di diritto canonico, commento giuridico-pastorale*, (Rome: Edizioni Dehoniane, 1996) 3: 104, n. 2; Gianpaolo Montini, "Alcune questioni in merito al can 1514," *Periodica* 92 (2003) 322–324; Joaquin Llobell, "La modificación "ex officio" de la formula de la duda, la certeza moral y la conformidad de las sentencias en la Instrucción *Dignitas Connubii*," *Ius Canonicum* 46 (2006) 139–148.

45. Ramos and Skoniecczny, 2/1: 139; Lüdicke-Jenkins, 241.

inviting the petitioner to seek a change in the grounds may be the safer course, it does seem a bit artificial and formalistic.[46] There are strong arguments that can be raised for the position adopted by Stankiewicz when he was still Dean of the Roman Rota that "in causes related to the public interest, such as marriage cases, it is still possible for the judge to change the terms, even ex officio (cf. c. 1452 §1), provided the other conditions established in canon 1514 are met." Nevertheless, all commentators are in agreement that among the conditions for a valid change of the grounds in the course of the process is that the parties, including the defender of the bond, be consulted.[47]

---

§3. If the case is to be handled through the ordinary process, the judicial vicar, by the same decree, is to arrange the constitution of a college of judges or of a single judge with two assessors according to can. 1673 §4.

§4. However, if the briefer process is decided upon, the judicial vicar proceeds according to the norm of can. 1685.

New canon 1676 §§3–4 charges the judicial vicar to determine whether the case that he has just accepted and for which he has set the grounds is to be treated according to the ordinary process before a college of judges or single judge or meets the criteria for being treated according to the new abbreviated process before the diocesan bishop. On the basis of the petition and any documentary evidence attached to it as well as any observations by the respondent, the judicial vicar must decide: a) whether the case has been submitted by both spouses or at least by one of them with the consent of the other, and b) on the basis of preliminary and fairly limited documentary evidence, whether the case seems to be one where the invalidity of the marriage is evident and for which a more rigorous investigation is not needed. (*Mitis Iudex*, c. 1683) If so, he issues a decree remitting the case to the abbreviated process and designating a judge-instructor and an assessor to carry out the instruction of the case in accord with the

---

46. Stankiewicz, "The Joinder of the Issues," in *Exegetical Commentary*, 4/2: 1159.

47. See Antoni Stankiewicz, "De nullitate dententiae 'ultra petita' prolatae," *Periodica* 70 (1981) 221–235.

norm of canons 1685–1686.[48] If the judicial vicar judges that the case does not meet the criteria for the abbreviated process, he is to issue a decree constituting a tribunal to hear and decide the case according to the ordinary process.

Can. 1677 §1. The defender of the bond, the legal representatives of the parties, as well as the promoter of justice, if involved in the trial, have the following rights: 1° to be present at the examination of the parties, the witnesses, and the experts, without prejudice to the prescript of can. 1559; 2° to inspect the judicial acts, even those not yet published, and to review the documents presented by the parties.

§2. The parties cannot be present at the examination mentioned in §1, n. 1.

This new canon 1677 repeats verbatim the originally promulgated canon 1678 and article 159 of the instruction *Dignitas connubii*.[49] The canon reflects the tendency of post-conciliar procedural law reform to equalize the status of the defender of the bond and the representatives of the parties during the process. All of the rights accorded to the both defender of the bond and the representatives of the parties by canon 1677 §1 and more were enjoyed only by the defender of the bond in the 1917 code's canons 1968–1969. Although the current law does go a long way toward equalizing the positions of the defender of the bond and the representatives of the parties, the defender of the bond still has a noteworthy advantage. If he or she is "not cited in cases which require their presence, the acts are invalid unless they actually took part even if not cited or, after they have inspected the acts, at least were able to fulfill their function before the sentence." (c. 1433; *Dignitas connubii*, art. 60). Although refusal to allow a party to have a legal representative at all or particularly egregious violations of the rights of a legal representative during the process may result in a sentence being declared irremediably null because of the denial of the right of defense (c. 1620, 7°), slights to the rights of the legal representatives of the parties are not treated as seriously by the law as are violation of the rights of defenders of the bond.

---

48. See the commentary on these canons by William Daniel in *The Jurist* 75 (2015) 539–591 and in this volume.

49. Joan Carreras, "Proofs," in *Exegetical Commentary*, 4/2: 1817–1821; Mario Ferrante, "Le prove in generale (art. 155–161)," in *Il giudizio*, 3: 314–320; Lüdicke-Jenkins, 273–275.

"Legal representative" is the translation chosen for the Latin *patronus* or *patrona*. The title is commonly used to denote a person who serves as both procurator and advocate for a party during a trial. The roles are somewhat different but not incompatible. A procurator is a legal representative who is empowered to perform legal actions on behalf of a client and thus can be said to have "power of attorney"; an advocate, on the other hand, is an expert in the law who assists a client in preparing his or her case, submitting the *libellus*, and arguing the case during the trial. Since parties with cases before the tribunals of the Holy See must have a procurator with a residence in Rome, the two functions of procurator and advocate are often joined in those called *defensor* for those who represent these parties before the Rota or Signatura. This usage has been extended to include those who join the two functions in other tribunals.

Can. 1678 §1. In cases of the nullity of marriage, a judicial confession and the declarations of the parties, possibly supported by witnesses to the credibility of the parties, can have the force of full proof, to be evaluated by the judge after he has considered all the indications and supporting factors, unless other elements are present which weaken them.

This new canon replaces, but only for marriage cases, the norm of canons 1536 §2 and article 180 §§1–2 of the instruction *Dignitas connubii* on the probative weight to be attributed to the judicial confessions or declarations of the parties.[50] Throughout the regime of the 1917 code, the testimony of the spouses themselves was viewed with considerable suspicion.[51] Article 117 of the 1936 instruction *Provida Mater* succinctly expressed the attitude of the 1917 code on the probative value of the party's judicial confessions and declarations: "The judicial deposition of the spouses is not suitable

---

50. Thomas Doran, "The Declarations of the Parties," in *Exegetical Commentary*, 4/2: 1216–1217; João Corso, "Le prove," in *Il Processo*, 612–615; Giordano, Caberletti, "La dichiarazioni della parte," in *Il giudizio*, 3: 352–357; Lüdicke-Jenkins, 306–311. See also Josef Gehr, *Die Bewertung des gerichtlichen Geständnisses und Parteierklärungen vor Gericht gemaß c. 1536 §2 CIC/1983* (St. Otilien: EOS Verlag, 1994).

51. See 1917 CIC, c, 1751 which is silent about any probative weight to accorded to the confessions of parties in marriage cases. 1917 CIC canons 1742–1746 which deal with the interrogations of the parties during a trial are not even included in the section of the code on Proofs but in a separate title.

for constituting proof against the validity of marriage." This quite negative evaluation of the party's own declarations and confessions was slowly eroded in the jurisprudence of the Roman Rota, but it was not until the promulgation of the 1983 Code that a more positive assessment of the weight of the depositions of the spouses was incorporated into the law itself. Canon 1536 §2 and article 180 §1 of the instruction *Dignitas connubii* established the principle that these depositions of the parties can have some probative weight, but not "the force of full proof . . . unless other elements are present which can thoroughly corroborate them." Both canon 1679 and article 180 §2 of the instruction *Dignitas connubii* helpfully suggested that "witnesses to the credibility of those parties in addition to other indications (*indicia*) and supporting factors (*admincula*)" might be sufficient to bolster the probative value of the depositions of the parties.[52] This somewhat more open attitude toward the weight of these depositions was still, however, rather guarded and it seemed to presume that that circumstances in which the deposition of a party could provide full proof would be rather rare.

The new canon 1678 §1 completely reverses the traditional standard for assessing the probative weight of the depositions of the parties. No longer are the parties to the marriage case considered suspect; no longer is it considered unusual that the depositions of the parties might be sufficient to provide full proof. Instead of stipulating that the depositions are capable of providing full proof only when they are fully corroborated by other indices and circumstances, the law now asserts simply that these depositions are capable of providing full proof "unless other elements are present which weaken them." Of course, it remains ultimately the prerogative of the judge, now unencumbered by limiting prescripts of the law, to determine in the light of the other indicia and circumstances of the case how much probative weight the parties' depositions deserve (c. 1608 §3). If the previous law's presumption was not to give probative weight to judicial depositions of the parties, the new law's presumption is for attributing probative weight to these depositions, especially when they are buttressed by witnesses to the credibility of the party or parties. These witnesses to the credibility of the parties or "testimonial witnesses" are persons who

---

52. Joan Carreras, "Proofs," in *Exegetical Commentary*, 4/2: 1822–1824; Lüdicke-Jenkins, 309–311.

have no direct knowledge of the relevant circumstances of the marriage now before the tribunal but who can attest to the party's credibility and reputation for honesty in the community. They may also have heard the petitioner recount the story of his or her failed marriage in the past and, therefore, be able to corroborate that the account of the marriage the party has given to the tribunal is consistent with what he or she had told others outside the tribunal at "non-suspect times." Such testimonial witnesses can lend even greater credibility to the deposition of a party itself.

The new canon 1678 §1 deals only with judicial confessions and declarations, i.e., those made to the judge or his delegate in the course of the trial. The evaluation of the probative value of extrajudicial confessions, i.e., those made outside the context of the trial but now brought into the trial by a document or the testimony of the other party or a witness, remain governed by canon 1537 and article 181 of the instruction *Dignitas connubii*: "After considering the circumstances, it is for the judge to decide how much value must be accorded to an extrajudicial confession introduced into the trial." Traditionally, the two critical criteria for assessing the weight of an extrajudicial confession are the reliability of the person or document bringing the confession into the trial and the time at which the confession itself was made, i.e., whether it was made at a suspect or a non-suspect time. A suspect time is one at which the party making the confession would be aware of the potential usefulness of his statement in a pending or soon to be pending process, e.g., while driving a witness to the tribunal office to testify; a non-suspect time is one at which the party would not be immediately aware of the juridic relevance of his or her statement.

---

§2. In the same cases, the testimony of one witness can produce full proof if it concerns a qualified witness making a deposition concerning matters done ex officio, or unless the circumstances of things and persons suggest it.

Canon 1791 §1 of the 1917 code stipulated: "The testimony of a single witness does not provide full proof, unless it is a qualified witness who deposes about things done *ex officio*." The ancient principle that "one witness is no witness" (*unus testis, nullus testis*) was quietly eroded by the jurisprudence of the Rota.[53] As a result, the traditional suspicion of the reliability of a

---

53. Pericle Cardinal Felice, "Juridical Formalities and Evaluation of Evidence in the Canonical Process," *The Jurist* 38 (1978) 156.

single witness was somewhat mitigated by canon 1573 of the 1983 code (*Dignitas connubii*, art. 202): "The testimony of one witness cannot produce full proof unless it concerns a qualified witness making a deposition concerning matters done *ex officio*, or unless the circumstances of things and persons suggest otherwise."[54] The new canon 1678 §2 completely eliminates the negative assessment of the testimony of a single witness and states simply that the testimony of a single witness can provide full proof if it is the testimony of a qualified witness or if the circumstances of the case and of the witness himself or herself that this testimony is worthy of full credence. A witness considered "qualified" (*qualificatus*) is one who testifies about what he or she did in an official capacity, e.g., a priest or deacon who testifies about how he performed a particular baptism. Canon 1572 and article 201 of the instruction *Dignitas connubii* suggest criteria to be used in evaluating whether a singular witness is worthy of full credence:

> 1° what the condition or reputation of the person is;
>
> 2° whether the testimony derives from personal knowledge, especially from what has been seen or heard personally, or whether from opinion, rumor, or hearsay;
>
> 3° whether the witness is reliable and firmly consistent or inconsistent, uncertain and vacillating;
>
> 4° whether the witness . . . is supported by other elements of proof.

If a judge is inclined to give the testimony of a singular witness the weight of full proof, he or she should explain in the sentence why he believes the circumstances of things or persons" warrant such confidence.

---

§3. In cases of impotence or defect of consent because of mental illness or an anomaly of a psychic nature, the judge is to use the services of one or more experts unless it is clear from the circumstances that it would be useless to do so; in other cases the prescript of can. 1574 is to be observed.

This new norm reproduces the former canon 1680 of the 1983 code with one noteworthy addition: an expert is to be used (*utatur*) not only in cases involving possible impotence or a defect of consent due to mental illness

---

54. Feliciano Gil de las Heras, "The Credibility of Evidence," in *Exegetical Commentary*, 4/2: 1324–1327; Corso, 617–620; Paola Moneta, "I testimoni," in *Il giudizio*, 3:371–386; Lüdicke-Jenkins, 343–344.

(*mentis morbum*) as in the former canon 1680 but also in cases involving a defect of consent due to an anomaly of a psychic nature. Thus, the new norm seems to incorporate the expansion of the requirement of canon 1680 by the instruction *Dignitas connubii*, art. 203 §1: "In causes concerning impotence or defect of consent because of *mentis morbum* or because of the incapacities described in can. 1095, the judge is to employ the assistance of one or more experts, unless from the circumstances this would appear evidently useless."[55]

Prior to the appearance of the instruction *Dignitas connubii*, some canonists had argued that, since it is the right to "appraise the proofs according to [his or her] own conscience" (c. 1608 §3), laws such as canon 1680 that restricted this right by limiting the judge's freedom in the evaluation of proofs should be interpreted strictly. This line of reasoning suggested that the term "mental illness" (*mentis morbum*) of former canon 1680 should be construed narrowly to require consultation with experts only in cases of psychoses and other such serious mental illness and not other psychic disturbances like personality disorders or gross immaturity. This line of reasoning was never adopted by the Roman Rota which employed the services of experts in most (but not all) cases being decided on the so-called "psychological" grounds mentioned in canon 1095. This Rotal practice was incorporated into article 203 of the instruction *Dignitas connubii* and now it has been added to the foundational canon itself.

Judges can dispense with consultation with one or more experts even in cases involving the defects of consent mentioned in canon 1095 if such consultation would be evidently useless (*inutilis evidenter*). A consultation with an expert might fairly be judged useless if evidence of a party's psychological condition is available from psychiatric or counseling records legitimately released by the party to the tribunal or because the psychological disturbance at issue was transitory in nature (e.g., drunkenness) as may sometimes be the situation in cases to be decided on the ground of canon 1095, 1°. While the decision about the validity or invalidity of a marriage is a legal issue that belongs exclusively to the judge, the law does

---

55. Kenneth Boccafola, "Experts, in *Exegetical Commentary*, 4/2: 1328–1331; Joan Carreras, "Proofs," in *Exegetical Commentary*, 4/2: 1825–1827; Umberto Tramma, "Perizie e periti," in *Il processo*, 625–632 Carlo Gullo, "Periti e le perizie," in *Il giudizio*, 3: 428–429; Lüdicke-Jenkins, 345–347; Augustine Mendonça, "The Apostolic Signatura's Recent Declaration of the Necessity of Using Experts in Marriage Nullity Cases," *Studia Canonica* 35 (2001) 33–58.

not suppose that the judge himself or herself has the expertise in psychology to be able to identify and assess the impact of psychic disturbance and irregularities on marital consent. Thus, the law's insistence on the use of experts in cases involving so-called "psychological" grounds is prompted by concern that, without the contribution of mental health professionals, judges may render decisions, both affirmative and negative, that are not solidly grounded in the facts. Although consulting an expert may lengthen the process and add to its expense, these are costs that must be borne to insure that the process gets to the truth of the matter.

The reference to canon 1574 at the end of the new canon 1678 §3 is a reminder that judges are free to seek the contribution of experts of various kinds even when the law does not require such consultations, but judges themselves may feel the need for an expert's insights to reach certainty in the matter before the court. These experts may be psychologists, psychiatrists or other mental health professionals but they may also be experts in other disciplines as exotic as cultural anthropology and as mundane as handwriting analysis. Article 203 §2 of the instruction *Dignitas connubii* stipulates: "[T]he assistance of experts is to be employed whenever, according to the prescriptions of the judge, their study and expert opinion, based on the precepts of their art or science, are required in order to establish some fact or to ascertain the true nature of something, as when an investigation of the authenticity of some written document is to be made."

---

§4. Whenever, during the instruction of a case, a very probable doubt arises as to whether the marriage was ever consummated, the tribunal, having heard both parties, can suspend the case of nullity, complete the instruction for a dispensation super rato, and then transmit the acts to the Apostolic See together with a petition for a dispensation from either one or both of the spouses and the votum of the tribunal and the bishop.

This new canon substantially repeats former canon 1681 and article 153 of the instruction *Dignitas connubii* with one noteworthy exception.[56] Former canon 1681 had authorized the tribunal that has uncovered evidence

---

56. Carmelo de Diego-Lora, "The Judgment and the Appeal," in *Exegetical Commentary*, 4/2: 1828–1837; Ferranti, "Le prove in generale," in *Il giudizio*, 3: 143–149 Lüdicke-Jenkins, 261–264.

prompting a probable doubt that the marriage had been consummated to suspend the marriage nullity process with the consent of the parties (*de consensu partium*). The new canon requires only that the tribunal consult the parties (*auditis partibus*) before suspending the marriage nullity process and preparing a petition for a dispensation of the ratified but unconsummated marriage from the Roman Pontiff. Although examining petitions for such dispensations and making recommendations to the Holy Father had long been within the competence of the Congregation for the Sacraments and Divine Worship, this responsibility was transferred by Benedict XVI in 2011 to a special office of the Roman Rota.[57]

ART. 4. THE JUDGEMENT, ITS APPEAL AND ITS EXECUTION

Can. 1679. The sentence that first declared the nullity of the marriage, once the terms as determined by cann. 1630–1633 have passed, becomes executive.

This new canon 1679 which replaces the former canon 1682 marks the most significant modification in the procedural law governing marriage cases in almost 300 years. Since Benedict XV's 1741 constitution *Dei miseratione*, couples who received affirmative decisions in marriage nullity cases involving defects of consent could not enter new marriages in the Church until the first decision had been confirmed by an appellate tribunal. Although between 1970 and 1983 particular law for the United States, Canada and some other countries mitigated the requirement of two conforming affirmative decisions before a spouse was allowed a new canonical marriage,[58] the universal law of the Church from 1741 to 1972 required the first instance defender of the bond to appeal any and all affirmative decisions to a higher tribunal. The defenders of the bond at the appellate court also had the right to appeal second affirmative decisions, if in their consciences they believed the cases had been wrongly decided. In his 1972 motu proprio *Causas matrimoniales*, Paul VI relieved the first instance defender of the bond of the strict obligation to appeal all affirmative decisions but charged

---

57. Benedict XVI, apostolic letter *Quaerit semper*, August, 30, 2011, art. 2–4: *AAS* 93 (2011) 570–571.
58. American Procedural Norms, Norm 23.II; *CLD* 7: 964; for Canada and Australia see Sacred Council for the Public Affairs of the Church, rescript, November 1. 1974, in *CLD* 8: 1170.

the judicial vicar of the tribunal that first declared the nullity of a marriage to forward all such cases along with any appeals received to the appellate court for a second instance process.[59] This provision of *Causas matrimoniales* was substantially incorporated into the 1983 code as canon 1682 and into the instruction *Dignitas connubii* as articles 264–267.[60] This so-called "mandatory appeal" of affirmative decisions in marriage cases has now been abrogated. If the peremptory period of fifteen (15) useful days from notice of the publication of the sentence has elapsed (c. 1630 §1) without an appeal being lodged against an affirmative decision either by the disgruntled respondent or by the defender of the bond, the parties are free to enter a new marriage in the Church.

One of the aims of Pope Francis' reform of procedural law for marriage nullity cases was to expedite the process. The elimination of a required second instance process for affirmative decisions will certainly have this effect. Depending on the caseloads and relative efficiency of appellate tribunals, the previous system of mandatory review of affirmative first instance decisions added several months to several years to the duration of the marriage nullity process. The elimination of the required second instance process will shorten the length of the process by that amount. At the extraordinary Synod of Bishops on The Vocation and Mission of the Family in the Church and The Contemporary World held in October of 2014 some synod fathers had objected strenuously to proposals that the annulment process be streamlined by dispensing the requirement of a second instance conforming sentence because, they feared, it "would not guarantee a reliable judgment" which reached "the truth about the validity of the marriage bond."[61] While it is too early to determine whether the abrogation of a mandatory second instance process some synod father feared, there is some evidence to suggest that it will not

---

59. Paul VI, *Causas matrimoniales*, VIII, §§1–3: *AAS* 63 (1971) 444; *CLD* 7: 972.

60. Carmelo Diego-Lora, he Judgment and the Appeal," 4/2: 1838–1854; Paolo Moneta, "L'appello," in *Il processo*, 771–795; Maria Teresa Romano, "La trasmissione della causa al tribunal di appello e la sua trattazione," in *Il giudizio*, 3: 576–590; Lüdicke-Jenkins, 423–433.

61. Synod of Bishops, The law does not suppose that the judge himself or herself have the expertise in psychology to be able to identify and assess the impact of psychic disturbance and irregularities on marital consent. Ordinary General Assembly, The Vocation and Mission of the Family in the Church and the Contemporary World, Instrumentum Laboris, §114, accessed August 14, 2015 at http://www.vatican.va/romancuria/synod/documents/rc_synod_doc_20150623_instrumentum-xiv-assemblyit.html.

notably increase the number of declarations of nullity granted. In recent years, the vast majority of affirmative decisions issued by first instance tribunals, not only in North America but throughout the world, were simply confirmed by decree at the appellate level rather than being admitted to the ordinary second instance process.[62]

A more real danger is that, in the absence of the oversight of first instance tribunal decisions that the mandatory second instance process insured, first instanced tribunal decisions will gradually grow rather sloppy. That this concern is not imaginary can be gleaned from the experience in the United States from 1970 to 1983 when the provision of the American Procedural Norms for dispensation from mandatory appeal virtually eliminated appeals of affirmative decisions, except those by dissatisfied respondents. In the absence of any real oversight, decision writing in some tribunals became extremely sloppy with narratives of the story of the marriage largely replacing reasoned argument. In his apostolic letter *Mitis Iudex*, Pope Francis expresses confidence in the ability and willingness of the diocesan bishop himself to exercise oversight over his tribunal as the one "who, due to his pastoral office, is with Peter the greatest guarantor of Catholic unity in faith and discipline." Whether busy diocesan bishops live up to the confidence the Holy Father has expressed in them remains to be seen.

Can. 1680 §1. The party who considers himself or herself aggrieved, as well as the promoter of justice and the defender of the bond, have the right to introduce a complaint of nullity of the judgment or appeal against the sentence, according to cann. 1619–1640.

Although the new canon 1679 abrogates the requirement of a second instance process for all affirmative decisions in marriage nullity cases, it retains the possibility for dissatisfied parties to lodge complaints of nullity or appeals against sentences, both those which declare the invalidity of a marriage and those which uphold its validity. A complaint of nullity (cc. 1619–1627; *Dignitas connubii*, art. 269–278) is a challenge to a definitive

---

62. Joaquin Llobell, "Prospettive e possibili sviluppi della *Dignitas connubii* sull'abrogazione dell'obbligo della doppia sentenza conforme," *Periodica* 104 (2015) 247–257.

sentence which alleges that the procedure followed by the tribunal in reaching the decision was so defective that the decision should be "thrown out" or vacated and the complainant granted a new trial or at least that the judge should be compelled to go back to the point in the original trial where the critical procedural error was made, correct the error, and proceed to a new decision. The new canon 1680 §1 leaves unchanged the norms of the code on reasons why a sentence might be declared null and on the procedure to be followed in lodging and resolving complaints of nullity. An exhaustive list of defects that might infect a sentence with nullity is found in canon 1620 for incurable or irremediable nullity and in canon 1622 for curable or remediable nullity. Sentences allegedly irremediably null can be challenged directly for up to ten years from notice of the publication of the sentence (c. 1621); sentences allegedly remediably null for up to three months. (c. 1623)

Complaints of nullity are normally to be lodged with the judge who issued the sentence being challenged. If the complainant has reason to fear that this judge who presided at the original trial and issued the sentence being challenged might be biased and, therefore, unwilling to admit having made a procedural error, he or she can demand that another judge or judges from the same tribunal be substituted to resolve the complaint. The complaint is resolved following the oral contentious process. A complaint of nullity can also be joined to an appeal of the definitive sentence. Although paragraphs 2 and 3 of the new canon 1680 do not specify the procedure to be followed should an appellate court be required to resolve a complaint of nullity, there is no reason to believe that the procedure for dealing with complaints of nullity attached to appeals has changed. Thus, once the appellate court receives an appeal to which a complaint of nullity is joined, the judicial vicar constitutes a tribunal of at least three judges. This tribunal first considers the complaint of nullity. If the complaint is found to have merit, the case is remanded to the first instance tribunal for a new trial; if the complaint of nullity is rejected, the tribunal proceeds to consider the appeal.[63]

---

63. See John P. Beal, "The Complaint of Nullity: A Hands-On Approach," in *Essays in Honor of Sister Rose McDermott, S.S.J.*, ed. Robert Kaslyn, Institutiones Iuris Canonici I (Washington: The Catholic University, 2010) 312–346. See also Antoni Stankiewicz, "Il procedimento della 'querela nullitatis': il giudice," in *La "querela nullitatis" nel processo canonico*, Studi Giuridici 69 (2005) 181–198; Roberto Palombi, "Il soggetti legittimati alla proposizione della querela

An appeal is a challenge to a definitive sentence that asks a higher tribunal to look a second (or third) time at the evidence gathered by the previous tribunal and to render a new—and, the appelant hopes, different—sentence. Unlike a complaint of nullity which addresses the procedure followed in reaching a decision, an appeal is a request for a new trial before a higher judge on the merits of the case. An appeal must be lodged within fifteen (15) useful days from the date when the party or defender of the bond received notice of the publication of the definitive sentence. (c. 1630 §1; *Dignitas connubii*, art. 281 §§1–2) If no appeal is lodged within this peremptory time frame, the sentence now can be executed. If a party or the defender of the bond does wish to exercise the right to appeal a first instance decision, the lodging and prosecution of the appeal remain governed by canons 1628–1634 and articles 279–285 of the instruction *Dignitas connubii*.[64]

The appeal is to be lodged with the tribunal which issued the sentence being challenged. Although appeals of first instance sentences can be made directly to the Roman Rota and potential appellants should be advised of their right to approach this Apostolic Tribunal, they are presumed to be made to the ordinary appellate court of the first instance tribunal whose decision is being challenged, unless the contrary is evident. (c. 1632; *Dignitas connubii*, art. 283 §§1–4) After lodging the appeal, the dissatisfied party or defender of the bond must prosecute or pursue the appeal before the higher tribunal within thirty (30) days. Little is required of the appellant to prosecute or pursue the appeal except to affirm his or her desire for the higher court to reverse the previous decision, state the reasons for objecting to the decision (a statement that may be as simple as "I believe the matter was wrongly decided by the Tribunal of X"), attach this statement to a copy of the decision, and send these documents to the appellate tribunal. (cc. 1633–1634; *Dignitas connubii*, art. 284–285) Although the law distinguishes between the lodging of an appeal and its prosecution, article 284 §2 of the instruction *Dignitas connubii* suggests that these two acts can be combined into one if the appellant's written statement lodging an appeal asks (or can be reasonably construed as asking) that the tribunal

---

di nullità," in Id., 199–213; Sebastiano Villegiante, "La trattazione incidentale delle querele di nullità," in Id., 215–229.

64. Paola Moneta, "The Appeal," in *Exegetical Commentary*, 4/2: 1566–1584; Egidio Turnaturi, L'appello," in *Il giudizio*, 3: 633–668; Lüdicke-Jenkins, 450–461.

a quo forward the case file along with the appeal itself to the appellate tribunal. At the very least, appellants should be advised clearly and precisely of what they need to do to pursue or prosecute their appeals.

In order to prosecute the appeal, the appellant must attach a copy of the definitive sentence being challenged to his or her letter to the appellate court. Since many tribunals, in an exaggerated concern about privacy, use strategies of dubious legality to publish definitive sentences, appellants may have some difficulty obtaining the copy of the definitive sentence to which there statement of an intent to pursue an appeal before the higher tribunal is to be appended.[65] If so, fairness demands that these tribunals of first instance should forward a copy of the sentence and the party's appeal with the acts of the case without quibbling about whether the appellant has done what is necessary to prosecute the appeal—and before being prodded to do so by the appellate tribunal itself.

---

§2. After the time limits established by law for the appeal and its prosecution have passed, and after the judicial acts have been received by the tribunal of higher instance, a college of judges is established, the defender of the bond is designated, and the parties are admonished to put forth their observations within the prescribed time limit; after this time period has passed, if the appeal clearly appears merely dilatory, the collegiate tribunal confirms the sentence of the prior instance by decree.

The abbreviated process introduced in Paul VI's *Causas matrimoniales* and continued in canon 1682 of the 1983 Code and article 265 of the instruction *Dignitas connubii* for confirming affirmative decisions by decree has now been abrogated by *Mitis Iudex*, except for cases in which the appellate tribunal deems the appeal to be "merely dilatory." Henceforth all other appeals of first instance decisions, both affirmative and negative, are to be dealt with at the appellate level only by what was called "the ordinary process."[66] Thus, when an appeal is received by an appellate court, the

---

65. See John P. Beal, "Publish or Perish: Transparency in the Marriage Nullity Process," *CLSA Proceedings* 75 (2013) 75–82 and William Daniel, "The Publication of the Definitive Sentence," *Studia Canonica* 42 (2008) 393–436.

66. Paolo Moneta, "The Appeal," in *Exegetical Commentary*, 4/2: 1594–1595; Francisco Ramos and Piotr Skonieczny, *Diritto Processuale Canonico* (Rome: Angelicum University

judicial vicar is to constitute a tribunal of three judges, a defender of the bond and a notary. The *praeses* or *ponens* of the panel is to advise (*moneantur*) the parties and the defender of the bond to propose any additional observations they may have about the case within a peremptory period of time set by him or her. This notice constitutes the citation of the parties for the appellate process. Once the time for making observations has elapsed, the judges must either move forward with the ordinary appellate process or declare the appeal to be a purely dilatory strategy by the appellant and confirm the first instance sentence by decree. Like all decrees which are not merely procedural in judicial processes, the decree confirming a sentence has no legal force unless it contains the reasons for its decision at least in summary form or "refer to reasons expressed in another act which has been properly published" such as the first instance sentence under appeal. (c. 1617; *Dignitas connubii*, art. 261; c. 1617)

Tribunals have long been familiar with—and frustrated by—appeals that seem to be purely dilatory in nature. Nevertheless, having an opportunity to appeal an adverse judgment is a fundamental right of participants in all judicial processes, ecclesiastical and secular, and a core component of the right of defense. As a result, decisions by appellate judges to dismiss appeals as dilatory which seem arbitrary or capricious can easily leave the second instance decisions open to complaints of nullity claiming denial of the right of defense. In such cases, the resolution of the complaint of nullity may prolong the process even more than the hearing of the dilatory appeal would have. Decisions that appeals are merely dilatory should be based on objective criteria. Since parties to tribunal processes in the Church are always free to "submit themselves to the justice of the court" and since the decision of the appellate court is usually based on the evidence gathered at the previous instance, the mere fact that parties have no new observations to offer at the outset of the appellate process cannot be fairly construed as a sign that the appeal was purely dilatory. However, if a respondent who has not offered a declaration or suggested witnesses during the first instance process appeals but fails to offer his or her declaration within the time set by the appellate judge, this fact may warrant the conclusion that his or her appeal was indeed dilatory. Although canon 1680 §2 does not mention explicitly an intervention of the defender of the bond before the

---

Press, 2014) 2/2: 284–307; Maria Teresa Romana, in *Il giudizio*, 3: 590–593; Lüdicke-Jenkins, 430–432.

appellate judges determine that an appeal was merely dilatory, it would be prudent to consult the defender prior to making such a determination.

When an affirmative sentence is confirmed by an appellate court, it can be executed immediately and the parties are free to enter new marriages recognized by the Catholic Church as soon as they are informed of the decision or decree. A further consequence of a sentence or decree confirming a first instance sentence is that the decision is no longer subject to further appeal. The only remedy remaining for a person still dissatisfied with a decision after it has been confirmed by an appellate court is to seek the favor of a new hearing of the case from the Roman Rota, a favor granted only if the party can bring forward sufficient new and substantial evidence or arguments to satisfy the Rota that a new hearing would probably result in a different decision than the two previous ones. Although the abbreviated appellate procedure introduced by Paul VI and continued in the 1983 code was available exclusively for confirming affirmative decisions by decree, this new norm of *Mitis Iudex* allows for confirming both affirmative and negative decisions by decree if the appellate judges legitimately determine that the appeal was merely dilatory. Allowing a first instance affirmative decision to become executive by confirming it by decree after a finding that the respondent's (or perhaps defender of the bond's) appeal had been merely dilatory is certainly keeping with the spirit of the procedural reform effected by *Mitis Iudex* with its emphasis on expediting the marriage nullity process. However, when an appellate tribunal confirms a negative decision by decree after finding a petitioner's appeal to have been merely dilatory, it leaves the petitioner with no option in the future except to request a new hearing of the case from the Rota.

---

§3. If an appeal is admitted, the tribunal must proceed in the same manner as the first instance with the appropriate adjustments.

§4. If a new ground of nullity of the marriage is alleged at the appellate level, the tribunal can admit it and judge it as if in first instance.

Once the appellate tribunal has determined that the appeal is not merely dilatory, it is to move on to resolve the appeal according to the norms for the ordinary appellate process in accord with the norms of canons 1640 and 1683 of the 1983 code and articles 226–268 of the instruction *Dignitas connubii.* As was explained above, the option given to appellate judges by Paul VI's *Causas matrimoniales* and the revised code to simply confirm an affirmative decision by decree has been abrogated by *Mitis Iudex.* All genuinely contested appellate cases are now to be handled according to the ordinary process to insure the appellant ample opportunity to make his or her case for a reversal of the original decision. Since the parties and defender of the bond were cited prior to the judges' determination that the appeal is not frivolous, the next task for the appellate tribunal is to join the issues. Normally, the doubt to be resolved at the appellate level is the same as the one established at the previous instance and so the formula of the doubt can be stated simply as "whether the sentence of the Tribunal of X should be confirmed or not." If the case was decided at first instance on multiple grounds, the appeal is presumed to be against all the grounds decided in the sentence, unless the contrary is evident. (c. 1637 §4)

Since the 1936 instruction *Provida Mater,* canon law has admitted an exception to the general principle that a new cause for petitioning cannot be admitted at the appellate level for marriage cases. (c. 1639 §1). Canon 1683 of the 1983 code and article 268 of the instruction *Dignitas connubii* stipulate that, if a new ground of nullity is alleged (*afferatur*) at the appellate level, the tribunal can admit the new ground and proceed to decide the case on that ground as if it were serving as a first instance tribunal.[67] This allowance for the introduction of a new ground of nullity at the appellate level is continued in the new canon 1680 §4 of *Mitis Iudex.* Although the canon is silent about who might propose a new ground at the appellate level, it seems to presume that the proposal will emanate from one of the parties or an advocate of a party and not by the judges of the appellate tribunal. Since most parties know little about the canonical grounds of nullity and their right to propose them and, in many, if not most, places, are not represented by advocates or at least by especially well trained advocates, to insist that only the parties can propose new grounds at the appellate level would effectively thwart the purpose of the law allowing the introduction of new grounds of nullity at the appellate level. In the course of the process, only the parties can propose changes to the *dubium* defined at the joinder of the issues (c. 1514). However, at the time of the joinder of

---

67. Paolo Moneta, "The Appeal," in *Exegetical Commentary,* 4/2: 1594–1595; Ramos and Skonieczny, 2/2: 298–307; Romano, in *Il giudizio,* 2/2: 592–593; Lüdicke-Jenkins, 433–434.

the issues itself, it is the judge who defines the *dubium* by his decree in the light of the claims made in the petition and any responses to the citations from the other party or the defender of the bond. (c. 1676 §2) One could argue then that, at the outset of the appellate process when the judges join the issue, they should be free to add a new ground of nullity suggested by the evidence gathered by the first instance court either at the prompting of a party or at their own initiative. Once the new doubt has been established, whether it contains new grounds or not, it is to be communicated to the parties and the defender of the bond.

If the appellate tribunal admits a new ground or grounds and proceeds "as if in first instance," it is still required to resolve the appeal of the decision on the ground established by the first instance court. The decision of the appellate court proceeding "as if in first instance," can be appealed by an unhappy party or defender of the bond. If there is an appeal of such a sentence, it is not referred to the ordinary appellate tribunal of the second instance court but to the Roman Rota, which will proceed to resolve the appeal "as if in second instance." (*Dignitas connubii*, art. 268 §2)[68] Failure to forward such an appeal to the Roman Rota is a violation of the norms of competence by grade of tribunal (c. 1440) and results in the irremediable nullity of the sentence of the offending appellate court. If no appeal is lodged against an affirmative decision on a new ground of nullity introduced at the appellate level within the peremptory fifteen useful days, however, it can, like any other unappealed affirmative first instance sentence, be executed.

Once the issues have been joined, the law foresees that the appellate process will proceed directly to the discussion of the case and a new decision by the appellate judges on the evidence that had been gathered by the first instance tribunal. (c. 1640) Nevertheless, the appellate judges do have the prerogative to reopen the case to gather new evidence "after the parties have been heard and provided that there is a grave reason and any threat of fraud or subornation is removed." (c. 1639 §1 and 1600 §1, 2°) If new evidence is gathered during the appellate process, there must also be a new publication of the acts, at least for the new evidence. (c. 1600 §3) After the discussion of the case by the submission of written arguments by any

---

68. Supreme Tribunal of the Apostolic Signatura, declaration, in *Roman Replies and CLSA Advisory Opinions 1998*, ed. Stephen Pedone and James Donlon (Washington: CLSA 1998) 17.

advocates and the defender of the bond, the appellate judges deliberate and reach a decision. (c. 1609 §§1–5) The *ponens* then drafts the sentence according to the same format as a first instance definitive sentence and all three appellate judges sign it. The appellate sentence is then published according to the norm of law. (c. 1615)

Can. 1681. If an executive sentence has been issued, one can go at anytime to a tribunal of the third level for a new proposition of the case according to the norm of can. 1644, provided new and grave proofs or arguments are brought forward within the peremptory time limit of thirty days from the proposed challenge.

Although *Mitis Iudex* has abolished the requirement introduced by Benedict XIV's *Dei miseratione* that two conformed affirmative decisions are needed before marriage nullity cases can be executed, it has not abrogated the principle also introduced by Benedict XIV that marriage cases never become *res iudicata* or finally judged matters. In principle, therefore, marriage cases can always be re-opened for a new decision at the request of an interested party no matter how long it has been since a decision had been executed. This extraordinary remedy against a sentence that has been executed is known as a request for "a new proposition of the case." However, when old cases are reopened, canons 1643–1644 and articles 290–294 of the instruction *Dignitas connubii*, the result can be disruptions to settled expectations and, more importantly, to the consciences of parties who have entered new marriages after the tribunal decision became executory. To minimize these upheavals the law requires that the one seeking a new hearing of the case must bear a fairly heavy evidentiary burden.[69] A new proposition of the case will be granted only if the one seeking it can bring forward new evidence or new arguments that probably would result in a different decision in the case.[70]

Whether a decision has been executed because no appeal was lodged within the peremptory time limit or by the appellate court following an

---

69. Carmelo de Diego-Lora, "Adjudged Matter," in *Exegetical Commentary*, 4/2: 1626–1644; Carlo, Gullo, "La 'nova causae propositio'," in *Il processo*, 797–823 Ramos and Skonieczny, 2/2: 353–381; Gian Paolo Montini, "La richiesta di nuovo esame della causa dopo una doppia decisione conforme," in *Il giudizio*, 2/2: 669–708; Lüdicke-Jenkins, 465–473.

70. See John P. Beal, "Remedial Readings: Challenges to the Sentence in Marriage Nullity Cases," *The Jurist* 59 (1999) 26–27 and Antoni Stankiewicz, "Le prove e gli argomenti nuovi e gravi per il riesame della causa," *Apollinaris* 68 (1995) 487–519.

appeal, the tribunal before which a new proposition of the case is sought is a tribunal of the third grade. For most of the Church, the sole ordinary tribunal of the third grade is the Roman Rota. Canon 1681 allows for a new proposition of the case "at any time" after a decision has become executory. A negative decision which has been executed does not pave the way to a new marriage in and recognized by the Catholic Church. As a result, a party to a marriage that received conforming negative decisions upholding the validity of the marriage will not usually threaten settled expectations or consciences by seeking a new proposition of the case before the Rota whenever he or she can bring forward new and serious evidence or arguments for the nullity of the marriage. The situation is more problematic with affirmative decisions which have already been executed. To avoid having marriage cases reopened after one of the parties had remarried in the Church, the second of the special faculties granted to the Roman Rota by Benedict XVI on February 11, 2013 stipulate: "It is not possible to propose a recourse before the Roman Rota for a New Proposition of a Cause after one of the parties has contracted a new canonical marriage."[71] Since, as a general rule, new laws do not abrogate special faculties granted by the Roman Pontiff, this faculty remains intact even after the promulgation of canon 1681 of *Mitis Iudex* and effectively precludes a new proposition of case when one of the parties has already entered a new marriage in the Catholic Church. However, the special faculties were granted by the rescript only for a period of three years. Whether these faculties will be renewed after they expire in February of 2016, remains to be seen.

The possibility that a respondent (or the defender of the bond) might petition for a new proposition of a marriage case after the other party has entered a new canonical marriage has long been a source of pastoral concern. The possibility of a new proposition of the case leaves the re-married spouse in a very precarious position. If the new proposition of the case is granted and leads to the original affirmative decision being reversed, the person's new marriage is presumptively invalid because of the impediment of prior bond. As a result, unless he or she separates from the new spouse, both are ineligible to receive Holy Communion. In practice, the Rota has been reluctant to grant the new proposition of a case when a new canonical marriage has already occurred, but the possibility of such an outcome

---

71. Secretariat of State, Rescriptum ex Audientia Sanctissimi, February 11, 2013, n. II: *AAS* 95 (2013). ET in *Roman Replies and CLSA Advisory Opinions 2013*, ed. Sharon Euart, John Alesandro, and Thomas Green (Washington: CLSA, 2013) 41.

causes a real crisis of conscience for affected members of the faithful. If the aim of the new law is extending mercy, renewal of the faculty precluding a new proposition of a case after a new canonical marriage would be the path of mercy.

Can. 1682 §1. After the sentence declaring the nullity of the marriage has been executed, the parties whose marriage has been declared null can contract a new marriage unless a prohibition attached to the sentence itself or established by the local ordinary forbids this.

§2. As soon as the sentence is executed, the judicial vicar must notify the local ordinary of the place in which the marriage took place. The local ordinary must take care that the declaration of the nullity of the marriage and any possible prohibitions are noted as soon as possible in the marriage and baptismal registers.

This new canon 1682 repeats with slight modifications to take into account the elimination of a mandatory appeal of all affirmative decisions the norm of the former canons 1684 §1 and 1685 and articles 300–301 of the instruction *Dignitas connubii*.[72] When an affirmative decision in a marriage nullity case becomes executory, the presumption that the previous union was an impediment to a new marriage is overturned and there is no further obstacle to the parties' new marriages in the Church. However, like its predecessor, canon 1682 §1 cautions that a new marriage may still be barred by a "prohibition" or *vetitum*. At the end of the nullity process, the judge may append to the sentence a clause that prohibits one or both parties from new marriages in the Catholic Church until certain conditions are met. Such judicial prohibitions are precautions to be used when the evidence gathered in connection with the nullity process indicates that the defect of consent that vitiated the first marriage has not been addressed and will probably infect the new marriage as well.[73] For example, when a marriage has been declared invalid because the respondent's alcoholism is judged to have deprived him of the due discretion for marriage but

---

72. Carmelo de Diego-Lora, "The Judgment and the Appeal," in *Exegetical Commentary*, 4/2: 1862–1875; Ramos and Skonieczny, 2/2: 441–452; Guido Lagomarsino, "L'annotazione della nullità di matrimonio e le formalità de premettere alla celebrazione del nuovo matrimonio," in *Il giudizio*, 767–786; Lüdicke-Jenkins, 483–486.

73. See John P. Beal, "The Tribunal Vetitum: A Practice in Search of a Theory," *The Jurist* 72 (2012) 377–427.

nothing has been done to address the alcoholism, the judge might well impose a prohibition on a new marriage by the respondent until he has suitably dealt with the alcohol problem. While the judge's vetitum affects particular persons, the local ordinary can, for a grave cause, prohibit a particular marriage. For example, when two minors are seeking to marry despite the objections of their parents, the local ordinary might prohibit the celebration of marriage until the couple has received appropriate premarital counseling. Unless they are issued by the supreme authority of the Church, however, prohibitions render marriages celebrated in contravention of them illicit but not invalid. (c. 1077 §2)

When a sentence declaring the invalidity of a marriage involving at least one Catholic has become executory, it is incumbent on the judicial vicar of the tribunal where the case initiated to notify the local ordinary of the place of the church where the marriage was celebrated and of the church or churches in which the party or parties were baptized so that appropriate notations of the declaration of nullity can be made in the sacramental registers of the church or churches. If a vetitum has been imposed that fact also should be recorded in the sacramental registers. In North America, it has become the customary practice for the judicial vicar of the tribunal in which a marriage nullity petition originated to notify the churches of Catholic marriage and baptism directly rather than sending notification through the local ordinary of the place where these churches are located.

ART. 6. THE DOCUMENTARY PROCESS

Can. 1688. After receiving a petition proposed according to the norm of can. 1677, the diocesan bishop or the judicial vicar or a judge designated by him can declare the nullity of a marriage by sentence if a document subject to no contradiction or exception clearly establishes the existence of a diriment impediment or a defect of legitimate form, provided that it is equally certain that no dispensation was given, or establishes the lack of a valid mandate of a proxy. In these cases, the formalities of the ordinary process are omitted except for the citation of the parties and the intervention of the defender of the bond.

Can. 1689 §1. If the defender of the bond prudently thinks that either the flaws mentioned in can. 1688 or the lack of a dispensation are not certain, the defender of the bond must appeal against the declaration of nullity to the judge of second instance; the acts must be sent to the appellate judge who must be advised in writing that a documentary process is involved.

§2. The party who considers himself or herself aggrieved retains the right of appeal.

Can. 1690. The judge of second instance, with the intervention of the defender of the bond and after having heard the parties, will decide in the same manner as that mentioned in can. 1688 whether the sentence must be confirmed or whether the case must rather proceed according to the ordinary method of law; in the latter event the judge remands the case to the tribunal of first instance.

With the exception of some slight editorial changes to take into account the changes in canon numbers resulting from the revisions effected by *Mitis Iudex*, these three canons reproduce verbatim the former canons 1686 to 1688 and articles 295–299 of the instruction *Dignitas connubii* on the documentary process.[74] The documentary process is an abbreviated judicial process that can be employed if a marriage can be shown to be invalid because of an undispensed diriment impediment, a defect in the legitimate canonical form or the absence of a proper mandate for a proxy standing in for one of the parties at the celebration of marriage through a document that is beyond challenge. Since this process, albeit, abbreviated, is a judicial process, a tribunal must be competent to decide the case on one of the bases mentioned in canon 1672. The documentary process begins with the submission of a petition in conformity with the norm of canon 1676. The judge is the diocesan bishop himself, the judicial vicar or a judge designated by either of them. After the acceptance of the petition, the citation of the respondent and the defender of the bond, and the joinder of the issues, the judge proceeds to a very abbreviated evidentiary phase of the process.

Since the documentary process is permitted only when the invalidating impediment or defect in the form or proxy mandate used in the celebration of the marriage can be demonstrated with a document whose authenticity and content are beyond challenge, the evidentiary phase consists of the introduction of the document that establishes the defect that

---

74. Carmelo Del Diego-Lora, "The Documentary process," in *Exegetical Commentary*, 4/2: 1876–1891; Piero Antonio Bonnet, "Il processo documentale," in *Il giudizio*, 2/2: 721–766; Lüdicke-Jenkins, 475–482.

invalidate the marriage. Such a document will almost always be a public document, either civil or ecclesiastical. The documentary process has been used most frequently by North American tribunals in cases where a marriage is alleged to be invalid because one of the parties was barred from marrying by the impediment of a prior bond. In these cases, the existence of the impediment can be often established by the civil marriage license or similar document for the marriage giving rise to the prior bond. Although the documentary process is an expeditious way to deal with such cases, the ordinary process can still be employed in situations where a document proving the existence of the alleged impediment or defect of form is not available and the tribunal must rely instead on the testimony of witnesses. This situation may occur in cases of prior bond where the respondent's prior marriage appears to be the source of the impediment but he or she refuses to cooperate in the process. Although the existence of the prior bond can often be proven by a public document such as the marriage license, some jurisdictions will, to protect privacy, provide marriage records only to the parties to the marriage. If it is impossible to obtain the public document, it may still be possible to prove the existence of the prior bond through the testimony of witnesses in an ordinary process.

After hearing the defender of the bond and any objections from the respondent, the judge in the documentary process issues a sentence either declaring the invalidity of the marriage or remanding the case to the tribunal to be dealt with by the ordinary process. It is not foreseen that the documentary process will result in negative decisions. Although the sentence in a case decided according to the documentary process can be quite brief, it must contain the essential elements of a sentence stipulated in canon 1612 and be publishes by one of the methods mentioned in canon 1615. If there is no appeal of the sentence by the respondent or the defender of the bond within fifteen days from notice of its publication, the sentence becomes executory. If there is an appeal of the sentence issued pursuant to the documentary process, the sentence and acts of the case are forwarded to the ordinary appellate tribunal of the first instance court with a written advisory that the case had been decided according to the norms for the documentary process. The judge at the appellate level is a single judge, the diocesan bishop or bishop moderator of the appellate tribunal, its judicial vicar or a single judge designated by either of them. After hearing the defender of the bond and the parties, the appellate judge either confirms the first instance decision by decree or remands the case to the first instance court for treatment according to the norms for the ordinary process. There are no negative decisions in cases treated according to the documentary process.

ART. 7. GENERAL NORMS

Can. 1691 §1. In the sentence the parties are to be reminded of the moral and even civil obligations binding them toward one another and toward their children to furnish support and education.

This new canon 1691 §1 repeats verbatim the norm of the previous canon 1689 and article 252 of the Instruction *Dignitas connubii*.[75] The canon was new to the 1983 code and reflected the Church's concern that spouses whose marriages have been declared invalid not neglect their obligations to their former spouses and any children born to the unions. The permission of the local ordinary is required for the celebration of marriages by persons with moral or civil obligations toward former partners or children arising from a previous union. (c. 1071 §1, 3°) Evidence that a party to a proposed marriage is delinquent in meeting these obligations would be a legitimate basis for the local ordinary to deny permission for the marriage or to prohibit its celebration. (c. 1067)

§2. Cases for the declaration of the nullity of a marriage cannot be treated in the oral contentious process mentioned in cann. 1656–1670.

This new canon repeats the former canon 1690 and article 6 of the instruction *Dignitas connubii* with the addition of the clarification that the oral contentious process is treated in canons 1656 to 1670 of the code.[76] This oral contentious process was an innovation of the 1983 code for expeditious resolution of incidental questions that might arise in the course of a trial or for other matters that do not require in depth investigation. Use of this simplified process for marriage nullity cases themselves is prohibited.

---

75. Joan Carreras, "General Norms," in *Exegetical* Commentary, 4/2: 1892–1893; Lüdicke-Jenkins, 409.

76. Lüdicke-Jenkins, 24.

Canon 1656 §2 reinforces this prohibition by declaring: "If the oral process is used outside cases permitted in law, the judicial acts are null." As a result, the sentence would also be invalid because "it was based on a null judicial act." (c. 1622, 5°) However, the nullity of the sentence is remediable, that is, it is sanated or healed by the passage of three months from the notice of the publication of the sentence unless a complaint of nullity has already been lodged. Despite the prohibition on its use for marriage nullity cases themselves, the oral process can, however, be employed to resolve complaints of nullity against sentences in marriage nullity cases (c. 1627; *Dignitas connubii*, article 277) and incidental cases which may arise in the course of trials. (c. 1590; *Dignitas connubii*, articles 224–225) In addition, some elements of this process have been incorporated into the new *processus brevior* for the resolution of marriage nullity cases before the diocesan bishop.[77]

---

§3. In other procedural matters, the canons on trials in general and on the ordinary contentious trial must be applied unless the nature of the matter precludes it; the special norms for cases concerning the status of persons and cases pertaining to the public good are to be observed.

This new norm reiterates the former canon 1691 with the curious exception of the deletion of its reference to the need to observe the norms for "cases pertaining to the public good."[78] The canons governing trials in general (1400–1500) and the ordinary contentious process (1501–1655) remain in force and are to be used in marriage nullity processes, except to the extent that they have been modified by the new norms of *Mitis Iudex*. (c. 6 §2) Since the instruction *Dignitas connubii* purports to be an instruction for those implementing the norms of the code governing marriage nullity processes, its articles remain authoritative interpretations of the norms of the code for practitioners on matters not dealt with in *Mitis Iudex*.

---

77. See the commentary on the new canons 1683–1687 by William Daniel in *The Jurist* 75 (2015) 539–591 and in this volume.
78. Joan Carreras, "General Norms," in *Exegetical Commentary*, 4/2: 1894–1895.

B. THE WAY OF PROCEEDING IN CASES REGARDING THE DECLARATION OF THE NULLITY OF A MARRIAGE

Art. 1. The bishop, under can. 383 §1 is obliged, with an apostolic spirit, to attend to separated or divorced spouses who perhaps, by the conditions of their lives, have abandoned religious practice. He thus shares, together with pastors (cf. can. 529 §1), the pastoral solicitude for these faithful in difficulties.

Canon 383 §1 states: "In exercising the function of pastor, a diocesan bishop is to show himself concerned for all the Christian faithful entrusted to his care, . . . [and] to extend an apostolic spirit to those who are unable to make sufficient use of ordinary pastoral care because of the condition of their life and to those who no longer practice their religion." In virtue of canon 529 §1, pastors have a similar obligation to share in "the cares, anxieties and griefs of the faithful" and to seek out "those weighed down by special difficulties." This article explicitly includes separated and divorced faithful among those with special needs requiring the pastoral solicitude of the diocesan bishop and, under his authority, pastors.

Art. 2. The pre-judicial or pastoral investigation, which in the context of diocesan and parish structures receives those separated or divorced faithful who have doubts regarding the validity of their marriage or are convinced of its nullity, is, in the end, directed toward understanding their situation and to gathering the material useful for the eventual judicial process, be it the ordinary or the briefer one. This investigation will be developed within the unified diocesan pastoral care of marriage.

This article calls for a comprehensive and integrated diocesan pastoral plan for marriage in which care for the separated and divorced is a prominent element. This pastoral plan should make available to separated and divorced faithful who either doubt the validity of their now broken marriage or are convinced of its invalidity what the current article calls a "pre-judicial" or "pastoral" investigation to assess their situations and, if appropriate, to assist them in preparing materials that may eventually become part of a petition for a declaration of nullity. This authorization of a "pre-judicial" or "pastoral" investigation prior to the initiation of a marriage nullity process constitutes a noteworthy relaxation of the structure of canon 1529 that "except for a serious reason, the judge is not to proceed to gather proofs before the joinder of issues." Article 120 of the instruction *Dignitas connubii* suggested very few reasons serious enough to warrant departure from this norm. The reasons for this prohibition on gathering evidence before and outside of the process itself were: 1) until the issues have been joined, it is not clear what evidence is relevant to the case and what questions should be posed to parties and witnesses and 2) outside the formal setting of a trial, the safeguards designed to insure the integrity and reliability of evidence gathered, including the intervention of the defender of the bond and the other party, will be missing and evidence gathered in this way may be tainted.

The law tacitly supposes that parties seeking declaration of nullity will be assisted by trained professional advocates to prepare their petitions and identify relevant documents and other evidence, as is the case in Italy. However, such advocates are not usually available in most of the world, not just in poor countries of the so-called "third world" but even in rich countries like those in North America. As a result, spouses are often left to draft their own petitions for a process whose details and requirements they do not understand with no professional assistance. To compensate for the absence of trained advocates to assist parties to prepare their petitions, many tribunals have conducted preliminary investigations. These preliminary investigations have, in turn, been the target of considerable criticism by the tribunals of the Holy See.[79]

Article 2 constitutes a frank acknowledgement that, if the marriage nullity process is to be realistically accessible to divorced Catholics throughout the world, they will need some kind of more or less professional assistance to navigate the tribunal process. In this respect Article 2 and the other introductory articles of the *Ratio Procedendi* appended to

---

79. Zenon Grocholewski, "Current Questions Concerning the State and Activity of Tribunals with Particular Reference to the United States of America," in *Incapacity for Marriage: Jurisprudence and interpretation*, ed. Robert Sable (Rome: Gregorian University Press, 1987) 246–247 and Id., "Canons 1505 and 1529: The Gathering of Proofs Before the Joinder of the Issues," in *Roman Replies and CLSA Advisory Opinions 1992*, ed. Kevin Vann and Lynn Jarrell (Washington: CLSA 1992) 128–129. See the discussion of this issue in John P. Beal, "Making Connections: Procedural Law and Substantive Justice," *The Jurist* 54 (1994) 154–159.

Mitis Iudex represent a return to the project initiated by Cardinal Rauscher of Vienna in the nineteenth century. Concerned that frivolous petitions were clogging tribunals in the Austro-Hungarian Empire while meritorious petitions of ordinary people were being rejected at the door or not presented at all because of their inability to retain trained canon lawyers to assist them, the Cardinal, with the approval of the Apostolic See, secured the promulgation of an instruction on matrimonial procedure for the Austrian Empire.[80] This instruction specifically called for a preliminary investigation of matrimonial petitions by a team consisting of a commissary or auditor, a notary and a defender of the bond who traveled about the territory "drumming up business" for the tribunal. Oral petitions were accepted and transcribed by the notary. When the preliminary investigation was completed, its results were forwarded to the competent tribunal to serve as a basis for acceptance or rejection of the petition.[81] This form of preliminary investigation was so successful in Austria that it was adopted in France,[82] the United States[83] and Spain[84] and continued to be used until it was abrogated by canon of 1730 of the 1917 code, the forerunner of the current canon 1529. The opening articles of the *Ratio Procedendi* seem to foresee a similar type of preliminary investigation at the diocesan or even parish level to assist people who lack access to professional advocates to prepare and present their cases to tribunals.

Art. 3. This same investigation is entrusted to persons deemed suitable by the local ordinary, with the appropriate expertise, though not exclusively juridical-canonical. Among them in the first place is the pastor or the one who prepared the spouses for the wedding celebration. This function of counseling can also be entrusted to other clerics, religious or lay people approved by the local ordinary.

One diocese, or several together, according to the present groupings, can form a stable structure through which to provide this service and, if appropriate, a

---

80. "Instructio pro iudiciis ecclesiasticis imperii Austriaci quoad Causas Matrimoniales," October 8, 1856: *Archiv für katholisches Kirchenrecht* 1 (1857) LVII–CXXXV.

81. Ibid., §141, C–CI.

82. See Robert Bassibey, *Cours complet de droit canonique* (Paris: H. Oudin, 1899) 12: 101.

83. *Acta et decretal concilii plenarii baltimorensis tertii, A.D. 1884* (Baltimore: J. Murphy, 1886) §304, 174: "Utiliter enim consuli poterit Instructio Austriaci in causis matrimonialibus, a 1855 (sic) a gravibus theologis et canonistis Romanis, lecet solo private suo iudicio commendata."

84. Robert Sanson, "The Preliminary Investigation for Marriage Annulments?" *Studia Canonica* 11 (1977) 40.

handbook *(vademecum)* containing the elements essential to the most appropriate way of conducting the investigation.

Article 3 continues the emphasis that pervades *Mitis Iudex* on the personal responsibility of diocesan bishops and pastors to provide pastoral care to the separated and divorced members of their flocks. The diocesan bishop is to oversee the training and appointment of pastoral ministers to conduct the pre-judicial or pastoral investigation preparatory to the submission of the petition to the tribunal. Pastors, especially those who prepared couples for their now broken marriages, are the first to be mentioned for this ministry to the divorced and separated. Other clerics, religious and lay people can also be approved for this role. Those who conduct the pre-judicial or pastoral investigation should have some competence in canon law but they should also be endowed with other skills. A determination that a marriage is irretrievably broken is to precede any petition to the tribunal. Thus, if those conducting the pre-judicial or pastoral investigation notice signs that the couple may be amenable to reconciliation, it would be helpful if they have counseling skills with which to help the separated and divorced to assess their situations. In addition, it cannot be overlooked that one of the critical responsibilities of those who conduct these investigations is to conduct pastoral outreach to people who may have become alienated from the Church because of their marital situations. These pastoral agents should, therefore, be people of faith with the personality and temperament for welcoming those who feel they are outcasts in the household of faith.

Thus, although knowledge of canon law and matrimonial jurisprudence are not the only, or even the most important, competences expected of those who conduct the pre-judicial or pastoral investigation, they should have enough knowledge of canon law to be able to explain the marriage nullity process to potential petitioners, to identify possible grounds of nullity embedded in the spouses' accounts of their marriages and their failures, to redact these accounts into formal petitions and to help the petitioner identify witnesses, documents and other evidence that might be useful for proving the invalidity of the marriage. A licentiate or doctorate in canon law is not necessary to perform these functions, but some formal canonical education like that provided by the annual two-week Institute on Matrimonial Tribunal Practice sponsored by the School of Canon Law at the Catholic University of America and similar non-degree or certificate programs offered elsewhere can be helpful as can various in-service and continuing education opportunities offered by academic institutions, canon law societies and dioceses.

Many of the responsibilities entrusted to those who conduct this pre-judicial or pastoral investigation of possible bases for marriage nullity cases are similar to those currently being carried out in many places either by parish priests or other pastoral ministers under a variety of more or less official, or perhaps official sounding, titles. Sometimes those who conduct these investigations are called "advocates," "field advocates," "auditors" or "pastoral assistants" and they may or may not have official recognition from the diocesan bishop. As the implementation of article 3 of the *Ratio Procedendi* moves forward, it would be helpful to develop an appropriate title for these pastoral agents and to formalize their relationship to the tribunal and to the diocesan bishop who is to entrust them with this task.

It probably would be advisable to avoid calling these pastoral agents "advocates." Canon 1483 stipulates that an advocate must be "a doctor in canon law or otherwise truly expert and approved by the [diocesan] bishop" of the tribunal before which he or she serves. In non-English speaking regions (including heavily Hispanic parts of the United States), the term "abogado" or "avocat" or "avvocato" is the generic word for "lawyer," a highly trained professional who represents parties especially in contentious matters and who charges a fee commensurate with his or her professional standing. The pastoral agents who conduct the pre-judicial or pastoral investigation are likely to have considerably less formal legal training than is expected of an advocate and the pervasive tone of *Mitis Iudex* suggests that they will not charge fees for their services. Moreover, unlike advocates whose role is restricted to the judicial arena, those who conduct these investigations have responsibilities that are not only juridical but pastoral. They are to ascertain that hope for restoration of conjugal life has disappeared and, if it has not, to foster reconciliation of the spouses. These pastoral agents are also to serve as part of the overall diocesan and parish pastoral outreach to the separated and divorced who may, because of their circumstances, feel alienated from the Church or have lapsed from active practice of the faith.

These pastoral agents will need some sort of formal preparation for the roles that they are to serve. It is the responsibility of the diocesan bishop to specify a program of preparation for these pastoral agents and to approve them for the task. The program of preparation may be carried out by several neighboring dioceses together and it is the sort of cooperative undertaking for which the episcopal conference could be an invaluable resource and agency of cooperation and coordination. Article 3 suggests that a diocese or groups of dioceses may want to prepare a handbook or *vademecum* for the use of the pastoral agents conducting the pre-judicial or pastoral investigation. Since *Mitis Iudex* encourages a return to the Metropolitan appellate system, it could be useful to have such a handbook for the tribunals of the appellate system so that there will be some standardization in the way these investigations are conducted throughout the province so that, when cases are appealed to the metropolitan tribunal, misunderstandings between the metropolitan and the suffragan tribunals can be avoided.

Art. 4. The pastoral investigation will collect elements useful for the introduction of the case before the competent tribunal either by the spouses or perhaps by their advocates. It is necessary to discover whether the parties are in agreement about petitioning nullity.

The pastoral investigation has two principal purposes: 1) to reach out to separated and divorced members of the faithful who may have been marginalized or alienated because of the circumstances of their lives so that they return to participation in the life of the Church in accord with their condition; and 2) to assist separated and divorced faithful to assess their situations with the possibility that this assessment may lead to a petition for a declaration of nullity. Even if the investigation strongly suggests that the marriage being assessed was invalid, however, it is only the spouse himself or herself who can submit a petition for a declaration of nullity to the tribunal.

The investigation should gather all of the essential elements for a possible petition for a declaration of nullity. These elements would include: a complete statement by the potential petitioner and, if he or she is involved at this stage, by the other spouse; baptismal certificates for the parties; civil and ecclesiastical marriage records; divorce decrees; records of counselling or psychiatric treatment or releases authorizing the tribunal to obtain these records; and documentary evidence that may be readily available. It would also be helpful for the pastoral agent to help the party to identify people who might be willing and able to serve as witnesses and the subjects about which they might offer testimony. Occasionally, the investigator might actually interview and take the testimony of a possible witness who may not be available later when the process is underway.

Art. 5. Once all the elements have been collected, the investigation culminates in the libellus, which, if appropriate, is presented to the competent tribunal.

The presumption of this article seems to be that a diligent pre-judicial or pastoral investigation of broken marriage will unearth sufficient evidence of the invalidity of the union to warrant petitioning a competent tribunal to declare the marriage invalid. The petition or *libellus* in which the investigation culminates should be drafted to meet the requirements of canon 1504.

Art. 6. Since the code of canon law must be applied in all matters, without prejudice to special norms, even the matrimonial processes in accord with can.1691 §3, the present ratio does not intend to explain in detail a summary of the whole process, but more specifically to illustrate the main legislative changes and, where appropriate, to complete it.

Article 6 is simply a reminder that the *Ratio Procedendi* does not purport to be a complete manual of procedure for marriage nullity cases but only attempts to highlight some of the changes in procedure effected by *Mitis Iudex*. For matters not treated in the new legislation, the norms of the 1983 code and the articles of the instruction *Dignitas connubii* remain in force.

TITLE I. THE COMPETENT FORUM AND TRIBUNALS

Art. 7 §1. The titles of competence in can. 1672 are the same, observing in as much as possible the principle of proximity between the judges and the parties.

This norm is not at all new but attempts to dispel a common misunderstanding about the enumeration of the titles of tribunal competence. Toward that end, the article reasserts the traditional principal that, where there are several tribunals potentially competent to hear and decide a case, the choice is left to the petitioner to determine in which of these tribunals he or she will introduce a petition for a declaration of nullity. (c. 1407 §3) When petitioners are choosing among competent tribunals, however, they should be mindful of the advantage of dealing throughout the process with a tribunal which is located in close proximity to the parties and witnesses. One of the principles motivating this most recent reform of procedural law was to minimize inconveniences and expenses for parties to marriage cases by making it possible for them to deal with tribunals geographically close to where they live.

---

§2. Through the cooperation between tribunals mentioned in can. 1418, care is to be taken that everyone, parties or witnesses, can participate in the process at a minimum of cost.

This article is a recognition that, despite the desire of the revised law to situate marriage nullity cases in close proximity to where the parties and witnesses reside, cases will inevitably arise in our mobile society when going to the office of the tribunal hearing the case to offer testimony or to perform other business will entail serious hardship or expense. Canon 1418 stipulates: "Any tribunal has the right to call upon the assistance of another tribunal to instruct a case or to communicate acts." The most common form of this request for assistance by one tribunal to another is what is often referred to as a request for a "rogatory commission," that is, the request of one tribunal that another appoint an auditor to take the testimony of a party or witness residing in its territory. This assistance may also take the form of a request by one tribunal that another oversee the review of the acts of a case by a respondent who lives in its territory but for whom going to the office of the tribunal hearing the case would be an undue hardship. Requests for assistance of these minds may well become common if tribunals make frequent use of the relaxed provisions for competence in canon 1672 which allow tribunals where petitioners have domiciles or quasi-domiciles to adjudicate cases even though the respondents and perhaps many witnesses live in the territories of dioceses in distant countries. Securing the testimony of these respondents and witnesses may require the assistance of the tribunals where these deponents reside.

Tribunals in North America have tried to minimize the time and expense entailed in conducting judicial interrogations in marriage nullity cases by asking parties and witnesses to provide information by completing written questionnaires and returning them to the tribunal after they have attested to their truthfulness in the presence of a notary public, a parish priest or some other ecclesiastical notary. Thus, the parties and witnesses do not offer judicial deposition but submit to the tribunal "affidavits" which are a kind of document.[85] Although the code does not mention the use of affidavits in ecclesiastical trials, article 185 §3 of the instruction *Dignitas connubii* does advert to them when it stipulates: "In causes of nullity of marriage any written document purposely prepared in advance in order to prove the nullity of marriage obtains the probative force of a private document, even if it was deposited with a notary public." Despite this somewhat grudging acknowledgement that affidavits constitute a legitimate means of proof, the tribunals of the Holy See have repeatedly complained about the use of affidavits by North American tribunals.[86] The almost exclusive use of such questionnaires and affidavits in North America has rendered requests for rogatory commission considerably less frequent than they once were. However, the relaxation of the requirements for the use of the forum of the domicile or quasi-domicile of the petitioner may lead to an increase in the number of requests from foreign tribunals for North American tribunals to take testimony from a party or witness living in their territory and from North American tribunals for other tribunals to take testimony of parties or witnesses who find preparing written responses to printed questionnaires difficult. The new article 7 §2 clearly expects tribunals to comply with such requests for assistance graciously and generously, even if they cause some inconvenience.

Art. 8 §1. In dioceses which lack their own tribunals, the bishop should take care that, as soon as possible, persons are formed who can zealously assist in setting up

---

85. *Black's Law Dictionary*, s.v. "affidavit:" "a written or printed declaration or statement of facts, made voluntarily and confirmed by the oath or affirmation of the party making it, taken before a person having authority to administer such an oath or affirmation."

86. See Beal, "Making Connections," 159–163. See also Grocholewski, "Canons 1528; 1530–1534; 1156–1570; and 1678: Interrogation of the Parties and Witnesses," in *Roman Replies and CLSA Advisory Opinions 1992*, 129; Id., "Current Questions," 245–247; and Antoni Stankiewicz, "La caratteristiche del Sistema probatorio canonico," in *Il processo*, 578–580.

marriage tribunals, even by means of courses in well-established and continuous institutions sponsored by the diocese or in cooperation with groupings of dioceses and with the assistance of the Apostolic See.

This article represents a strong exhortation to diocesan bishops who have hitherto been unable to establish tribunals in their own dioceses because of a shortage of trained personnel to take the necessary steps to prepare an adequate tribunal staff.

---

§2. The bishop can withdraw from an interdiocesan tribunal constituted in accordance with can. 1423.

In some places, several dioceses which found themselves unable to establish and staff well-functioning tribunals of their own have joined together and pooled their resources to establish interdiocesan tribunals of first instance to displace their respective diocesan tribunals. Sometimes these interdiocesan tribunals came about at the initiative of the participating bishops themselves; in other cases, they resulted from the prodding of the Apostolic Signatura. The establishment and functioning of these interdiocesan tribunals is now governed by canon 1423. Article 8 empowers diocesan bishops to withdraw or secede from such an interdiocesan tribunal at his own initiative. The article does not expressly explain the reason or reasons why a bishop might want to withdraw from an interdiocesan tribunal. Nevertheless, the context of the article suggests that the primary motivation would be that the bishop is now able to establish and staff a diocesan tribunal of his own.

This empowerment of bishops to withdraw unilaterally from interdiocesan tribunals applies only to interdiocesan tribunals of first instance, the only ones dealt with in canon 1423. In the United States, several interdiocesan appellate tribunals were established shortly before the provisions of the 1983 code abrogated the American Procedural Norms which had for the previous decade virtually eliminated mandatory appeals of affirmative decisions in marriage nullity cases. The establishment of these interdiocesan tribunals was prompted by concern that the traditional metropolitan appellate system would be unable to deal efficiently with the anticipated volume of appeals. Although these interdiocesan tribunals of second instance were established pursuant to Apostolic Signatura's 1970 Norms on Interdiocesan and Regional Tribunals, they are now governed by canon 1439. Because these tribunals constitute the appellate structure for several dioceses and have effectively replaced the metropolitan tribunal, they cannot be simply dismantled until an alternate appellate structure such as a return to the metropolitan model has been agreed on by all participants. As a result, the norms of *Mitis Iudex* do not authorize unilateral withdrawals from these interdiocesan appellate tribunals by participating bishops. However, since *Mitis Iudex* encourages that "the appeal to the metropolitan be restored . . . [as] a distinctive sign of collegiality in the church," the desire of bishops currently participating in an interdiocesan appellate court to return to the metropolitan system would surely receive favorable consideration from the Apostolic Signatura. The dismantling of an interdiocesan appellate tribunal requires: 1) the agreement of the participating bishops to dismantle the existing structure and adopt an alternative, 2) a favorable vote of the episcopal conference (which, in virtue of canon 1439, now has authority to establish and dis-establish these tribunals), 3) the approval of the Apostolic Signatura, and 4) the promulgation of the decree of the episcopal conference.

TITLE II. THE RIGHT TO CHALLENGE A MARRIAGE

Art. 9. If a spouse dies during the process with the case not yet concluded, the instance is suspended until the other spouse or another person, who is interested, insists upon its continuation; in this case, a legitimate interest must be proven.

Article 9 reiterates canon 1518, 1° of the 1983 code and article 143 §1, 1° of the instruction *Dignitas connubii* to make provision for the situation where one of the spouses dies while the trial is in progress. The new canon 1674 §3 had already adverted to the fact that the prescriptions of canon 1518 are to be followed if a spouse dies while a marriage nullity trial is in process. If the death occurs after the trial has begun by citation but before the decree concluding the evidentiary phase of the process has been issued, the trial is suspended until the other spouse or an interested party resumes it. In this respect the article completes the new canon 1674 §3 by specifying what is to be done when a party dies while the trial is in progress. Article 9 is, however, curiously silent about what is to be done if a party dies after the evidentiary phase of the process has been completed. Canon 1518, 2° and article 143 §1, 2° of the instruction *Dignitas connubii* stipulate that, if the evidentiary phase has already been concluded at the time of the party's death, the judge proceeds to a decision after citing the procurator for the deceased, if there is one, or his or her heir. (c. 1518, 2°) In North America and other places where the decisions of ecclesiastical tribunals have no civil effects, resumption of a marriage nullity trial after the death of one of the spouses will be an exceedingly rare occurrence. Since spouses in these countries seek declarations of nullity solely to be free to enter a new marriage in the Catholic Church, that end is already achieved with the death of one of the spouses.

TITLE III. THE INTRODUCTION AND INSTRUCTION OF THE CASE

Art. 10. The judge can admit an oral petition whenever a party is prevented from presenting a libellus: however, the judge himself orders the notary to draw up the act in writing that must be read to the party and approved, which takes the place of the libellus written by the party for all effects of law.

Article 10 is little more than a summary of canon 1513 which allows for the submission of an oral petition and its application to marriage nullity cases. Historically, canon law has made provision for oral petitions to accommodate the situations of those who were unable to write. One presumes that this reminder will be of greatest practical value in regions with a large number of potential petitioners who are either not literate or who do not express themselves in writing well.

Art. 11 §1. The libellus is presented to the diocesan or interdiocesan tribunal which has been chosen according to the norm of can. 1673 §2.

In most cases, the first instance tribunal to be approached with a petition for the declaration of the nullity of a marriage is the tribunal of the diocese in which the marriage was celebrated, in which either the respondent or the petitioner has a domicile or quasi-domicile, or in which the majority of the evidence is to be gathered. However, a diocesan bishop unable to establish an effective tribunal for his own diocese may have opted, in virtue of canon 1673 §2, to have joined together with other neighboring bishops to establish an interdiocesan tribunal for their territories or to approach a neighboring bishop to have cases dealt with in his tribunal. The latter approach has often been used when a new diocese has been created by dividing one or more existing dioceses and, until the new diocese can assemble an adequate staff for its own tribunal, the original diocese's tribunal handles cases from the newly established one. If the diocesan bishop has chosen one of these alternatives to an ordinary diocesan tribunal, petitions for declarations of nullity from faithful in his diocese are to be submitted to the interdiocesan or diocesan tribunal chosen by the bishop.

---

§2. A respondent who remits himself or herself to the justice of the tribunal, or, when properly cited, once more, makes no response, is deemed not to object to the petition.

In canonical marriage nullity processes it is incumbent on the petitioner to bring forward sufficient evidence to overturn the presumption that, once properly celebrated, a marriage is valid. Moreover, it is the duty of the judge to take the initiative in "furnishing proofs or in lodging exceptions whenever [he or she] considers it necessary in order to avoid a gravely unjust judgment." (c. 1452 §§2–3) As a result, a respondent can waive his or her right to submit evidence in support of the validity or the marriage and instead can remit himself or herself "to the justice of the tribunal." Article 11 §2 asserts a presumption that respondents who, after being properly cited, exercise their prerogative to remit themselves to the justice of the court are, by that fact, saying that they do not contest the petitioner's claim.

When a respondent offers no response whatsoever to the initial citation beginning a marriage nullity process, the judge is to ascertain that he or she has received the original citation and perhaps repeat the citation. If the respondent makes no answer even to this second citation, the judge is to declare him or her absent from the trial. (cc. 1592–1593; *Dignitas connubii*, art. 138–141) Article 11 §2 stipulates that such a non-responsive respondent is also presumed, in virtue of his or her silence, to have no objections to the petitioner's claim. Nevertheless, the respondent declared absent is still entitled to receive the formulation of the grounds for the case and a copy of the definitive sentence. (*Dignitas connubii*, art. 134 §3)

TITLE IV. THE SENTENCE, ITS APPEALS, AND EXECUTION

Art. 12. To achieve the moral certainty required by law, a preponderance of proofs and clues is not sufficient, but it is required that any prudent doubt of making an error, in law or in fact, is excluded, even if the mere possibility of the contrary is not removed.

Article 12 reaffirms the now traditional norm that a judge can declare a marriage invalid only if he or she has reached moral certainty about the invalidity of the marriage being challenged on the basis of the evidence adduced in the acts of the case. If the judge cannot reach this moral certainty, he or she must issue a negative decision upholding the validity of the marriage. Moral certainty is a standard of proof essentially different than the preponderance of evidence which is the standard used in most civil cases in our secular courts. The preponderance of evidence means simply that the weight of the evidence tilts, however slightly, toward the claim of one or the contending parties. The preponderance of evidence yields probability but not real certainty. By contrast, moral certitude is similar to the standard of "proof beyond reasonable doubt" in our secular jurisprudence. A now classic explanation of the notion of moral certainty was given by Pius XII in his allocution to the Roman Rota in 1942:

> Between the two extreme of absolute certainty and quasi-certainty or probability, if that *moral certainty* which is usually involved in the cases submitted to your tribunal, and of which We principally wish to speak. It is characterized on the positive side by the exclusion of well-founded doubt or reasonable doubt, and in this respect it is essentially distinguished from the quasi-certainty which has been mentioned; on the negative side, it does admit the absolute possibility of the contrary, and in this it differs from absolute certainty. The certainty of which we are now speaking is necessary and sufficient for the rendering of a judgment, even though in the particular case it would be impossible either directly or indirectly to reach absolute certainty. Only thus is it possible to have a regular and orderly administration

of justice, going forward without useless delays and without laying excessive burdens on the tribunal as well as on the parties.[87]

The judge is to derive this moral certitude not from *ex parte* communications or educated "hunches" or "gut feelings" but solely from the evidence adduced in the course of the trial and collected in the acts of the case. (c. 1608 §2; *Dignitas connubii*, art. 247 §3) Judges are free to "appraise the proofs according to [their] own conscience, without prejudice to the prescripts of law concerning the efficacy of certain proofs" (c. 1608 §3; *Dignitas connubii*, art. 247 §4), but often no single piece of evidence, even when it is generously weighed, is sufficient to generate the moral certainty required for marriage cases. Nevertheless, they may still reach certitude through the prudent application of the principal of sufficient reason, a principle that Pius XII characterized as "absolutely secure and universally valid."[88] The principle of sufficient reason allows judges to derive certainty from

> an aggregate of indications and proofs which, taken singly, do not provide the foundation for true certitude but which, when taken together, no longer leave room for doubt on the part of a man of sound judgment. . . . [I]t is rather to recognize that the simultaneous presence of all these separate indications and proofs can have a sufficient basis only in a common origin or foundation from which they spring, that is in objective truth and reality.[89]

Thus, judges trying to reach moral certainty must attend not only to the various pieces of evidence gathered in the course of the trial individually but also to the pattern or concatenation these pieces of evidence form.

Art. 13. If a party expressly declares that he or she objects to receiving any notices about the case, that party is held to have renounced of the faculty of receiving a copy of the sentence. In this case, that party may be notified of the dispositive part of the sentence.

---

87. Pius XII, allocution ad praelatos auditors ceterosque officiales et administros tribunalis S. Romanae Rotae necnon eiusdem tribunalis advocatos et procuratores, October 1, 1942: AAS 34 (1942) 339–340. ET in CLD 3: 607–608.
88. Pius XII, AAS 34 (1942) 340; CLD 3: 608.
89. Ibid.

This article of *Mitis Iudex* incorporates article 258 §3 of the instruction *Dignitas connubii*. In an effort to insure that the right of defense of respondents was not violated, the previous law had required tribunals to make a copy of the definitive sentence available to parties who had been declared absent from the trial, even to those who had clearly asked that they not be contacted by the tribunal and had been declared absent from the trial. (c. 1593 §2) Article 258 §3 of *Dignitas connubii* and this new article 13 relax this requirement of notification for respondents who expressly request that they receive no further notices from the tribunal. In these cases, the tribunal should respect the respondents' clear wishes by refraining from any further communications about the case. The tribunal is absolved of its obligation to publish the sentence to the respondent. A respondent's *express* declaration that he or she desires no further communication from the tribunal may be explicit or implicit. However, judges have the discretion to notify such respondents of the dispositive parts of the sentences, i.e., the parts that simply state whether the marriages were declared invalid or not.

ART. VI. THE DOCUMENTARY PROCESS

Art. 21. The competent diocesan bishop and the judicial vicar are determined in accordance with can. 1672.

This article is simply a reminder that, even though it is considerably truncated, the documentary process is a true judicial process. As a result, the tribunal approached by the petitioner must be competent to hear the case by one of the titles mentioned in canon 1672.

ABSTRACT

The apostolic letter Mitis Iudex *effects a significant revision of the procedural law governing marriage nullity cases. In addition to introducing a new abbreviated process for cases where the nullity of a marriage is clear, the apostolic letter makes major modifications in the grounds for tribunal competence and in the introductory phase of the process. It eliminates the mandatory appeal of all affirmative decisions and enhances the probative weight to be attributed to the declarations of the parties and of a single witness. Perhaps most importantly, it calls for a much greater personal or "hands-on" involvement in the work of tribunals by the diocesan bishop than has hitherto been typical.*

WILLIAM L. DANIEL*

The Abbreviated Matrimonial Process before the Bishop in Cases of "Manifest Nullity" of Marriage

Among the proposals advanced by some of the fathers of the third extraordinary assembly of the synod of bishops on pastoral challenges to the family in the context of evangelization, held in Rome on October 5–19, 2014, was that there be instituted "a simple process to be used in cases where nullity is clearly evident."[1] This proposal was received by the supreme legislator into the general legislation of the Church in the institution of the *processus matrimonialis brevior coram Episcopo*, the abbreviated matrimonial process before the bishop.[2] This institute, as such, is a pure novelty in the Church's modern legislation and thus merits extensive attention in the canonical science. This study offers a modest examination of it, one which can only be considered preliminary, due to the fact that, as of this writing, there has been no experience of its application, and there are already clarifications being offered by the Apostolic See about its correct implementation, of which there are surely more to come.

This preliminary study strives to introduce the new juridical institute from various perspectives. First, there is a consideration of the nature of the process and the identity of the judge. Second, there is an examination of the material presupposition to the abbreviated process, namely,

---

* Assistant Professor, School of Canon Law, The Catholic University of America, Washington, DC.

1. III Extraordinary General Assembly of the Synod of Bishops, *"Relatio Synodi." The Pastoral Challenges of the Family in the Context of Evangelization* (Vatican City: 2014) at no. 48.

2. Francis, motu proprio *Mitis iudex Dominus Iesus*, August 15, 2015 (Vatican City: Libreria Editrice Vaticana, 2015) at cc. 1683–1687; idem, motu proprio *Mitis et misericors Iesus*, August 15, 2015 (Vatican City: Libreria Editrice Vaticana, 2015) at cc. 1369–1373.

the matter of the manifest nullity of marriage due to a defect of consent. Third, the dynamic elements of the process are analyzed.

I. The Nature of the Process and the Identity of the Judge (*pars statica*)

The demeanor of some tribunals according to which the declaration of nullity of marriage has been treated as if it were a favor has led to a misconception of the nature of the marriage nullity process throughout the Church. In particular, there could be a temptation to think that the use of a judicial process is a mere construct of the past, long overdue for updating. The reform of Pope Francis not only gives an occasion for revisiting this question but also demands it, since the abbreviated process bears only partial resemblance to the ordinary judicial process of the canonical system. This first section thus first expounds upon the juridical nature proper to the marriage nullity process in general—whether ordinary, abbreviated or documentary—and the characteristics of the abbreviated process in particular. After that there is a discussion of the bishop as judge since bishops do not ordinarily exercise judicial power personally. Included within this discussion therefore is the question of whether he can delegate his judicial power to those accustomed to adjudicating causes of nullity of marriage.

A. Juridical Nature of the Process Declaring the Nullity of Marriage

1. The Necessarily Judicial Nature of the Process

In the preamble of the above-cited motu proprios establishing the reform, Pope Francis stresses his fundamental continuity with the reform of his predecessors, who consistently ensured that the alleged nullity of marriage would be examined by means of a judicial process. He declares:

> We have brought this about certainly following in the footsteps of Our Predecessors, who willed that causes of nullity of marriage be treated in a judicial manner, not an administrative one. This is not because the nature of the matter requires it, but rather the demand for greatly protecting the truth of the sacred bond urges it; the precautions of the judicial order rightly provide for this.[3]

---

3. "Quod fecimus vestigia utique prementes Decessorum Nostrorum, volentium causas nullitatis matrimonii via iudiciali pertractari, haud vero administrativa, non eo quod rei natura

This statement serves, in fact, as a response to the third extraordinary assembly of the synod of bishops, which proposed that certain causes could be handled by means of an "administrative procedure." Indeed, some synod fathers wondered about, *inter alia*, "the possibility of establishing an administrative means under the jurisdiction of the diocesan bishop."[4] In order to retain the time-tested method for best arriving at the truth of the alleged nullity of the matrimonial bond, however, Pope Francis wisely confirmed the judicial pathway.

The above-quoted statement from the motu proprios raises the question of the nature of the examination of the alleged nullity of marriage (*rei natura*), stating that a judicial treatment is not necessary, even if that is his legislative choice. The nature of juridical things (*de re iuridica*) is an object of study of the canonical science, and its examination is thus within the competence of jurists. And so this statement in the motu proprios may be subject to some critique. Assuredly, the divine law does not somehow dictate that a supposed lack of validity of marriage be examined within a judicial process; but the divine law of the indissolubility of marriage does have implications that correspond with the Church's consistent discipline demanding that this matter be treated within a judicial process. This can be demonstrated by a more profound consideration of the distinction between judicial power and administrative power, since these powers, respectively, are marked principally by formality and freedom. And the proper nature of the marriage nullity process raises the question of whether the decision is governed *ex natura rei* by some objective standard dictated with reference to something outside the will of the competent authority, or whether such a decision may flow from the free disposition of the authority.

The distinction between these two powers has been treated in great depth by the influential jurist Klaus Mörsdorf.[5] Reflecting on his teaching

---

id imponat, sed potius postulatio urgeat veritatis sacri vinculi quammaxime tuendae: quod sane praestant ordinis iudicarii cautiones." This is the text from *Mitis iudex Dominus Iesus*. It is stated almost verbatim in *Mitis et misericors Iesus* at the paragraph that begins: "Quidquid autem his Litteris statuimus, id fecimus vestigia . . . ."

4. III Extraordinary General Assembly of the Synod of Bishops, "Relatio Synodi." *The Pastoral Challenges of the Family in the Context of Evangelization* (Vatican City: 2014) at no. 48.

5. Cf. Klaus Mörsdorf, *Rechtssprechung und Verwaltung im kanonischen Recht* (Freiburg im Breisgau: Verlag Herder, 1941). The ideas from this book were reiterated and developed in subsequent publications, such as in the 1953 paper he gave at the fourth centenary of the

with application to our topic, we can examine the question employing three intrinsic distinguishing elements between judicial and administrative or executive power: (1) the material object of the decision, (2) the formal object of the decision, and (3) the motive for the decision.

The *material object* of judicial power (whether expressed by a sentence or a decisional decree) is the *cognitio veri*. The substance of the intrinsic purpose of the act is the identification, manifestation, and authoritative declaration of what the judge has discovered to be the truth.[6] Here it is not primarily a question of ontological truth but of "procedural truth"; that is, the judge is charged with explaining what has been demonstrated to be the truth vis-à-vis the allegation(s) in the trial. The diligent fulfillment of this task is, incidentally, good for the ecclesial society, but the aim of the judge's act is not proximately the realization of some good for the Church or the parties. The material object of an administrative decision, on the other hand, is the *volitio boni*. Intrinsic to the act of the public administra-

---

Gregorianum, "De relationibus inter potestatem administrativam et iudicialem in iure canonico," in *Questioni attuali di diritto canonico. Relazioni lette nella Sezione di Diritto Canonico del Congresso Internazionale per il IV Centenario della Pontificia Università Gregoriana, 13–17 ottubre 1953*, Analecta Gregoriana 69 (Rome: Pontificia Universitas Gregoriana, 1955) 399–418, and in his "De actibus administrativis in Ecclesia," in *Ius Populi Dei. Miscellanea in honorem Raymundi Bidagor* (Rome: Università Gregoriana Editrice, 1972) 3: 13–19.

With particular application to causes of nullity of marriage, see Manuel Jesús Arroba Conde, "Apertura verso il processo amministrativo di nullità matrimoniale e diritto di difesa delle parti," *Apollinaris* 75 (2002) 745–777; Frans Daneels, "La natura propria del processo di nullità matrimoniale," in *La nullità del matrimonio: temi processuali e sostantivi in occasione della "Dignitas connubii,"* ed. Hector Franceschi, Joaquín Llobell and Miguel Ángel Ortíz (Rome: Università della Santa Croce, 2005) 15–26; idem, "Osservazioni sul processo per la dichiarazione di nullità del matrimonio," *Quaderni di diritto ecclesiale* 14 (2001) 77–88; Velasio De Paolis, "I fondamenti del processo matrimoniale secondo il Codice di diritto canonico e l'Istruzione *Dignitas connubii*," in *Il giudizio di nullità matrimoniale dopo l'Istruzione "Dignitas connubii." Parte Prima: I principi*, ed. Piero Antonio Bonnet and Carlo Gullo, Studia Giuridici 75 (Vatican City: Libreria Editrice Vaticana, 2007) 47–78; *L'Istruzione "Dignitas connubii" nella dinamica delle cause matrimoniali*, ed. Juan Ignacio Arrieta, Studi 4 (Venice: Marcianum Press, Istituto di Diritto Canonico San Pio X, 2006) *passim*; G. Paolo Montini, *De iudicio contentioso ordinario. De processibus matrimonialibus. I. Pars statica* (Rome: Editrice Pontificia Università Gregoriana, 2014) 9–14. See also the recurring analyses of Joaquín Llobell in his writings on the "administrativization" of the marriage nullity process (e.g., "'Quaestiones disputatae' sulla scelta della procedura giudiziaria nelle cause di nullità del matrimonio, sui titoli di competenza, sul libello introduttorio e sulla contestazione della lite," *Apollinaris* 70 [1997] 581–622).

6. Exceptions to this are those intraprocedural acts of the judge called ordinatory decrees (*decreta ordinatoria*). These are not decisions but provide some important development for the progression of the trial—for example, making some provision (e.g., appointing an advocate *ex officio* or prescribing a time limit) or ordering a party to do something (e.g., present a document).

tion is the realization of some good, primarily for the community or at least without prejudice to the community. The establishment, alteration or suppression of some juridical institute aims at bringing about some good or at least of avoiding some harm that could be brought upon the community or exacerbated within it. The provision of offices or other institutes has this aim in the purest form, and the concession of favors, too, seeks to provide some good or prevent some evil for the benefit of individual physical or juridical persons without causing harm to the society. The public administration, in carrying out administrative activity, ordinarily does not have as its aim the declaration of truth as the primary end in itself.

The *formal object* of judicial power is the application of the law to the concrete case. In issuing the norm (*ius*), the legislator establishes or identifies what is just (*iustum*) for the generality of cases. When an ordinary contentious cause is treated, in the definitive sentence the judge applies this just norm to the proven facts of the case; that is, after discovering the true facts, he applies the law to them and objectively arrives at the truth about whether a juridical fact has been proven or a right injured, as the case may be. In principle, this applicative declaration of the truth results in justice (*iustitia*). On the other hand, the formal object of administrative power resides not so much in the application of the law but in the evaluative process of the administrative authority. The law states what is just—what is due or binding upon each interested person—but it does not declare every possible good that may be at stake in every situation; this would be impossible. Taking the norm of law as the starting point in order to ensure justice, the public administration weighs all the goods at stake and all the circumstances in order to arrive at a prudent judgment (*prudens arbitrium*) about what is suitable, useful and good. Since the legislator cannot exercise prudence in concrete cases, it is left to the public administration to discern the most fitting course of action.

The *motive of the act* of judicial power—that is, the judicial decision—corresponds with the material object; the judge discerns and declares what is true based on moral certitude about the objectively established truth of things, which is reached by evaluating the proofs. This certitude entails the elimination of every founded, reasonable doubt—that is, doubt about what is true. The judge is motivated to decide because of a demonstrable conviction about what is true with respect to the allegation(s) in view of the proper application of the law. The motive of the singular administrative act is the demonstrable conviction of the administrative authority about what is good and about how that good is best achieved. While this presupposes justice—that each is given what is his or her due—and an appreciation of the truth about the circumstances and facts of the situation, the administrator is motivated to act in order to obtain the good(s) at stake or avoid some evil threatening that good.

If the alleged nullity of marriage could be treated via an administrative procedure, the ecclesiastical decision would amount to a disposition about what is good for the society of the Church and the local community and what is good for the spouses and their families. It would be the result of the authority's evaluation of the circumstances of the case and the possible consequences of one decision or another. And this would all be the fruit of the prudent discretion of the authority, who could make a disposition of the will about whether the marriage is null or not. In effect, *he* would be the one to establish its nullity. Evidently, this would be a disordered approach to the marriage nullity process, since no man can make a marriage null once it has been validly entered, not even one of the spouses, considering that such an act would amount to a dissolution of the indissoluble bond of marriage.

In fact, the authority entrusted with the grave duty of examining the alleged nullity of marriage does not himself cause the marriage to become null or assert its perduring validity. For the object of the decision about the alleged nullity of marriage is a declaration of the discovered truth about the alleged nullity. It is a declarative, not a constitutive judgment. This declaration is the result of an application of the law to the proven facts of the case, such that, after weighing what in law is considered a cause of nullity of marriage, the authority can carefully examine whether such a cause is proven to exist in the case of a given marriage. The definitive answer flows not from the free disposition of the authority as an act of his prudent discretion but from his attainment (or not) of moral certitude about the nullity of marriage, eliminating any prudent doubt about its nullity or declaring the existence of remaining doubts.

Bearing all of this in mind, we can say that the alleged nullity of marriage *ex natura rei* is always to be examined according to a process that carefully brings to light the facts that could redound to the nullity of marriage. This process is under the direction of a qualified, competent expert attributed with the authority in a community needed for discerning and declaring the truth about whether the alleged nullity is established beyond any reasonable doubt. And in the canonical tradition, this is a matter of a judicial process concluding with a judicial pronouncement and never a mere administrative procedure concluding with an administrative disposition. The final decision necessarily has a declarative nature, pronouncing what is proven to be or not to be, and not a constitutive nature, since the divine law renders man absolutely incompetent to dissolve a marriage that is *ratum* and consummated, or to declare null what is in fact valid. And since the abbreviated process before the bishop does in fact result in the declaration of nullity of marriage, unless such nullity is not proven (cf. *CIC* c. 1687 §1, *CCEO* c. 1373 §1), it is a judicial process that results (again, when proven) in a declaration of nullity of marriage in virtue of the attainment of moral certitude.

2. The "Special" Character of the Abbreviated Process

The basic pattern for the Church's administration of justice is the ordinary contentious trial, which consists of a thorough, detailed, orderly treatment of any question pending before the competent judge. The norms regulating it have the character of general judicial norms, which is verified by the legislative technique of *remission* in the context of other procedural institutes. Thus, the norms governing many other processes frequently acknowledge their own inadequacy, that is, the existence of *quasi-lacunae legis*, and resolve this problem by incorporating the canons of the ordinary contentious trial into themselves, *mutatis mutandis*. This occurs in the other generic form of trial, the oral or summary contentious process (cf. *CIC* c. 1670, *CCEO* c. 1356), as well as the many special judicial processes (*processus speciales*), such as those regulating the treatment of the alleged nullity of marriage (*CIC* c. 1691 §3, *CCEO* c. 1377 §3), the separation of spouses when this process is requested (*CIC* c. 1693 §1, *CCEO* c. 1379 §1), the alleged nullity of sacred ordination (*CIC* c. 1710, *CCEO* c. 1386 §2), the imposition or declaration of a penalty (*CIC* c. 1728 §1, *CCEO* c. 1471 §1),[7] the processes proper to the Supreme Tribunal of the Apostolic Signatura, such as

---

7. Related to this is the case of dismissal of an Eastern monk (c. 501 §4), of members of Eastern orders and congregations (c. 553), and of societies of common life after the manner of religious (c. 562 §3), which, if requested, is to be treated via the penal process governed, in part, by the canons on the ordinary contentious trial.

the contentious-administrative process,[8] and, with regard to the gathering of proofs, causes of beatification and canonization.[9] Notable in the context of the contemporary canonical system is the fact that the nullity of marriage due to a defect of consent has until now been treated before local tribunals solely according to the norms of the ordinary contentious trial.

The reform of Pope Francis, however, has now created a bifurcation of causes of nullity of marriage due to a defect of consent.[10] They may be treated now either via the ordinary contentious process or via the abbreviated process before the bishop, *servatis servandis*. The fundamental material criterion for electing one process over the other, which shall be explored below, is whether the nullity of consent is "manifestly evident." At the same time, the reform repeats the norm according to which causes of nullity of marriage cannot be treated via the oral (summary) contentious process prescribed in the codes (see *CIC* c. 1691 §2, *CCEO* c. 1377 §2). Indeed, the illegitimate use of the oral contentious process is not merely considered illicit but in fact causes the nullity of the acts: "If the oral process is used outside of the cases permitted by law, the judicial acts are null" (*CIC* c. 1656 §2, *CCEO* c. 1343 §2, *DC* art. 269). And the nullity of the acts redounds at least to the remediable nullity of the definitive sentence (see *CIC* c. 1622, 5°; *CCEO* c. 1304 §1, 5°), if not its irremediable nullity if such a violation of the law amounts to a denial of one of the parties' right of defense (cf. *CIC* c. 1620, 7°; *CCEO* c. 1303 §1, 7°).[11]

---

8. Cf. Benedict XVI, motu proprio *Antiqua ordinatione*, June 21, 2008: *AAS* 100 (2008) 538, art. 122 (hereafter *Lex propria STSA*); *CIC* c. 1402.

9. Cf. Congregation for the Causes of Saints, instruction *Sanctorum Mater*, May 17, 2007 (Rome: Libreria Editrice Vaticana, 2007) at art. 1 §3; *CIC* c. 1403 §2.

10. It seems likely that the addition of this process will induce new confusion among the faithful and thus create new pastoral challenges. Already prior to this reform, members of the faithful who approached tribunals were often bewildered by their perception that, while their cause is protracted for about one year, the cause of their friend or relative was completed in just a few months or less. Prior to the present reform, it was possible (though not always easy) to explain that the nullity of some marriages is evident due to the fact that it was attempted outside the Church without a dispensation from canonical form or because of a diriment impediment or the priest's or deacon's lack of a ministerial faculty, whereas other causes concern the more complicated and subtle matter of a defect of consent. Now there are two processes by which a defect of consent can be examined, and it would not be at all surprising if this were to give rise to confusion about which causes qualify for the abbreviated process, creating a sense of inequality among the faithful.

11. Cf. Gianpaolo Montini, "La querela di nullità (artt. 269–278)," in *Il giudizio di nullità matrimoniale dopo l'Istruzione "Dignitas connubii." Parta terza: La parte dinamica del processo*, Studi Giuridici 77 (Vatican City: Libreria Editrice Vaticana, 2008) 608–610; Zenon Grocholewski,

What, however, is the real, substantial difference between the dynamic steps of the abbreviated process before the bishop and the oral (or summary) contentious process? They are both introduced with a *libellus* that briefly, fully and clearly explains the facts, indicates the proofs that the judge can collect immediately, and presents supporting documentation.[12] Then, after formulating the doubt, the judge cites all the parties and witnesses to be present at the session/hearing, which is to take place not more than 30 days later.[13] Not less than three days before the session, the parties may propose points that are to be investigated during the session in support of their interests.[14] All of the proofs are collected at the session, and, as a rule, the parties and their advocates may be present during all the questioning.[15] The only substantial differences reside in the discussion of the cause and the issuance of the decision: whereas the oral contentious process involves an oral discussion and an immediate announcement of the decision by the judge (later put into writing with motivation), the abbreviated process prescribes written argumentation and the issuance of a definitive sentence by the bishop.

"Illegittimo uso del processo sommario come motivo di nullità della sentenza," in *Cause incidentali e processo contenzioso sommario ossia orale nella dinamica della revisione del diritto processuale canonico*, Studia et Documenta Iuris Canonici XIV, Annali di Dottrina e Giurisprudenza Canonica VIII (Rome: Officium Libri Catholici, 1988) 169–175.

In some causes judged before the Roman Rota, while the use of the oral contentious process is not the explicit cause of nullity of the sentence, it has been pointed out that the parties' right of defense is thoroughly denied due to the illegitimate abbreviation of the time limits prescribed by law without the consent of the parties (cf. *CIC* c. 1465 §2). In one cause, for example, the whole ordinary contentious matrimonial process lasted just one month! This left no reasonable periods of time for the *contestatio litis*, the presentation of proofs, and the inspection of the acts (cf. Tribunal of the Roman Rota, Decree *c*. Boccafola, February 4, 1993: *RRDecreta* 11: 21, no. 13).

It has also been suggested that the illegitimate use of the oral or summary process is in fact a question of absolute incompetence *ratione materiae*, since the judge lacks jurisdiction for judging the matter of the nullity of marriage with that procedural instrument. Cf. Antoni Stankiewicz, "Il processo contenzioso orale," in *I procedimenti speciali nel diritto canonico*, Studi Giuridici 27 (Vatican City: Libreria Editrice Vaticana, 1992) 41, no. 4; idem, "Chapter I. The Plaint of Nullity of the Judgement," in *Exegetical Commentary on the Code of Canon Law*, ed. Ángel Marzoa, Jorge Miras and Rafael Rodríguez-Ocaña, Gratianus Series (Montréal: Wilson & Lafleur/Chicago: Midwest Theological Forum, 2004) IV/2: 1545.

12. See *CIC* cc. 1658, 1684; *CCEO* cc. 1344, 1370.
13. See *CIC* cc. 1661 §1, 1685; *CCEO* cc. 1347 §1, 1371.
14. See *Ratio procedendi* (*RP*) art. 17, *CIC* c. 1661 §2, *CCEO* cc. 1347 §2.
15. See *RP* art. 18, *CIC* c. 1663 §2, 1664; *CCEO* cc. 1349 §2, 1350.

In many cases the very text of the oral contentious process is simply taken up into the abbreviated process.¹⁶ In this comparative table, the principal dynamic steps of both processes are juxtaposed, and the differences are roughly indicated for the convenience of the reader:¹⁷

Abbreviated Process	Oral Contentious Process
Can. 1684. Libellus quo processus brevior **introducitur, praeter ea quae in can.** 1504 **recensentur, debet:** 1° **facta** quibus petitio innititur **breviter, integre et perspicue exponere;** 2° **probationes,** quae statim a iudice colligi possint, indicare; 3° documenta quibus petitio innititur in adnexo exhibere.	Can. 1658—§ 1. **Libellus quo** lis **introducitur, praeter ea quae in can.** 1504 **recensentur, debet:** 1° **facta** quibus actoris petitiones innitantur, **breviter, integre et perspicue exponere;** 2° **probationes** ~~quibus actor facta demonstrare intendit, quasque simul afferre nequit, ita~~ indicare ut statim colligi a iudice possint. § 2. Libello adnecti debent, ~~saltem in exemplari authentico,~~ documenta quibus petitio innititur.

16. The influence of the oral contentious process is further demonstrated in the new norm on the citation of the parties in the ordinary contentious marriage nullity process, both of which are notable for their minimization of the act of citation:

| *Novus* Can. 1676 § 1. Recepto libello, Vicarius iudicialis **si aestimet eum aliquo fundamento niti, eum admittat et, decreto ad calcem ipsius libelli apposito, praecipiat ut exemplar** notificetur defensori vinculi et, nisi libellus ab utraque parte subscriptus fuerit, parti conventae, eidem dato termino quindecim dierum ad suam mentem de petitione aperiendam. | Can. 1659 — § 1. ~~Si conamen conciliationis ad normam can. 1446, § 2 inutile cesserit,~~ iudex, **si aestimet libellum aliquo fundamento niti,** ~~intra tres dies,~~ **decreto ad calcem ipsius libelli apposito, praecipiat ut exemplar** petitionis notificetur parti conventae, facta huic facultate mittendi, intra quindecim dies, ad cancellariam tribunalis scriptam responsionem. |

17. The main textual transferences or similarities are indicated with bold font, and expressions taken out of the oral process norms in order to create the abbreviated process norms are crossed out to illustrate the editing work that seems to have been done.

For the sake of simplicity, only the canons of the Latin code are cited in this table; but the same details are recognizable in the Eastern norms, *mutatis mutandis*.

Can. 1685. Vicarius iudicialis, eodem decreto quo **dubii formulam determinat**, instructore et assessore nominatis, **ad sessionem non ultra triginta dies** iuxta can. 1686 celebrandam omnes citet qui in ea interesse debent.	Can. 1661 — ~~§ 1. Elapsis terminis, de quibus in cann. 1659 et 1660,~~ iudex, ~~perspectis actis,~~ formulam dubii determinet; dein ad audientiam, **non ultra** triginta dies celebrandam, omnes citet qui in ea interesse debent~~, addita pro partibus dubii formula~~.
[RP] Art. 17. **In citatione** ad mentem can. 1685 expedienda, **partes certiores fiant se posse, tribus saltem ante** sessionem instructoriam **diebus**, articulos argumentorum, nisi libello adnexi sint, **exhibere**, super quibus interrogatio partium vel testium petitur.	Can. 1661 § 2. **In citatione partes certiores fiant se posse, tres saltem ante audientiam dies,** aliquod breve scriptum tribunali **exhibere** ~~ad sua asserta comprobanda~~.
[RP] Art. 18. § 1. **Partes earumque advocati assistere possunt excussioni ceterarum partium et testium**, nisi instructor, propter rerum et personarum adiuncta, censuerit aliter esse procedendum. §2. **Responsiones partium et testium redigendae sunt scripto a notario, sed summatim et in iis tantummodo quae pertinent ad matrimonii controversi substantiam.**	Can. 1663 § 2. **Pars eiusque advocatus assistere possunt excussioni ceterarum partium, testium** ~~et peritorum~~. Can. 1664 — **Responsiones partium, testium,** ~~peritorum, petitiones et exceptiones advocatorum,~~ **redigendae sunt scripto a notario, sed summatim et in iis tantummodo quae pertinent ad substantiam** rei controversae, ~~et a deponentibus subsignandae~~.
Can. 1686. Instructor una sessione, quatenus fieri possit, **probationes colligat** et terminum quindecim dierum statuat ad animadversiones pro vinculo et defensiones pro partibus, si quae habeantur, exhibendas.	Can. 1663 — § 1. **Probationes colliguntur** in audientia, ~~salvo praescripto can. 1418~~.

Can. 1687 § 1. **Actis receptis**, Episcopus dioecesanus, collatis consiliis cum instructore et assessore, perpensisque animadversionibus defensoris vinculi et, si quae habeantur, defensionibus partium, si moralem certitudinem de matrimonii nullitate adipiscitur, sententiam ferat. Secus causam ad ordinarium tramitem remittat.	Can. 1667—**Probationibus collectis**, fit in eadem audientia discussio oralis.

What is striking about this comparison is the fact that very few substantive elements distinguish a process the use of which (for causes of nullity of marriage) has nullifying consequences from a process that has no such consequences. In a concrete case of abuse of the abbreviated process, the competent superior judge could examine the question of whether a wrongfully used abbreviated process had the character, in reality, of an illegitimate use of the oral contentious process, redounding to the nullity of the definitive sentence.

B. The Bishop Exercising the Function of Judge in Causes of Nullity of Marriage

Now that the fittingly judicial nature of the new abbreviated process has been explained, it is appropriate to dwell upon the figure of the bishop as judge. For, while the process is moderated by the judicial vicar and the instructor, who may be the judicial vicar (RP art. 16) or another (cf. c. 1685), and is instructed by the instructor, the one who issues the decision is the bishop. Related to this is the question of whether the bishop can and, if so, should delegate this judicial power to another. These questions are thus treated in sequence.

From the moment of episcopal ordination, bishops are entrusted with the functions not only of sanctifying and teaching but also of governing (*munus regendi*). The episcopal character itself entails a share in the governance of the Church, though the power needed for this is conferred apart from the sacramental act of ordination, through the conferral of a canonical mission. Indeed, this governing function, which is always to be exercised in communion with the head and members of the college of bishops, is given "juridical determination" when a bishop is entrusted with a concrete office or determined subjects. This occurs *par excellence* in the entrusting of a particular Church to the pastoral care of a bishop, conferring upon him the office of diocesan or eparchial bishop. Such a provision bestows upon the bishop the fullness of the power of governance within the limits of his competence, constituting him as the legislator, the primary organ of public administration, and the judge.[18]

Accordingly, the diocesan or eparchial bishop is innately or naturally a judge (*iudex natus*) over the flock entrusted to his total pastoral care.[19] In the juridical language of the Church, the diocesan or eparchial bishop is the judge of first instance in his diocese or eparchy. He may exercise this judicial function himself (*per se*) or through the judicial vicar and others upon whom he confers the office of judge.[20] In saying that he may exercise it himself (*per se*), the supreme legislator certainly presupposes that his exercise of this power would be done always according to the norm of procedural law; thus, he could as a rule (cf. *CIC* c. 1673 §3, *CCEO* c. 1359 §3) only conduct a trial and issue the definitive sentence in an ordinary contentious matrimonial trial within a college of judges (presumably as the *praeses*). Outside of the case of necessity described in §4 of the just cited canons, he would personally and solely judge a cause legitimately treated via the abbreviated process (*CIC* cc. 1683–1687, *CCEO* cc. 1369–1373) and the documentary process (cf. *CIC* c. 1688, *CCEO* c. 1374). Ordinarily, however, the bishop refrains from personally administering justice, and up to now in the modern period, he has thus rarely exercised his judicial power

---

18. See Second Vatican Ecumenical Council, dogmatic constitution *Lumen gentium*, November 21, 1964: *AAS* 57 (1965) 25 and 32–33, nn. 21 and 27, as well as the *Nota explicativa praevia* in ibid., 73, no. 2. Cf. Wilhelm Bertrams, "De potestatis episcopalis constitutione et determinatione in Ecclesia, sacramento salutis hominum," *Periodica* 60 (1971) 399–400; Dario Composta, "Teologia del diritto divino positivo. La *potestas iurisdictionis*," *Apollinaris* 45 (1972) 251; Antonio Souto, "El *munus regendi* como función y como poder," in *Acta conventus internationalis canonistarum, Romæ diebus 20–25 maii 1968 celebrati*, ed. Pontificia Commissio Codici iuris canonici recognoscendo (Vatican City: Typis Polyglottis Vaticanis, 1970) 244–247.

19. The old law included among the powers of the residential bishop the *potestas iudiciaria*: *CIC*/17 c. 335 §1; Pius XII, motu proprio *Cleri sanctitati*, June 2, 1957: *AAS* 49 (1957) 433–603, at 500 *sub* c. 399 §1. And the same power, identified as the *potestas iudicialis*, is likewise listed among the powers of the diocesan or eparchial bishop in the current law: see *CIC* c. 391 §1, *CCEO* c. 191 §1.

20. "Can. 1419 § 1. In unaquaque dioecesi et pro omnibus causis iure expresse non exceptis, iudex primae instantiae est Episcopus dioecesanus, qui iudicialem potestatem exercere potest per se ipse vel per alios, secundum canones qui sequuntur" (*CCEO* c. 1066 §1). "Can. 391 [. . .] § 2. . . . exercet ipse Episcopus . . . potestatem iudicialem sive per se sive per Vicarium iudicialem et iudices ad normam iuris" (cf. *CCEO* c. 191 §2).

himself. His relationship to the judicial forum has typically been administrative, expressed in his activities of providing for judicial offices and exercising vigilance over the correct administration of justice in his tribunal (cf. DC art. 33).[21]

The fundamental reason that the bishop ordinarily does not exercise judicial power is the natural positioning of the administration of justice outside the general governance of the particular Church. The legislative and administrative functions are those that are directed toward making dispositions for the public good of the community entrusted to his care, whether through establishing norms ("policies") in all areas of ecclesial life, or through organizing pastoral care, or resolving or responding to individual cases or requests. Judicial power, even while pertaining to the public good especially in causes of nullity of marriage, is directed toward the resolution of particular controversies that have a highly limited scope of interest, aside from the universal thematic relevance of the validity of marriage and the stability of the family. As a result, the mode of exercising power in judicial causes is quite distinct from the common mode of governance. Whereas in the latter the bishop as legislator or public administrator makes a general or singular disposition out of his prudent judgment in view of the common good and the particular interests at stake, the bishop as judge would be bound to make decisions according to the objective

---

21. Cf. Raymond Leo Burke, "Il Vescovo come moderatore del tribunale," *Ius Ecclesiae* 23 (2011) 13–32; Luigi Chiappetta, *Il Codice di diritto canonico. Commento giuridico-pastorale*, ed. F. Catozzella et al., 3rd ed. (Bologna: Edizioni Dehoniane, 2011) 1: 187, no. 979 and 3: 24, no. 5143; Carmelo de Diego-Lora and Rafael Rodríguez-Ocaña, *Lecciones de Derecho procesal canónico. Parte general* (Pamplona: EUNSA, 2003) 270–271; Thomas J. Green, "Article 2: Diocesan Bishops [cc. 381–402]," in *The Code of Canon Law. A Text and Commentary*, ed. James A. Coriden, Thomas J. Green and Donald E. Heintschel (New York/Mahwah: Paulist Press, 1985) 331; Zenon Grocholewski, "Art. 1. The Judge," in *Exegetical Commentary*, IV/1: 717–720; idem, "Guiding Principles of Book VII of the Code of Canon Law," *Forum* 10 (1999) 63–64; José Luis Gutiérrez, "Art. 2. Diocesan Bishops," in *Code of Canon Law Annotated*, ed. Ernest Caparros, Michel Thériault and Jean Thorn, 2nd ed. (Montréal: Wilson & Lafleur Ltée/Woodridge: Midwest Theological Forum, 2004) 335; Montini, *De iudicio contentioso ordinario*, 104–110, 128–130; Pio Vito Pinto, "Titolo VIII. La potestà di governo," in *Commento al Codice di diritto canonico*, ed. Pio Vito Pinto (Rome: Urbaniana University Press, 1985) 82; Francisco J. Ramos, *I tribunali ecclesiastici. Costituzione, organizzazione, norme processuali, cause matrimoniali*, (Rome: Pontificia Università S. Tomasso D'Aquino, 1998) 105–109; Gordon Read, "Art. 2. Diocesan Bishops," in *The Canon Law Letter & Spirit. A Practical Guide to the Code of Canon Law*, ed. Gerard Sheehy et al. (Collegeville, MN: The Liturgical Press, 1995) 224; Francesco Viscome, "Il Vescovo come giudice nella propria diocesi," *Quaderni dello Studio Rotale* 16 (2006) 123–124.

standard of moral certitude, pronouncing not what may seem best in the case but what corresponds to the truth of the matter.

One practical reason that bishops have not, up to now, habitually decided causes of nullity of marriage is the fact that many of them are not canonists or, even if they are, may have limited experience in the judicial forum or experience only in the distant past. As is known, a bishop need not be completely prepared in canon law in order to be eligible for selection as a bishop (cf. *CIC* c. 378 §1, 5°; *CCEO* c. 180, 6°). He presumably has a well-developed sense of what is just in the ecclesial society, but this does not guarantee learning in the Church's sacred discipline in the areas of matrimonial and procedural law. As we read in the 2004 Directory for the Pastoral Ministry of Bishops, "The administration of canonical justice is a duty of grave responsibility that demands, first and foremost, a profound sense of justice, but also sufficient canonical expertise and experience," and concretely a doctorate or at least a licentiate in canon law.[22] It has thus long been the natural inclination of the Church not to burden the bishop with the personal exercise of judicial power, while always demanding that he exercise personal and diligent attention over the administration of justice.

Indeed, this practical distance of the bishop from the concrete work of the administration of justice in the particular Church was even stated in the first codification. We read in canon 1578 of the 1917 code that "the bishop himself can always personally preside over the tribunal; but it is greatly expedient that he leave causes to be judged to the ordinary tribunal, especially criminal and contentious causes of serious importance, over which the officialis or vice-officialis is to preside."[23] When in the revision of the 1917 code some suggested that this norm be included in the new code, it was decided that the norm is superfluous, since bishops are accustomed to leaving judicial causes to their tribunals; and so the suggestion

---

22. Congregation for Bishops, Directory for the Pastoral Ministry of Bishops *Apostolorum Successores*, February 22, 2004 (Vatican City: Libreria Editrice Vaticana, 2004) 195, no. 180, where cc. 1420 §4 and 1421 §3 are cited.

23. "Can. 1578. Exceptis causis de quibus in can. 1572, par. 2, Episcopus semper potest tribunali ipse per se praeesse; sed valde expedit ut causas, praesertim criminales et contentiosas gravis momenti, iudicandas relinquat tribunali ordinario, cui praesit officialis vel vice-officialis." The exceptions cited in c. 1572 §2 are causes concerning the rights or goods of persons close to the bishop, viz., those in his retinue (*mensa*) or curia, for the judgment of which he would clearly be impeded (cf. *CIC*/17 c. 1613 §1).

was rejected.[24] This principle has consistently been applied to causes of nullity of marriage in the contemporary period. Article 14 §3 of the 1936 instruction *Provida Mater Ecclesia* approved by Pius XI declared the expediency of the bishop not presiding in a cause of nullity of marriage "unless special reasons demand it."[25] This same norm was restated in the 2005 instruction *Dignitas connubii* approved by John Paul II.[26]

Nevertheless, the reform of Pope Francis, and in particular the institution of the abbreviated process before the bishop, is in some discontinuity with this. For it entrusts the very judgment of the cause to the bishop: "The diocesan [or eparchial] bishop himself is competent to judge causes concerning the nullity of marriage with the abbreviated process . . . ." (*incipit* of CIC c. 1683 and CCEO c. 1369). The rationale for this, as stated in the preamble to the motu proprios establishing the reform, is that the bishop, who is not only the pastor and head of his particular Church but also her judge, should "offer a sign of the *conversion* of ecclesiastical structures" called for by Pope Francis in no. 27 of his post-synodal apostolic exhortation *Evangelii gaudium*. For it is his will that the bishop "not leave the judicial function in matrimonial matters entirely delegated to offices of the curia." The abbreviated process is one major implication of this, since the bishop himself is to issue the decision in the cause.

One could question whether this proximity to individual judicial causes will truly bring the hoped-for benefits to realization. Surely experience with the application of this new procedure will be illustrative. Certain concerns, however, could be noted *in limine*:

(1) The principle of proximity stressed in several places in the motu proprio would seem not to be applied in the abbreviated process. For

---

24. *Communicationes* 10 (1978) 229: "Nonnulli suggesserunt ut repristinetur norma can. 1578 CIC qua consulitur Episcopis ut causas, praesertim criminales et contentiosas gravis momenti, iudicandas relinquant tribunali ordinario, cui praesit officialis vel vice-officialis. Consultores censent hanc normam esse superfluam quia Episcopi generatim ita agunt."

25. Sacred Congregation for the Discipline of the Sacraments, instruction *Provida Mater Ecclesia*, August 15, 1936: *AAS* 28 (1936) 317: "Quamvis Episcopus possit eidem tribunali praeesse, valde expedit ne id faciat, nisi speciales causae id exigant (cfr. can. 1578)."

26. Pontifical Council for Legislative Texts, instruction *Dignitas connubii*, January 25, 2005 (Vatican City: Libreria Editrice Vaticana, 2005), hereafter cited as *DC*: "Art. 22–§1. In unaquaque dioecesi iudex primae instantiae pro causis nullitatis matrimonii iure expresse non exceptis est Episcopus dioecesanus, qui iudicialem potestatem exercere potest per se ipse vel per alios, ad normam iuris (cf. can. 1419, § 1). §2. Expedit tamen, nisi speciales causae id exigant, ne ipse id per se faciat. §3. Ideo omnes Episcopi pro sua dioecesi constituere debent tribunal dioecesanum."

while the bishop in one sense is closer to the cause, it is arranged such that there is never any personal encounter between the parties (i.e., the spouses and the defender of the bond) and the bishop-judge. It is the instructor who meets with the spouses, and the bishop, from a hidden and distant position, issues the decision. Tribunals have long been accused of deciding such personal matters "from an ivory tower"; and now the bishop may be given direct participation in that critique, and it may result in one more hindrance to the receptivity of the contemporary faithful to the principal expressions of his apostolic ministry of proclaiming the Word of God, administering the sacraments, and building up the unity of the presbyterate.

(2) The bishop is obliged personally to decide whether he is morally certain of the alleged nullity of marriage. Unlike so many matters in his daily governance of the particular Church, he cannot rely principally on the counsel of advisors for making this decision. It is true that he receives the counsel of the instructor and the assessor, but he also must personally examine the acts, study the arguments of the defender of the bond and of the spouses and their advocates, and decide whether all prudent doubt about the alleged nullity of marriage has been eliminated (cf. *CIC* c. 1687 §1, *CCEO* c. 1373 §1). One would think this a significant burden added to daily episcopal governance; but the reform seems to be insisting that the bishop must make time for it.

(3) The obligation of the defender of the bond to appeal an affirmative decision of the bishop not based on demonstrably objective moral certitude, which obligation is implicit in the law[27] and has been stressed both by Pope John Paul II in his January 25, 1988 discourse to the Roman Rota[28] and by Pope Francis in his 2013 discourse to the Apostolic Signatura,[29] becomes socially difficult or possibly even subjectively imprudent for the defender of the bond in the abbreviated process. The dynamic is not so very different from that of a pastor or other diocesan official who wishes to make hierarchical recourse against

---

27. *CIC* cc. 1432, 1628; *CCEO* cc. 1096, 1309.

28. Cf. *Papal Allocutions to the Roman Rota, 1939–2011*, ed. William H. Woestman (Ottawa: Saint Paul University, 2011) 202 (cited hereafter as *Papal Allocutions*).

29. See Francis, discourse to the Plenary Session of the Supreme Tribunal of the Apostolic Signatura, November 8, 2013: *AAS* 105 (2013) 1153, where he mentions the defender of the bond's "duty to appeal, even to the Roman Rota, against a decision he considers injurious to the truth of the bond." See also Francis, discourse to the Faculty of Canon Law at the Pontifical Gregorian University, January 24, 2015: *AAS* 106 (2015) 193.

the bishop's decision to remove him from office. It is a juridically protected right, and it is possible for people to remain detached and professional about it; but it cannot but have a personal component or even a prevailingly personal character. For it is the bishop's own, much considered decision, and to challenge it before a hierarchical superior can seem threatening and intimidating to the bishop's authority, which places the recurrent in a most awkward position, especially in the event of a decision favorable to the appeal. The defender of the bond is appointed by the bishop and, in secular terms, is his employee; he is dependent upon the bishop for his employment and livelihood. It would be socially natural, therefore, for the defender of the bond habitually to avoid appealing decisions he finds unfounded or dubious. This dynamic is likely one that the bishop would ordinarily prefer to avoid as well.

These observations and others that could be made could cause one to question the suitability of the positioning of the bishop as the judge, the sole judge, of certain causes of nullity of marriage. If the bishop deems it imprudent in a particular case to issue the decision, if he is ill at ease with his new judicial responsibility, or if he is genuinely over burdened with urgent matters of diocesan or eparchial governance, can he legitimately delegate the power to decide such causes to another, in whole or in part?

C. Delegation by the Bishop of the Power to Judge a Cause to be Treated via the Abbreviated Process

In articulating the threefold distinction of the powers of governance in the Church, in canon 135 of the Latin code and canon 985 of the Eastern code, the supreme legislator prescribes certain general rules for their legitimate exercise. Included among these are rules governing the delegation of powers. Legislative power cannot be validly delegated, unless the law provides otherwise (§2); judicial power "cannot be [validly (*CCEO*)] delegated, except for completing acts preparatory to a decree or sentence" (§3);[30] and executive power, as is well known, can be broadly delegated and

---

30. This is reiterated and unaltered in the instruction *Dignitas connubii*: "Art. 32—§1. Potestas iudicialis, qua gaudent iudices aut collegia iudicialia, exercenda est modo iure praescripto, et delegari nequit, nisi ad actus cuivis decreto aut sententiae praeparatorios perficiendos (can. 135, §3)."

subdelegated (cf. *CIC* c. 137, *CCEO* c. 988). The judicial power that cannot be delegated is that exercised precisely to issue judicial decisions, whether they are interlocutory or decisional decrees or interlocutory or definitive sentences; what can be delegated is non-decisive judicial "power" (*rectius*: authority), especially acts of judicial instruction.

The prohibition on the delegation of judicial power in the cited canons of the codes may seem evident in itself: decisive, judicial power cannot be delegated. The problem with this seemingly absolute prohibition, though, is the fact that the same legislator that established that prohibition makes legislative provisions precisely for the delegation of judicial power.[31] This fact leads to the logical conclusion that the aforementioned, apparently absolute prohibition is not so absolute as it may seem. Indeed, the codes explicitly acknowledge that the Roman Pontiff himself can delegate his judicial power in saying that he may make judicial decisions himself, through the apostolic tribunals "or through judges delegated by him" (*"vel per iudices a se delegatos"*—*CIC* c. 1442, *CCEO* c. 1059 §1). Nor is this possibility limited to the supreme judge of the whole Catholic world. When there is a contentious cause introduced between two provinces of the same clerical institute of pontifical right, the supreme moderator may instruct and decide the cause himself or through his delegate (*"per se ipse vel per delegatum"*—*CIC* c. 1427 §2). Two classes of ecclesiastical authority may delegate their judicial power—one of whom has the episcopal character, the other of whom is an authority with limited jurisdiction. This gives rise to the question of whether the diocesan or eparchial bishop may delegate his judicial power.[32] He is a judge, and the general norm says that judges cannot delegate their judicial power; but it does not seem rational that the Roman Pontiff and especially supreme moderators would be exempt from this general prohibition, which is clearly not absolute, while bishops, who are vicars of Christ and successors to the Apostles, would not.

---

31. This would seem to be a case of the lack of cohesion that is sometimes observed between the results of the various *Coetus studiorum* of the code commission; nevertheless, both elements are part of the pontifical legislation and thus cannot be discounted.

32. As doctrine routinely observes, this question applies likewise to those equivalent in law to a bishop, namely, the superiors who govern the entities listed in c. 368, as well as the head of a mission *sui iuris*, a personal prelature, and a military or personal ordinariate, whether or not they have the episcopal character.

A minority of doctrine insists that the bishop cannot delegate his judicial power in virtue of the cited general norm.[33] Their chief arguments are four. (1) There is a parallelism between the general norm on the delegation of legislative power and that on judicial power, such that, just as the Roman Pontiff may delegate his legislative power while the bishop may not, so likewise with judicial power. (2) The legislator says that the bishop, who is the judge of first instance for his diocese or eparchy, may exercise his power himself or through others "according to the canons which follow" (*CIC* c. 1419 §1) or "according to the norm of law" (*CIC* c. 391 §2). That is taken to mean that, when exercising it through others, he must do so through those vicarious organs established in the codes, that is, the collegial organs of the hierarchically related tribunals and the personal organs of the judicial vicar and the other judges. Thus he may not establish special tribunals or extend his judicial power to individual persons for one or more cases. (3) The general norm prohibiting delegation refers to the power "which judges and judicial colleges enjoy," and the bishop is a judge; therefore, it applies to him. (4) The norms on delegated tribunals (*CIC*/17 cc. 1606–1607) were abrogated in the revision of the 1917 code.

These arguments, in addition to being in the minority, are not convincing, because they do not account for a number of factors. Argument (1) ignores the fact that it is not only the Roman Pontiff who can delegate his judicial power but, as was noted, also the supreme moderator of a clerical religious institute of pontifical right. Argument (2) employs a strict interpretation of "according to the canons which follow" and "according to the norm of law" that is unwarranted in view of canon 18 (*CCEO* c. 1500). The cited canons declaring the bishop's enjoyment of judicial power do not amount to a restriction of rights but rather promote the right of the faithful to a judicial process (cf. *CIC*, c. 221, *CCEO* c. 24); and there is no question

---

33. See, e.g., Juan Ignacio Arrieta, "Title VIII. The Power of Governance," in *Code of Canon Law Annotated*, ed. Ernest Caparros, Michel Thériault and Jean Thorn, 2nd ed., (Montréal: Wilson & Lafleur Ltée/Woodridge: Midwest Theological Forum, 2004) 119; Julio García Martín, *Le norme generali del Codex Iuris Canonici*, 5th ed. (Rome: EDIURCLA, 2006) 485, 511; Javier Ochoa, "I processi canonici in generale," *Apollinaris* 57 (1984) 213; Santiago Panizo Orallo, "La *Dignitas connubii*. Los títulos I a III de la Instrucción. Presentación y novedades (arts. 8 a 91)," in *Procesos de nulidad matrimonial. La Instrucción "Dignitas connubii." Actas del XXIV Curso de Actualización en Derecho Canónico de la Facultad de Derecho Canónico (Pamplona, 24–26 octubre de 2005)*, ed. Rafael Rodríguez-Ocaña and Joaquín Sedano (Pamplona: EUNSA, 2006) 114.

whatsoever of an exception to the law or the imposition or declaration of penalties. On the contrary, the manner in which the bishop exercises his power through others should be understood broadly, since the diocesan (or eparchial) bishop "in the diocese [or eparchy] entrusted to him has all the ordinary, proper and immediate power which is required for the exercise of his pastoral function" (*CIC* c. 381 §1), not excluding the delegation of his power to resolve judicial controversies arising in his particular Church, such as the alleged nullity of marriage of one of his subjects or a marriage celebrated in his particular Church. The weakness of the positivistic arguments (3) and (4) is evident in view of what has just been said in response to arguments (1) and (2).

In fact, the majority of canonical doctrine supports the right of the diocesan or eparchial bishop to delegate his judicial power. The one who has written the most prolifically on this question is Joaquín Llobell.[34] He demonstrates that the phenomenon of the delegation of judicial power has been a peacefully accepted practice in the Church for centuries, including its explicit regulation in the 1917 code in a brief but distinct chapter entitled "*De tribunali delegato*," comprised of canons 1606–1607. He underscores the fact that the *Coetus "de processibus"* charged with revising the Church's general procedural law maintained that the diocesan bishop retained the right to delegate his judicial power. Indeed, in the context of its treatment of the hierarchy of tribunals, a consultor observed the absence of delegated tribunals as a lacuna. In response, the reporter declared that the *Coetus* avoided this topic on purpose "so that, as far as possible, the public order not be disturbed by special jurisdictions which, as is indeed evident, are not prohibited. Moreover, the fact that there can be a tribunal delegated by the Holy See *or by the Bishop* is taken both from the general norms and because in canon 102 §2 (on General Norms) only judges are prohibited

---

34. See Joaquín Llobell, "La delega della potestà giudiziaria nell'ordinamento canonico," in *Escritos en honor de Javier Hervada. Ius Canonicum: Revista del Instituto Martín de Azpilcueta*, special volume (Pamplona: EUNSA, 1999) 459–472; idem, "La delegación de la potestad judicial 'decisoria' y la reconvención en las causas de nulidad del matrimonio tras la Instr. *Dignitas connubii*. Brevas notas," *Ius Canonicum* 94 (2007) 495–503. These arguments are echoed by Miguel Ángel Ortiz in his commentary on *DC* art. 32; see *Norme procedurali canoniche commentate*, ed. Massimo del Pozzo, Joaquín Llobell, Jesús Miñambres (Rome: Coletti a San Pietro, 2013) 304–305; see also his "La potestà giudiziale in genere e i tribunali (artt. 22–32)," in *Il giudizio di nullità matrimoniale dopo l'Istruzione "Dignitas connubii." Parte Seconda: La parte statica del processo*, ed. Piero Antonio Bonnet and Carlo Gullo, Studi Giuridici 76 (Vatican City: Libreria Editrice Vaticana, 2007) 100–102.

from delegating judicial power" (emphasis added).[35] The exclusion of the diocesan bishop from the restriction of what would become canon 135 §3 was already evident to those drafting the code and would have seemed to them superfluous. Llobell's major argument, however, is the fact that a number of canons of the *De processibus* of both codes demand the delegability of power by the one endowed with proper judicial power, inasmuch as they presume the existence of delegated judges.[36] Interesting in our context is Llobell's threefold explanation for why it is fitting for the bishop not to judge causes personally: 1) to save him time when he is already greatly burdened with the governance of the diocese, 2) to spare him from entering into matters that may be outside of his expertise, and 3) to protect his pastoral and paternal relationship toward the faithful, which could be compromised by needing to resolve a formal controversy and give either or both parties the impression of being "condemned" by their spiritual father.

The other authors echo much of what has been said already. They are recounted here in brief:

— Rodríguez-Ocaña notes that the cited general norm refers to the judge, and this is not a word used in law to identify the diocesan

---

35. "Aliquis notavit in schemate fere unquam mentionem fieri de tribunali delegato et petiit ut haec lacuna impleatur. Relator respondet Coetum consulto id fecisse ita ut, quantum fieri possit, non turbetur ordo publicus per iurisdictiones speciales, quae quidem, ut evidens est, non vetantur. Quod autem dari possit tribunal delegatum a S. Sede vel ab Episcopo eruitur sive ex normis generalibus sive quia in can. 102 §2 (de Normis Generalibus) soli iudices vetantur ne potestatem iudicialem delegent" (*Communicationes* 10 [1978] 243).

That discussion was held on May 15, 1978. In fact, 12 years earlier, on May 27, 1966, there was some discussion concerning the different opinions among the authors about whether judicial power could be delegated. The matter was dismissed, though, because the 1917 code in fact recognized its delegability. The relator did think it valuable perhaps to make it clear that the prohibition of delegation was restricted to judges appointed by an authority with ordinary judicial power ("Rev.mus Relator vellet hoc vel aliquid simile sancire: 'Iudex a Superiore constitutus, qui potestate ordinaria fruitur, non potest illam delegare'"). But there was no agreement about the matter, and the discussion was deferred until a later time.

36. See especially *CIC* cc. 1495 and 1512, 3° and *CCEO* cc. 1102 §2, 1157, and 1312.

Julio García Martín proposes that the uses of "delegated judge" or "delegated tribunal" in the law, on the contrary, refer to judges to whom an individual cause has been entrusted, not to individuals upon whom judicial power has been conferred for one cause (see his *Le norme generali del Codex Iuris Canonici*, 5th ed. (Rome: EDIURCLA, 2006) 485). This argument, however, attributes to the legislator an imprecise and analogous application of the term "delegate" to cases of truly ordinary judges being assigned to a cause by the judicial vicar.

bishop. He also observes that it does not make sense to say that what a supreme moderator can do (cf. c. 1427 §1) a bishop cannot. Moreover, the Latin code refers to judge delegates in norms that would be applicable in diocesan tribunals (see cc. 1495 and 1512, 3°).[37]

— Montini, in addition to referring to these and other norms as well as the code revision process, cites the praxis of the Apostolic See to delegate judges, which supports the position that the restriction of canon 135 §3 is not an absolute one.[38]

— Acebal states that the derogation of the norms of the 1917 code governing delegated tribunals (cc. 1606–1607) was intended to contribute to the better ordering of the regular administration of justice but cannot be taken as a restriction on the power of the bishop. This is evident from the above-cited text of the code commission.[39]

— De Paolis and D'Auria hold that the restriction of canon 135 §3 pertains to those with ordinary vicarious judicial power, not to the bishop, who is the first titular of judicial power in the diocese. He may therefore entrust one or more specific cases to individual qualified subjects or to a college.[40]

---

37. See de Diego-Lora and Rodríguez-Ocaña, *Lecciones de Derecho procesal canónico*, 321 (see 20 for the latter's authorship). For support of this teaching, see Carlos M. Morán Bustos and Carmen Peña García, *Nulidad de matrimonio y proceso canónico. Comentario adaptado a la Instrucción "Dignitas connubii"* (Madrid: Dykinson, S.L., 2008) 84–85, which is authored by the first mentioned.

38. See Montini, *De iudicio contentioso ordinario*, 125–127.

39. See Juan Luis Acebal, "Art. 1.—Del juez," in *Código de Derecho Canónico. Edición bilingüe comentada*, 11th ed. (Madrid: Biblioteca de Autores Cristianos, 1992) 697.

40. See Velasio De Paolis and Andrea D'Auria, *Le norme generali. Commento al Codice di diritto canonico. Libro primo*, Manuali-Diritto 22 (Rome: Urbaniana University Press, 2008) 437. In the same sense, see Albert Gautier, *I principi generali dell'attività giuridica nella Chiesa (Commentario dei canoni 96–203 del Libro I del Codice di Diritto Canonico)* (Rome: Pontificia Università San Tommaso, 1993) 79; José Miguel Pinto Gómez, "La giurisdizione," in *Il processo matrimoniale canonico*, Studi Giuridici 17 (Vatican City: Libreria Editrice Vaticana, 1988) 61, sub 25.2°, and in *Il processo matrimoniale canonico. Nuova edizione riveduta e ampliata*, ed. P.A. Bonnet and C. Gullo, Studi Giuridici 29 (Vatican City: Libreria Editrice Vaticana, 1994) 127, sub 25.B.2°; Antoni Stankiewicz, "I tribunali (artt. 22–64)," in *Il giudizio di nullità matrimoniale dopo l'Istruzione "Dignitas connubii." Parte Seconda: La parte statica del processo*, 49; Francisco Javier Urrutia, *De normis generalibus. Adnotationes in Codicem: Liber I* (Rome: Pontificia Universitas Gregoriana, 1983) 93; Myriam Wijlens, "Title VIII. The Power of Governance [cc. 129–144]," in *New Commentary on the Code of Canon Law*, ed. John P. Beal, James A. Coriden and Thomas J. Green (New York/Mahwah: Paulist Press, 2000) 189.

— Chiappetta observes that the legislator explicitly foresees the possibility of the delegation of judicial power by a supreme moderator of a clerical religious institute of pontifical right. And he notes that the delegation of judicial power was manifestly permitted in the 1917 code, while there was no clear intent to reform that matter.[41]
— Grocholewski compares the diocesan bishop to the Roman Pontiff in this matter, implicitly suggesting that those with the capital offices (i.e., those with the fullness of power in their field of competence) may equally delegate their judicial power.[42]
— Similarly, Arroba Conde asserts that the matter is solved by relying on canon 1442 as a parallel place (cf. c. 17). That is to say, just as the Roman Pontiff can delegate his judicial power, so can the diocesan bishop, since they are both exercising the same episcopal power, even if the scope of the power is diverse.[43]

In view of these arguments and the prevailing doctrine, there is no outstanding reason to doubt that the diocesan or eparchial bishop may delegate his judicial power to others. With application to our subject matter, it is certain that a cause of nullity of marriage legitimately treated according to the norms of the new canons 1683–1687 (*CCEO* cc. 1369–1373) may be decided by one to whom the bishop delegates the power to do so. Given the fact that the supreme legislator has deliberately entrusted this matter to the bishop, with particular stress placed on the role of the bishop as judge by divine right, it would nevertheless seem to be against the spirit of the law for the bishop to delegate this faculty *ad universitatem causarum* without a grave reason.

It is always for a delegating authority to determine who is suitable to be a delegate. As a rule, though, it would seem highly imprudent for the bishop to select someone who does not fulfill all the law's requirements for the office of judge. And, relying on a parallel place, since the delegate would be a sole judge, he must be a cleric (cf. *CIC* c. 1673 §4, *CCEO* c. 1359 §4). Accordingly, the delegate should be a priest (*sacerdos*) or deacon with

---

León del Amo takes it for granted that the bishop has this power (see "Chapter I. The Tribunal of First Instance," in *Code of Canon Law Annotated*, 1104).

41. See Chiappetta, *Il Codice di diritto canonico. Commento giuridico-pastorale*, 1: 188–189, no. 987 and 3: 22, no. 5138.

42. See Grocholewski, "Art. 1. The Judge," in *Exegetical Commentary*, IV/1: 718, no. 4.

43. See Manuel Jesús Arroba Conde, *Diritto processuale canonico*, 5th ed. (Rome: Editiones Institutum Iuridicum Claretianum, 2006) 93.

a doctorate or at least a licentiate in canon law, enjoying a good reputation and proven prudence and zeal for justice (cf. *CIC* c. 1421 §3, *CCEO* c. 1087 §3). A natural institutional choice would be the judicial vicar, who constitutes "one tribunal" with the bishop (*CIC* c. 1420 §2, *CCEO* c. 1086 §2), though other suitable clerics may be chosen.

II. Essential Material Presupposition to the Use of the Abbreviated Process: "Manifest" Nullity of Matrimonial Consent

The new canon 1683 of the *CIC* and canon 1369 of the *CCEO* establish two essential presuppositions to the legitimate use of the abbreviated process. The *essential formal presupposition* is the explicit consent of both spouses to use the abbreviated process, since that process contains far fewer procedural guarantees than the ordinary contentious process; and it must be clear that both spouses are willingly renouncing them. The *essential material presupposition* is that the nullity of marriage requires minimal judicial investigation and is in fact manifest at the outset of the abbreviated trial.

The formal presupposition is sufficiently clear in itself, but the material presupposition requires much further exploration. For it would seem to be in discontinuity with the canonical tradition, which has consistently considered a defect of consent to be difficult to prove, and even common sense, which finds the hidden reality of an act of the will placed in the past to be an inherently obscure matter, especially when masked by the public, external act of consent manifested apparently *scienter et volenter*. This section accordingly examines the principle of the objective difficulty of proof of a defect of matrimonial consent. This principle demands some analysis of article 14 §1 of the *Ratio procedendi*, which offers a list of cases of possibly manifest nullity. Finally, it is worthwhile in this context to investigate the title of competence of the Apostolic Signatura in virtue of which it can declare the nullity of marriage when there is no need for a deeper examination or investigation, since this may seem to resemble the new abbreviated process.

A. The Objective Difficulty of Proving a Defect of Matrimonial Consent

Prior to entering into the detailed dynamic norms governing the abbreviated matrimonial process, a fundamental matter needs to be explored and given careful reflection by those entrusted with the grave duty of administering justice in diocesan and eparchial tribunals, especially judicial vicars, who are the veritable gateway to the abbreviated process. It is a question of the legitimate use of the abbreviated process. The ordinary contentious process has been and remains the standard instrument of the Church for examining the alleged nullity of marriage due to a defect of consent; and thus it should be presumed that this is how such causes will typically be handled throughout the Church even after December 7, 2015.[44] The legitimate use of the abbreviated process depends, in part, upon the verification of a particular quality of facts presented with notable clarity. Indeed, the canonical legislator declares that the abbreviated process is meant "to be applied to cases in which the alleged nullity of marriage has for itself a basis of particularly evident arguments" (preamble, "IV.—*Processus brevior*," §1). He states elsewhere that it is used when the circumstances of the case "do not require a deeper examination or investigation and render nullity manifest" (*CIC* c. 1683, 2°; *CCEO* c. 1369, 2°). The ascertainment of the "manifest nullity" of consent must be done in continuity with the canonical science and forensic experience.

Prescinding from the question of whether it is in fact principally intended for regions of the Church that have no functioning tribunal despite being integrated into universal legislation, what is perhaps most perplexing about the institution of the abbreviated process is this notion of the manifest nullity of matrimonial consent. For as a rule, the nullity of consent is not something that is manifest, self-evident or, even within an ordinary judicial process, easily proven. Arriving at the truth about facts of the past always involves the reception by the judge of information in a form determined by its instrument (a person or a document), the judge's decoding of its real meaning, and the discernment of its juridical value in relation to other probative instruments.[45] Also, on account of the sensitive

---

44. "[T]he brief process is an exception to the general norm." Pontifical Council for Legislative Texts, Letter on the Consent of the Petitioner and the Respondent for the Use of the *processus brevior*, October 1, 2015 (Prot. N. 15138/2015): *The Jurist* 75 (2015) 664 and this volume, 368.

45. Cf., e.g., Emilio Colagiovanni, "Il giudice e la valutazione delle prove," in *I mezzi di prova nelle cause matrimoniali secondo la giurisprudenza rotale*, Studi Giuridici 38 (Vatican City: Libreria Editrice Vaticana, 1995) 10; Aidan McGrath, "From Proofs to Judgement: The Arduous Task of the Judge," in *The Art of the Good and Equitable. A Festschrift in Honor of Lawrence G. Wrenn*, ed. Frederick C. Easton (Washington, D.C.: The Canon Law Society of America, 2002) 147–173; Antoni Stankiewicz, "Le caratteristiche del sistema probatorio canonico," *Apollinaris*

and at times intense interpersonal implications of a marriage nullity trial, there are frequently practical difficulties at arriving at the truth about the alleged nullity of marriage. For example, this task can be hindered by "the bad faith of one of the parties who does not appear in the trial in acceptance of his responsibilities and who forbids parents and friends to testify and make their contribution to the search for the truth."[46]

The objective difficulty of proving nullity of marriage due to a defect of consent is often emphasized by jurisprudence, for example, in the context of examining the simulation of consent. In one place we read this standard observation of Rotal jurisprudence: "Proof of exclusion ... is difficult since it concerns an internal act in itself known fully to God alone."[47] This difficulty is something quite easily grasped upon reflection; for it is a hidden reality to which the simulator bore false public witness in the nuptial rite: "Simulation is not always easily proven, since the true internal will of a certain contracting party, not manifested externally, must be proven; for simulation occurs when a person reveals externally a will other than the one which he intended in his internal mind."[48] Indeed, proof of willfully defective consent is difficult and is even more difficult when some of the basic elements of proof are missing, such as a judicial confession: "If one of these or another is lacking, proof does not become impossible but, *since it is in itself already difficult (difficilis), becomes more difficult (difficilior)*" (emphasis added).[49]

Nor is this by any means limited to simulation but is true of any ground of defect of matrimonial consent. Proof of the incapacity to consent, for example, involves not only an examination of the hidden will of

---

67 (1994) 89–122. See also *La prova della nullità matrimoniale secondo la giurisprudenza della Rota Romana*, Studi Giuridici 91 (Vatican City: Libreria Editrice Vaticana, 2011) *passim*.

46. See Paolo Bianchi, "È più facile, col nuovo Codice di diritto canonico, dimostrare la nullità di un matrimonio? I canoni 1536, par. 2, e 1679," *Quaderni di diritto ecclesiale* 3 (1990) 395.

47. "Exclusionis boni sacramenti, sicuti cuiuscumque simulationis, difficilis est probatio cum agatur de actu interno plene per se soli Deo noto." Definitive Sentence *c*. Funghini, *Mediolanen*., December 18, 1991: *RRDec* 83: 793, no. 7.

48. "Simulatio non semper facile probatur, quoniam vera voluntas interna, extra non manifestata, cuiusdam contrahentis probanda est; simulatio enim evenit quando persona extra patefacit aliam voluntatem ab illa quam in animo suo interno intendit." Definitive Sentence *c*. Alwan, *Regien. in Aemilia-Guastellen.*, January 18, 2005: *RRDec* 97: 14, no. 8.

49. "Si una vel altera ex his deficiat probatio haud impossibilis evadit sed, cum iam difficilis ex sese sit, difficilior evadit." Definitive Sentence *c*. Davino, *Romana*, February 18, 1983: *RRDec* 75: 36–37, no. 4.

the person but also the existence of a psychic anomaly and its possible impact on the proper functioning of the intellective and volitive faculties of those contracting marriage. The direct proof of this, moreover, is ordinarily not immediately accessible to the judge but is drawn from the conclusions of experts in psychology and psychiatry, the juridical value of which conclusions is itself by no means self-evident; such conclusions, which can even be contradictory, demand critical evaluation. This is, as was stated by the celebrated and much-cited 1987 discourse of John Paul II to the Roman Rota, an "arduous task" since such are "difficult cases."[50] Indeed, whenever it is a question of a defect of consent, "it is not a matter of [cases] . . . which can easily be included in the category of notorious or evident cases."[51]

It is for these reasons that John Paul II declared in his February 4, 1980 discourse to the Roman Rota that reaching moral certitude in causes of nullity of marriage in general is a "difficult task." The evaluation of the proofs, he declares, is "the most demanding and delicate phase of the trial."[52] When reflecting on the new abbreviated process, it is critical for the Church to be "attentive to the gravity and difficulty of causes of nullity of marriage" (DC art. 33, *incipit*). Accordingly, notwithstanding the constitution of this procedural institute of the abbreviated process, it would seem to be in fact quite rare that the nullity of marriage due to a defect of consent is manifest or evident at the time of the submission of the *libellus*. Ordinarily, such nullity becomes evident only after the completion of the careful instruction of the cause, a technical discussion about it, and the judicial evaluation of the proofs as demonstrated for the parties in the definitive sentence—in other words, after the completion of the ordinary contentious process.

In North America, where "faster is better," canonists advising bishops on these matters, especially judicial vicars, should be deeply mindful of

---

50. *Papal Allocutions*, 195. Cf. Zenon Grocholewski, "Cause matrimoniali e '*modus agendi*' dei tribunali," *Ephemerides iuris canonici* 49 (1994) 134–138; Aidan McGrath, "Assisting Judges in Their Arduous Task: *Dignitas connubii* and the Assistance It Offers in Cases Based on Canon 1095," *Studies in Church Law* 4 (2008) 109–142.

51. See Zenon Grocholewski "Dichiarazioni di nullità di matrimonio in via amministrativa da parte del Supremo Tribunale della Segnatura Apostolica," *Ephemerides iuris canonici* 37 (1981) 196, *sub* 2). This was stated in the context of the Apostolic Signatura's competence to declare the nullity of marriage by a single executable decree without conducting a judicial process. On this topic, *vide infra* II.C.

52. *Papal Allocutions*, 161, no. 5.

the fact that a broad application of the abbreviated process would be irresponsible and would assuredly weaken the diligent search for the truth about the alleged nullity of marriage. Proof of nullity of marriage is a complicated matter, and the ordinary judicial process is the Church's time-tested instrument for ascertaining the truth about a matter of such importance, delicacy and obscurity. This was taught eloquently by John Paul II in his just-cited 1980 discourse to the Roman Rota. He declared:

> To limit as much as possible the margins of error in fulfilling the precious and delicate service performed by you, the Church has elaborated a procedure which, with the intention of ascertaining the objective truth will, on the one hand, ensure the parties the greatest security in advancing their own arguments, and on the other, consistently respect the divine command: 'Therefore what God has joined together, let no one separate' (Mk 10:9).[53]

In other words, unjustly supplanting the ordinary contentious process with the abbreviated process would widen the margin of error, weakening the ability of the judge to discover the truth. In this situation, the bishop may not discover the truth as could have been done in a more elaborate process, possibly leaving him to declare his lack of moral certitude about the alleged nullity of a truly null marriage, delaying that subsequent investigation unnecessarily after remitting the cause to an ordinary examination before the tribunal in first instance (cf. *CIC* c. 1687 §1, *CCEO* c. 1373 §1). Or worse, under the influence of false compassion and false charity, he may be tempted to declare the nullity of a marriage that is not proven to be null and that is truly valid, thus surrendering, as John Paul II taught in the same discourse, to a divorce-oriented mentality.[54] Anyone who has diligently carried out the work of the tribunal and examined these matters with any depth knows that the nullity of matrimonial consent is not something that

---

53. *Papal Allocutions*, 160, no. 2.
54. See *Papal Allocutions*, 162, no. 6. Later, in 1990, he would declare that "people also have the right not to be deceived by a judgment of nullity which is in conflict with the existence of a true marriage. Such an unjust declaration of nullity would find no legitimate support in appealing to love or mercy. Love and mercy cannot put aside the demands of truth. A valid marriage, even one marked by serious difficulties, could not be considered invalid without doing violence to the truth and undermining thereby the only solid foundation which can support personal, marital, and social life. A judge, therefore, must always be on guard against the risk of false compassion that would degenerate into sentimentality, and would be pastoral in appearance alone. The roads leading away from justice and truth end up in serving to distance people from God, thus yielding the opposite result from that which was sought in good faith" (ibid., 211, no. 5).

is ordinarily evident. And so it would be erroneous or disingenuous to see the reform as offering a means for the more simple declaration of nullity of marriage, when in the majority of case that nullity is not manifestly evident.

B. The Problem of Article 14 §1 of the *Ratio procedendi*

In this context, it is natural to reflect upon the norm of art. 14 §1 of the *Ratio procedendi* attached to both motu proprios, since they propose concrete scenarios (*factispecies*) in which the nullity of marriage may be manifest. It reads:

> Among the circumstances of events and persons which permit a cause of nullity of marriage to be treated according to the pathway of the abbreviated process of canons 1683–1687 [*CCEO* canons 1369–1373], the following are listed by way of example: a defect of faith which can give rise to simulation of consent or an error determining the will, the brevity of the common conjugal life, abortion procured in order to avoid procreation, an obstinate continuation of an extramarital relationship at the time of the wedding or immediately subsequent to it, deceitful concealment of sterility or of a serious contagious illness or of children from a previous relationship or of imprisonment, a motive for marrying that is entirely extraneous to the conjugal life or an unforeseen pregnancy, physical violence inflicted in order to coerce consent, a defect of the use of reason proven by medical documentation, etc.[55]

Many of these scenarios are quite familiar to ministers of justice, since some of them arise rather frequently in forensic experience. Their presentation in this way, however, brings not clarity but new questions. What is the character of this list? Does it establish new grounds of nullity? Does verification of any particular scenario on the list demand that the judicial

---

55. "Art. 14 §1. Inter rerum et personarum adiuncta quae sinunt causam nullitatis matrimonii ad tramitem processus brevioris iuxta cann. 1683–1687 pertractari, recensentur exempli gratia: is fidei defectus qui gignere potest simulationem consensus vel errorem voluntatem determinantem, brevitas convictus coniugalis, abortus procuratus ad vitandam procreationem, permanentia pervicax in relatione extraconiugali tempore nuptiarum vel immediate subsequenti, celatio dolosa sterilitatis vel gravis infirmitatis contagiosae vel filiorum ex relatione praecedenti vel detrusionis in carcerem, causa contrahendi vitae coniugali omnino extranea vel haud praevisa praegnantia mulieris, violentia physica ad extorquendum consensum illata, defectus usus rationis documentis medicis comprobatus, etc."

vicar decree use of the abbreviated process for the eventual decision of the diocesan or eparchial bishop?

In the first place, it should be clear that it is by no means certain that the supreme legislator intends to establish new grounds of nullity of marriage consent by means of the cited article 14 §1. From a formal perspective, this listed bears no resemblance to the legislative technique of the Latin and Eastern Codes according to which defects of consent are stated in law. The legislator, by his own standards as received from canonical tradition and demanded in justice, is bound to state in certain terms that a given law renders an act invalidating or a person juridically incapable: "Only (*tantum*) those laws are invalidating or juridically incapacitating by which it is expressly stated that an act is null or a person is juridically incapable" (*CIC* c. 10, *CCEO* c. 1495, emphasis added).[56] As regards defects of matrimonial consent, this is accomplished in the codes by means of consistent, clear formulae, such as: *matrimonium irritum reddit, invalide contrahit/ celebrat, invalidum est matrimonium, sunt incapaces matrimonii contrahendi/ celebrandi*, and the like (cf. *CIC* cc. 1095–1107, *CCEO* cc. 817–827). Nothing in the quoted art. 14 §1 resembles such expressions or declares any new grounds of nullity.

From a material perspective, the attentive reader notices that the list contains some scenarios that correspond with defects of consent already stated in the codes or recognized by apostolic jurisprudence, while others are events or circumstances that do not univocally pertain to the matrimonial will at the time of the wedding (*matrimonium in fieri*). The simulation of consent or an error determining the will perhaps related to a defect of faith (cf. *CIC* cc. 1099, 1101 §2; *CCEO* cc. 822, 824 §2), deceitful concealment of sterility (*CIC* cc. 1084 §3, 1098; *CCEO* cc. 801 §3, 821) or of children from a previous relationship, physical violence inflicted in order to coerce consent (cf. *CIC* c. 1103, *CCEO* c. 825) and a defect of the use of reason (*CIC* c. 1095, 1°; *CCEO* c. 818, 1°) are already recognized as defects of consent. Even these, however, are not typically known to be easily proven with evident arguments. For instance, the example of the defect of faith giving rise

---

56. Also, strictly speaking, this norm is not a *lex*, which is the object of the cited c. 10 of the *CIC* and c. 1495 of the *CCEO*: "Irritantes aut inhabilitantes eae tantum *leges* habendae sunt. . . ." Rather, it is a supreme administrative norm, as I suggest in my "An Analysis of Pope Francis' 2015 Reform of the General Legislation Governing Causes of Nullity of Marriage," *The Jurist* 75 (2015) *supra* in this fascicle, at section III.D.1.

to simulation may be treated in apostolic jurisprudence under the heading of partial simulation against the sacramental dignity of marriage; and the nullity of marriage on such a ground is usually found not to be verified after an ordinary contentious trial, to say nothing of being manifestly evident.[57]

The others, however, are particular fact patterns that the common jurisprudence recognizes as *possible indications of a defect of consent* but not defects of consent themselves. "The brevity of the common conjugal life" is a subsequent circumstance that could be indicative of some defect of consent but could just as likely be attributed to the willful abandonment of a valid marriage, which is particularly realistic and verifiable with tragic frequency in divorce-oriented cultures. Likewise, an "abortion procured in order to avoid procreation" could be indicative of partial simulation *contra bonum prolis* when it is proven that the abortion was procured in execution of a positive exclusion of procreation at the time of the wedding; but it could just as likely be the rejection of the gift of life in an isolated instance having no proven connection to the matrimonial will. The scenario of "an obstinate continuation of an extramarital relationship at the time of the wedding or immediately subsequent to it" may correspond with the ground of partial simulation *contra bonum fidei*; but these may also in a particular case be only commissions of grave sin by one who had elicited an integral act of matrimonial consent, since—as the common jurisprudential maxim states it—"*praxis adulterina est argumentum sat aequivocum.*"[58] The "deceitful concealment of a serious contagious illness or . . . of imprisonment" may be examples of the ground of *dolus*, but it is not evident that these facts would always "by their very nature gravely disturb conjugal life" (*CIC* c. 1098, *CCEO* c. 821). The existence of "a motive for marrying that is entirely extraneous to the conjugal life" could in extreme cases constitute indirect total simulation or some kind of partial simulation; but the nullifying consequences of such a fact depend upon other factors,

---

57. Cf. Definitive Sentence *c.* Carberletti, *Bratislavien.-Tyrnavien.*, October 24, 2003: *RRDec* 95: 623, no. 4; Definitive Sentence *c.* Boccafola, *Brunen.*, May 6, 2004: *RRDec* 96: 278 and 279, nn. 7 and 9; Definitive Sentence *c.* Turnaturi, *Ferrarien.-Comaclen.*, July 21, 2005: *RRDec* 97: 403–407, nn. 14–18; Definitive Sentence *c.* De Angelis, *Veronen.*, March 10, 2006: *RRDec* 98: 38–40, nn. 7–8; Definitive Sentence *c.* Yaacoub, *Bononien.*, November 27, 2007: *RRDec* 99: 331, no. 9.

58. Sacred Roman Rota, Definitive Sentence *c.* Sabattani, *Southvarcen.*, November 13, 1959: *RRDec* 51: 503, no. 4.

especially whether there was a prevailing proximate motive to simulate (*causa simulandi*). And the fact of "an unforeseen pregnancy," which is a frequently occurring phenomenon, has often accompanied many Rotal decisions decided in the negative and, as a motive for marriage, has in fact even been placed in a relatively positive light as the exercise of personal responsibility for the good of the child to be born.[59]

Whatever the case may be, the judicial vicar who is considering the admission of a *libellus* to the abbreviated process should take careful note of the fact that such scenarios are not in and of themselves manifest causes of nullity of consent but are in fact merely examples that the legislator is proposing as imaginable (though not certain) scenarios of manifest nullity. They could only be seen to be such if all the other circumstances supported such a conclusion at the outset of the trial (cf. *CIC* c. 1683, 2°; *CCEO* c. 1369, 2°).

C. The Declaration of Nullity of Marriage by the Apostolic Signatura without a Trial

One part of the new canon on the introduction of a cause of nullity of marriage for treatment via the abbreviated process declares that that process may be used when the circumstances "do not require a deeper examination or investigation," using the phrase *"accuratiorem disquisitionem aut investigationem non exigant"* (*CIC* c. 1683, 2°; *CCEO* c. 1369, 2°). This expression is part of canonical tradition, having been used to describe a past title of competence of the Sacred Congregation for the Discipline of the Sacraments. Among its other titles of competence in regard to marriage, questions concerning the validity of marriage could be deferred to it, though it was to remit to a competent tribunal cases that demanded a deeper examination or investigation: "Pariter ad eam deferri possunt quaestiones de validitate matrimonii, quas tamen, *si accuratiorem disquisitionem aut investigationem exigant*, ad tribunal competens remittat" (*CIC*/17 c. 249 §3, emphasis added).[60]

Paul VI's 1967 reform of the Roman Curia transferred this title of competence to the Supreme Tribunal of the Apostolic Signatura, seeing

---

59. See especially the Definitive Sentence *c.* Ferreira Pena, *Bogoten.*, April 19, 2002: *RRDec* 94: 258–259, nn. 8–9 and 265, no. 19.

60. This text is substantially the same in the parallel Eastern norm. See Pius XII, motu proprio *Cleri sanctitati*, June 2, 1957: *AAS* 49 (1957) 491, at c. 196 §3.

that it was and is an aspect of the function of exercising vigilance over the administration of justice in the Church, in particular the more rapid administration of justice when the faithful in a particular region have no tribunal to approach, especially in mission territories.[61] A later pontifical provision would refine the Signatura's manner of treating such cases: "It appears opportune that the decisions in the matter be made by the [Prefect in] *Congresso*, with a prior *votum 'pro rei veritate,'*" that is, not by the plenary body of the Signatura, "for two reasons: *a)* because it is a question of cases that are simple and evident; *b)* because such cases in general require a rapid procedure."[62] This title of competence has been and remains the Signatura's, whose proper law says that this faculty may be used for "cases which do not require a deeper examination and investigation" (*"accuratiorem disquisitionem vel investigationem non exigant"*).[63]

In the experience of the Apostolic Signatura, such cases are quite rare. Within the period of August 1967 to June 2011, there were only 22 declarations of nullity in virtue of this title of competence.[64] And it is its praxis ordinarily to admit such causes only when they originate from a region

---

61. Cf. Paul VI, apostolic constitution *Regimini Ecclesiæ universæ*, August 15, 1967: *AAS* 59 (1967) 921, no. 105.

62. See Paul VI, rescript, Prot. N. 5374/74 VAR, March 21, 1974: *Leges Ecclesiae post Codicem iuris canonici editae*, ed. Javier Ochoa (Rome: Institutum Iuridicum Claretianum, 1980) 5: 6784–6785, no. 4277.

On this history and a thorough analysis of the matter and the jurisprudence of the Signatura, see Zenon Grocholewski, "La facoltà del Congresso della Segnatura Apostolica di emettere dichiarazioni di nullità di matrimonio in via amministrativa," in *Investigationes theologico-canonicae* (Rome: Università Gregoriana Editrice, 1978) 211–232; idem, "Dichiarazioni di nullità di matrimonio," 177–204; Raymond L. Burke, "La procedura amministrativa per la dichiarazione di nullità del matrimonio," in *I procedimenti speciali nel diritto canonico*, 93–105.

63. See art. 118 of the *Lex propria STSA*.

64. From 1967 to 1981, there were 16 declarations of nullity of marriage (see Grocholewski, "Dichiarazioni di nullità di matrimonio," 195, *sub* 1; for a chronicle of negative responses given to petitions for such a declaration of nullity, see ibid., 200–203); from 1981 to 1991, there were five (see Burke, "La procedura amministrativa," 101; there were also two negatives during that period [ibid., 104–105]); and from 1991 to 2007 there was only one (see Frans Daneels, "La vigilanza sui tribunali: Introduzione al Titolo V della *Lex propria*," in *La "Lex propria" del S.T. della Segnatura Apostolica*, ed. Piero Antonio Bonnet and Carlo Gullo, Studi Giuridici 89 (Vatican City: Libreria Editrice Vaticana, 2010) 209–210). Cf. Joaquín Llobell, "Articoli preliminari [di *Dignitas connubii*]," in *Norme procedurali canoniche commentate*, 273.

In the cited study, Frans Daneels, who is the secretary of the Supreme Tribunal, notes that some requests were sent after the publication of the instruction *Dignitas connubii*, likely because of art. 5 §2 of that document; but these were not truly cases that did not demand a deeper examination or investigation.

lacking functioning tribunals and to deny a declaration of nullity of marriage when there is a functioning tribunal available to the parties, even if the alleged nullity seems well established.[65] For this is the limit of its competence. At times, though, a cause may be admitted before the Signatura when there is a functioning tribunal which, however, cannot suitably handle the cause due to personal and local circumstances (e.g., the risk of public bewilderment were the cause to be handled locally).[66]

The precise object of such causes of nullity of marriage is not too diverse. The cited studies published by Grocholewski and Burke reveal that the most common *caput nullitatis* is force or grave fear, of which there have been 13 cases reported. There have also been four cases of the impediment of impotence. Apart from these, there is one of each of the following: partial simulation *contra bonum sacramenti*, unspecified simulation, total simulation,[67] and grave defect of discretion of judgment.[68] What is characteristic of all of these cases is the fact that at the beginning of the Apostolic Signatura's treatment of the cause, it was already thoroughly instructed, or it was instructed to a significant degree and the Signatura called upon the local authority (usually the local bishop or nuncio) to supplement the instruction. Such instruction usually consisted of sworn statements of the spouses and witnesses taken before the bishop, and sometimes of expert reports when the case warranted it. These cases fell within the Signatura's competence not because the nullity of marriage was in itself obvious or manifest but because the conclusive proofs of nullity were already largely gathered, while, for the most part, there was no competent tribunal in a position to carry out a trial.

This title of competence of the Apostolic Signatura seems somewhat to resemble the "manifest nullity" anticipated by the abbreviated process

---

65. Cf. Daneels, "La vigilanza sui tribunali," 209; Llobell, "Articoli preliminari," 272–273; G. Paolo Montini, "La nuova legge della Segnatura Apostolica a servizio della retta e spedita trattazione delle cause matrimoniali," *Quaderni di diritto ecclesiale* 23 (2010) 492–493; Nikolaus Schöch, "Presentazione della *Lex propria* del Supremo Tribunale della Segnatura Apostolica," *Anuario Argentino del Derecho Canónico* 15 (2008) 224.

66. Grocholewski observes that this was verified in two causes *Chilavenses* (see "La facoltà del Congresso," 226–228).

67. The decree of the Apostolic Signatura in this case is published in *Il diritto ecclesiastico* 102–II (1991) 487–489.

68. See Burke, "La procedura amministrativa," 100–101, at notes 33 and 34, where the author lists each cause, providing the protocol number, the originating diocese, the ground of nullity, and the date of the decree.

instituted by Pope Francis. It may be that this competence of the Signatura even inspired some aspects of the abbreviated matrimonial process before the diocesan or eparchial bishop. For, as was observed, in many of these cases the proofs were assembled by the local bishop, though he did not proceed to declare the nullity of the marriage but rather transmitted the cause to the Apostolic See, where it was taken up before the Apostolic Signatura. An application of the principle of subsidiarity may lead one to wonder why the bishop should have to send the matter to Rome and not simply decide the cause himself with his innate judicial power.

There is even a procedural parallel between the two institutes. For the need for no deeper examination or investigation amounts to the need for no judicial treatment of the cause, or a trial. For its part, the Signatura can carry out some investigation, by requesting additional information and proofs from the parties; but it would remit the cause to a competent tribunal or entrust the cause to a relatively incompetent tribunal if it judged that a trial were needed, that is, if the Signatura were not morally certain of the alleged nullity without a deeper investigation.[69] Similarly, the diocesan or eparchial bishop who does not reach moral certitude about the alleged nullity of marriage after examining the acts and the arguments from the abbreviated process entrusts the cause to the competent tribunal so that the matter may be examined via the ordinary contentious trial (CIC c. 1687 §1, CCEO c. 1373 §1). Given this similarity, one may wonder if the Signatura's jurisprudence and praxis in this matter would be a valuable source for implementing the abbreviated process.

In fact, despite some similarities, it is not appropriate to see in the competence of the Apostolic Signatura a precedent for the declaration of "manifest nullity" via the abbreviated matrimonial process before the diocesan or eparchial bishop. For, as was explained, the causes introduced before the Signatura typically have already been instructed extrajudicially before the local bishop, sometimes with the aid of the nunciature or even an interested dicastery of the Roman Curia, such as the Congregation for the Evangelization of Peoples, under whose jurisdiction many

---

69. See DC art. 5 §2. Cf. Grocholewski, "La facoltà del Congresso," 222, 229–230; idem, "Dichiarazioni di nullità di matrimonio," 191–192; Burke, "La procedura amministrativa," 96–97; Velasio De Paolis, "Amministrazione della giustizia e situazione dei tribunali ecclesiastici," in Curso de derecho matrimonial y procesal canónico para profesionales del foro (XVIII), ed. Myriam Cortés Diéguez and José San José Prisco, Bibliotheca Salamanticensis, Estudios 300 (Salamanca: Universidad Pontificia, 2007) 444.

of the petitioning parties and bishops are situated. This is legitimate in these cases, since the local authorities ordinarily have no tribunal before which a cause of nullity of marriage can be adjudicated; and they simply gather proofs in an authentic manner in preparation for the judgment of the Apostolic Signatura. In the abbreviated process before the bishop, however, proofs may not licitly be gathered extrajudicially. It is true that there may be "a prejudicial or pastoral investigation" which may include the collection of "elements useful for possibly carrying out an ordinary or abbreviated judicial process," namely, with the aid of suitable persons approved by the local ordinary or hierarch (*RP* artt. 2–5). This, however, is the preparatory work of the party carried out with the aid of knowledgeable, approved persons, especially in places that do not have easily accessible experts who can be hired as an advocate. The *libellus* only indicates the proofs that *will* be gathered in the process; apart from any documents that may be submitted at the outset, the proofs may not be submitted with the *libellus* (cf. *CIC* c. 1684, *CCEO* c. 1370). The judicial gathering of proofs is always under the moderation of the judge or auditor (instructor); and in the abbreviated process this is done at the live session conducted by the instructor (*CIC* c. 1686, *CCEO* c. 1372). For these reasons, it is, *stricto sensu*, inconceivable that the elements introducing the abbreviated process could lead to the conclusion that no deeper examination or investigation is needed—that the circumstances and facts proposed *"accuratiorem disquisitionem vel investigationem non exigant."* For even in the face of a *libellus pro processu breviori*, the investigation or the examination of the parties and witnesses still has to be carried out.

Another major difference between the two processes is the matter of the existence of a functioning tribunal. The Signatura's competence typically presupposes the inexistence of a functioning tribunal or at least the moral unavailability of such a tribunal. The reformed norms, at least *ad litteram*, presuppose the existence of a tribunal in the diocese or eparchy whose bishop is handling the cause or at least his ability to call upon a neighboring tribunal (cf. *CIC* cc. 1673 §2, 1687 §1; *CCEO* cc. 1359 §2, 1373 §1).

Moreover, the Signatura is the most qualified (*peritissima*) for ascertaining these matters due to the highest expertise with which its officials are endowed and its long experience with promoting the use of a correct jurisprudence in all the tribunals of the world. The individual diocesan or eparchial bishop may have little or no experience or learning in these matters. It should not be thought that just any ecclesiastical authority can critically evaluate and weigh proofs in a cause of nullity of marriage with the skill of an apostolic dicastery of justice.

The existence of a process predicated on the "evident nullity" of marriage justifies that a final point be underlined. An examination of the literature on the Signatura's competence in this matter reveals the more proper sense in which the "manifest" or "evident" nullity of marriage is to be understood. This title of competence is mentioned in art. 5 §2 of the instruction *Dignitas connubii* which uses the phrase, "for cases in which it is apparent that nullity is evident" (*nullitas evidens appareat*). The above cited authors Daneels, Montini, Schöch, Llobell and Baura,[70] who are all officials of the Apostolic Signatura, recognize that this expression was not incorporated into the Signatura's proper law issued three-and-a-half years after the publication of that instruction, since it could obscure the fact that moral certitude is necessary and sufficient for deciding in favor of nullity. That is, it could give the impression that a higher degree of certitude is required, namely, that the alleged nullity is observable without the need for any evaluation of the proofs or facts. In reality, moral certitude is the standard used before the Signatura in such causes, and it is likewise the standard to be used by the bishop (see *RP* art. 12). It would seem highly unlikely that a petition introducing the abbreviated process before the bishop could make the nullity of marriage consent plain at first glance without the need for evaluation, which would seem to be the proper sense of "evident nullity." More accurately—and I suspect this is what the legislator truly has in mind—such a petition would enjoy a strong *fumus boni iuris*, rendering it likely that moral certitude can be reached even in an abbreviated or summary process.

III. The Phases of the Abbreviated Process (*pars dynamica*)

The judicial process has four principal phases, each of which contribute to the gradual development of the investigation for the truth of the contested matter. They are the following: 1) the *introductory phase*, which includes the

---

70. See Daneels, "La vigilanza sui tribunali," 209; Montini, "La nuova legge della Segnatura Apostolica," 492–493; Schöch, "Presentazione della *Lex propria*," 224; Llobell, "Articoli preliminari," 273; Eduardo Baura, "Le sanzioni disciplinari, i ricorsi gerarchici, le dichiarazioni di nullità del matrimonio," in *La "Lex propria" del S.T. della Segnatura Apostolica*, 366–367.

introduction of the *libellus*, the citation of the parties and the formulation of the doubt, 2) the *instructional phase*, which consists of the gathering of proofs in a way that is marked with publicity vis-à-vis the parties, 3) the *discussion phase*, in which the parties and advocates propose arguments, and 4) the *decisional phase*, in which the competent judge reaches a decision and communicates it to the parties.[71] While these are marked with greater solemnity and formality in the ordinary process, they also inform the oral contentious and abbreviated matrimonial process and ensure its rational sequence. A brief examination of these phases are the object of this final section.

In examining these phases, the primary point of reference is obviously the norms of the process enunciated in the two motu proprios in the section on the abbreviated matrimonial process before the bishop. Just as important, however, are the norms of the ordinary contentious trial, which is stated by the reform itself as a general norm to be applied unless the nature of the matter suggests otherwise (see CIC c. 1691 §3, CCEO c. 1377 §3). And as will be observed below, some cross reference to other matrimonial procedural norms is necessary.

A. Introductory Phase

As was observed above, the essential formal and material presuppositions to the legitimate use of the abbreviated matrimonial process are, respectively, the explicit consent of both spouses and the verification of manifest nullity without the need for a deeper examination or investigation. These presuppositions are obviously elements that are to be assessed by the judicial vicar *in limine iudicii brevioris* and are here examined from a procedural point of view. In addition, the rights of the defender of the bond at the outset of the trial are examined, since he or she, too, is a party to the abbreviated process.

---

71. This pattern is describe crisply in the following terms by Zenon Grocholewski: "In processu distingui possunt quattuor periodi: introductoria, instructoria seu probatoria (colliguntur probationes), discussoria (disceptatio fit inter partes et defensorem vinculi atque promotorem iustitiae si iudicio intersint) et decisoria (fertur decisio)." See his "De periodo initiali seu introductoria processus in causis nullitatis matrimonii," *Periodica* 85 (1996) 83.

1. The Libellus and the Consent of the Respondent

As with any judicial cause, in view of the principle *nemo iudex sine actore*, the abbreviated process is introduced by, or presupposes, the submission of a *libellus* (CIC c. 1684, CCEO c. 1370) by one or both of the spouses, or by the promoter of justice if the case warrants it (cf. CIC c. 1674 §1, 2°; CCEO c. 1360 §1, 2°). This *libellus* may include a request that the cause be treated via the abbreviated process, but this is not necessary. Indeed, the proposal of such a process would seem to be ordinarily the initiative of one or both spouses (cf. CIC c. 1683, 1°; CCEO c. 1369, 1°); but even without such a request, the judicial vicar, in weighing the *libellus*, may propose that the cause be treated via the abbreviated process (*RP* art. 15). Even in such a case, though, both spouses must be notified of the eventual use of the abbreviated process and consent to it. And it is necessary that at least one of them in fact wish to pursue the abbreviated process by submitting a suitable *libellus* which indicates more specifically the proofs that the judge can gather immediately (ibid.; CIC c. 1684, 2°; CCEO c. 1370, 2°).

In any case, unlike in the ordinary contentious trial, the spouse who has not introduced the cause must consent to the use of the abbreviated process and not merely not object to it. The norm of CIC c. 1683, 1° and CCEO c. 1369, 1° makes this clear with the expression *altero consentiente*, not *altero non excipiente* or something similar.[72] This expression must be read strictly, since it treats an exception to the ordinary pathway of the ordinary contentious trial and since it involves limitations of the defender of the bond's procedural rights, which are far fewer in the abbreviated process (cf. CIC c. 18, CCEO c. 1500). Accordingly, the inability to locate the respondent impedes the use of the abbreviated process.[73]

---

72. "The brief process cannot be used, if the respondent remains silent, [and] does not sign the petition or declare his consent. The new canon 1683 and Art. 15 of the procedural norms make clear that the consent of the petitioner and the respondent (whether given by a joint signature of the parties or by other means) is a preliminary condition to initiate the brief process. The consent of both parties required to initiate this procedure is a condition *sine qua non*. This explicit consent is foremost necessary because the brief process is an exception to the general norm." Pontifical Council for Legislative Texts, Letter on the Consent of the Petitioner and the Respondent for the Use of the *processus brevior*, October 1, 2015 (Prot. N. 15139/2015): *The Jurist* 75 (2015) 665 and this volume, 369.

73. "If the whereabouts of a respondent are unknown, the case cannot be accepted for the *processus brevior*." Pontifical Council for Legislative Texts, Letter on the Conversion of a Formal Canonical Proces into a *processor brevior* and Consent of the Petitioner and the

This essential, explicit assent of both spouses is a natural consequence of *the right of the spouses to the ordinary contentious trial*, such that a party's demand for such a trial impedes the use of the abbreviated process.[74] Indeed, the presence of such assent is seen in each of the follow scenarios:

1) The abbreviated process is requested by both spouses, in which case they clearly both consent (*CIC* c. 1683, 1°; *CCEO* c. 1369, 1°);
2) It is requested by one spouse and the other consents (ibid.);
3) It is proposed by the judicial vicar and both spouses consent or at least one of them prepares a proper *libellus* and the other then consents (*RP* art. 15);
4) It is requested by the promoter of justice who has submitted the *libellus*, and, if the judicial vicar does not reject the request, he proposes it to the parties according to the norm of art. 15 of the *RP*.

The eventual joint submission of the *libellus* by the spouses (*consortium litis activum*) could give rise to a fear of collusion between them in order to obtain a declaration of nullity being sought by them both. This, however, would concretely be a problem of the integrity of the proofs, which will be treated below.

2. Assessment of Supposedly Manifest Nullity

Upon receipt of a *libellus* requesting the abbreviated process, or even of a *libellus* requesting an ordinary process, the foundational matter to be weighed by the judicial vicar is whether there is truly any question of "manifest nullity" or the existence of particularly "evident arguments." As was demonstrated above, this would not be a common occurrence, since the nullity of marriage due to a defect of consent is rarely certain at the outset, much less evident. And so the judicial vicar should be prepared to admit causes to the ordinary process as a standard course of action, even if the spouses request the abbreviated process on the basis of a simplistic understanding of the nullity of marriage or a facile invocation of one of the scenarios mentioned in art. 14 §1 of the *RP*. When weighing the supposed manifest nullity of matrimonial consent, the judicial vicar will attend carefully to the circumstances of fact (*species facti*) described

---

Respondent for the Use of the *processus brevior*, October 1, 2015 (Prot. N. 15138/2015): *The Jurist* 75 (2015) 664 and this volume, 368.

74. Cf. *CIC* c. 1656 §1, *CCEO* c. 1343 §1.

in the *libellus*, the specific proofs that are proposed, as well as any related probative documentation. Examples of this that can be imagined, *positis ponendis*, include the following.

(1) A *libellus* revealing the case of a person afflicted with a well-documented, serious mental disability or personality disorder, hospitalized several times prior to and after consent, who was nevertheless admitted to marriage in the Church while lacking any ability for a conjugal relationship, could be a case well supported with a strong *fumus boni iuris*. The abbreviated process could be justified when the *libellus* promises the testimony of the parents, siblings and peers of the ill person, who will all testify to the consistent illness and disturbing behavior of their loved one, incapable of normal interpersonal relationships.

(2) The same could be true of a *libellus* that displays the clear coercion inflicted on a 17-year-old young woman by her aggressive father, who was enraged by her premarital pregnancy, when her total dependence upon him for her material and emotional well-being is indisputable from the circumstances. The *libellus* promises the confession of the father and the testimony of both families about the lack of a conjugal relationship between the spouses and the extreme brevity of their common life.

Other examples could be imagined. As is known to any experienced minister of justice, however, the majority of *libelli* received at the tribunal are far more subtle. And the same *libelli*, while they may enjoy the *fumus boni iuris*, not infrequently raise more questions than they answer, thus demanding a careful, thorough judicial investigation.

3. Rights of the Defender of the Bond

Although the defender of the bond is a party equal to the spouses (cf. *CIC* c. 1434, *CCEO* c. 1098), he or she is unfortunately not treated as such at the introductory stage of the abbreviated process. It is true that the defender of the bond has a right to be heard prior to the decision about which process is to be used, namely, the ordinary or the abbreviated (see *CIC* c. 1676 §§1–2, *CCEO* c. 1362 §§1–2). Indeed, in his or her *votum praevium*, he or she may legitimately observe that the nullity of marriage is not manifestly evident or that the consent of the respondent is missing or uncertain and thus insist that the ordinary process be used. Nevertheless, this public minister of justice does not enjoy the same peremptory faculty to request the ordinary contentious trial as the spouses. In other words, the defender of the bond's objection or non-consent to the use of the abbreviated process does not impede its use. This is a departure from the spirit of the judicial system which, in application of the *favor matrimonii*, treats the public minister of justice as an equal party, especially in a matter so foundational to the process.[75]

Nevertheless, the defender of the bond maintains the right to make recourse against the decree of the formulation of the doubt in which the judicial vicar determines that the abbreviated process is to be used. For such a decree[76] does not merely give impulse to the process, like a decree of instruction, a decree establishing a time limit, or another ordinatory decree. Rather, it is a decision that is prejudicial against the bond, which will enjoy far fewer protections in the trial than it would via the ordinary contentious trial. And so, especially if the arguments against use of the abbreviated process stated in his or her *votum praevium* went unheeded by the judicial vicar, the defender of the bond may make recourse.

The recourse in question is not an appeal, which remedy is not immediately available against this decree inasmuch as it lacks the force of a definitive sentence, or the criterion of finality (cf. *CIC* c. 1629, 4°; *CCEO* c. 1310, 4°; *DC* art. 280 §1, 4°). Rather, this is a procedural recourse, which is a standard element of any judicial process. The problem is the identification of the authority competent to receive and judge the recourse. Ordinarily, recourse against a decree of one judge is made to the college of judges.[77] At this introductory stage of the process, however, there is no college of judges, which is only constituted after the judicial vicar has decreed the formulation of the doubt and the use of the ordinary contentious process (cf. *CIC* c. 1676 §3, *CCEO* c. 1362 §3). The recourse may not be directed to

---

75. Indeed, in a cause of the separation of spouses, it is not only the spouses but also the promoter of justice who can request the ordinary contentious process and thus inhibit the use of the oral or summary contentious process (*CIC* c. 1693 §1). While the promoter of justice is not named in the parallel Eastern norm, he or she in fact has this right also before an Eastern tribunal, since the parallel norm (*CCEO* c. 1379 §1) says that a party may request the ordinary process, and the promoter of justice is a party and must intervene in that process (cf. cc. 1098, 1382).

76. Cf. *CIC* c. 1617; *CCEO* c. 1300; *DC* art. 261.

77. Cf. Tribunal of the Roman Rota, Decree *c.* Pompedda, *Florentina*, July 8, 1986: *RRDecreta* 4: 118–119, no. 10; *DC* art. 221 §2.

the diocesan or eparchial bishop, since the judicial vicar constitutes one tribunal with him; he is not a hierarchically related judicial organ. Nor may the recourse be directed to the appellate tribunal, since this would transfer the cause to the jurisdiction of another tribunal, which may only be done after the jurisdiction of the tribunal *a quo* has ceased through issuance of an act having the force of a definitive sentence or a legitimate *avocatio causae*. Indeed, since the judicial vicar in this matter is the sole judge and personifies the tribunal (cf. *CCEO* c. 1092), recourse may only be made immediately to him, which resembles a request for a *beneficium novae audientiae* or which could amount to a complaint of nullity against the decree, if the case warrants it. Should the judicial vicar reject the recourse, the defender of the bond would justly raise the objection again in his or her observations to be made for the bishop's deliberations. And he or she would retain the right to appeal an eventual affirmative decision of the bishop on the basis of the illegitimate use of the abbreviated process, especially if the nullity of marriage still remains objectively in doubt.

B. Instructional Phase

Potentially by means of a single decree, or in distinct decrees issued at about the same time, the judicial vicar establishes the formulation of the doubt, determines that the abbreviated process is to be used, appoints the instructor (perhaps himself—*RP* art. 16) and the assessor, and summons the parties, witnesses and, where needed, expert(s) to the instructional session (*sessio instructoria*).[78] The summons is communicated individually to each of the parties (the spouses and the defender of the bond) and the witnesses and expert(s), who must appear at the appointed date and time or offer a just excuse for not being able to do so, which the judge either admits or rejects. Rejection of such an excuse may take the form of an admonition to appear or a declaration of the person's absence.[79] The instructor can and must cite persons and order the presentation of documents which he deems necessary for the discovery of the truth, even if the spouses have neglected or refuse to introduce them (cf. *CIC* c. 1452, *CCEO* c. 1110). The parties have a right to know the names of all the witnesses who will be deposed at the instructional session (cf. *CIC* c. 1554, *CCEO* c. 1235) and may

---

78. Cf. *CIC* c. 1676 §2, 1685; *CCEO* cc. 1362 §2, 1371.
79. Cf. *CIC* cc. 1556–1557, *CCEO* cc. 1237–1238, *DC* art. 142.

suggest questions to be proposed to them and to the spouses no less than three days prior to the session (*RP* art. 17).

The process is considered abbreviated principally because of the expedience with which the instruction is carried out. As soon as possible after the formulation of the doubt, but no more than thirty days later, it is to be carried out entirely on one day—if possible, at a single session (*"una sessione"*—*CIC* c. 1686, *CCEO* c. 1372). Such a session may last a full day, but the circumstances of persons and places may demand a follow-up session; nor would it seem extraordinary for the instructor to need to issue rogatorial letters so that another tribunal may assist with the instruction of the cause (cf. *CIC* c. 1418, *CCEO* c. 1071). Since this could cause delays in what is meant to be an abbreviated process, the called upon tribunal may consider whether it should prioritize the completion of the rogatorial commission (cf. *CIC* c. 1458, *CCEO* c. 1117).

The instructional session has the same external dynamics as any judicial examination, wherein the instructor administers an oath and questions the deponent. The notary, at the direction of the instructor, writes the responses of the deponent that pertain to the substance of the case, legitimately omitting peripheral comments, opinions, and other irrelevant information (cf. *RP* art. 18 §2, *DC* art. 173 §1). The defender of the bond and the advocates, if there are any, are present but may not speak during the interrogation. They may quietly propose questions for the instructor to ask, but he or she may refrain from doing so if they seem superfluous, irrelevant or inappropriate (cf. *CIC* c. 1561, *CCEO* c. 1242).

In principle, the spouses are present for the judicial examination of each other and of the witnesses and expert(s). However, the instructor may insist that the spouses and advocates be absent during some or all of the interrogations if there is any concern that their presence may influence the candor or honesty of the deponent (cf. *RP* art. 18 §1). One would in fact expect it to be an ordinary practice to insist that the spouses be absent for all the interrogations, while their advocates would remain present in order to protect the right of defense. For human nature would ordinarily lead one to be disinclined to declare the full truth with total openness to the instructor when there could be immediate social consequences. If a party or witness is giving responses only before the instructor, assessor, notary, defender of the bond and the advocates, he or she may speak openly and fearlessly, and the act of the deposition may justly omit those more delicate statements which in fact may have little to do with the central questions in the case. Moreover, if there has been any collusion between the spouses and the witnesses, this could be more easily discovered in the absence of any private parties, since the social expectation induced by the presence of the one or both spouses would be eliminated, and the instructor's more probing scrutiny would be more efficacious.[80]

When the instructor prudently decides that the spouses are not to be present at the judicial examinations, it is necessary to take special care lest their right of defense be denied. For there is no publication of the acts in the abbreviated process. At a minimum, as was observed, the presence of the advocate(s) at the interrogations would ensure protection of the right of defense. Beyond this, it would seem licit for the judge to offer the spouses an opportunity individually to examine the acts, since they have been drawn up by the notary (cf. RP art. 18 §2) and could be inspected under supervision of the instructor.

It could happen that a ground of nullity of marriage not stated in the formulation of the doubt would be discovered during the instructional session. This would give rise to a possible modification of the formulation of the doubt, if the nullity of marriage on the new ground is likewise considered to be manifest in the case. The modification could only validly occur at the request of one of the spouses, after having heard the other spouse and the defender of the bond, with a formal declaration by the judge, which is to be put in writing (cf. *CIC* c. 1514, *CCEO* c. 1196). Evidently, this could be done quite conveniently, since all the interested parties would be present at the tribunal on the occasion of the modification of the grounds.

C. Discussion Phase

The discussion of the cause is that technical interpretative dialogue that occurs between the public minister of justice (typically in this case, the defender of the bond) and the advocates and the spouses under the moderation of the judge. Ordinarily, it involves the presentation of arguments, the (opportunity for) mutual response to the arguments of the others, and the final response of the defender of the bond (cf. *CIC* cc. 1601, 1603; *CCEO*

---

80. Daneels prudently observes in this regard: "Non sembra che nelle cause per la dichiarazione della nullità del matrimonio la raccolta delle prove in presenza delle parti sia la strada migliore per scoprire la verità circa questioni spesso molto delicate" ("Osservazioni sul processo," 84).

cc. 1284, 1286). This true dialogue aids the judge in refining the principal questions and in discovering the more rational arguments that support (or not) the allegation(s) in the case.

In the abbreviated process, no real dialogue among the parties is envisioned. Rather, at the end of the instructional session, the instructor issues a decree establishing a time limit of fifteen days for the presentation of the arguments. These are not exchanged but are simply submitted to the instructor, who presents them to the diocesan or eparchial bishop together with all the acts (cf. *CIC* cc. 1686, 1687 §1; *CCEO* cc. 1372, 1373 §1). The arguments are carefully examined also by the instructor and the assessor, who offer their counsel to the bishop. While there is no exchange of arguments, this is a welcome element of the abbreviated process since the written, unlike the oral, presentation of arguments best affords the judge the opportunity for a serene evaluation of the principal questions in the case and thus fosters the discovery of the truth about the alleged nullity of marriage.[81]

D. Decisional Phase

The diocesan or eparchial bishop, or the one legitimately delegated by him, has a single function in the cause, and it is the most serious one: the determination of whether or not the manifest nullity of marriage in the case is objectively proven beyond any reasonable doubt. The instruments available to him for deciding this question are the following: the proofs gathered by the instructor, the arguments proposed by the defender of the bond and the advocates, and the counsel of the instructor and the assessor (cf. *CIC* c. 1687 §1, *CCEO* c. 1373 §1).

It is critical for the bishop to recall at this moment that he is not making a decision based on a prudent judgment about what brings the highest benefit to all the parties in the case. Such would be the method for issuing an administrative decision. Rather, he is bound to determine what is proven by the aforementioned instruments to be the demonstrable truth in the case. This is a question of moral certitude of whether the manifest nullity of marriage in the case is established from the acts. And the ever

---

81. "[L]e difese scritte e le osservazioni scritte del difensore del vincolo garantiscono meglio al giudice la possibilità di valutare criticamente gli argomenti *pro* e *contra* di quanto possa fare la discussione soltanto orale della causa." Daneels, "Osservazioni sul processo," 85.

valuable source for understanding what that certitude entails is the classic October 1, 1942 discourse of Pius XII to the Roman Rota, reiterated also by John Paul II on February 4, 1980.[82]

What needs to be carefully and diligently kept in mind, since it can often be lost sight of, is that the bishop does not reach his decision based on a subjective conviction about the nullity of marriage but on a judgment about what is certain and demonstrable from the proofs and arguments that have been brought forward in the process. This is a judgment that is personal to the bishop. While he can delegate his judicial power for such causes, he may not delegate his analytical judgment in causes that he is deciding. Thus, while the counsel of the instructor and assessor is sure to be quite helpful, especially if they are highly learned in matrimonial law and jurisprudence, he is bound personally to examine the acts and read and weigh the arguments.[83]

Like in the documentary process, the only definitive decision the bishop may make is that the nullity of marriage is established, which decision is executable if it is not appealed after fifteen days from publication of the definitive sentence. The definitive sentence has the very same structure and style as one issued at the conclusion of the ordinary process: after invoking the divine name, it presents the basic factual scenario and procedural history (*species facti*), the pertinent juridical principles found in the Church's magisterium, the law, Rotal jurisprudence and approved doctrine (*in iure*), and the argumentation identifying and defending what proven facts support the alleged nullity and exclude any doubt to the contrary (*in facto*) (cf. *CIC* cc. 1611–1612, *CCEO* cc. 1294–1295). Within one month of reaching the decision (*RP* art. 20 §2), an authentic copy of the full text of the definitive sentence—"*integer sententiae textus*" (*CIC* c. 1687 §2, *CCEO* c. 1373 §2)—is published to the spouses and the defender of the

---

82. See *Papal Allocutions*, 17–22, 159–164.

For an analysis of this concept and a bibliography, see William L. Daniel, "The Notion of Moral Certitude in Canonical Tradition and in the Dynamism of the Judicial Process," *Studies in Church Law* 6 (2010) 209–268.

83. All canonists who are serious about their ecclesial ministry are to avoid the formalism and reductionism according to which the function of the bishop is considered that of merely signing the definitive sentence. Unless he delegates the judicial faculty, he is the judge and thus must examine the proofs and the arguments and make the decision. If he, in practice, entrusts the preparation of the text of the sentence to another, it nevertheless reflects his own evaluation of the cause.

bond by handing it over to them personally or by transmitting it to them via a certain and secure method, such as certified mail, courier, or the like (*CIC* c. 1615, *CCEO* c. 1298). The bishop may find it to be of highest pastoral advantage to hand it over to them personally in a private meeting, where he can employ additional means of encouragement and paternal care (cf. *RP* art. 20 §1).

When the bishop is not morally certain of nullity of marriage in the cause—that is, when even one reasonable doubt remains about the alleged nullity—he issues a decree briefly articulating these doubts and deferring it to the competent tribunal approached by the petitioner so that it may conduct an ordinary contentious trial.[84] That decree is subject to no appeal, since it lacks the force of a definitive sentence (cf. *CIC* c. 1629, 4°; *CCEO* c. 1310, 4°). Once the cause has been received by the judicial vicar, he constitutes the college of judges and orders the instruction of the cause, if this is necessary. Presumably the formulation of the doubt would be the same as it was in the abbreviated process, but the parties could propose a new formulation at this moment if new questions arose during the abbreviated process.

E. Challenge

Beyond the full course of any trial, an additional phase could be identified, namely, the challenge phase. This is true likewise in the abbreviated matrimonial process, in which the right of appeal is expressly recognized.

An appeal is a judicial action (an introductive juridical act within a trial) by which one of the parties, who deems him or herself aggrieved by the sentence, requests the total or partial emendation of the sentence from the superior judge (cf. *CIC* cc. 1628, 1634 §1; *CCEO* cc. 1309, 1315 §1). While the diocesan bishop has no ordinary superior below the Roman Pontiff, positive law establishes the metropolitan archbishop as his judicial superior, as it does the bishop of the oldest suffragan see over the metropolitan.[85] Obviously, the Roman Rota is the superior in any case. As the case

---

84. The natural model for this decree is found in the Rotal decrees by which an affirmative sentence is not confirmed but is admitted to an ordinary examination (cf. *CIC vetus* c. 1682 §2, *CCEO vetus* c. 1368 §2), many of which are published in the *RRDecreta*.

85. Cf. *CIC* cc. 1438, 1°, 1687 §3; Pontifical Council for Legislative Texts, Letter on the Meaning of Senior Suffragan Bishop, October 13, 2015 (Prot. N. 15155/2015): *The Jurist* 75 (2015) 666–667 and this volume, 370–371. In regard to Eastern Churches, see *CCEO* cc. 1064 §1, 1373 §3.

may be, it is for this competent bishop or the Dean of the Roman Rota to make a judgment *in limine* about *the admission of the appeal* against the declaration of nullity of marriage via the abbreviated process. The question before him is whether it is evidently apparent that the appeal is *"mere dilatoria,"* that is, merely a delay-tactic (*CIC* c. 1687 §4, *CCEO* c. 1373 §4). Since the right of appeal demands that this expression be understood strictly (cf. *CIC* c. 18, *CCEO* c. 1500), the superior bishop rejecting an appeal would need to establish positively that the appellant is not aggrieved by the decision but seeks only to delay the execution of the affirmative sentence. This would ordinarily be difficult to assess, since the very juridical situation of being a spouse or the defender of the bond carries with it an easily demonstrable interest in the decision. Thus, for example, if the respondent strove to defend the validity of the marriage and appealed against an affirmative sentence of the bishop, presumably his appeal would at least partially be directed toward further protecting the validity of the marriage and not merely toward delaying a future marriage of the petitioner.

The rejection of an appeal that is judged to be merely a delay tactic is a decree that has the force of a definitive sentence, inasmuch as it prevents a new level of the trial, namely, the second degree of jurisdiction (cf. *CIC* c. 1618, *CCEO* c. 1301). Accordingly, it is itself subject to appeal (cf. *CIC* c. 1629, 4°; *CCEO* c. 1310, 4°), which appeal suspends the execution of the rejection of the appeal (cf. *CIC* c. 1638, *CCEO* c. 1319), leaving the original declaration of nullity of the sentence unexecutable. Appeal against the metropolitan's rejection of an appeal, or that of the bishop of the oldest suffragan see, is ordinarily directed to the Roman Rota (cf. *CIC* c. 1444 §1, 2°; *CCEO* c. 1065) or, in patriarchial or major archepiscopal Churches *sui iuris*, to the ordinary appellate tribunal of those Churches (*CCEO* c. 1063 §3).

However, if the appeal against the affirmative sentence is made immediately to the Roman Rota and the Dean rejects the appeal as a mere delay tactic, or if the Dean confirms the rejection of an appeal, it is less clear to which authority one may make recourse. The rejection of an appeal amounts, in part, to a declaration that the appeal is illegitimate and thus that the affirmative decision has given rise to a *res quasi-iudicata*. The remedy against such a declaration is a new proposition of the cause. Thus, when the Dean rejects an appeal or confirms the rejection of an appeal, a recurrent may make a new proposition of the cause before the Roman

Rota in accord with the norm of canon 1681 (*CCEO* c. 1367). Were this to be rejected by the Rota and one still found himself aggrieved, he could approach the Supreme Tribunal of the Apostolic Signatura.[86]

The superior bishop (like the Dean of the Roman Rota) is absolutely incompetent to confirm or overturn the affirmative decision immediately. If he judges that the appeal is not merely a delay tactic, he admits the cause to an ordinary examination in second instance, that is, an appellate process to be judged before the competent tribunal according to the norm of the ordinary contentious trial (*CIC* c. 1687 §4, *CCEO* c. 1373 §4). This is an exception to the principle of the correspondence of instances, since there is no abbreviated appellate process. Which tribunal is competent to handle the appeal? While one might think the matter would be entrusted to the ordinary appellate tribunal, it would presumably remain within the jurisdiction of the bishop who admitted the appeal, since his judicial power is exercised by his own tribunal and his admission of the appellate amounts to a mandate to exercise his power. Thus, the tribunal of the oldest suffragan see operates as an appellate tribunal for causes judged via the abbreviated process and admitted to appeal by its bishop.[87]

In addition to the appeal, it should be noted that the other remedies of law are available to the spouses and the defender of the bond. In particular, an affirmative sentence of the bishop that has been executed after the passage of the time limits for appealing can still be challenged by making a new proposition of the cause at any time before the Tribunal of the Roman Rota (cf. *CIC* c. 1681, *CCEO* c. 1367). And complaints of irremediable and remediable nullity may likewise be proposed according to the norm of law.[88]

---

86. Cf. *Lex propria STSA* art. 33, 3°.

87. When two or more suffragan sees are equally the oldest, it could be argued that the appellant has his or her choice of which bishop will receive the appeal, since the choice of equally competent fora is a principle operative in the canonical judicial system (cf. *CIC* cc. 1407 §3, 1632 §1). It would be suitable for the bishops involved to have a pre-established method for distributing the appeals in the event that an appeal makes no indication of the suffragan bishop to which appeal is being made.

88. Cf. *CIC* cc. 1620–1623, *CCEO* cc. 1303–1304, *DC* artt. 269–278.

Conclusion

In one respect, the most innovative aspect of the Franciscan reform of the marriage nullity process is the institution of the abbreviated matrimonial process before the bishop. For it eliminates several elements of the ordinary matrimonial trial, especially the need for a college of judges, the normative instruction of the cause in the absence of the spouses, the publication of the acts, the full discussion of the cause and, like the revised ordinary process, the need for a double conformity of affirmative sentences prior to executing a declaration of nullity of marriage.

In another respect, however, a careful examination of the institute reveals that its use is designed to be exceptional and even somewhat rare in practice. For the elements that are presuppositional to the legitimate use of the process are quite strict and occur with relative infrequency. The material presupposition in particular would likely be verified in few cases, since the nullity of marriage due to a defect of consent is ordinarily something difficult to prove inasmuch as it is almost always a hidden event of the past. The formal presupposition, too, may not be very common, since respondents often oppose the process and wish to defend the validity of their marriage or are even altogether absent from the process or unlocatable.

It is expected that the actual application of the norms governing the abbreviated process will give rise to many new practical questions and problems, and the Apostolic See is sure to offer direction or even supplementary norms in the months and years ahead. It will be interesting to see from appeals made to the Roman Rota against affirmative sentences of the bishop if a common jurisprudence develops concerning any number of particular questions. It would not be surprising to begin observing some jurisprudential trends in the matter of what does and does not constitute manifest or evident nullity of matrimonial consent and cases in which a delay-motived appeal is verified.

One area that is worthy of additional attention, and which is a general point of critique of the abbreviated process, is the protection of the indissolubility of marriage. For, even while the abbreviated process may promote the celerity of a judicial examination of nullity of marriage and foster the accessibility of the process especially to spouses residing in regions without efficiently functioning tribunals, it is the protection of marriage that is potentially most curtailed in this process. For, not only may one sustain the concern that tribunals operating out of a divorce-oriented mentality may overuse or misuse the process; but, institutionally speaking, the defender of the bond is offered fewer opportunities to defend the bond within the process, and it may now be socially quite difficult for him or her to appeal the decision, since it is issued by the bishop as head of the particular Church. It is hoped that subsequent normative interventions may promote the proactive defense of the bond by this public minister of justice, as a means of safeguarding the dignity of marriage and the family founded on marriage.

ABSTRACT

The abbreviated matrimonial process before the bishop is the most novel element introduced by Pope Francis in his August 15, 2015 reform of the marriage nullity process. Among other things, it situates the diocesan or eparchial bishop in the position of judge in the trial. According to the prevailing doctrine, however, the bishop can delegate his judicial power, and that applies also to the power to judge such causes. In any case, such causes are of an inherently judicial nature inasmuch as they are directed toward the procedural discovery of the objective truth of the alleged nullity of marriage and are thus necessarily of a declarative nature. The essential presuppositions of the process are the explicit consent of both spouses and the verification of a very strong fumus boni iuris *already in the* libellus *(called "manifest nullity" in the new law). The abbreviated process, while not providing all the hoped-for guarantees for the protection of the matrimonial bond, follows an ordered sequence in accord with the judicial patrimony of the canonical system.*

— Appendix —

**Sample Documents for
the Abbreviated Matrimonial Process before the Bishop
(*CIC* cc. 1683–1687; cf. *CCEO* cc. 1369–1373)**

Nota bene: These fictional acts are only examples meant to illustrate the progression of the abbreviated matrimonial process. While they pertain to the same fictional marriage, they are not always mutually consistent. In particular, the last four acts illustrate the different decisions that can be made by the Bishop and by the Appellate Bishop. The last four acts are a first instance definitive sentence *pro nullitate*, a first instance decree admitting the cause to an ordinary examination, a second instance decree of admission of the appeal, and a second instance decree of rejection of the appeal.

★ ★ ★

Diocese of X. Tribunal
[Address]

Libellus introductorius

Very Reverend and dear Judicial Vicar of the Diocese of X.:

Some months ago, through the services of University of X. Newman Center in [City, State], the undersigned Procurator-Advocate became acquainted with MARY SMITH (who resides in X. at [address]). After several conversations, she resolved with my counsel to challenge the validity of her marriage to PETER JOHNSON (who resides in Y. at [address]). In virtue of the attached Mandate, I hereby carry out her wish.

Mary Smith met Peter Johnson in September 2010, when they enrolled in the same high school. These two baptized non-Catholics did not know each other well but were acquainted inasmuch as they had many common friends. During the course of their secondary studies, they would at times become closer friends, but then their friendship would wane when one of them would step out with someone in a temporary youthful courtship. In June 2013, however, there was a celebration of the end of the academic year among those who were about to enter their last year of high school, at which both Mary and Peter were present. They indulged in alcohol and, in the middle of the night while the celebration was carrying on with increased fervor, surrendered to lustful passions by engaging in sexual intercourse. The celebration came to a close, and in subsequent weeks Mary and Peter quickly reached a mutual understanding that the encounter was no indication of a more serious relationship but only a passing, even regrettable experience.

In late August of the same year, after consulting her older sister with great distress, Mary came to the realization that she was pregnant. She had had intercourse on no other occasions and so was certain of Peter's paternity. With immense trepidation, being aided by her sister, she disclosed her pregnancy to her parents. While her mother was deeply disappointed and at the same time filled with compassion, her father, Thomas, was uncompromisingly enraged. He stormed from the family home, and returned four hours later prepared to utter his decree, namely: Mary and Peter, whose parents he had confronted and consulted, would marry in a quiet ceremony before Thomas' brother, the local Justice of the Peace; Mary would be homeschooled during her senior year of high school, and the baby would in the meantime be considered her parents' child; Mary and Peter would not present themselves as spouses but would see one another only under supervision of the families; after high school graduation, they would live with Mary's parents and Peter would work for his father, for whom he was already an apprentice in the family trade. It was clearly implicit that failure to comply with this plan would result in Mary's banishment from the family home—a grave consequence for which Peter would feel responsible.

Mary and Peter were altogether opposed to this arrangement, since they sustained no conjugal love for one another. At the same time, they were completely lacking in freedom, due to Thomas' immutable decision ratified by Peter's father. It was entirely clear to both of them that the only way to escape the paternal decree would be to flee from their homes and embark upon unknown paths alone—not at all a realistic solution. Thus, they yielded to the plan and took part in the above-described ceremony on Friday, August 23, 2013 at 8:45 p.m., when the offices of the local courthouse were closed, and no one but the fathers (as witnesses) and the uncle officiant were present (cf. enclosed marriage certificate).

There was in fact no common life, in view of the arrangement made by the fathers: throughout the duration of the parties' final year of high school, Mary lived with her parents, while Peter lived with his. Moreover, the parties rarely even spent time with one another, since she was homeschooled and never permitted to socialize with her former group of friends, while he carried on with his schooling and work. The only occasions on which they would see one another were scheduled monthly visits, when the families would gather for a common meal, in the interest of promoting a social bond between the families and the couple. Finally, a healthy baby boy was born to the couple on March 2, 2014 (cf. enclosed birth certificate), and Peter was permitted to be present for the birth, though subsequently he could only see the baby on the weekends, accompanied by his mother.

Despite the fact that the parties loved the child and wished each other well, they could not consent to this coerced marriage or continue pretending that they ever had. They thus conspired to flee from the parents' grasp with the aid of others. Upon graduation, Peter would move to a neighboring town to work in his best friend's family business, while Mary would live with a sympathetic aunt, with whose aid she would be able to pursue university studies. In June 2014, the parties divorced quietly and this plan was effectively carried out, to the great dismay and even sorrow of their parents, who had deceived themselves into thinking that their children would simply execute the vision they had contrived for their lives. Moreover, Mary's uncle who had performed the nuptials was confronted by his superior who eventually discovered that the local courthouse was used in an immoral way for private family interests. He was thus removed from office, and the families, seeing the rotten fruits of their ill-conceived plan, came to regret their actions.

Once she had matriculated in the local university, Mary met John, a Catholic, whom she wished to marry one day. With the aid of the Reverend Chaplain of the university's Newman Center, she and John learned about the marriage nullity process, and Mary's aunt hired the undersigned to assist her in introducing this petition.

Therefore, in accord with the norm of can. 1685 of the CIC as reformed by His Holiness Pope Francis in the August 15, 2015 motu proprio *Mitis iudex Dominus Iesus*, the undersigned Procurator-Advocate accuses this marriage of nullity due to force and grave fear imposed on both parties (cf. can. 1103) and requests the expeditious ministry of the X. Tribunal in the matter. Peter was hesitant to sign this *Libellus*, being unfamiliar with the Church's discipline in this matter, but he has privately declared his consent to the process and is willing to be questioned in the matter, since he wishes for this grave injustice to be identified and declared for the sake of closure and family healing. As the enclosed notarized affidavits indicate, all four parents, Mary's uncle-officiant, Mary's sympathetic aunt, and the friend whose father is employing Peter are all willing to testify, since I have made them understand the purpose of this process and its importance for Mary, who suffered unjustly; and they are all prepared to receive and promptly respond to the summons of the Tribunal.

Respectfully submitted on December 31, 2015 in X.

Procurator-Advocate of the Petitioner, R.S.
[address]

Enc.: Procuratorial Mandate, Documents

Diocese of X.
Tribunal

[Address]
[Address]
email@email.org
tel.: (000) 000-0000

Nullitatis matrimonii
(Smith–Johnson)

Prot. no. 2016-0001

DECREE

On this day, a *Libellus* accusing the above captioned marriage of nullity was received at the Chancery of this Diocesan Tribunal. Therefore,

In virtue of the norm of cann. 1432-1434, and 1676 §1 of the CIC;

The undersigned Judicial Vicar decrees:

The function of Defender of the Bond in the case is entrusted to the Respected Mr. J. N., who stably holds that office in this Diocese.

Given at [City, State] from the seat of the Diocesan Tribunal on January 4, 2016.

Judicial Vicar

Notary

DIOCESE OF X.
TRIBUNAL

[Address]
[Address]
email@email.org
tel.: (000) 000-0000

Nullitatis matrimonii
(Smith–Johnson)

Prot. no. 2016-0001

DECREE

On January 4, 2016, there arrived at the Chancery of this Diocesan Tribunal the woman-Petitioner's *Libellus*, in which the use of the abbreviated matrimonial process before the Most Reverend Bishop Moderator of this Tribunal was requested. Now,

Since the *libellus* is marked with a very strong *fumus boni iuris*;

However, having observed that, notwithstanding what was asserted in the *Libellus*, the mind of the man-Respondent is not yet directly known to this Tribunal;

In accord with the norm of cann. 1507 §1, 1676 §1 and 1683, 1° of the CIC;

The undersigned Judicial Vicar decrees:

The *Libellus* is admitted, and the Respected Defender of the Bond and the man-Respondent are hereby cited and are to reply in writing by January 22, 2016.

Given at [City, State] from the seat of the Diocesan Tribunal on January 7, 2016.

_____
Judicial Vicar

_____
Notary

DIOCESE OF X. [Address]
TRIBUNAL [Address]
email@email.org
tel.: (000) 000-0000

Nullitatis matrimonii
(Smith–Johnson)

Prot. no. 2016-0001

DECREE

On January 7, 2016, the undersigned Judge called the Respected Defender of the Bond and the man-Respondent to trial. Now,

Having duly weighed the *Votum* of the Respected Defender of the Bond, in which he declares that nothing prohibits the legitimate use of the abbreviated matrimonial process, even while cautioning the Judge as to possible difficulties in obtaining the testimony of two of the proposed witnesses;
Having observed that the man-Respondent consents to use of the abbreviated process (cf. can. 1683, 1°) and is prepared to appear at the instructional session;
In accord with the norm of cann. 1676 §2 and 1685 of the CIC and of artt. 16–17 of the *Ratio procedendi*, the undersigned Judicial Vicar decrees:

1) The cause is to be treated via the abbreviated matrimonial process before the Bishop, to be conducted by the undersigned Judge as the Instructor and the Rev. Sister Mary Y. Z. as the Assessor.
2) And the terms of the controversy are established according to the following formula: *"Whether nullity of the marriage in the case is established due to force and grave fear imposed on the parties (cf. can. 1103 CIC)."*
3) The parties and witnesses are hereby summoned for the instructional session to be conducted at this Tribunal on January 29, 2016 at 9:00 A.M.

Within three days of receipt of this decree, the spouses and the Respected Defender of the Bond may submit to this Tribunal any matters to be investigated in the aforementioned session.

Given at [City, State] from the seat of the Diocesan Tribunal on January 15, 2016.

_____
Judicial Vicar

_____
Notary

DIOCESE OF X. [Address]
TRIBUNAL [Address]
email@email.org
tel.: (000) 000-0000

Nullitatis matrimonii
(Smith–Johnson)

Prot. no. 2016-0001

DECREE

Now that this instructional session has been concluded;

Having observed that none of the parties propose any additional proofs;

In accord with the norm of can. 1686 of the CIC;

The undersigned Instructor decrees:

The Respected Defender of the Bond is to submit his Observations, and the Respected Procurator-Advocate his argumentation, by February 15, 2016.

Given at [City, State] from the seat of the Diocesan Tribunal on January 29, 2016.

_____
Instructor

_____
Notary

Diocese of X.
Tribunal

[Address]
[Address]
email@email.org
tel.: (000) 000-0000

Nullitatis matrimonii
(Smith–Johnson)

Prot. no. 2016-0001

DECREE

Having received the Observations of the Respected Defender of the Bond and the argumentation of the Respected Procurator-Advocate;

In view of the norm of can. 1687 §1 of the CIC;

The undersigned Instructor decrees:

The acts of the cause are hereby transmitted to the Most Reverend Bishop for his decision in the case.

Given at [City, State] from the seat of the Diocesan Tribunal on February 18, 2016.

_____
Instructor

_____
Notary

DIOCESE OF X. [Address]
OFFICE OF THE BISHOP [Address]
email@email.org
tel.: (000) 000-0000

Nullitatis matrimonii
(Smith–Johnson)

Prot. no. 2016-0001

DEFINITIVE SENTENCE

In the Name of the Lord. Amen.

While POPE FRANCIS is happily reigning, the Undersigned Most Reverend Judge, in the fifth year of his governance of the Diocese of X., as regards the alleged nullity of the marriage of:

— MARY SMITH, a baptized non-Catholic having a domicile at [address], being legitimately represented by her Procurator-Advocate R. S., and

— PETER JOHNSON, a baptized non-Catholic having a domicile at [address];

— with the Respected Mr. J. N. intervening in the cause as Defender of the Bond,

issued the following definitive sentence at the first level of jurisdiction.

---

1. – **The Facts.** – Mary Smith and Peter Johnson, both baptized non-Catholics, met at the age of 14 as freshmen in high school in the city of Y. They originate from stable close families. Her father was a strong figure both in his family and in the community, and he enjoyed the respect of many. His father was much devoted to his family and always sought their welfare. These two fathers, who did not know each other well, would soon find themselves conspiring to resolve a difficulty induced by their children's indulgence in illicit passion.

In the summer at the end of their third year of high school, Mary and Peter engaged in sexual intercourse, leading to her pregnancy with their son Frederick. The parties' fathers, without the objection of their wives, wishing to spare their children the difficulty of pre-mature parenthood, established a plan for their secret marriage, the removal of any occasion of bewilderment in the community, and provision for their future common conjugal life of reparation. The two youths, finding themselves powerless, yielded to this situation and contracted marriage but fled when the opportunity arose according to what was explained in the *Libellus*.

2. – Now, wishing to enter marriage as an exercise of her personal freedom with a man she loves, Mary accuses the marriage of nullity.

Indeed, on January 4, 2016, the *Libellus* of Mary Smith arrived at the Chancery of the Tribunal, signed by her Procurator-Advocate, by which she accused her marriage to Peter Johnson of nullity and expressly requested use of the abbreviated matrimonial process.

Once the Respected Defender of the Bond had been deputed and he and the man-Respondent were cited, on January 15, 2016 the doubt to be resolved in the case was established according to the following formula: *"Whether nullity of the marriage in the case is established due to force and grave fear imposed on the parties (cf. can. 1103 CIC)."*

The instructional session was carried out on January 29, 2016 by the Very Reverend Instructor according to the norm of law, and the arguments have been obtained. Now, having examined the acts and weighed the law and the facts with the aid of the same Instructor and the Reverend Sr. Assessor, it is for the Undersigned Bishop to decide whether nullity of the marriage in the case is established or whether the cause is to be admitted to an ordinary examination.

3. – **The Law.** – The Church, in application of her teaching on just liberty as belonging to the essential dignity of the human person, has declared that every person, especially members of Christ's faithful, have a right to be free from coercion in electing a state of life (see can. 219 CIC). The Church's solicitude for the stability and dignity of marriage and the family founded on marriage furthermore moves her to defend the right of the human person to this same freedom in choosing a prospective spouse and in exchanging matrimonial consent with the one chosen. A lack of such freedom is contrary to the natural law governing marriage, the spouses' consent to which can be supplied by no human power (cf. can. 1057 §1 CIC).

Thus, when it is the force of a human will extraneous to the spouses that is the efficient cause of marriage, the marriage is vitiated by the sanction of nullity. Indeed, as we read in can. 1103 of the CIC, "A marriage is invalid that is entered due to force or grave fear inflicted from the outside, even if unintentionally, by which one is coerced to choose marriage in order to free himself."

4. – According to the Church's constant jurisprudence, the nullity of consent on this basis is known to have occurred when it is judicially established that 1) a grave evil, or at least the loss of esteem in a superior in a case of reverential fear, is threatened 2) from outside the person by another human agent, such that 3) the marriage is the only avenue for escaping the threatened consequence.

In assessing the gravity of the force and the fear suffered as a result of it, the Judge is to attend not only to the objective gravity of the matter but also its subjective gravity. That is, there is to be a careful consideration not only of the threatened evil in itself but also of the personal character of the one suffering the fear so as to discern how vulnerable he would have been to the coercion. This includes an examination of whether he is of feeble character, his degree of emotional stability, his sex, level of education, and degree of dependence on others.

On the other hand, when faced with a particularly weak person suffering fear, there must be certitude that the fear is not merely a subjective phenomenon. That is, it cannot be self-imposed or the result of one's own imagination. "[I]nvalidating fear must be inflicted *from without*, that is, by an external and free cause, namely, another person, by a person distinct from the one suffering the fear, as the common and constant jurisprudence teaches" (Tribunal of the Roman Rota, Definitive Sentence c. Stankiewicz, *Nullitatis matrimonii, Maceraten.-Toletina-Recineten.-Cingulana-Treien.*, November 25, 2005: *RRDec* 97: 585, no. 8).

The third above-mentioned element refers to the *inevitability* of the marriage. In other words, for one wishing to be spared the threatened evil, the celebration of marriage is "unavoidable (*inevitabilis*), such that marriage is celebrated precisely because of the fear, by the person who has no other true refuge" (see Definitive Sentence c. Ciani, *Nullitatis matrimonii, Mediolanen.*, May 21, 2003: *RRDec* 95: 324, no. 8).

5. – In investigating the alleged imposition of force and grave fear, one is to pay careful attention to whether those inflicting and those suffering the fear confess, respectively, to what they did and what they suffered. The accuracy of such confessions is necessarily weighed in view of the antecedent, concomitant and subsequent circumstances.

A critical element of confirming proof is whether the forced party or parties experience aversion toward the celebration of marriage with the other person. For, "It cannot be understood how an intimate communion of life and love, directed toward obtaining the good of the spouses and the other ends of marriage, can arise when one is forced to live in a marital union with an unloved person, toward whom he deeply experiences an aversion to enter marriage, for the sole reason that he sees no other remedy for fleeing the grave evil that weighs upon him" (Definitive Sentence c. Bottone, *Nullitatis matrimonii, Rheginen.-Boven.*, May 15, 2003: *RRDec* 95: 311, no. 12).

Such aversion, however, need not amount to repulsion to the person of the other spouse, who may even be loved on some level. Rather, it is a question of having an aversion *to entering marriage with that person*. As we read: "Nevertheless, that *aversion* in the mind of the contracting party does not necessarily pertain to *the very person* with whom one is unjustly compelled to celebrate the sacred covenant. For a will entirely contrary to contracting marriage can exist even without aversion toward the very person imposed on someone; rather, it suffices that the contracting party be against *the celebration of marriage* with this person" (Definitive Sentence c. Wynen, *Nullitatis matrimonii, Assisien.*, July 26, 1951: *RRDec* 43: 577, no. 3).

6. – **The Argument.** – The Very Reverend Judicial Vicar acted justly in admitting the cause for treatment in the abbreviated matrimonial process. For the account relayed by the Respected Procurator-Advocate was quite thorough and gave rise to a very strong *fumus boni iuris*. Numerous facts advanced in the *Libellus* were elaborated upon and further explained in the instructional session and brought probative support to the petition.

7. – The young spouses and their fathers openly offered their judicial confessions before the Instructor, and these were supported by other witnesses.

The woman-Petitioner confessed: "I was stupid to have had sex with Peter that night. I didn't want a relationship with him at all; it was something I was avoiding for a long time. But in the heat of the moment and the social pressures of the party, I messed up. He's a good guy, and he will make someone very happy someday. But I married him only because my father made me" (p. 32, no. 6).

The man-Respondent likewise denounces himself: "I let myself get too much into the drinking and the partying and I lost my head. I actually liked another girl at the time and didn't plan to date Mary. When I found out she was pregnant, though, there was no turning back. Our fathers set the train moving, and we were going to be married no matter what" (p. 38, no. 4).

The woman's father, who was the principal instigator of the coercion, admits: "This marriage happened because of me. Even worse than their giving in to fornication was my giving in to rage. I love my daughter, but that turned into a jealous attitude of control when I thought her life was ruined. I was going to be sure to help her start over, as far as possible. But I didn't trust her, so I knew I had to make it happen." He admits that his realization of having alienated his daughter, having stifled her maturity in remedying the situation himself, and having cost his brother his career led to his change of heart. "I apologized to her once I saw what I had done, and I hope she forgives me some day" (pp. 52 and 55, nn. 5 and 14).

The man's father, too, admits his will to control the situation and to help with the full execution of that plan (cf. p. 44, no. 3).

Mary's maternal aunt, who would provide for Mary after her graduation, observed this whole dynamic and testifies to it at length (cf. pp. 57–63). And her credibility and good character are well supported by testimonial letters attached to the *Libellus* (see pp. 10–13).

8. – The objective and subjective gravity of what was threatened are converging elements, in the case, in view of the vulnerable personal condition of the spouses, namely, inasmuch as they were both minors and dependents at the time of the coercion. They relied upon their fathers for shelter, for material support (food, clothing), for the financial provision for their education and, in the case of the man, for future employment. It is clear, therefore, that the marriage was truly inevitable in this sense, for the spouses had no true means of escaping the displeasure of their parents apart from getting married. And they also feared that they could be cast out of their homes, given the acute nature of the coercion, inflicted, as it was, in an emotionally intense and temporally brief span of time.

9. – One could reasonably question, as did the Respected Defender of the Bond (see p. 65, no. 3), whether the means of escape to which they eventually had recourse were available before wedding. That is, could the woman have gone to live with her aunt and the man begun work with his friend's family before and instead of agreeing to the wedding? If so, this would at least cast into doubt the inevitability of the marriage.

As regards the woman, it is clear from the aunt's testimony that this remedy was not morally available in the circumstances of the summer of 2013. It is true that the aunt was in the habit of welcoming Mary to live with her during the month of July each summer; but this was always something to which her parents consented, and it was consistently done under joyful and peaceful circumstances. The event of Mary's pregnancy dominated that whole summer, and so her parents forbade her from leaving their home until a solution to the problem was decided upon. The aunt was and is a loving and even venerable figure in the family, but she would not interfere directly in the parenting decision of her relatives. Her eventual intervention was motivated by the same providing spirit that motivated Thomas' act of coercion, but the aunt's intervention was directed toward aiding one who was now legally an adult and who ought not be so dominated by her father, especially in so grave a matter as marriage. Once Mary graduated from high school, therefore, the aunt felt more free to come to her aid.

As regards the man, it is certain that the position with his friend's family business would not yet have been available to him, who had not completed high school. So that means of escape was not practically available to the man.

10. – Having thoroughly weighed everything pertaining to the law and the facts, the Undersigned Judge, having God alone before his eyes and having invoked the name of Christ, in response to the proposed doubts, definitively declares:

AFFIRMATIVELY, that is, that nullity of the marriage in the case is established due to force and grave fear on the part of both parties.

Each party has the right to appeal this decision to the Metropolitan Archbishop of Y. or to the Tribunal of the Roman Rota. They also enjoy the right to propose a complaint of nullity against it before the Undersigned Judge (can. 1624) or by joining such a complaint with an appeal to the designated Appellate Tribunal (can. 1625).

This Declaration of Nullity does not in any way affect the natural obligation of either party toward the child born of this putative marriage. The Undersigned Bishop therefore exhorts the parents to keep their parental obligations as a matter of justice and always to treat their children with Christian charity.

Given at [City, State] from the seat of the Diocesan Chancery on February 26, 2016.

_____

Bishop of X.

_____

Chancellor

DIOCESE OF X. [Address]
OFFICE OF THE BISHOP [Address]
email@email.org
tel.: (000) 000-0000

Nullitatis matrimonii
(Smith–Johnson)

Prot. no. 2016-0001

DECREE

1. – **The Facts.** – Mary Smith and Peter Johnson, both baptized non-Catholics, met at the age of 14 as freshmen in high school in the city of Y. They originate from stable close families. Her father was a strong figure both in his family and in the community, and he enjoyed the respect of many. His father was much devoted to his family and always sought their welfare. These two fathers, who did not know each other well, would soon find themselves conspiring to resolve a difficulty induced by their children's indulgence in illicit passion.

In the summer at the end of their third year of high school, Mary and Peter engaged in sexual intercourse, leading to her pregnancy with their son Frederick. The parties' fathers, without the objection of their wives, wishing to spare their children the difficulty of pre-mature parenthood, established a plan for their secret marriage, the removal of any occasion of bewilderment in the community, and provision for their future common conjugal life of reparation. The two youths, finding themselves powerless, yielded to this situation and contracted marriage but fled when the opportunity arose according to what was explained in the *Libellus*.

2. – Now, wishing to enter marriage as an exercise of her personal freedom with a man she loves, Mary accuses the marriage of nullity.

Indeed, on January 4, 2016, the *Libellus* of Mary Smith arrived at the Chancery of the Tribunal, signed by her Procurator-Advocate, by which she accused her marriage to Peter Johnson of nullity and expressly requested use of the abbreviated matrimonial process.

Once the Respected Defender of the Bond had been deputed and he and the man-Respondent were cited, on January 15, 2016 the doubt to be resolved in the case was established according to the following formula: *"Whether nullity of the marriage in the case is established due to force and grave fear imposed on the parties (cf. can. 1103 CIC)."*

The instructional session was carried out on January 29, 2016 by the Very Reverend Instructor according to the norm of law, and the arguments have been obtained. Now, having examined the acts and weighed the law and the facts with the aid of the same Instructor and the Reverend Sr. Assessor, it is for the Undersigned Bishop to decide whether nullity of the marriage in the case is established or whether the cause is to be admitted to an ordinary examination.

3. – **The Law.** – The Church, in application of her teaching on just liberty as belonging to the essential dignity of the human person, has declared that every person, especially members of Christ's faithful, have a right to be free from coercion in electing a state of life (see can. 219 CIC). The Church's solicitude for the stability and dignity of marriage and the family founded on marriage furthermore moves her to defend the right of the human person to this same freedom in choosing a prospective spouse and in exchanging matrimonial consent with the one chosen. A lack of such freedom is contrary to the natural law governing marriage, the spouses' consent to which can be supplied by no human power (cf. can. 1057 §1 CIC).

Thus, when it is the force of a human will extraneous to the spouses that is the efficient cause of marriage, the marriage is vitiated by the sanction of nullity. Indeed, as we read in can. 1103 of the CIC, "A marriage is invalid that is entered due to force or grave fear inflicted from the outside, even if unintentionally, by which one is coerced to choose marriage in order to free himself."

4. – According to the Church's constant jurisprudence, the nullity of consent on this basis is known to have occurred when it is judicially established that 1) a grave evil, or at least the loss of esteem in a superior in a case of reverential fear, is threatened 2) from outside the person by another human agent, such that 3) the marriage is the only avenue for escaping the threatened consequence.

The third element just mentioned refers to the *inevitability* of the marriage. In other words, for one wishing to be spared the threatened evil, the celebration of marriage is "unavoidable (*inevitabilis*), such that marriage is celebrated precisely because of the fear, by the person who has no other true refuge" (see Tribunal of the Roman Rota, Definitive Sentence *c.* Ciani, *Nullitatis matrimonii, Mediolanen.*, May 21, 2003: *RRDec* 95: 324, no. 8).

If the one allegedly coerced had some practical alternative path to follow aside from entering marriage, doubt of the alleged nullity arises. For the person would seem to have freely elected marriage, albeit in inopportune or strained circumstances, instead of the alternate path. Marriage would thus constitute the object of a fundamentally free exercise of the will.

5. – In investigating the alleged imposition of force and grave fear, one is to pay careful attention to whether those inflicting and those suffering the fear confess, respectively, to what they did and what they suffered. The accuracy of such confessions is necessarily weighed in view of the antecedent, concomitant and subsequent circumstances.

A critical element of confirming proof is whether the forced party or parties experience aversion toward the celebration of marriage with the other person. For, "It cannot be understood how an intimate communion of life and love, directed toward obtaining the good of the spouses and the other ends of marriage, can arise when one is forced to live in a marital union with an unloved person, toward whom he deeply experiences an aversion to enter marriage, for the sole reason that he sees no other remedy for fleeing the grave evil that weighs upon him" (Definitive Sentence c. Bottone, *Nullitatis matrimonii, Rheginen.-Boven.*, May 15, 2003: *RRDec* 95: 311, no. 12).

If such aversion is lacking, doubt of the nullity of consent further arises, since the one marrying finds himself not opposed to the marriage, even if certain circumstances render the choice of spouse or of the timing of the marriage less free than it would ideally be.

6. – **The Argument.** – The Very Reverend Judicial Vicar acted justly in admitting the cause for treatment in the abbreviated matrimonial process. For the account relayed by the Respected Procurator-Advocate was quite thorough and gave rise to a very strong *fumus boni iuris*. Numerous facts advanced in the *Libellus* were elaborated upon and further explained in the instructional session and brought probative support to the petition.

Nevertheless, the same session also introduced certain doubts in the cause, which admittedly may not be indicative of a lack of foundation to the petition but which, in the judgment of the Undersigned, demand deeper investigation (cf. can. 1683, 2° CIC).

7. – In the first place, the Respected Defender of the Bond rightly observes that the avenues of escape available to the spouses after their high school graduation are not proven to have been unavailable prior to marriage (see p. 65, no. 3). Indeed, the Petitioner was clearly in communication with her sympathetic aunt in the earliest stages of this dramatic situation of her life.

For the Petitioner herself explains that, after she had first told her sister about the pregnancy, the two of them went almost immediately to that aunt for counsel. "She was known in the family to be a wise and loving person," relates the sister, "and we knew she would know what to do. But she actually was somewhat unsure at this time but urged Mary to tell our parents before deciding anything" (p. 41, no. 2).

The Respondent, too, was aware of this: "I was a little mad at Mary for telling two other people about her pregnancy before telling me. She told me that she had already talked to her sister and her aunt before coming to me. We weren't very close but, c'mon, it was my baby!" (p. 39, no. 7).

The aunt, for her part, explained by way of self-introduction, "Mary and I have always been close and she knew she could always come to me. Our friendship was deepened over the years, since her parents let us spend the month of July each summer together" (no. 57, no. 1).

The question thus remains answered with probability as to whether Mary could have had recourse to the aunt at the time of the pregnancy, instead of agreeing to marriage. She likely had the opportunity to call upon the aunt, and this would have potentially satisfied her parents' aspiration for secrecy.

8. – Secondly, the instructional session not only elaborated upon the account related in the *Libellus* but also revealed the existence of other witnesses who could provide a fuller understanding of the circumstances. In particular, the Respondent

and his parents insinuate a possible lack of aversion in the parties and imply certain witnesses to that fact.

The Respondent himself states, "I didn't want to marry Mary under pressure like that, and we didn't know each other very well, but I did care for her. I really came to love her through those family visits during her pregnancy, and finally leaving her and Freddie was really hard, but I knew it was for the best" (p. 40, no. 8).

His father declares: "Peter had a few relationships in high school, but after his freshman year his friends would always tease him about Mary and how she made him nervous and blush in public. I didn't really know Mary but I gathered she was a girl that he liked" (p. 44, no. 1). His mother further relates that she "once saw Mary and Peter together that summer talking intimately. There seemed to be something between them and I figured she was becoming his girlfriend" (p. 46, no. 2).

In view of these indications, therefore, the matter of his aversion is highly doubtful, and even her alleged aversion merits further examination also in view of what was discussed in no. 7 above.

9. – Finally, it is not clear why the woman-Petitioner's mother was absent from the instructional session. As is indicated in the acts, despite the summons issued by the Instructor, no legitimate excuse was ever made by the witness, nor did her husband offer any explanation on the day of the session. Due to the relationship of the witness both to the Petitioner and to the aunt, her own sister, this matter needs to be attended to, and the testimony of the woman should be sought.

10. – In view of these reasons, the undersigned Bishop, having thoroughly examined the acts of the cause and the arguments, to the questions proposed, hereby decrees:

To the first: *Negatively*; to the second: *Affirmatively*; that is, that nullity of the marriage in the case is not established, and that the cause is to be admitted to an ordinary examination before the Diocese of X. Tribunal.

Given at [City, State] from the seat of the Diocesan Tribunal on February 26, 2016.

_____

Bishop of X.

_____

Chancellor

ARCHDIOCESE OF Y. [Address]
OFFICE OF THE BISHOP [Address]
email@email.org
tel.: (000) 000-0000

Nullitatis matrimonii
(Smith–Johnson)

Prot. no. 2016-0001

DECREE

On February 26, 2016, the Most Reverend Bishop of the Diocese of X. issued an affirmative decision declaring nullity of marriage in the above captioned cause according to the norms governing the abbreviated matrimonial process. The definitive sentence was published to the parties on March 16, 2016, and on March 22 of the same year the Respected Defender of the Bond presented his appeal, which was prosecuted the next day before the Undersigned Archbishop. Therefore,

Having attentively weighed both the acts of the cause and the appeal, which is based on arguments raised both at the outset of the process, when the Defender of the Bond urged the use of the ordinary process, and in his Observations, wherein he proposed the existence of certain doubts about the alleged nullity of the marriage;

In virtue of the norm of can. 1687 §4 of the CIC;

The Undersigned Archbishop decrees:

The appeal is admitted for treatment according to the ordinary appellate process. The acts are hereby transmitted to the Judicial Vicar of the Archdiocese of Y.

Given at [City, State] from the seat of the Archdiocesan Chancery on April 6, 2016.

_____
Archbishop of Y.

_____
Chancellor

ARCHDIOCESE OF Y. [Address]
OFFICE OF THE BISHOP [Address]
email@email.org
tel.: (000) 000-0000

Nullitatis matrimonii
(Smith–Johnson)

Prot. no. 2016-0001

DECREE

On February 26, 2016, the Most Reverend Bishop of the Diocese of X. issued an affirmative decision declaring nullity of marriage in the above captioned cause according to the norms governing the abbreviated matrimonial process. The definitive sentence was published to the parties on March 16, 2016, and on March 22 of the same year, the Respected Defender of the Bond presented his appeal, which was prosecuted the next day before the Undersigned Archbishop. Now, however:

— Having observed that the introductory *Libellus* was justly admitted and the cause treated according to the norms of cann. 1683–1687 §§1–3 CIC;

— Considering that the infliction of force and fear by the fathers of the Petitioner and of the Respondent is clearly asserted in the same *Libellus* and well-established in the acts, especially through the confessions of the fathers and other supporting indications;

— Since, in the judgment of the Undersigned, the gravity of the consequences, the defect of any means of escaping the wedding, and the aversion of both spouses are certainly demonstrated in the acts, as is accurately explained in the affirmative sentence;

— Having weighed the argument in the appeal of the Respected Defender of the Bond according to which the acts are lacking the testimony of sister in whom the Petitioner first confided about her pregnancy; nevertheless, considering that:

- The sister is most qualified to testify to the fact of the pregnancy and the Petitioner's immediate negative reaction to it, which facts are not in doubt;
- The testimony of the sister would seem to be otherwise superfluous;

- The supposition of the Defender of the Bond that the sister's testimony would introduce doubt about the Petitioner's aversion lacks any foundation;
- It is notable that the same Defender never proposed the citation of that witness, neither at the time of the citation, nor during the instructional session, nor in his Observations;

Since, therefore, admission of the appeal would merely delay the execution of the just affirmative sentence issued at the first level of jurisdiction;[89]

In virtue of the norm of can. 1687 §4 of the CIC;

Having attentively weighed the *votum praevium* of the Reverend Defender of the Bond of this Archdiocese;

The Undersigned Archbishop decrees:

The appeal is rejected at the outset and the affirmative sentence is hereby confirmed.[90]

---

89. Contrary to initial impressions, the notion of the "merely dilatory appeal" as one made as a delay-tactic seems insufficient. For such an understanding risks an unwarranted rupture with the common understanding of the canonical judicial process as one oriented toward the discovery of the truth. Accordingly, if the appellate bishop should receive an appeal that is motivated merely by a desire to delay the process while at the same time sees that the affirmative sentence is not sufficiently founded since the alleged nullity of marriage remains in doubt, he should not reject the appeal but should admit the cause to an ordinary examination. The "merely dilatory appeal" is better understood as one that, if admitted, would *merely delay* the execution of a just affirmative sentence, independent of whether or not the appellant has obstructionistic motives. For initial doctrinal treatments dedicated to the question, see the soon to be published studies of Gian Paolo Montini, ("'*Si appellatio mere dilatoria evidenter appareat*' (cann. 1680 §2 e 1687 §4 MIDI: alcune considerazioni iniziali," *Periodica*, publication pending), and William L. Daniel ("The '*Appellatio mere dilatoria*' in Causes of Nullity of Marriage. A Contribution to the General Theory of the Appeal against a Definitive Sentence," *Studia canonica*, publication pending).

90. This decree is characterized in c. 1687 §4 (cf. *CCEO* c. 1373 §4) as a decree of rejection of the appeal ("*eam a limine decreto suo reiciat*"). This introduces some difficulties that need further exploration in doctrine and jurisprudence, especially since it at first glance suggests that in the abbreviated matrimonial process there is no firm right of appeal, contrary to the norm of c. 1628 (*CCEO* c. 1309), and, by extension, that there is no possibility of obtaining a double conforming sentence in a matter so grave as the dignity of marriage and one's status in the Church. In this author's opinion, it is better suited to the rationality of the canonical system to understand this "decree of rejection" as essentially the same as the decree of confirmation

This decree is subject to no appeal. The matter is thus returned to the Most Reverend Judge in the case so that he may attend to the execution of the sentence.

Given at [City, State] from the seat of the Archdiocesan Chancery on April 6, 2016.

_____

Archbishop of Y.

_____

Chancellor

---

of the ordinary process, such that it is the implicit petition of the appellant for an appellate trial that is rejected, while the affirmative sentence is confirmed as regards its merits.

JOHN P. BEAL*

The Ordinary Process According to *Mitis Iudex*: Challenges to Our "Comfort Zone"

Human institutions, like the human beings who create and shape them (and, in turn, are shaped by them), are creatures of habit. They develop ways for dealing with routine and recurring tasks and situations and usually persist in these behaviors unless external factors force reconsideration and revision. Indeed, change in these ingrained habits can be wrenching, for both individuals and institutions. The iron grip of the familiar and the comfortable can be so strong that extraordinary effort—and sometimes intense outside pressure—are needed to overcome inertia and resistance and prompt adaption to changed circumstances.

Over the past fifty years the Church's marriage tribunals in North America have faced the challenge of changing and adapting their familiar and comfortable procedures for dealing with marriage nullity cases over and over again. Soon after the close of the Second Vatican Council, the episcopal conference of the United States in collaboration with the Canon Law Society of America proposed to the Holy See a series of changes in procedural law for marriage nullity cases. When given provisional approval by the Holy See as particular law for the United States during the period while the 1917 Code of Canon Law was under revision, this innovative

---

* Ordinary Professor, School of Canon Law, The Catholic University of America, Washington, DC.

procedural scheme became known as the American Procedural Norms.[1] These norms as well as Paul VI's provisional reform of marriage nullity procedure in the motu proprios *Causas matrimoniales* for the Latin Church[2] and *Cum matrimonialium* for the Eastern Churches[3] were intended to simplify the often cumbersome contentious process imposed by the 1917 code and the instruction *Provida Mater*[4] and to expedite thereby the resolution of marriage cases.

These new norms eventually had their desired effect, but not before tribunals whose officials had been trained in and had come to feel at home with this procedural framework had struggled mightily to adapt to the revised norms and the new way of thinking they embodied. By the time most North American tribunals had achieved a certain "comfort level" with the procedural changes of the post-conciliar era, the 1983 Code of Canon Law was promulgated. The abrogation of the American Procedural Norms and other provisional particular procedural laws effected by the revised code required tribunals once again to re-tool their procedures to bring their practice into conformity with the new norms. Among the most wrenching adjustments for these tribunals was learning anew how to deal with second instance cases—and to deal with them in volume. Throughout the years when the American Procedural Norms were in force, tribunals in the United States had made liberal use of Norm 23, II which allowed the diocesan bishop to request from the episcopal conference a dispensation from the obligation to appeal an affirmative decision, if he and the defender of the bond were convinced that such an appeal would be "superfluous."[5] Although it had been foreseen that such a dispensation would be sought only rarely and for cases that were "open and shut," it quickly became used for almost every case receiving an affirmative decision. As a result, for over a decade very few affirmative decisions in marriage nullity cases were dealt with at the appellate level.

---

1. American Procedural Norms, Sacred Council for the Public Affairs of the Church, rescript, April 28, 1970, Prot. No. 3320/70: *CLD* 7: 950–966. Similar, but less generous, provisional norms were also granted to other episcopal conferences by the Holy See for the period during which the 1917 Code was undergoing revision.
2. Paul VI, motu proprio *Causas Matrimoniales*, March 27, 1971: *AAS* 63 (1971) 441–446.
3. Paul VI, motu proprio *Cum matrimonialium*, September 8, 1973: *AAS* 65 (1973) 577–581.
4. Sacred Congregation for the Sacraments, instruction *Provida Mater Ecclesiae*, August 15, 1936: *AAS* 28 (1936) 313–361.
5. American Procedural Norms, Norm 23, II.

Even before many tribunals had adjusted completely to the changes necessitated by the procedural norms of the revised code, they were confronted in 2005 with the instruction *Dignitas connubii*.[6] Although this instruction did not purport to change the law, its provisions did suggest to many attentive canonists that existing practice in many tribunals was not entirely in harmony with the expectations of the law and needed to be modified. Adjustments to tribunal practice prompted by the instruction *Dignitas connubii* had only just begun when the unexpected appearance of Pope Francis' apostolic letters *Mitis Iudex*[7] and *Mitis et Misericors Iesus*[8] once again "upset the applecart" for tribunals and necessitated yet another round of rethinking and retooling of their standard operating procedures.

The two apostolic letters have retained the judicial process as the normative vehicle for addressing cases of possible marriage nullity. "[T]he unparalleled need to safeguard the truth of the sacred bond"[9] is cited as the reason for not acceding to many requests for an even more streamlined administrative procedure for marriage cases. Nevertheless, the norms of the two apostolic letters do attempt to streamline this process to "enhance the speed of the process as well as the simplicity due them, lest the clouds of doubt overshadow the hearts of the faithful awaiting a decision regarding their state because of a delayed sentence."[10] To assist tribunals in the adjustments dictated by these most recent jolts to their comfortable routines, it will be useful to highlight the most significant changes the two apostolic letters effect in the previous procedural law governing the ordinary process for deciding marriage nullity cases; other articles in this issue will address the new *processus brevior*.

European canonists distinguish between what they call the *pars statica* and the *pars dynamica* of the judicial process. The first consists of the complex of norms that governs the organization, personnel and rules of operation of tribunals; the second of the norms governing the unfolding of the actual contentious trial. The changes brought about by the two apostolic

---

6. Pontifical Council for Legislative Texts, instruction *Dignitas Connubii*, January 25, 2005 (Vatican City: Libreria Editrice Vaticana, 2005).

7. Francis, motu proprio *Mitis Iudex Dominus Iesus*, August 15, 2015 (Vatican City: Libreria Editrice Vaticana, 2015). English translation in *Origins* 45/24 (November 12, 2015) 418–423.

8. Francis, motu proprio *Mitis et Misericors Iesus*, August 15, 2015 (Vatican City: Libreria Editrice Vaticana, 2015).

9. Francis, *Mitis Iudex*, prologue.

10. Ibid.

letters of Pope Francis in each of these "parts" of the judicial process will be treated in turn

I. Tribunal Organization: The So-Called *Pars Statica*

A. The First Instance Tribunal

The apostolic letters of Pope Francis highlight the responsibility of the diocesan bishop himself "with an apostolic spirit, to attend to separated or divorced spouses."[11] An important element of the diocesan bishop's pastoral solicitude is providing the means by which these divorced faithful can resolve their status in the Church through a judicial process. Although much of the attention of commentators since the appearance of the apostolic letters has been on the new *processus brevior* in which the diocesan bishop himself serves as the judge,[12] the more fundamental obligation of the diocesan bishop is to insure that an accessible and reasonably efficient tribunal is available to the faithful who need its services.[13] He may do this by establishing and staffing a traditional diocesan tribunal with a staff of judges distinct from the diocesan bishop or with the diocesan bishop himself as one of the judges.[14] The apostolic letters stress the importance of insuring that tribunals are readily accessible to the faithful, especially that

---

11. Francis, apostolic letter *Mitis Iudex*, September 8, 2015: *Ratio Procedendi* art. 1; Francis, apostolic letter *Mitis et Misericors Dominus Iesus*, September 8, 2015, *Ratio Procedendi*, art. 1.

12. See Massimo del Pozzo, *Il processo matrimoniale più breve davanti al vescovo*, Subsidia Canonica 19 (Rome: EDUSC, 2016); William Daniel, "The Abbreviated Matrimonial Process before the Bishop in Cases of 'Manifest Nullity' of Marriage," *The Jurist* 75 (2015) 539–592; Geraldo Nuñez, "El proceso *brevior*: exigencies y estructura," *Ius Canonicum* 56 (2016) 135–155; Javier Ferrer Ortiz, "Valoración de las circumstancias que pueden dar lugar al proceso abreviado," *Ius Canonicum* 56 (2016) 157–192; Philippe Toxé, "La réforme des procès en nullité de mariage en droit canonique latin selon le motu proprio *Mitis Iudex Dominus Iesus*," in *La réforme des nullités de mariage: une étude critique*, ed. Cyrille Dounot et François Dussaubat (Paris: Artège Lethielleux, 2016) 89–142; Emmanuel Tawil, "Le motu proprio *Mitis Iudex* au regard de l'arrêt Pellegrini de la CEDH," in *La réforme des nullités de mariage*, 203–216; Alessandro Giraudo, "La scleta della modalità con cui trattare la causa di nullità: processo ordinario o processo più breve," in *La riforma dei processi matrimoniali di Papa Francesco: Una guida per tutti* (Milan: Ancora, 2016) 47–66; Paolo Bianchi, "Lo svolgimento del processo breve: la fase istruttoria e di discussione della causa," in *La réforme*, 67–90; Guillermo Rodríguez R., "Del proceso de nulidad matrimonial más breve ante el Obispo. Elementes estructurales," *Revista Mexicana de Derecho Canonico* 21 (2015) 339–348.

13. MI. c. 1673 §2; MMDI, c. 1359 §2.

14. MI, c. 1673 §§1–2; MMDI, c. 1359 §§1–2.

they are geographically close to where the parties, particularly petitioners, live so that they can approach them without undue difficulty.¹⁵ Nevertheless, the dearth of qualified personnel may prevent some bishops from establishing their own diocesan tribunals or at least from establishing effective ones. As a result, the law has long offered bishops the possibility of pooling their resources to establish interdiocesan first instance tribunal to take the place of their several diocesan tribunals.¹⁶ The apostolic letters now afford a diocesan bishop who cannot establish his own tribunal the additional possibility of approaching another nearby and, presumably, better staffed diocesan tribunal to serve as the ordinary tribunal for all cases introduced by the faithful of his diocese.¹⁷

Previously, the faculty to extend or prorogue the competence of a tribunal to hear a case for which it was otherwise incompetent was reserved to the Apostolic Signatura.¹⁸ Now, however, the revised law recognizes the faculty of the diocesan bishop to approach another tribunal, either a nearby diocesan tribunal or a nearby interdiocesan tribunal, at his own initiative (*salva facultate ipsius Episcopi accedendi ad aliud dioecesanum . . . vicinius tribunal*) and without the prior authorization of the Holy See. Of course, the approval of the diocesan bishop of the other tribunal or, in the case of an interdiocesan tribunal, the moderator would still be required and the Apostolic Signatura should be informed.¹⁹ However, if a diocesan bishop intends for an existing interdiocesan tribunal established in accord with the norm of canon 1423 to be the stable first instance tribunal for his diocese, he would have to join formally with the other bishop participants

---

15. MI, introduction: "The desire for this reform is fed by the great number of Christian faithful who as they seek to assuage their consciences are often kept back from the juridical structures of the church because of physical and moral distance. Thus charity and mercy demand that the church, like a good mother, be near her children who feel themselves estranged from her;" MMDI: "The restoration of the proximity between the judge and the faithful will never reach its desired result unless episcopal synods offer encouragement and assistance to individual bishops so that they may carry out the reform of the matrimonial process."

16. CIC, c. 1423; CCEO, c. 1067.

17. MI, c. 1673 §2; MMDI, c. 1359 §2.

18. John Paul II, apostolic constitution *Pastor Bonus*, June 28, 1988, art. 124, 3°: *AAS* 90 (1988)

19. See Appendix 4.2 "Decree to entrust the competence for marriage cases to an existing diocesan tribunal," in Apostolic Tribunal of the Roman Rota, *Subsidium for the application of the M. p. Mitis Iudex Dominus Iesus*, (Vatican City: Libreria Editrice Vaticana, 2016) 61–62.

in the tribunal. Becoming such a stable participant would require approval of the competent authority of the interdiocesan tribunal.

Commentators on *Mitis Iudex* and *Mitis et Misericors Iesus* have focused exclusively on the faculty enjoyed by the diocesan bishop who is unable to establish any tribunal at all in his own diocese to entrust cases initiated by faithful of his diocese to a near-by tribunal on a stable basis. However, even when a diocesan bishop is able to establish a tribunal capable of dealing with the majority of cases arising in his diocese, there may be occasional cases for which he is unable to establish a suitable tribunal. For example, should a case involving a member of the tribunal staff come to the tribunal, it is likely that all the other members of the tribunal would have to recuse themselves because of at least the perception of bias. As a result, it would be impossible to constitute a tribunal to hear and decide the case. The diocesan bishop could, of course, appoint judges and other court officials from other dioceses to serve for this case in his own tribunal, but even that strategy might not entirely remove the perception of bias. Another approach has been to seek from the Apostolic Signatura prorogation of the competence of another tribunal to hear the case. The two recent apostolic letters recognize the faculty of the diocesan bishop to seek the assistance of near-by tribunal and to entrust to it competence to hear and decide all cases arising from within his diocese without prior recourse to the Apostolic Signatura. It is a general principle of law that one who is authorized to do more can also do less.[20] Thus, if a bishop can entrust all cases to a near-by tribunal without the prior approval of the Apostolic Signatura, he can certainly do so an individual case as well.

Diocesan bishops who are already part of an interdiocesan first instance arrangement or who join one in the future, as well as those who have entrusted the responsibility for marriage cases presented by the faithful of their dioceses to another near-by diocesan tribunal, are now free to withdraw from first instance interdiocesan tribunals or from their agreement with a neighboring diocesan bishop simply by informing the other bishop participants in the tribunal and the Apostolic Signatura of his intention to do so.[21] One presumes that the motivation for withdrawal from an

---

20. *In VI°*, Regulae Iuris 53: "Cui licet, quod est plus, licet utique quod est minus."

21. MI, *Ratio Procedendi*, art. 8 §2; MMDI, *Ratio Procedendi*, art. 8 §2. See Appendix 4.3 "Decree for withdrawal from an inter-diocesan Tribunal and access to a nearer Tribunal," in *Subsidium*, 63–66.

interdiocesan tribunal or a stable relationship with a nearby tribunal will be that the diocesan bishop in question now has the resources to establish his own diocesan tribunal.

B. Second Instance Tribunals

One of the major innovations of the two apostolic letters is the elimination of the requirement, part of canon law since Benedict XIV's bull *Dei miseratione* in 1741, that all affirmative decisions in marriage nullity cases receive a second conforming decision before the parties are permitted to enter new marriages in the Church. They do not, however, eliminate altogether the need for a hierarchically organized system of appellate courts. Even in the new dispensation, there will be negative decisions that disappointed petitioners will want to appeal and affirmative decisions that disgruntled respondents and conscience-stricken defenders of the bond will feel the need to appeal. Since Patristic times, appeals from decisions of the bishop's court have been directed to the tribunal of the Metropolitan, appeals from decisions of the Metropolitan to the tribunal of a suffragan or to a stably designated tribunal outside the province. This Metropolitan appellate structure was the predominant, if not the exclusive, model in the Church until quite recently. In the United States, by the early 1980s it had become clear both that the revised code soon to be promulgated would restore the requirement of two conforming affirmative decisions before a sentence in a marriage nullity case could be acted on and that many Metropolitan tribunals would not be able to deal in an expeditious manner with the volume of appellate cases that would be coming their way once the revised Code was promulgated. Concerned bishops and tribunal officials responded to this looming threat by establishing interdiocesan appellate tribunals pursuant to the 1970 norms issued by the Apostolic Signatura or by devising hybrid appellate structures to effect an equitable distribution of the burden of resolving appellate cases.[22] While these alternate appellate structures have served their purpose reasonably well during the years since 1983, the rationale for adopting them has been largely eliminated by the recent apostolic letters: the volume of appeals of affirmative decisions

---

22. Apostolic Signatura, *Normae pro Tribunalibus interdioecesanis vel regionalibus*, December 28, 1970: *AAS* 63 (1971) 486–492. See also John P Beal, "Making Connections: Procedural Law an Substantive Justice," *The Jurist* 54 (1994) 129–142.

will probably be greatly reduced by the elimination of the mandatory second instance process. This change in circumstances will, no doubt, prompt at least some diocesan bishops to consider whether to retain their existing appellate systems or to return to the traditional Metropolitan appellate model.

The recent apostolic letters do not, in themselves, alter existing appellate systems. Alternate appellate models are still permissible and, where they have already been established, continue in existence. Diocesan bishops cannot unilaterally alter these arrangements. The faculty of bishops to withdraw from interdiocesan tribunals mentioned in article 8 §2 of the *Ratio Procedendi* of both of the apostolic letters applies only to first instance interdiocesan tribunals, i.e., those established in accord with the norm of canon 1423 of the Latin code and canon 1067 §§1–4 and canon 1068 §§1–3 of the Eastern Code, but not to second instance tribunals, i.e., those established in accord with the norm of canon 1439 of the Latin code and canon 1067 §5 and 1068 §4 of the Eastern code. The recent apostolic letters do, however, state a strong preference for retaining or, where an alternate model has been installed, returning to the traditional metropolitan appellate structure:

> It is necessary (*oportet*) that the appeal process be restored to the metropolitan see, especially since that duty, insofar as the metropolitan see is the head of the ecclesiastical province, stands out through time as a stable and distinctive sign of synodality in the Church.[23]

Although most of the existing interdiocesan tribunals in the United States were established prior to 1983 by the interested bishops themselves with the approval of the Apostolic Signatura pursuant to the 1970 *Normae* of the Signatura, the revised Code now vests authority to establish and, one presumes, to abolish or modify interdiocesan appellate courts to the episcopal conference with the *recognitio* of the Apostolic Signatura.[24] Changes in the appellate model, even though they involve a return to the Metropolitan model, still require: 1) the consent of the Metropolitan

---

23. ME, V; MMDI: "The appeal process to the Metropolitan See, insofar as it has been a capital duty of the ecclesiastical province through the centuries and a prime mark of the synodality of the Eastern Churches, should, by that reason, be maintained and fostered."

24. CIC, c. 1439. Since the Eastern Churches do not have episcopal conferences, CCEO, cc. 1067–1068 entrust competence to erect interdiocesan appellate courts to the Patriarch or Major Archbishop in their territories or the Holy See.

archbishop to become the appellate court for all suffragans; 2) agreement of the (arch)bishop or (arch)bishops whose tribunals will become the appellate courts for the Metropolitan tribunal; 3) the approval of this choice of a stable appellate tribunal by the Apostolic Signatura; 4) a favorable vote of the participating bishops and, in the case of an interdiocesan tribunal, a favorable vote of the episcopal conference; and 4) approval of the new appellate system by the Apostolic Signatura.

C. Composition and Competence of Tribunals

1. Lay People As Judges

Since the promulgation of 1917 code, the norm has been that marriage nullity cases are reserved to tribunals of at least three judges. The two apostolic letters retain this strong preference for collegiate tribunals at first instance. To facilitate the formation of such panels in places where clergy trained in canon law are in short supply, the apostolic letters authorize the formation of three-judge panels with lay judges. The use of one lay man as a member of a turnus had been authorized by Paul VI in his post-conciliar motu proprios *Causas matrimoniales*[25] and *Cum matrimonialium*.[26] Despite considerable opposition, especially from the German episcopal conference,[27] canon 1421 §2 of the revised code incorporated this allowance for the use of lay judges and expanded it to permit both men and women to serve as judges. The recent apostolic letters have further expanded the possibility of using lay judges by authorizing the use not of only one but of two lay judges along with one clerical judge to form collegial tribunals. The cleric on the panel can be either a priest or a deacon.

Both Paul VI's motu proprio *Causas matrimoniales* and the revised Latin code had required the favorable vote of the episcopal conference before a diocesan bishop could appoint lay persons to serve as judges in his tribunal.[28] Some commentators on the recent apostolic letters hold that

---

25. Paul VI, *Causas matrimoniales*, V §1.
26. Paul VI, *Cum matrimonialem*, V §1.
27. "Prima Quaestio Specialis: De participatio laicorum in exercito potestatis regiminis," in *Congregatio Plenaria diebus 20–29 octoboris 1981 habita*, ed. Pontifical Council for the Revision of the Code of Canon Law, (Vatican City: Typis Polyglottis Vaticania, 1991) 35–97 and "Examen primae Quaestionis," in *Congregatio Plenaria*, 190–229.
28. Paul VI, *Causas matrimoniales*, V., 1; CIC, c. 1421 §2. Since the Eastern Churches do not have episcopal conferences, there was no provision for episcopal conference approval of the use of lay judges either in Paul VI's *Cum matrimonialium* or in the CCEO. Instead, *Cum*

these new norms abrogate the requirement of a prior favorable vote of the episcopal conference before a diocesan bishop can appoint lay people as judges, but they offer no reason for this opinion.[29] In fact, the opinion appears to lack a solid foundation.

Certainly the apostolic letters have effected a change in the previous law governing the use of lay judges in marriage cases (but not in other cases reserved by the law to a panel of at least three judges). However, canon 1421 of the Latin code and canon 1087 of the Eastern code where the possibility of lay judges is addressed deal primarily with the qualifications for appointment to the office of judge. Paragraph one stipulates that the diocesan bishop (or bishop-moderator of the tribunal) is to appoint "diocesan judges, who are to be clerics." Paragraph 2 inserts an exception to the norm that diocesan judges are to be clerics: "The conference of bishops can also permit the appointment of lay persons as judges; when it is necessary one of them can be chosen to form a college."[30] Paragraph 3 requires that judges, whether lay or clerical, must be "of unimpaired reputation and doctors or at least licensed in canon law."[31] Although they have expanded the possibilities for the use of lay persons as judges by allowing two lay persons instead of only one to be assumed to form a collegiate tribunal, the recent apostolic letters do not alter the qualifications for appointment to the office of judge (or to other tribunal offices). In fact, the change allowing the use of two lay persons as judges to form collegiate tribunals is found in canons of the apostolic letters which deal not

---

matrimonialium V. §1 stipulated: "[T]he patriarch or major archbishop, after having heard the permanent synod, is granted the faculty to permit the constitution of a panel made up of two clerics and one lay man in the above-mentioned instances. Outside of the patriarchate or archbishopric, the same faculty is enjoyed by the metropolitan after he has heard the two bishops of the province who are senior by order of precedence. In other cases recourse should be had to the Apostolic See." After minor revisions, this provision was incorporated as canon 1087 §2 of the CCEO.

29. Klaus Lüdicke, "Prozessrecht Eheverfahren," in *Münsterische Kommentar*, 1673/3; Toxé, in *La réforme*, 108.

30. CIC, c. 1421 §2; CCEO 1087 §2 states: "The patriarch, having consulted with the permanent synod, or the metropolitan who presides over a metropolitan Church *sui iuris*, having consulted the two eparchial bishops senior by episcopal ordination, can permit that other members of the Christian faithful also be appointed as judges. When it is necessary, one of them can be assumed to form a collegiate tribunal; in other cases, the Apostolic See is to be approached regarding this matter."

31. CIC, c. 1421 §1; CCEO, c. 1067 §3. The Eastern code adds, "and known for prudence and zeal for justice."

with qualifications for appointment as judge but with the constitution of tribunals,[32] norms that roughly parallel canon 1425 of the Latin code and canon 1084 of the Eastern code. Thus, the recent apostolic letters do not seem to have abrogated or to have completely reordered the requirement that the diocesan bishop or bishop-moderator receive authorization from a higher authority before he proceeds to appoint lay judges.[33]

2. Single-Judge Tribunals

The American Procedural Norms, Paul VI's two post-conciliar motu proprios enacting interim reforms of matrimonial procedure and the two codes all recognized that, even with the use of lay judges, it might well be impossible to establish collegial tribunals to hear all the cases that might come before a marriage tribunal and to resolve these cases expeditiously. As a result, they all authorized diocesan bishops to resort to the constitution of single judge tribunals to decide marriage nullity cases.[34] Pope Francis' two apostolic letters continue this authorization of the use of single judge tribunals: "The bishop moderator, if a collegial tribunal cannot (*nequeat*) be constituted in the diocese or in a nearby tribunal chosen according to the norm of §2, is to entrust cases to a single clerical judge."[35] Like all the previous post-conciliar legislation authorizing the use of single judge tribunals in marriage nullity cases, the two recent apostolic letters reserve the authority to constitute single-judge tribunals to the diocesan bishop or bishop moderator of a tribunal and not to the judicial vicar. This and other tribunal functions reserved to the diocesan bishop can, of course, be delegated to the judicial vicar. Nevertheless, the continued reservation of the authority to constitute single-judge tribunals to the diocesan bishop is a pointed reminder that the assignment of marriage nullity cases to single-judge tribunals, whether for an individual case or as a general practice, is not a decision to be taken lightly. One noteworthy change that is effected by *Mitis Iudex* is its elimination of the requirements of the prior approval

---

32. MI, c. 1673; MMI, c. 1359.
33. CIC, c. 6; CCEO, c. 6.
34. APN, Norm 3; Paul VI, *Causas matrimoniales*, V 2; *Cum matrimonialium*, V §2; CIC, c. 1425 §4; CCEO, c. 1084 §3.
35. MI, c. 1673 §4; MMI, c. 1359 §4.

of the episcopal conference before a diocesan bishop or bishop moderator actually appoints single-judges in marriage cases.[36]

Like the prior law of the two codes, the recent apostolic letters authorize the use of single judges in marriage nullity cases only when a collegiate tribunal cannot be (*nequeat*) established. Bishop Thomas Paprocki has insisted that the law permits the use of a single judge for marriage nullity cases only when there is an absolute impossibility of forming a collegiate tribunal to hear any case of marriage nullity.[37] Paprocki holds that the fact that a tribunal's judges live in disparate parts of the diocese may render their convening as a collegiate tribunal to discuss and resolve a case inconvenient, but not impossible. Similarly, he argues that the steep cost of hiring lay canonists to provide a small diocese with the three judges needed to establish a collegiate tribunal is a factor that renders forming a college difficult, but not impossible. With all due respect, Bishop Paprocki's reasoning is unconvincing.

In his argument against resort to single judge tribunals in marriage nullity cases, he seems to adopt an understanding of "impossible" that is quite abstract rather than, as is typical in the interpretation of canon law, one that is relative to the concrete circumstances of persons and things. He also focuses exclusively on the impossibility of forming a collegiate tribunal to hear an individual case that might be presented to a tribunal and ignores the broader question of the impossibility of dealing expeditiously with the volume of cases which may reasonably be expected to be presented to a tribunal. Since the possibility of constituting single-judges for marriage nullity cases was first opened in the 1970s, the source of the "impossibility" cited North American first instance tribunals to justify their regular, indeed almost exclusive, use of single judges to decide marriage cases in first instance has not been the unavailability of sufficient qualified personnel to constitute a collegial tribunal for an individual case.

---

36. MI, c. 1673 §4. The motu proprio comments: "In the first instance, the responsibility of appointing a single judge, who must be a cleric, is entrusted to the bishop, who in the pastoral exercise of his juridical powers must guard against all laxism." MMI, c. 1359 §4 similarly eliminates CCEO, c. 1085 §3's requirement of prior approval by the patriarch or metropolitan for an eparch to constitute single judge tribunals. Roman Rota, *Subsidium*, 20: "*If the Bishop decides to constitute a sole Judge, must he seek the authorization of some competent authority? No.*"

37. Thomas Paprocki, "Implementation of *Mitis Iudex Dominus Iesus* in the Diocese of Springfield in Illinois," *The Jurist* 75 (2015) 595–599 and this volume, 343–347.

Rather, it has been the unavailability of sufficient qualified personnel to constitute collegial tribunals for all of the marriage nullity cases on their dockets without protracting the process unduly. The "impossibility" of establishing a collegial tribunal has been a prerequisite for the constitution of single-judge tribunals in marriage nullity cases, even with the availability of lay judges. This has been part of canonical procedural law since Paul VI's 1971 motu proprio *Causas matrimoniales*,[38] and *nequeat* is also the word used to express this "impossibility" in canon 1425, §4 of the Latin code.[39] There is no reason to think that the use of *nequeat* in the two recent apostolic letters is meant to suggest a greater degree of "impossibility" than it did in the previous law.

If they carry out their function as the law requires, associate judges in collegial tribunals do more than gather at the phase of decision to deliberate and decide the case. While they have few defined duties during the introductory and evidentiary phases of the process, these associate judges may be assigned particular roles in the course of the trial by the presiding judge.[40] More importantly, when they arrive for the deliberation of the collegiate tribunal, not only are the associate judges to have studied the acts of the case carefully enough to engage in the discussion and resolution of the case; they are also to "submit their written conclusions on the merits of the case with the reasons in law and in fact which led them to their conclusions," documents which will be preserved in the *acta causae*.[41] In other words, these associate justices are expected to prepare at last an initial draft of what might become the definitive sentence in every case in which they participate. Moreover, besides having an adequate staff of qualified judges, marriage tribunals must employ one or more defenders of the bond who, like judges, must possess at least a licentiate in canon law.[42] Although the defender of the bond can fulfill the minimal requirements of his or her office by reviewing the acts prior to the decision and submitting a written brief during the discussion phase of the process, the law expects that defenders of the bond to be actively involved in the case throughout

---

38. Paul VI, *Causas matrimoniales*, V §2.
39. CCEO, c. 1084 §3 says "si collegium constitui *non potest*" as did *Causas matrimoniales*, V §2 and *Cum matrimonialium*, V §2.
40. See CIC, c. 1428 §1; DC, art. 47 §2; CCEO, c. 1093 §1.
41. CIC, c. 1609 §2; CCEO, c. 1292 §2.
42. CIC, c. 1435; CCEO, c. 1099 §2.

the process and not to be content with a merely perfunctory fulfillment of the minimal requirements of their office.[43] If carried out diligently, the responsibilities of their offices would place tremendous demands on the time and energy of judges and defenders, even if the conditions of their dioceses permitted them to be assigned to the tribunal on a full-time basis.

If a tribunal with six qualified judges (including the diocesan bishop himself) and one defender of the bond like the one described by Bishop Paprocki[44] were to constitute collegial tribunals for all of the one hundred twenty cases submitted to it in an average year, each of the judges would have to prepare sixty draft sentences and revise and edit a substantial number of them into definitive sentences. Moreover, the one defender of the bond would have to be able to intervene in and draft briefs for all one hundred twenty cases that came through the tribunal in that year, a work load that, in its responses to annual reports of activity submitted by diocesan tribunals, the Apostolic Signatura has often characterized as unreasonable. Since few modestly sized dioceses (the sort that might receive about one hundred twenty cases per year) can afford the luxury of assigning five priests to the tribunal on a full-time basis and since few diocesan bishops can devote the time required to serve effectively as a judge on sixty cases per year, most of these judges would have to juggle responsibilities for several offices, thus diminishing the time (and energy) available to devote to tribunal work. It is hard to see how such a tribunal could manage to constitute collegial tribunals for every case submitted without thwarting one of the central purposes of the reforms effected by the two apostolic letter, viz., to favor "the speed of processes as well as the simplicity due them, lest the clouds of doubt overshadow the hearts of the faithful awaiting a decision regarding their state because of a delayed sentence."[45] In other words, for a tribunal of a modest sized North American diocese receiving about one hundred twenty new marriage nullity cases per year, constituting collegiate tribunals for all of these cases would seem to be truly "impossible."

Bishop Paprocki also holds that a legitimate resort to single-judge tribunals requires not only that it be impossible to form a collegial tribunal

---

43. CIC, cc. 1433–1444; DC, art. 56 §§1–4; CCEO, cc. 1097–1098.
44. Paprocki, 598 and this volume, 346.
45. MI.

in the diocesan bishop's or bishop moderator's own tribunal but that it be impossible as well to establish a collegial tribunal by approaching "a nearby tribunal chosen according to the norm of §2."[46] Although the recent apostolic letters reaffirm the value of collegial decisions in marriage nullity cases, they also emphasize other values that their procedural changes are designed to foster. Prominent among these are the rehabilitation of the role of the diocesan bishop as "judge of those entrusted to his pastoral care" and "the restoration of the proximity between the judge and the faithful."[47] The goals of giving prominence to the bishop's own judicial role and the restoration of this proximity between judge and faithful would be thwarted if a diocesan bishop was required to surrender his own judicial responsibility and refer cases to another, even nearby, tribunal or an interdiocesan tribunal simply because he was unable to form a collegial tribunal in his own diocesan tribunal. Besides, when one considers that almost all tribunals are plagued by chronic shortages of trained personnel, resorting to the services of a near-by tribunal would only pass the problem of constituting collegiate tribunals to a new venue.

3. Use of Assessors

The apostolic letters call for the use of officials known as "assessors" in both the ordinary process and in the so-called *processus brevior*.[48] Assessors

---

46. Paprocki, 598 and this volume, 346. MI, c. 1673 §4; MMI, 1359 §4. The §2 to which §4 refers recognizes the faculty of the diocesan bishop "to approach another nearby diocesan or interdiocesan tribunal" if he cannot establish one for his own diocese. Although the clause to which Bishop Paprocki calls attention is not found in either code, neither is it the complete innovation he suggests. Canon 1425 §4 of the 1983 code addressed the impossibility of establishing a collegial tribunal "in the first instance of a trial," whether that first instance occurs in a diocesan tribunal, an interdiocesan tribunal, or some alternate arrangement, and it spoke of the judgement of the impossibility of forming a collegial tribunal by "the bishop," a term inclusive of the diocesan bishop and the bishop moderator of another sort of tribunal. Thus, canon 1425 §4 already required that the "impossibility" of forming a collegial tribunal be judged in light of the various options available "in the first instance of trial." However, since *Mitis Iudex*, canon 1673 §4 speaks explicitly of the impossibility of establishing a collegial tribunal "in the diocese," it has to go on to mention explicitly the other first instance options available to a diocesan bishop as well. Thus, the phrase to which Paprocki calls attention does not really constitute a new obligation. There were no commentators on the previous law who held that a diocesan bishop unable to establish collegial tribunals in his own diocesan tribunal was obligated to work with neighboring bishops to establish an interdiocesan first instance tribunal or to share personnel with a nearby diocese in order to do so.
47. MI; MMI.
48. See Lüdicke, 1673/6.

are court officials with whom the judge discusses and deliberates about the case before reaching a decision. Their function is like that of associate judges of a collegial tribunal, but without a deliberative vote, or that of the pastor-consultors with whom the diocesan bishop is required to discuss cases of possible removal or transfer of pastors.[49] To fulfill their function, assessors are entitled to unrestricted access to the acts of the case. Consequently, they are bound by the same obligation of maintaining confidentiality about the details of the case as are other tribunal officials.[50] They are also barred from serving as assessor or judge in a case in which they were involved in one instance at a subsequent instance[51] and should recuse themselves—or be subject to recusal—in cases where they have a conflict of interest.[52] Since they are now to be appointed by the judicial vicar when he constitutes a single judge tribunal, their names should be made known to the parties and the defender of the bond so that they can raise exceptions to their participation in the case.

Neither code offers a description of the role of or qualifications for the appointment of assessors, except to suggest that they can be clerics or lay people and do not have to have degrees in canon law to be appointed to this function. The two recent apostolic letters stipulate that these assessors are to be "of upright life, expert in juridical or human sciences [and] approved by the bishop for this task."[53] The requirement that the diocesan bishop or bishop moderator appoint a pool of assessors from which judges can draw as need is clearly new. At least one commentator has suggested that, by including expertise in the human sciences among the competences of assessors, the law was subtly offering an alternative to the use of psychological experts in marriage nullity cases.[54] This suggestion seems erroneous. Although assessors trained in the human sciences may well assist the judge in discerning significance of patterns of behavior exhibited by a party and gauging the severity of psychic disorders and their impact on the party's decision making process, their discussions with the judge are

---

49. CIC, cc. 1742 §2, 1745, 2° and 1750; CCEO, cc. 1391 §2, 1394, 2°, 1399 §1.
50. CIC, c. 1455; CCEO, c. 1113.
51. CIC, c. 1447; CCEO, c. 1105.
52. CIC, c. 1448 §2; CCEO, 1106 §2.
53. MI, c. 1673 §4; MMI, 1359 §4.
54. Francis G. Morrisey, "The Motu Proprio *Mitis Iudex Dominus Iesus*," in *The Simplification of Marriage Nullity Procedures* (Ottawa: Faculty of Canon Law Saint Paul University, 2015) 10–11.

ex parte communications which will not be made known to the parties or the defender of the bond and cannot, therefore, be rebutted by them. The report of the court appointed psychological expert, on the other hand, becomes a part of the record of the case, is available to the parties or at least to their advocates at the time of the publication of the acts, and can be rebutted by contrary arguments or the opinion of others experts. To allow the *ex parte* communications from an assessor to substitute for the report of a duly appointed expert would be a grave violation of the right of defense.

The two apostolic letters urge that, in the ordinary process, single judges are, "where possible, to employ two assessors" (*ubi fieri possit, duos assessors. . . sibi asciscat*).[55] The obligation of the single judge to employ assessors seems to be no greater in the new law than it had been in the prior law. A single judge is obligated only "where possible." Nevertheless, the new law of the two apostolic letters stipulates that two assessors are to be appointed for a single judge by the judicial vicar when he constitutes a single-judge tribunal for the ordinary process.[56] Although there is no explicit requirement that the single judge in the ordinary process actually consult these assessors the judicial vicar has appointed for him, a judge who failed to consult such assessors in the deliberative stage of the process would at least be acting contrary to the spirit of the law. Consultation with the duly appointed assessor is not, however, facultative in the so–called *processus brevior*. The judicial vicar is to appoint an assessor at the same time he remits the case to this *processus brevior*,[57] and the bishop-judge is to consult the assessor before reaching a decision.[58]

4. Composition of Appellate Tribunals

As was the case in the previous law, tribunals at the appellate level must always be constituted of at least three judges for validity, except in cases of

---

55. MI, c. 1673 §4; MMI, c. 1359 §4. Both codes had originally suggested that a single judge should avail himself of the assistance of "an assessor and an auditor" in cases normally reserved by law to a collegial tribunal. CIC, c. 1425 §4; CCEO, c. 1084 §3. The provision for two assessors by the apostolic letters seems to be derived from c. 1424 of the Latin code and canon 1089 of the Eastern code that provide that, "[i]n any case, a single judge can employ two assessors."

56. MI, c. 1676 §3; MMI, c. 1362 §3.

57. MI, c. 1685; MMI, c. 1371.

58. MI, c. 1687 §1; MMI, c. 1373 §1.

appeal of decisions decided according to the documentary process.⁵⁹ The invalidity of the sentence resulting from the use of a single judge at the appellate level is remediable or curable.⁶⁰ As a result, unless the defender of the bond or the unhappy party challenges the appellate sentence issued by a single judge within three months from notice of the publication of the sentence, the nullity of the sentence will be sanated or healed by the passage of time.⁶¹

5. Tribunal Competence or Jurisdiction

The two apostolic letters do not alter existing provisions of the law rendering diocesan tribunals absolutely incompetent to hear certain types of cases and reserving cognizance of them to a particular judge or tribunal.⁶² Violations of this reservation result in the irremediable nullity of the sentence. Fortunately, few of these reserved cases are likely to involve issues of marital nullity. In fact, only the marriage cases in which "those who hold the highest civil office of a state" are parties, which are reserved to the Roman Pontiff personally and are, in practice, delegated by him to the Roman Rota, are likely to be submitted to ordinary first instance tribunals.⁶³ In the United States, such cases for which regular first instance tribunals are absolutely incompetent would include those involving the president of the United States and the governors of the several states. In addition, Latin tribunals are absolutely incompetent to hear cases involving two Eastern Catholics, unless the Eastern Catholics lack a hierarch and their pastoral care has been entrusted to a Latin ordinary or the Apostolic Signatura has prorogued or extended the competence of a Latin tribunal to decide cases involving certain Eastern Catholics; and Eastern tribunals are absolutely incompetent to hear cases involving two Latin Catholics. Finally, when a decision is rendered by an appellate tribunal that is not the duly designated appellate court for the tribunal from which the appeal resulted, that decision is irremediably null.

The apostolic letters do make some significant modifications of the conditions under which tribunals can claim to be relatively competent to

---

59. MI, c. 1673 §5; MMI, c. 1359 §5.
60. CIC, c. 1622 1°; CCEO, c. 1304 §1, 1°.
61. CIC, c. 1623; CCEO, c. 1304 §2.
62. CIC, c. 1620, 1°; CCEO, c. 1303 §1, 1°.
63. CIC, c. 1405 §1, 1°; CCEO, c. 1060 §1, 3°.

judge marriage nullity cases. Although they retain unchanged the forum of the place where the marriage was celebrated and the forum of the place where the respondent has a domicile or quasi-domicile as possible bases for claiming competence in marriage cases, the apostolic letters notably change the conditions under which tribunals can invoke the forum of the petitioner and the forum where the majority of proofs are to be gathered as the basis for competence. First, the letters expand the forum of the petitioner to include not only the place where the petitioner has a domicile but also the place where he or she has a quasi-domicile. Second, they eliminate the requirement that, before a tribunal claims competence as the forum of the petitioner or of the place where the majority of proofs are to be gathered, it seek the consent of the judicial vicar of the respondent. Finally, the letters eliminate the restriction of the previous law that allowed for competence on the basis of the domicile of the petitioner only in cases where both the petitioner and the respondent resided in the territory of the same episcopal conference or, for Eastern tribunals, the territory of the same nation.

The removal of these restrictions on the use of the forum of the petitioner as a basis for competence has been welcomed by North American tribunals, especially since it enables them to provide a pastoral response to the situation of immigrants whose marriages were celebrated in their countries of origin and whose former spouses reside in places without effectively functioning marriage tribunals. The relaxation of the requirements for the use of this basis for competence is not, however, without its dangers. The restrictions on the use of the forum of the petitioner as a basis for competence were originally inserted into the law in response to complaints to the Holy See about abuses by American tribunals operating under Norm 7 of the American Procedural Norms which had allowed unrestricted use of the forum of the petitioner as a basis for competence.[64] These complaints focused in particular on abridgements, if not outright

---

64. American Procedural Norms, Norm 7. See Apostolic Signatura, "litterae ad Praesidem Conferentiae Episcopalis Mexicana," in *Documenta recentiora circa rem matrimonialem et processualem* (Rome: Gregorian University Press, 1980) 2: nn. 53456–5462 and Zenon Grocholewski, "Declaration of the Apostolic Signatura on the Competence of Ecclesiastical Tribunals in the United States of America," *Monitor Ecclesiasticus* 104 (1979) 142–159. See also Rafael Rodríguez-Ocaño, "*Mitis Iudex*: Fuero competente y sistema de apelaciones," *Ius Canonicum* 56 (2016) 109–110 and Toxé, 103–104.

denial, of the right of defense of respondents living outside the United States. Now that the restrictions on the use of the forum of the petitioner as a basis for competence have been removed, it will be important for tribunals to be attentive to the right of defense of respondents residing in other countries, especially those who may not speak English or may not be especially adept at expressing themselves in writing. North American tribunals who claim competence on the basis of the forum of the petitioner must also be alert to possible civil effects of annulments granted here where the respondent lives in a country whose concordat with the Holy See provides for the civil recognition of annulments such as Italy, Spain, and Columbia or where the civil law defers to religious authorities in matters of family law.[65]

II. The Revised Ordinary Process: The So-Called *Pars Dynamica*

In addition to effecting changes in the ways tribunals are structured, the two recent apostolic letters make significant changes in the procedure to be followed in the contentious process for adjudicating marriage cases.

A. The Introductory Phase

1. Allocation of Responsibilities

Mitis Iudex and *Mitis et Misericors Iesus* have radically altered the allocation of responsibilities for carrying out the several steps of the introductory phase of the contentious judicial process used for marriage nullity cases. In the two codes promulgated, respectively, in 1983 and 1990, the norms governing the introductory phase of this process foresee that, once a petition is submitted to a tribunal, the judicial vicar will constitute a tribunal consisting of a judge or judges, a defender of the bond and a notary and that the single judge or *praeses* will proceed to accept (or reject) the case, cite the respondent, join the issues and move on to gather evidence in the probatory phase of the process.[66] The apostolic letters alter this traditional division of labor by concentrating every step of the introductory phase in the hands of the judicial vicar. He alone determines whether the

---

65. See Tawil, 203–215.
66. CIC, cc. 1505, 1507, 1513 and 1677; CCEO, cc. 1188, 1190, 1195, and 1363.

tribunal is competent to hear the case, accepts or rejects the petition, cites the respondent, joins the issues, decides whether the case is to be heard according to the ordinary process or is to be deferred to the bishop for a decision pursuant to the *processus brevior*. Only then does the judicial vicar constitute a tribunal by appointing the various officials needed to hear and decide the case.[67]

2. Communication of the Libellus to the Respondent

Both canon 1508 §2 of the Latin code and canon 1191 §2 of the Eastern code stipulate that, when the judge cites the respondent at the beginning of the process, he is to attach a copy of the libellus to the citation "unless for grave causes the judge determines that the *libellus* must not be made known to the party before that party makes a deposition in the trial."[68] Under this provision of the former law, tribunals in North America have considered all of the initial submissions of the petitioner, including the rather extended narrative known as a "marital history," as elements of the "petition" and then relatively routinely deferred (with, but usually, without a decree from the judge) communicating the libellus to the respondent until after he or she had testified during the trial or even until the publication of the acts. The justification for this skirting of the requirement for the law has usually been that, if the petitioner's extended narrative history of the marriage were shared with the respondent at this early stage of the process, he or she would be inclined to use his own declaration to try to refute the petitioner's assertions point by point rather than offering his or her own narrative account of the marriage. (This rationale subtly presumes, of course, that every case presented to the tribunal will be decided on one of the "psychological" grounds described in canon 1095 of the Latin code and canon 818 of the Eastern code.)

The new norms for marriage cases contain no provision for deferral of the communication of the libellus to the respondent. In fact, by stipulating that the "decree [of citation is to be] appended to the bottom of the libellus itself," the new norms seem to preclude such a deferral.[69] It is difficult to see how a tribunal could comply with this provision of the law without

---

67. MI, c. 1676 §§1–5; MMI, c. 1362 §§1–5.
68. CIC, c. 1508 §2; CCEO, c. 1191 §2.
69. MI, c. 1676 §1; MMI, c. 1362 §1.

making a copy of the petition available to the respondent. The purpose of communicating the petition to the respondent at the time of the citation is to enable him or her to make an informed initial response to the petitioner's claim that their marriage was invalid. This aim can be achieved without making available to the respondent everything in the petitioner's original submission. The two codes take a decidedly minimalist approach to what the petition introducing the cases must contain.[70] Adapting these requirements for marriage cases, the instruction *Dignitas connubii* stipulates that the libellus must

> describe the object of the cause, that is, specify the marriage in question, present a petition for a declaration of nullity, and propose—although not necessarily in technical terms—the reason for petitioning, that is, the ground or grounds of nullity on which the marriage is being challenged . . . [and] indicate at least in a general way the facts and proofs on which the petitioner is relying in order to demonstrate what is being asserted.[71]

This information can usually be digested from the longer narrative prepared by the petitioner into a few paragraphs of a one or two page document containing the necessary formalities for a libellus. The narrative itself is not the libellus but a preliminary supporting declaration or affidavit. Nor are documents submitted in connection with the petition part of the petition itself. As a result, there is no need to communicate these materials to the respondent at the time of the citation.[72] Instead, they can be withheld until the publication of the acts at the end of the probatory phase of the process. Tribunals desiring to bring their practice into compliance with the new law while avoiding unnecessary contentions between the parties might consider taking this less expansive view of what "the petition" encompasses and attaching the decree of citation to the brief summary statement of the petitioner's position described in canon 1504 of the Latin code and canon 1187 of the Eastern code.

---

70. CIC, c. 1504; CCEO, c. 1187.
71. DC, art. 116 §1, 2°–3°.
72. Pontifical Council for Legislative Texts, Two Questions about the Procedural Norms and About Can. 1676 § of the Motu Proprio *Mitis Iudex Dominus Iesus*, April 8, 2016, (Prot. N. 15363/2016): *The Jurist* 76 (2016) 291–292 and this volume, 380.

3. Changing Grounds in the Course of the Process

The recent apostolic letters entrust to the judicial vicar the case the responsibility of joining the issues or setting the grounds on which the case will be heard and decided. Only after the grounds have been set does the judicial vicar proceed to constitute a tribunal consisting of a judge or judges, a defender of the bond, and other court officials for the case. As a result, the judges may find that they disagree with the judicial vicar's choice of grounds. Anticipating such a disagreement, a judicial vicar in the United States inquired of the Pontifical Council for Legislative Texts whether a judge, once constituted, was free to change the grounds established by the judicial vicar. On November 26, 2015, the Council sent the judicial vicar a private response:

> While the new canon 1676 regards cases for the declaration of nullity of marriage, canons 1513 and 1514 regard the ordinary contentious trial and are not affected by the changes in the canons affected by the change in canons concerning special processes, i.e., marriage cases. While the judicial vicar decrees the initial doubt in marriage cases, the faculty of the judge to change the doubt or add another is not affected by the modification introduced with the MP *Mitis Iudex*.[73]

This response has led some to the erroneous conclusion that judges are authorized to modify the decrees joining the issues unilaterally when they receive the case from the judicial vicar or at any point in the course of the process. This conclusion fails to advert to canon 1514 to which the response refers:

> Once established, the terms of the controversy cannot be changed validly (*mutari valide nequeunt*) except by a new decree, for a grave cause, at the request of a party, and after the other parties have been heard and their arguments considered.

Thus, although judges can change the grounds in the course of the process, they can do so validly only at the request of one of the parties.[74]

---

73. Pontifical Council for Legislative Texts, private response, November 26, 2015, (Prot. N. 15210/2015), unpublished.

74. Even after the promulgation of the 1983 Latin code and the 1990 Eastern code, many North American canonists have continued have continued to operate in the spirit of the 1970 American Procedural Norms which gave judges considerable leeway to modify the decree of joinder in the course of the process. Norm 11 had stipulated: "During the course of the trial

In North America, parties to marriage nullity cases are unlikely to be well versed in the intricacies of matrimonial jurisprudence or to be represented by advocates well-grounded in this jurisprudence. Moreover, parties are not permitted to review regularly the evidence in their cases as it accumulates in the case file and advocates often do not monitor the progress of their clients' cases on a regular basis. As a result, it is unlikely that parties will request changes in the grounds at their own initiative or at the prompting of their advocates. The judge who becomes aware that the grounds set by the judicial vicar at the introductory phase of the process do not fit well with the facts emerging during the instruction of the case could notify the petitioner or his or her advocate of this fact and suggest a request for a change of grounds. Such a gambit is, however, rather awkward. The Roman Rota has, at least to date, not sanctioned sentences with irremediable nullity when they were issued after the judge had taken the initiative to change the decree of joinder during the process, as long as the parties were informed and given the opportunity to object to the change.[75]

4. Involvement of the Defender of the Bond

Since at least Benedict XIV's 1741 constitution *Dei miseratione*, the involvement of a defender of the bond in marriage nullity and dissolution processes has been necessary for the validity of the process. Many North American tribunals comply with this requirement by making the complete acts of the case available to the defender of the bond during the phase of discussion toward the end of the process.[76] While this practice may be minimally sufficient to prevent the nullity of the sentence, it is not the sort of involvement in the process the law foresees. In fact, the law stipulates that the defender of the bond has the right to be cited for and to be present at every significant moment in the process, including the hearing of parties, witnesses and experts, and to be heard by the judge whenever the parties are to be heard.[77] The recent apostolic letters give some specific indica-

---

the judge may add an additional basis or bases for nullity." *CLD* 7: 957. This provision of the APN has, of course, been abrogated. Nonetheless, some tribunals continue to act as if judges had this power to add (or delete) grounds unilaterally.

75. Antoni Stankiewicz, "De nullitate sentenriae 'ultra petita' prolatae," *Periodica* 70 (1981) 222–235.

76. CIC, c. 1433; CCEO, c. 1097.

77. CIC, c. 1432: CCEO, c. 1098.

tions of moments during the introductory phase of the process when the defender of the bond is to be heard: the defender is to be cited and receive a copy of the petition at the outset of the process[78] and is to be heard before the judicial vicar issues the decree joining the issues.[79]

As is the case with other moments in the process where the defender of the bond is to be heard, failure to cite the defender at the outset of the process results in the nullity of the act. Although this nullity can be corrected if the defender, "after [he or she has] inspected the acts, at least [was] able to perform [his or her] function,"[80] the apostolic letters' mentions of specific involvements by the defender of the bond during the introductory phase of the process are clearly meant to highlight the particular importance of the defender in the streamlined marriage nullity process introduced by the two recent apostolic letters. With the elimination of a mandatory second instance review of affirmative decisions, much of the responsibility for providing "quality control" in the process has devolved to the defender of the bond. Without the involvement of the defender, not just in the phase of discussion of the case but throughout the trial, the integrity of the process can be easily jeopardized. This heightened importance of the intervention of the defender of the bond has recently prompted the Apostolic Signatura to deny, on at least one occasion, an extension of the dispensation of a defender of the bond who lacked the required academic degree in canon law. In denying this extension, the Signatura noted: "[T]he new procedural norms for the handling of marriage nullity cases will require even more diligence and greater competency on the part of the defender of the bond."[81]

One of the puzzling consequences of the decision of the apostolic letters to entrust responsibility for the whole of the introductory phase of the process to the judicial vicar and to defer the constitution of a tribunal to the end of this phase is that the judicial vicar is required to consult with the defender of the bond before accepting or rejecting the case and before joining the issues but no defender has yet been designated with whom he

---

78. MI, c. 1676 §1; MMI, c. 1362 §1. The instruction *Dignitas connubii*, article 119 §2 had previously recommended that the defender of the bond be heard by the judge prior to his acceptance or rejection of the petition.
79. MI, 1676 §2; MMI, c. 1362 §2.
80. CIC, c. 1433; CCEO, c. 1097.
81. Apostolic Signatura, letter, December 2015. Unpublished.

can consult. One can only presume that the judicial vicar will consult with one of the defenders of the bond stably appointed by the diocesan bishop for service in the tribunal during the introductory phase of the process and then formally designate this defender for the case when he constitutes a tribunal at the end of this phase of the process.

5. Possible Stances of the Respondent

The two apostolic letters provide some helpful directives to tribunals on how to assess some of the stances respondents' may take to the initial citation. First, the apostolic letters foresee that, in some cases at least, the respondent may be the co-presenter of the petition or may explicitly consent to it, either at the time it is presented or subsequently.[82] If so, the judicial vicar can consider deferring the case to the *processus brevior* if the other conditions for the use of this extraordinary process are met. The Pontifical Council for Legislative texts has made clear that this consent by the respondent must be explicit: "Though the consent of the respondent can be given by several means, those means must however guarantee publicly and unequivocally his or her will."[83] Second, the respondent can answer the citation by expressing a willingness to participate in the process without agreeing (or necessarily disagreeing) with the claims of the petitioner. In this case, he or she enjoys unqualified use of the right of defense. Third, a respondent who "remits himself to the justice of the tribunal, or, when properly cited, once more, makes no response" is presumed "not to object to the petition."[84] Nonetheless, unless he or she has been legitimately declared absent from the trial, such a respondent is still entitled to receive the decree formulating the doubt, any new petitions presented in the course of the process, the decree of publication of the acts, and the definitive sentence as well as any other decisions of the single judge or panel of judges.[85] Fourth, a respondent declared absent according to the norm of law is also presumed not to object to the petition[86] but is

---

82. MI, c. 1683, 1°; MMI, c. 1369, 1°.

83. Pontifical Council for Legislative Texts, letter, P.N. 15138/2015, October 1, 2015: *The Jurist* 75 (2015) 664 and this volume, 368.

84. MI, *Ratio Procedendi*, art. 11 §2; MMI, *Ratio Procedendi*, art. 11 §2.

85. DC, art. 134 §3.

86. MI, *Ratio Procedendi*, art. 11 §2 and MMI, *Ratio Procedendi*, art. 11 §2 do not expressly mention the situation of a respondent who has been declared absent from the trial. Nevertheless, they do mention the respondent who "when properly cited once more makes no

entitled to receive only the formulation of the doubt and the definitive sentence.[87] Finally, "[i]f a party expressly declares that he or she objects to receiving any notices about the case, that party is held to have renounced of the faculty of receiving a copy of the sentence. In this case, that party can, but need not, be notified (*notificari potest*) of the dispositive part of the sentence."[88] Most tribunals will welcome this clarification of how to deal with the respondent who answers the initial citation (or subsequent citations) by asking (or sometimes demanding) that he or she not be contacted again.

6. Do We Have to Do it This Way?

There is no escaping the fact that the two recent apostolic letters have radically altered the allocation of responsibility for the various moments of the introductory phase of the marriage nullity process. Hitherto, the judicial vicar himself played a rather modest role in this phase of the process: he constituted a tribunal consisting of a judge or judges, a defender of the bond and a notary and then stepped aside to allow this tribunal to deal with the case until its conclusion. Now, however, responsibility for the whole preliminary phase rests with the judicial vicar himself and the judge or judges assigned to the case become involved only when the evidentiary or probative stage of the process is about to begin. No explanation has been offered for this enhancement of the role of the judicial vicar in the introductory phase of the process. One must presume, however, that the drafters of the revised law thought the changes would somehow expedite the process.

Whatever the motives for the changes, they confront many North American tribunals with some particular challenges. In many these tribunals, the judicial vicar is also a pastor and so comes to the tribunal office only a few times per week while the administration of the tribunal is entrusted to the moderator of the tribunal chancery or tribunal administrator, usually a lay person who may or may not have received academic

---

response," a phrase which describes the respondent who is subject to being declared absent in accord with the norms of CIC, c. 1592 and CCEO, c. 1272.

87. DC, art. 134 §3.

88. MI, *Ratio Procedendi*, art. 13; MMI, *Ratio Procedendi*, art. 13. This provision for honoring the respondent's express wish not to be contacted corresponds to the provision of DC, art. 258 §3.

formation in canon law. This arrangement has worked reasonably well as long as the judicial vicar's role in the process was over once he had constituted tribunals for cases recently submitted to his tribunal. Now, however, the process is likely to slow to a snail's pace unless the now part-time judicial vicar can devote sufficient time to the several tasks in the introductory phase of the process for all the cases submitted to the tribunal. As a result, there will be a strong temptation to ignore the clear directives of the two recent apostolic letters and continue to process marriage cases "the way we always have done it."

Since the traditional allocation of responsibility for the introductory phase of the process to the presiding or single judge after the judicial vicar has constituted a tribunal remains the norm for non-matrimonial cases, it would not seem that ignoring the norms of the two apostolic letters and allowing the single or presiding judge to continue to accept the petition, cite the respondent and join the issues would result in the nullity of the sentence. Moreover, the part-time (or, perhaps, merely nominal) judicial vicar could probably delegate the moderator of the tribunal chancery to constitute tribunals on his behalf. However, a tribunal's decision to ignore the provisions of the revised law that it finds inconvenient would seem to suggest that such a tribunal and its diocesan bishop have opted for "business as usual" rather than committing themselves to "the conversion of ecclesiastical structures" called for by Pope Francis.[89]

B. The Probatory Phase

The two apostolic letters make few changes to the existing norms on the gathering of evidence in the course of the trial. They do, however, significantly modify the norms governing the weight to be given to certain types of evidence.

1. Declarations and Confessions

The new norms stipulate that

> a judicial confession and the declarations of the parties, possibly supported by witnesses to the credibility of the parties, can have the force of full proof, to be evaluated by the judge after he has considered all the indications

---

89. MI, introduction, III; MMI, introduction.

(*indiciis*) and supporting factors (*adminculis*), unless other elements are present which weaken them.[90]

These norms represent a rather remarkable reversal in the way the law views the declarations or confessions of the parties. The 1936 instruction *Provida Mater* had asserted flatly that "a judicial deposition of the consorts is not admissible (*non est apta*) to constitute proof against the validity of marriage."[91] The 1983 Latin code and the 1990 Eastern code made cautious moves toward enhancing the probative value of the declarations and confessions of parties in marriage nullity cases but retained the principal that "the force of full proof cannot be attributed to them" except under rather stringent conditions.[92] Where the prior norms allowed for attributing the weight of full proof to the declarations or confessions of parties only when "other elements are present that thoroughly corroborate them," the revised norms allow the judge to consider these declarations or confessions fully probative "unless other elements are present which weaken them." This change should go a long way toward eliminating the awkward conflict situations, not infrequent in the past, in which petitioners were certain in conscience that their marriages were invalid but are unable to prove this fact in the external forum because the weight of their own declarations were heavily discounted or because of a lack of corroborating witnesses. Such conflict situations have long been cited as the justification for resort to the "internal forum" approach to marriage cases mentioned briefly by Pope Francis in his apostolic exhortation *Amoris Laetititia*.[93]

2. Testimony of a Single Witness

The new norms also upgrade the weight that judges can attribute to the deposition of a single witness. The ancient maxim that "one witness is no

90. MI, c. 1678 §1; MMI, c. 1364 §1.
91. Congregation for the Sacraments, instruction *Provida Mater Ecclesiae*, art. 117, August 15, 1936: AAS 28 (1936). More obliquely, canon 1751 of the 1917 CIC had asserted: "Si agatur de negotio aliquot private et in causa non sit bonum publicum, confessio iudicialis unius partis, dummodo libere et considerate facta, relevant alteram ab onere probandi." Since marriage case were not merely private matters and did involve the public good, the confession of one party did not relieve the other of the burden of proof. The same awkwardly phrased norm was found in the previous law for the Eastern Churches promulgated as Pius XII, motu proprio *Sollicitudinem nostram*, January 6, 1950: AAS 42 (1950) c. 273.
92. CIC, c. 1536 §2; CCEO, c. 1217 §2.
93. Francis, apostolic exhortation *Amoris Laetitia*, §300, March 19, 2016: *Origins* 45/46 (April 21, 2016) 821.

witness" has been thoroughly discredited and replaced by the principle that "the testimony of a single witness can produce full proof . . . if the circumstances of things and persons suggest it."[94] This provision too should eliminate many of the conflict cases that have prompted suggestions that parties who are convinced of the invalidity of their broken marriage but cannot prove it to the satisfaction of a tribunal because of a paucity of witnesses should resort to "internal forum" solutions.

3. Use of Experts

The two apostolic letters address the circumstances when tribunals must seek the assistance of experts. The former canon 1680 of the Latin code and canon 1366 of the Eastern code had stipulated: "In cases of impotence or defect of consent because of mental illness (*mentis morbum*), the judge is to use (*utatur*) the services of one or more experts unless it is clear from the circumstances that it would be useless to do so." Many tribunals interpreted the expression "mental illness" strictly to include only the most serious mental disorders such as psychoses but not less severe psychic disturbances such as immaturity or personality disorders. This strict interpretation did not correspond to the practice of the Roman Rota which rather routinely required an expert's report in all cases being tried on grounds listed in canon 1095 regardless of the nature of the alleged psychic irregularity. This Rotal practice was extended to lower tribunals by the 2005 instruction *Dignitas connubii* which held: DC, art. 203 §1: "In causes concerning impotence or a defect of consent because of *mentis morbum* or because of the incapacities described in can. 1095, the judge is to employ the assistance of one or more experts, unless from the circumstances this would appear evidently useless."[95]

Proponents of a more restrictive interpretation of "mental illness" could still argue that after all *Dignitas connubii* was only an "instruction" and, as such, to the extent that it "cannot be reconciled with the prescripts of laws, [it] lack[s] all force."[96] Although the provision of *Dignitas connubii* does go somewhat beyond the letter of the canons promulgates in 1983 and 1990 respectively, it does reflect the exhortations of John Paul II in

---

94. MI, c. 1678 §2; MMI, c. 1364 §2.
95. DC, art. 203 §1.
96. CIC, c. 34 §2.

his frequently cited allocutions to the Roman Rota,[97] the *stylus and praxis* of the Roman Rota itself, and the 1998 declaration of the Apostolic Signatura.[98] The argument for a very narrow reading of the codes' requirement for the use of experts has become untenable after the appearance of the two recent apostolic letters. They stipulate: MI, c. 1678 §3 "In cases of impotence or defect of consent because of mental illness or an anomaly of a psychic nature, the judge is to use the services of one or more experts unless it is clear from the circumstances that it would be useless to do so."[99]

C. The Decisory Phase

The most dramatic and most publicized change in the marriage nullity process effected by the two apostolic letters is their elimination of the requirement that all affirmative decisions in marriage nullity cases receive conforming decisions at the appellate level before the parties are declared free to enter new marriages. Now, once the peremptory time of fifteen useful days from notice of the publication of the sentence has elapsed without an appeal being lodged either by the respondent or the defender of the bond, an affirmative decision can be executed, i.e., the parties are to be notified by the judicial vicar of the tribunal issuing the first affirmative sentence that they are free to enter new marriages in the Church.[100] While the elimination of mandatory second instance review of affirmative decisions in marriage cases will, no doubt, expedite the resolution of these cases, it will also require tribunal officials to be more attentive to the peremptory time limits for making appeals than they have been hitherto. When all affirmative decisions had to be forwarded to the appellate court *ex officio* whether a party lodged an appeal or not, it was possible to treat the time limit for lodging an appeal rather casually. In the new dispensation, however, it is important to know with certainty when the respon-

---

97. John Paul II, allocution, February 5, 1987: *AAS* 79 (1987)1454–1455 and John Paul II, allocution, January 25, 1998: *AAS* 80 (1988) 1178–1185.

98. Supreme Tribunal of the Apostolic Signatura, declaration, June 16, 1998: *Periodica* 87 (1998) 619–622. For commentary on this declaration see Urban Navarrete, "Commentarium," *Periodica* 87 (1998) 624 and Augustine Mendonça, "The Apostolic Signatura's Recent Declaration on the Necessity of Using Experts in Marriage Nullity Cases," *Studia Canonica* 35 (2001) 33–58.

99. MI, c. 1678 §3; MMI, 1364 §3.

100. MI, c. 1679; MMI, c. 1365.

dent and the defender of the bond received notice of the publication of the sentence. Since the right to appeal is extinguished with the elapse of the peremptory fifteen days, the notification of the publication of the sentence should clearly inform the respondent and the defender of the bond of the inevitable consequence of delay in lodging an appeal. While the judge can shorten the time limit for lodging an appeal at the request of the parties, he has no authority to extend the time for lodging an appeal: "*Fatalia legis*, that is, the time limits established by law for extinguishing rights, cannot be extended."[101] As a result, the only remedy remaining for a respondent or defender who has allowed the time for appeal to elapse is to request the favor of a new hearing before the Roman Rota,[102] a remedy which will probably be unavailable if the other party has already entered a new marriage in the Church.[103] To obtain such a new hearing, the party or defender will have to bear the evidentiary burden of submitting "new and grave proofs or arguments" which show that a different decision would result from the granting of a new hearing.[104]

Since the time for lodging an appeal begins to run only with notification to the parties of the publication of the sentence, tribunals must insure that their methods of publishing the sentence comport with the law. The current law foresees only two methods for publishing the sentence: "by giving a copy of the sentence to the parties or their procurators or by sending them a copy" in the mail."[105] In either case, the law requires that a copy of the definitive sentence in its entirety to be available to the parties to do with what they will. Other methods of publishing the sentence may pass muster in exceptional cases as long as the parties are given sufficient information about the sentence to lodge a well-informed appeal.[106] Nevertheless, absent exceptional circumstances, failure to make a copy of the sentence available to the parties means that the time for appeal does not

---

101. CIC, c. 1465 §1; CCEO, c. 1124 §1.

102. MI, c. 1681; MMI, c. 1367.

103. See Francis, "Rescritto del Santo padre Francesco sul compliment e l'osservanza della nuova legge del processo matrimoniale, 11.12. 2015," II, 3, December 7, 2015: http://press.vatican.va/content/salastampa/en/bolletino/pubblico/2015/12/11/0981/02193.html.

104. CIC, c. 1644 §1; CCEO, c. 1325 §1. See Antoni Stankiewicz, "Le prove e gli argomenti nuovi e gravi per il riesame della causa," *Apollinaris* 68 (1995) 499–513.

105. CIC, c. 1615; CCEO, c. 1298.

106. See William Daniel, "The Publication of the Definitive Sentence," *Studia Canonica* 42 (2008) 393–436 and John P. Beal, "Publish or Perish: Transparency and the Marriage Nullity Process," *CLSA Proceedings* 75 (2013) 75–82.

even begin[107] and the possibility of an appeal of the decisions will hang over the case in perpetuity.

Although the two apostolic letters abolish the requirement of appellate review of all affirmative decisions in marriage nullity cases, dissatisfied parties, both petitioners and respondents, retain the right to appeal adverse decisions and the defender has the right to appeal an affirmative decision. What has been virtually eliminated by the two apostolic letters is the abbreviated appellate procedure introduced by Paul VI's motu proprio *Causas matrimoniales* and continued in both the Latin and the Eastern code for confirming affirmative first instance decisions in marriage nullity cases by decree.[108] Except in the rare case where the appellate judges deem an appeal to be merely dilatory, all appeals, whether of affirmative or negative decisions, are to be dealt with by the ordinary appellate process and conclude not with summary decrees ratifying or confirming the previous decision but with full-blown sentences.

When an appeal is received by an appellate court, the judicial vicar constitutes a tribunal of three judges as well as a defender of the bond and a notary to hear and decide the case. The *praeses* of the panel notifies the parties of their right to offer additional observations on the case within a peremptory time period set by the judges. This notification functions as the citation in the appellate process. After consulting with the appellate defender of the bond, the judges determine by decree whether the appeal is merely dilatory or is to be admitted to the ordinary process.[109] The apostolic letters provide no criteria for deciding that an appeal is "merely dilatory."[110] These criteria will, therefore, have to be worked out on a case by case basis by jurisprudence. However, the failure of an appellant to respond at all to the initial notification, especially if he or she had not offered testimony in the first instance trial, might well be one criterion for a determination that the appeal was merely dilatory. If they determine that the appeal was "merely dilatory," the judges hear the defender of the bond and proceed to confirm the original sentence, whether it was affirmative or negative, by decree.

---

107. CIC, c. 1614; CCEO, c. 1297.
108. Paul VI, *Causas matrimoniales*, VII; CIC, c. 1682; CCEO, c. 1368.
109. MI, c. 1680 §2; MMI, c. 166 §2.
110. See Rodríguez-Ocaña, 120–122.

If the judges remit the case to the ordinary appellate process, they or the *praeses* or *ponens* moves on to set the grounds or join of the issues for the appellate process. Normally, the decree of joinder is: "Whether the decision of the prior tribunal should be confirmed or not." The appellate judges do, however, have the discretion to add a new ground of nullity that was not considered by the first instance tribunal and to proceed "as if in first instance."[111] Nevertheless, should an appellate court avail itself of this option, any appeal of its decision on this new ground is directed not to its ordinary appellate tribunal but to the Roman Rota which, although normally a third instance court, will proceed "as if in second instance."[112] An appellate trial typically moves directly from the joinder of issues to the discussion of the case without the intermediary of an evidentiary phase, and the judges then decide the case on the basis of the evidence gathered in the course of the first instance process. They do, however, have the faculty to gather new evidence during the appellate process if "it is like that the new sentence will be unjust" if they do not do so.[113] If new evidence is gathered, it must be published to the parties and a new decree concluding the case issued. As in a first instance trial, the appellate process proceeds to the phases of discussion and decision and concludes with the issuance of a sentence and its publication.

There are several possible outcomes for the appellate process. First, the appellate court may confirm a negative decision upholding the validity of the marriage. If so, the unhappy petitioner has no further right of appeals but can petition for a new hearing of the case before the Roman Rota.[114] Second, the appellate court may confirm an affirmative decision declaring the invalidity of the challenged marriage. If so, the disgruntled respondent or defender of the bond can still request a new hearing of the case before

---

111. MI, c. 1680 §4; MMI, c. 1366 §4.

112. Apostolic Signatura, declaration, in *Roman Replies and CLSA Advisory Opinions 1998*, ed. F. Stephen Pedone and James Donlon (Washington: CLSA, 1998) 16–17. See also Klaus Lüdicke and Ronny Jenkins, *Dignitas Connubii: Norms and Commentary* (Washington: CLSA, 2006) 434 and John P. Beal, "Remedial Readings: Challenges to Sentences in Marriage Nullity Cases," *The Jurist* 59 (1999) 22–23.

113. CIC, c. 1639 §2 and c. 1600; 1320 §2 and c. 1283.

114. MI, c. 1681. MMI, c. 1367 speaks of making this recourse to "the tribunal of third grade" since the Rota is the third instance tribunal for eparchies of the Eastern Churches outside the territory of the Patriarch or Major Archbishop. However, within their territories, the Patriarch and major Archbishop are empowered to establish their own tribunals of second and subsequent instance. See CCEO, cc. 1062–1065.

the Roman Rota, but the parties may still enter new marriages in the Catholic Church as soon as they are notified. Third, the appellate court may overturn a first instance negative decision by issuing a decision declaring the nullity of the marriage. A dissatisfied respondent or defender can still appeal this decision to the Roman Rota. If there is no appeal within the peremptory fifteen days from notice of the publication of the sentence, however, the parties can remarry as soon as they are notified that the decision has become executive. Finally, the appellate court may overturn a first instance affirmative decision with a negative decision upholding the validity of the marriage. If this should occur, the petitioner has the right to appeal the new decision to the Rota.

As was noted above, there is no longer a right to appeal in the strict sense of the term after a decision, affirmative or negative, in a marriage nullity case against which no appeal has been lodged within the peremptory fifteen days from notice of the publication of the sentence or one which has received a second conforming decision at appellate level. The only remedy left for parties dissatisfied with such decisions is a petition for a new hearing of the case before the tribunal of the third instance which almost always is the Roman Rota. In order to be granted a new hearing, the one seeking the new hearing must be able to produce "new and grave proofs or arguments" that show that a different decision would probably be issued if the new hearing is granted. The possibility that a respondent in a marriage nullity case will pursue a new hearing of the case even after the other party has entered a new canonical marriage has long been a pastoral concern for canonists. Pope Francis minimized the chances that a marriage case will be reopened for a new hearing after one of the parties has entered a new marriage in the Catholic Church in a Rescript from an Audience with the Dean of the Roman Rota on December 11, 2015. This rescript stipulates: "Recourse for a new hearing of the case before the Roman Rota is not admitted after one of the parties has contracted a new canonical marriage, unless the injustice of the decision is clear."[115]

D. A Note on the "Pre-Judicial Process"

One of the innovations found in the two apostolic letters is the provision in articles 1 to 5 of their appendices entitled *Ratio Procedendi* for a

---

115. Francis, "Rescriptum ex Audientia," December 11, 2015 II, 3.

"pastoral" or "pre-judicial" process.[116] As the inclusion of these articles in legal documents designed to revise and streamline the marriage nullity process suggests, the "pastoral" or "pre-judicial" process is intended, in part, to assist members of the faithful to organize their accounts of their now broken marriages into coherent narratives and gather possible supporting evidence in preparation for eventual submissions of petitions to marriage tribunals. In this respect, the "pre-judicial" process appears to weaken the prohibition of canon 1529 of the Latin code and canon 1210 of the Eastern code on gathering evidence prior to the joinder of the issues and to validate the practice of many North American tribunals of conducting extensive preliminary investigations of petitions prior to accepting them and citing the respondent. As a result, many tribunals have seen the introduction of the "pre-judicial" process as a vindication of their existing practice and have not seen any need to modify this practice.

However, the "pre-judicial" process of the two recent apostolic letters is only partly aimed at preparing the ground for a possible marriage nullity petition. It is seen as an important component of a larger "unified pastoral plan for the care of marriage."[117] Responsibility for this pastoral outreach to "separated and divorced spouses who perhaps by the condition of their lives have abandoned religious practice" rests with the diocesan bishop and other pastors.[118] The "pastoral" or "pre-judicial" process outlined in the apostolic letters is not an additional diocesan or parish "program" designed to bring the skills of experts to bear to solve the "problem" of those who have suffered marital shipwreck but a commitment of the diocesan and parish community to "accompany" separated and divorced faithful on their journey. Although the "pre-judicial" process may result in a well-documented petition ready for a tribunal, the process is to be entrusted not to officials of the diocesan tribunal but to

> Persons deemed suitable by the local ordinary, with appropriate expertise, *though not exclusively juridical-canonical*. Among them in the first place is the pastor or the one who prepared the spouses for the wedding celebration.

---

116. See Pedro A. Moreno García, "El servicio de indagación prejudicial: aspectos jurídico-pastorales," *Ius Canonicum* 56 (2016) 65–85; Eugenio Zanetti, "La consulenza previa all'introduzione di unacausa di nullitá matrimoniale," in *La riforma dei processi matrimoniali*, 9–28.

117. MI, *Ratio Procedendi*, art. 2; MMI, *Ratio Procedendi*, art. 2.

118. MI, *Ratio Procedendi*, art. 1; MMI, *Ratio Procedendi*, art. 1.

This function of counseling can also be entrusted to other clerics, religious or lay people approved by the local ordinary.[119]

The mention of the "counseling" as among the roles of those entrusted with the "pre-judicial" process suggests that, before examining the possibility of pursuing a declaration of nullity, those accompanying the separated and divorced should attempt to pursue the possible reconciliation of the spouses and the resumption of common life. If these efforts prove fruitless, it will be clear, should a petition for a declaration of nullity eventually be introduced, that "the marriage has irreparably failed, such that conjugal living cannot be restored."[120] Since the pastoral outreach connected with the "pre-judicial" process is meant to help those who feel alienated from the Christian community because of their situation be re-integrated and feel welcomed in the life of that community, the process cannot be a merely bureaucratic response to personal catastrophe. Those entrusted with this process should be men and women of faith who are capable of communicating their faith and are willing to accompany the separated and divorced whether they opt to pursue a declaration of nullity or not.

Conclusion

If, in early 2015, North American tribunals had drawn up a wish list of procedural reforms to streamline the marriage nullity process and expedite the resolution of cases, it is hard to identify an item from this list of desiderata that has not been granted by *Mitis Iudex* and *mitis et Misericors Iesus*. All of the usual suspects are here: expanded possibilities for the use of lay people as judges, fewer restrictions on the use of the forum of the petitioner as a basis for competence, greater respect for the probative weight of the declarations of parties and the depositions of a single witness, elimination of the mandatory review of affirmative decisions, a possibility for dismissing merely dilatory appeals, and even an abbreviated process for dispatching those so-called "open and shut" cases. Of course, the two apostolic letters also contain innovations that it is unlikely North American canonists would have included on their wish lists for procedural reform, most

---

119. MI, *Ratio Procedendi*, art. 3; MMI, *Ratio Procedendi*, art. 3.
120. MI, c. 1675; MMI, c. 1361.

notably the reallocation of the responsibilities for the introductory phase of the process from the single judge or *praeses* to the judicial vicar. Tribunals cannot simply "cherry pick" those elements of Pope Francis' reform that they find congenial and ignore the rest. As occurred with the previous reforms of matrimonial procedure, tribunal practitioners will have to accept the bitter with the sweet and learn new ways of dealing with cases.

When promulgating these reforms of matrimonial procedure, Pope Francis recognized that streamlining and simplifying marriage nullity procedure carries the inherent risk of undermining the principal of marital indissolubility. He was willing to take this risk, however, because of his enormous confidence in his brother bishops, individually and collegially, not just to oversee but to be actively engaged in the marriage nullity process to insure "catholic unity with Peter in faith and discipline."[121] As the implementation of the two apostolic letters unfolds, we will see whether the Holy Father's confidence in his brother bishops was warranted.

ABSTRACT

The apostolic letters Mitis Iudex Dominus Iesus *and* Mitis et Misericors Iesus *have effected significant revisions in the procedure tribunals are to follow in resolving marriage nullity cases. This article identifies the most significant revisions in the law and explains the adjustments that tribunals will have to make in dealing with cases according to the "ordinary" process. It deals with changes in the organization and staffing of tribunals, tribunal competence, responsibility for the several steps of the introductory phase of the process, the weighing of evidence and appeals.*

---

121. MI, V.; MMI.

WILLIAM L. DANIEL*

The Notion of Canonical Jurisprudence and its Application to the Tribunal of the Roman Rota and Causes of Nullity of Marriage

I. Introduction

Those engaged in the governance of and the administration of justice in the Church are bound by the duty of their office to act always in accord with the sacred discipline of the Church. That discipline cannot be reduced to the bald text of the canons of the codes but, in the first place, presupposes a profound appreciation for what is just (*iustum*) in the societal relationships of Christ's faithful. One critical source for attaining such an appreciation is the body of jurisprudence that is an integral portion of the canonical tradition and science.

In the contemporary ecclesial milieu, where the stability and nullity of marriage have been called into question in a public way reminiscent of the 1960s and 1970s,[1] and where the norm of procedural law governing causes of nullity of marriage has just undergone some profound modifications,[2] the stability of ecclesiastical jurisprudence, especially in the area of marriage, seems also to have been impacted. Accordingly, the time is most

---

* Assistant Professor, School of Canon Law, The Catholic University of America, Washington, DC.

1. Cf. III Extraordinary Assembly of the Synod of Bishops, *Relatio post disceptationem*, October 13, 2014 (Vatican City: Libreria Editrice Vaticana, 2014).

2. Cf. Francis, motu proprio *Mitis iudex Dominus Iesus*, August 15, 2015 (Vatican City: Libreria Editrice Vaticana, 2015); idem, motu proprio *Mitis et misericors Iesus*, August 15, 2015 (Vatican City: Libreria Editrice Vaticana, 2015).

appropriate for an investigation into the notion of canonical jurisprudence, keeping in mind especially the Church's jurisprudence concerning the nullity of marriage due to a defect of consent, being one of the most frequently examined matters in her judiciary.

After laying out some basic premises, this study will first expound upon various facets of the notion of jurisprudence in the canonical system. The meaning of this for the universal Church will then be explored through an analysis of the expression "unity of jurisprudence," the promotion of which is a function entrusted by the supreme legislator, on the basis of canonical tradition, to the Tribunal of the Roman Rota. A proper understanding of jurisprudence also has implications for the administration of justice in the particular Church, thus justifying a consideration of the question of local jurisprudence. Finally, certain recent developments pertaining to matrimonial jurisprudence will be identified and their ability to impact jurisprudence examined. This study pertains to the jurisprudence concerning the nullity of marriage, but its analyses and conclusions are applicable, *mutatis mutandis*, to all areas of law, including penal and contentious-administrative jurisprudence.

II. Basic Premises to the Notion of Jurisprudence

Legislation is by its nature general and abstract. That is to say that the legislative norm aims to provide a juridical institute or rule of conduct applicable to all persons and all cases in view of the common good (generality). And it largely omits consideration of what may be needed for a just application of the norm in the concrete case, leaving the judgment about the correct application of the norm to the individual competent authority (abstractness). It foresees and establishes what is, as a rule, just for all cases.

In the context of the administration of justice, the authority competent to apply the law is the judge, whether it be a college of judges or an individual judge. The judge, who knows the general and abstract norm, stands as *dominus* over the judicial process, which he directs, and ultimately issues the definitive sentence at its culmination. The definitive sentence is notable for its very objective tone and structure, inasmuch as it analyzes the proofs and lays out the whole question in the manner of a syllogism (major premise—minor premise—conclusion). In preparing the definitive sentence, the judge declares what juridical principles govern the case at hand (*in iure*), which is the major premise. Then he externalizes his objective examination of the proofs (*in facto*), which is the minor premise. Finally, he draws the logical conclusion in stating the dispositive part of the sentence, in effect declaring and juridically establishing what the law means (*ius dicere*) for the parties' juridical situation, by an act of judicial authority (*iuris dictio*). Evidently, the foundation to this act of judicial power is the ensemble of juridical principles at play in the case, and so identifying these is of primary practical importance.

It would be simplistic to reduce this primary task of identifying juridical principles to the mere citation of the canons of the Code of Canon Law that apply to the case. This is due not only to the generality and abstractness of the legislative norm but also because of the living juridical patrimony flowing from the Church's long experience of the judicial treatment of controverted questions. In other words, lying between the general legislation and the particular judicial application there is a system of complex substantive and procedural rules that guide the exercise of the judicial function, which can be called *maxims of jurisprudence*. These are rules formulated over the course of time and by means of consistent decision-making, which direct the most just and effective manner for discerning what has been proven and for verifying the juridical effects of what has been proven (juridical facts). They are not for the most part incorporated into the legislation for a few reasons. (1) Many of them are not absolute (or purely general) but pertain to an ensemble of diverse facts, which can only be verified in a particular case. (2) They reveal the dynamic vitality of law in the society, since they reveal how the law rightly applies to real social situations; accordingly, they are subject to continual, if very gradual, development.[3] It would thus be inopportune for them to be codified, since the good order of society demands that legislation have the mark of stability. (3) The canonical system holds in high esteem the particular prudential operations of the human judge, especially in regard to his free evaluation of proofs. In view of these principles, maxims of jurisprudence are not

---

3. Cf. Francesco Finocchiaro, "La giurisprudenza nell'ordinamento canonico," in *La norma en el derecho canonico. Actas del III Congreso internacional de derecho canonico, Pamplona, 10–15 octubre de 1976* (Pamplona: EUNSA, 1979) 1: 989–1007, esp. 991, no. 1.

part of the general legislation of the Church, but they are not for this reason dispensable.

In causes of nullity of marriage, at the decisional moment—or moments: 1) when the individual judge draws up his *votum*, and 2) when the college of judges convenes under secrecy to discuss the cause[4]—the judge in general determines whether or not he is morally certain that the alleged nullity of the marriage in the case is objectively established. This is of course a matter of discerning whether what is proven (*probata*) corresponds with what the general legislation states in regard to the nullity of marriage on a particular ground (e.g., whether the proofs demonstrate that a spouse perpetrated total simulation). *Nevertheless, it is of preliminary importance that the judge also discern whether he is morally certain about what juridical principles govern his examination of the cause*: "In order to have the moral certitude necessary by law . . . it is required that any prudent doubt whatsoever truly be excluded with respect to *the law* and the facts . . ." (DC art. 247 §2, emphasis added).[5] The judge accordingly may only justly proceed in issuing his *votum* and subsequently, as a college, the definitive sentence when he is certain that he knows and has rightly applied the juridical principles applicable to the case. This is a matter not only of having a general understanding of the text of the relevant canons of the code but also of having a grasp of the jurisprudence that relates to the case at hand.[6] Hence, one can see the great importance of knowing and continually studying jurisprudence.

---

4. Cf. CIC c. 1609 §§2–3, CCEO c. 1292 §§2–3, DC art. 248 §§2–3. DC is used as the abbreviation for the Instruction *Dignitas connubii*: Pontifical Council for Legislative Texts, *Instructio "Dignitas connubii" servanda a Tribunalibus diœcesanis et interdiœcesanis in pertractandis causis nullitatis matrimonii*, January 25, 2005 (Vatican City: Libreria Editrice Vaticana, 2005). On the enduring force of most of the norms of this instruction even after the Franciscan reform of August 15, 2015, see William L. Daniel, "An Analysis of Pope Francis' 2015 Reform of the General Legislation Governing Causes of Nullity of Marriage," *The Jurist* 75 (2015) 456–464 and this volume, 27–64.

5. The whole norm reads: "Ad certitudinem autem moralem iure necessariam, non sufficit praevalens probationum indiciorumque momentum, sed requiritur ut quodlibet quidem prudens dubium positivum errandi, *in iure* et in facto, excludatur, etsi mera contrarii possibilitas non tollatur" (emphasis added). It is repeated verbatim in art. 12 of the *Ratio procedendi* attached to the two above-mentioned motu proprios of August 15, 2015.

6. Cf. Joaquín Llobell, "Perfettibilità e sicurezza della norma canonica. Cenni sul valore normativa della giurisprudenza della Rota Romana nelle cause matrimoniali," in *Ius in vita et in missione Ecclesiae. Acta Symposii Internationalis Iuris Canonici, in Civitate Vaticana celebrati diebus 19–24 aprilis 1993*, ed. Pontificium Consilium de legum textibus interpretandis (Vatican City: Libreria Editrice Vaticana, 1994) 1258.

III. The General Notion of Canonical Jurisprudence

The general notion of canonical jurisprudence is here explored by stating a definition of it, as proposed by canonical doctrine. In explaining this definition, both positive and negative approaches are useful, and so there is a discussion of what jurisprudence is and what it is not. Because of its importance in the canonical system, the general legislation stipulates the extent of its juridical force, while doctrine helps to explain its moral-persuasive force on the rational plane.

A) A Definition of Jurisprudence

In Roman law, the emperor was both the legislator and the font of understanding of the law. In the earlier period of the empire, this latter function was assumed by the *iuris consulti* or *iuris periti* or *iuris prudentes*, who gave responses for the emperor (*ius respondendi*). Eventually, the judicial function became more defined through developments in the office of magistrate, who issued decisions according to the common pattern of deciding similar cases. Accordingly, the decision of an imperial magistrate not only resolved the case at hand but could also create a rule binding upon all. This sense of Roman jurisprudence thus had a precedential and even a normative value. This understanding seems to have been applied in the medieval period to the decisions and replies of the Supreme Pontiff, whose responses were seen to be binding on all judges deciding similar cases.[7]

In the contemporary canonical system, jurisprudence is justly defined, in the terms given by the Capuchin jurist Zaccaria Varalta, as "the complex of uniform decisions, that is, those uniformly issued by tribunals in the effective exercise of their jurisdictional function" (*"complexus decisionum uniformium seu uniformiter latarum a tribunalibus, in effectivo exercitio propriae functionis iurisdictionalis"*).[8] Pope St. John Paul II in his 1984 discourse to

---

7. Cf. Zaccaria Varalta, "De iurisprudentiae conceptu," *Periodica* 62 (1973) 41–43, nn. 3–5. See also Arthur Caron, "Jurisprudence in Canon Law," *The Jurist* 18 (1958) 89–90; Gérard Fransen, "La valeur de la jurisprudence en droit canonique," in *La norma en el derecho canonico*, 197–212, esp. 204, no. 12; Charles Lefèbvre, "Pauli VI verba de rotali iurisprudentia necnon de studiis iuris canonici," *Periodica* 59 (1969) 117–142, at 119.

8. Varalta, "De iurisprudentiae conceptu," 40. This is the objective sense. The author also indicates the formal (or, better, subjective) sense as referring to the authority that issues such decisions.

the Roman Rota similarly described jurisprudence as an "ensemble of concordant decisions" (*"insieme di sentenze concordanti"*).[9]

Varalta's expression "complex of uniform decisions" has elements of distinct importance that must be taken adequately into account. *Complex*: as a rule, it is a matter not of any one decision on a particular question but of an indeterminate grouping of decisions issued over the course of time by diverse judges.[10] This is due to the fact that when numerous judges treat a particular question according to the same principles, such principles cannot be reduced to the opinion of individuals but are rooted in the prudence of presumably learned jurists. *Uniform decisions*: inevitably a tribunal repeatedly deals with the same questions, given the fact that litigation reflects societal patterns; but it is not merely the repeated treatment of the same questions that gives rise to jurisprudence. Rather, jurisprudence is created from the fact that those same questions are examined and decided in the same way, according to common rules of prudence.

Moreover, avoiding all formalism, one should bear in mind that it is not a question of a certain number of sentences "but a proportion between the number of sentences, time, and the recurrence of the same question."[11] Thus, it is a multiplicity of decisions on the same matter issued over the course of time that gives rise to jurisprudence. Even the course of time cannot be quantified by way of general principle. For if a tribunal finds itself issuing the same kind of decision frequently during the course of some months, its jurisprudence on a particular point may emerge. It is more likely, though, that the development of a common jurisprudence occurs over the course of several years or even decades.

See also Caron, "Jurisprudence in Canon Law," 95–97; Heinrich Ewers, "De quibusdam quaestionibus ad rectam iurisprudentiae canonicae constitutionem et aestimationem spectantibus," *Periodica* 68 (1979) 641–642; Antoni Stankiewicz, "The Unity of Jurisprudence and the Role of the Roman Rota," in *Matrimonial Law and Canonical Procedure*, ed. Patricia M. Dugan and Luis Navarro, Gratianus Series (Montréal: Wilson & Lafleur Ltée, 2013) 22.

9. Allocutio ad Praelatos Auditores S. Romanae Rotae coram admissos, January 26, 1984: *AAS* 76 (1984) 647, no. 6.

10. One could argue, though, that a single sentence or judicial decree that treats a question for the first time constitutes the jurisprudence on that point, (cf. Joaquín Llobell, *Los procesos matrimoniales en la Iglesia* [Madrid: RIALP, 2014] 134, *sub* 3.2); but such jurisprudence could evidently be subject to evolution or consolidation with the issuance of subsequent decisions in similar matters.

11. See Carlo Gullo, "Interpretazione evolutiva o evoluzione del diritto? Contributo alla teoria dell'interpretazione nel diritto canonico," *Ephemerides iuris canonici* 26 (1970) 371.

In explaining the common doctrine on the notion of jurisprudence, one author writes that "Rotal jurisprudence is not constituted by a single Rotal decision or by a few decisions but by a manner of judging which is consistent in many decisions during a given period of time."[12] Similarly, another author writes that "'jurisprudence' is not the act of judging nor one isolated sentence"; rather "jurisprudence exists or the jurisprudence is formed when there is a *unity* of criteria . . . among various decisions."[13] As has already been stressed, no one sentence ordinarily constitutes jurisprudence, nor does a single sentence in itself bring about an evolution in already existing jurisprudence.[14] Rather, jurisprudence is the ensemble of consistent juridical principles that can be derived from a collection of decisions on the same matter.[15] It was for these reasons that one past Dean of the Roman Rota, then-Msgr. William Theodore Heard, prohibited the publication of individual Rotal sentences "since only one who reads all the sentences pronounced over a period of time by different *Turni* can catch the line of jurisprudence, not only those written by a particular [Judge]."[16]

---

12. Raymond L. Burke, *Lack of Discretion of Judgment Because of Schizophrenia: Doctrine and Recent Rotal Jurisprudence*, Analecta Gregoriana 237 (Rome: Editrice Pontificia Università Gregoriana, 1986) 21. In the same sense, see Juan Ignacio Arrieta, "Amministrazione della giustizia e comunione tra i tribunali della Chiesa," in *"Veritas non auctoritas facit legem." Studi di diritto matrimoniale in onore di Piero Antonio Bonnet*, ed. Giuseppe dalla Torre, Carlo Gullo and Geraldina Boni, Studi Giuridici 99 (Vatican City: Libreria Editrice Vaticana, 2012) 67; Francesco Coccopalmerio, "La Rota Romana e la sua funzione nell'interpretazione della legge canonica," *Quaderni dello Studio Rotale* 18 (2008) 123.

13. See Rafael Rodríguez-Ocaña, "El Tribunal de la Rota Romana y la unidad de la jurisprudencia," *Ius Canonicum* 60 (1990) 437–438. See also Eduardo Baura, "Riflessioni sul valore canonico della giurisprudenza," in *"Iustitia et iudicium." Studi di diritto matrimoniale e processuale canonico in onore di Antoni Stankiewicz*, ed. Janusz Kowal and Joaquín Llobell, Studi Giuridici 90 (Vatican City: Libreria Editrice Vaticana, 2010) 3: 1388; Velasio De Paolis, "La giurisprudenza del Tribunale della Rota Romana e i tribunali locali," *Quaderni dello Studio Rotale* 18 (2008) 151; Llobell, "Perfettibilità e sicurezza," 1257, *sub* a); Urbano Navarrete, "Independencia de los jueces eclesiásticos en la interpretación y aplicación del Derecho," *Estudios eclesiásticos* 74 (1999) 671.

14. See Juan Arias, "Jurisprudencia eclesiástica y nulidad de matrimonio," in *La norma en el derecho canonico*, 1020.

15. In his final discourse to the Roman Rota, Paul VI mentions "your decisions and the jurisprudence that derives from them": "Dobbiamo, forse, ricordare che *le vostre decisioni e la giurisprudenza che ne deriva*, fanno testo e, a volersi restringere al solo settore tecnico, sono per gli altri (singoli studiosi, Facoltà Universitarie, Sedi Giudiziarie) un punto di riferimento ed un argomento di studio?" Allocutio ad Tribunalis Sacrae Romanae Rotae Decanum, Praelatos Auditores, Officiales et Advocatos, ineunte anno iudiciali, January 28, 1978: *AAS* 70 (1978) 185, emphasis added.

16. See Burke, *Lack of Discretion of Judgment*, 21, note 26, quoting the then-contemporary Dean of the Rota, Msgr. Arturo De Jorio. See also idem, "Canon 1095, 1° and 2°. Presentation

When one reads an individual Rotal sentence or decree for scientific purposes (including its citation in an act of judicial power or in written argumentation), it is necessary first to verify what contribution it truly makes to the common jurisprudence and to discern whether it corresponds with the common jurisprudence. At times a canonist will cite a particular decision of the Roman Rota and presume that he is basing his argument on "the jurisprudence of the Roman Rota." Or there will be a scholarly examination of a newly issued decision of the Rota, and it is presumed that the author is presenting the "new jurisprudence" of the Roman Rota on a particular point. It is necessary, however, not to over-simplify the matter. When citing or analyzing a decision, the merit of the principles it contains must be contextualized within the constant jurisprudence of the Roman Rota on a given point. Without prejudice to the undeniable juridical value of the Rotal decision in the life of the judicial cause, the scientific merit of a single decision standing alone may in fact be reducible to that of a scholarly opinion.

It is critically important that the minister of justice or scholar, in the study of jurisprudence, not unduly associate novelty with value, that is, holding the position that only the newest decisions are those that matter. Canonists from common law nations (such as the United States of America) are mistaken if they expect canonical jurisprudence to operate in the same manner as the jurisprudence of our secular courts. That is, tribunal decisions, including those of the Roman Rota, should not be presumed to have an *innovative character*. It is not the place of the judiciary in the Church to be innovative with respect to the general legislation; rather, it is bound to apply it. The ecclesiastical judicial function consists in the application of the law and explores the cause at hand in wholly objective terms in a manner that protects the stability of the law. Thus, rather than develop the law, it yields to its prescripts. This is not to minimize the importance of becoming aware of recent developments in jurisprudence; and in fact it is highly valuable to discover how the Rota treats questions of very contemporary moment (e.g., new developments in psychology, or the impact on matrimonial consent of the habitual use of certain kinds of

---

III: Jurisprudence," in *Incapacity for Marriage. Jurisprudence and Interpretation. Acts of the III Gregorian Colloquium*, ed. Robert M. Sable (Rome: Pontificia Universitas Gregoriana, 1987) 129–130.

contraception or the habitual indulgence in pornography, etc). However, there is a wealth of jurisprudence already published and readily available to well-prepared canonists, and it is that jurisprudence that typically forms the basis even for treating novel questions. Thus one should not exaggerate the fact that the publication of decisions by the Roman Rota has long been 5–10 years "behind." This is a situation that is worthy of being remedied,[17] but it should not be too troubling as if we were left resourceless.[18]

Accordingly, in view of the general notion of canonical jurisprudence, one can identify certain errors to be avoided when studying or relying on jurisprudence: 1) identifying jurisprudence with any one decision of the Roman Rota, 2) identifying jurisprudence with the consistent thought of any one judge of the Roman Rota,[19] 3) presuming that a divergent decision of the Rota constitutes a change in jurisprudence, and 4) searching out only the newest decisions as if they constitute the most or only relevant jurisprudence.

B) The Rational Authority of Jurisprudence

Jurisprudence emanates from an ensemble of judicial sentences and decrees of judges issued in particular causes. In this respect, it can be said that jurisprudence is not juridically binding on the judge, since the judicial decision binds only those persons for whom it is issued, or the parties in

---

17. The Rota has long sought to reduce this gap in time. Cf., e.g., Mario F. Pompedda, "Dopo novanta anni dalla dua ricostituzione, la Rota Romana sulla soglia del terzo millennio: Retrospettive e problematiche attuali," *Ius Ecclesiae* 11 (1999) 678–679, no. 20. As of this writing, there is approximately a seven year gap.

18. Ironically, it is not difficult to find *In iure* sections in the definitive sentences of local tribunals that quote only or mostly Rotal decisions issued prior to 1983.

19. This may be a matter of a collection of sentences and decrees authored by a judge or of published studies of a Rotal judge, which do not constitute jurisprudence even if they may identify it. In regard to the latter, we read: "For judges themselves lay out their opinion as private persons in journals or other means of publication, while jurisprudence is only expressed by way of sentences or decrees. And therefore the field is indeed fertile due to various and countless Rotal decisions, by which alone jurisprudence directs trials in the Church for the entire ecclesial community" ("Ipsi enim iudices opinionem patefaciunt tamquam personae privatae in diurnariis vel ceteris mediis notitiarum vulgationis dum iurisprudentia tantum per sententias vel decreta exprimitur. Ideoque ager quidem fecundus est ob varias ac innumeras decisiones rotales per quas tantum iurisprudentia pro universo coetu ecclesiali moderatur iudicia in Ecclesia"—Decree c. Verginelli, *Torontina, Nullitatis matrimonii, Nullitatis sententiae et novae causae propositionis*, December 6, 2001: *RRT Decreta* 19: 152, no. 7). On the precedence in authority of jurisprudence over the opinions of authors, even if the authors are also apostolic judges, see Gullo, "Interpretazione evolutiva," 374.

the cause. Indeed, this is a general norm of law, as stated in canon 16 §3 of the Latin Code (cf. CCEO c. 1498 §3): "An interpretation in the form of a judicial sentence . . . , though, does not have the force of law and binds only the persons and affects the matters for which it was given."[20] In other words, the judge and even the whole judicial system that creates ecclesiastical jurisprudence do not assume legislative power in the exercise of their function. In this regard, we read:

> The function of the judge is not the function of the legislator. The judge is not a legislator but only an interpreter of the law, and indeed only for the individual controversy about which he pronounces in the trial. That is, in exercising his function of declaring what is just (*ius dicendi*), he truly becomes also like a legislator, though not of the law in itself but of the law interpreted. For, in applying the law, he defines what is just and indicates the law by which the parties are bound, but only for the individual situation about which he concretely judges and decides [CIC/83 cc. 16 §3, 1642 §2].
>
> Therefore, the jurisprudence which is indicated by the conforming and constant praxis of tribunals does not obtain the force of law, even when it concerns the constant praxis received in the Apostolic Tribunals of the Sacred Roman Rota and the Apostolic Signatura, which, when they judge, employ the jurisdiction directly conferred upon them by the Supreme Pontiff. Indeed, nor can the force of law be attributed to the sentences issued in a conforming manner by the Roman Pontiff, even if they constitute the supreme norm of jurisprudence.[21]

Rather, the ordinary authority of jurisprudence resides in its resplendence in illustrating juridical rationality (*ratio iuris*). It is meant to have an influence on juridical thought and decision-making in the Church, especially in her tribunals, through the convincing power of reason exercised consistently.[22] "The authority of jurisprudence must be extolled

---

20. Interpretatio autem per modum sententiae iudicialis aut actus administrativi in re peculiari, vim legis non habet et ligat tantum personas atque afficit res pro quibus data est.

21. See Varalta, "De iurisprudentiae conceptu," 46–47, no. 10. See also Arias, "Jurisprudencia eclesiástica," 1018–1019; Ewers, "De quibusdam quaestionibus," 639, 644.

With regard to the Roman Pontiff, however, being the supreme legislator he could conceivably issue general norms or generally binding authentic interpretations of the law in conjunction with a judicial decision after the manner of a Roman emperor in the issuance of an imperial *decretum*. Cf. H. F. Jolowicz and Barry Nicholas, *Historical Introduction to the Study of Roman Law*, 3rd ed. (New York: Cambridge University Press, 1972) 368.

22. On this theme, see Benedict XVI, Allocutio ad omnes participes Tribunalis Romanae Rotae, January 26, 2008: *AAS* 100 (2008) 86–87.

and its function obtains great importance, in regard to what it effectively influences and excellently brings together to establish a correct and uniform interpretation and application of law in the decision-making of tribunals."[23] For it is the common jurisprudence that indicates what is just in a particular set of factual circumstances. And when a judge is faced with the same or a very similar collection of facts, it would presumably be unjust to diverge from the common jurisprudence.[24]

In other words, the indications of the common jurisprudence are binding, if not in a formal juridical way, to the extent that they display what reason demands in particular scenarios.[25] This is what is intended by the famous expression of Cardinal Sabattani, according to which jurisprudence is binding *non ratione imperii, sed imperio rationis*.[26] The jurisprudence of the Roman Rota, or other jurisprudence properly speaking, must be applied to other cases not merely because of the authority from which it emanates but because it is endowed with reason and consistency. Thus, while the lower-level judge is not strictly and formally bound by the jurisprudence of a superior judge when issuing a decision in a concrete cause,[27] it would be "imprudent" and "rash" for the judge to spurn this authority of jurisprudence.[28] In other words, it could be said that the lower-level judge is morally bound to act in accord with the juridical logic of the canonical order.

On the other hand, the canonical system highly protects the principles of the independence of the judge, the free evaluation of proofs, and the obligation to act according to conscience.[29] That is, the judge before whom the cause is pending is alone entrusted with giving the authoritative judicial response to the doubts; he discerns whether he is morally certain

---

23. See Varalta, "De iurisprudentiae conceptu," 48, no. 10.

24. Tomás García Barberena, "Norma en sentido material y en sentido formal," in *La norma en el derecho canonico*, 669: "La razón vinculante de la jurisprudencia reside, pues, fundamentalmente, en que non puede haber dos normas, dos justicias distintas para dos casos iguales."

25. Cf. Baura, "Riflessioni sul valore canonico della giurisprudenza," 1389–1390.

26. See Aurelio Sabattani, "L'évolution de la jurisprudence dans les causes de nullité de mariage pour incapacité psychique," *Studia canonica* 1 (1967) 145.

27. Cf. Caron, "Jurisprudence in Canon Law," 96–97; Varalta, "De iurisprudentiae conceptu," 51, no. 13.

28. See Varalta, "De iurisprudentiae conceptu," 49, no. 11.

29. Cf. CIC c. 1608, CCEO c. 1291, DC art. 247; Pius XII, Allocutio ad Praelatos Auditores ceterosque officiales et administros Tribunalis S. Romanae Rotae necnon eiusdem advocatos et procuratores, October 1, 1942: *AAS* 34 (1942) 338–343.

about the allegation from his own diligent examination of the acts and from what is seen to be proven (*ex actis et probatis*); and he himself—not the Bishop Moderator, not the Roman Rota—must place the juridical acts of the judicial *votum* and the definitive sentence based on his own examination of the cause and knowledge of the law and jurisprudence. Therefore, hypothetically a judge could, in a particular case, be morally certain that some reasoning in contrast with the constant jurisprudence of the Roman Rota is sounder than the latter and act accordingly.[30] The judge's obligation to act according to conscience, however, firmly presupposes a thorough understanding of that jurisprudence and a strong ability of argumentation; and so such an occurance is to be held as being highly exceptional and most rare. It is essential that the judge hold himself rigidly to these just mentioned conditions, lest he pollute his ministry of justice with arbitrariness, placing himself above the common jurisprudence and even the norm of law. The common jurisprudence of the Roman Rota cannot be taken as one among many considerations but as the direction to be habitually followed when carrying out the free evaluation of proofs and drawing juridical conclusions from what is proven.[31]

C) The Normative Value of Rotal Jurisprudence

Although jurisprudence does not ordinarily have a normative character, it can constitute a juridical source that may be used to supply a *lacuna legis*. This is stated in the general norm of canon 19 of the Latin Code (cf. CCEO c. 1501): "If an express prescript of universal or particular law or a custom are lacking in a certain matter, the cause, unless it be penal, is

---

30. As is stated in one Rotal decree: "Moreover, jurisprudence is not legislation but is only an interpretation of already extant legislation. And also, if absolute adherence to the prevailing opinion of jurisprudence were to be demanded, then all progress in jurisprudence itself would be impeded, and the stability of decisions would easily be removed through a corruption of law" ("Ceterum iurisprudentia non est lex, sed est tantum legis iam exsistentis interpretatio, et insuper si absoluta adhaesio praevalenti opinioni iurisprudentiae exigenda esset, omnis eiusdem iurisprudentiae progressus impediretur, et facile iudiciorum firmitas, per corruptelam iuris, vanificeretur"— Decree *c.* Bruno, *Parisien.*, *Nullitatis matrimonii, Novae causae propositionis*, October 26, 1995: *RRT Decreta* 13: 131, no. 6). Cf. Baura, "Riflessioni sul valore canonico della giurisprudenza," 1401.

31. Cf. De Paolis, "La giurisprudenza del Tribunale della Rota Romana," 134–135; Gian Paolo Montini, "La Rota Romana e i tribunali locali," in *La giurisprudenza della Rota Romana sul matrimonio (1908–2008)*, Studi Giuridici 87 (Vatican City: Libreria Editrice Vaticana, 2010) 57–58.

to be resolved in light of laws issued in similar matters, the general principles of law observed with canonical equity, *the jurisprudence and praxis of the Roman Curia*, and the common and constant opinion of the learned" (emphasis added).[32] The pre-eminent and perennial example of such jurisprudence, especially in the matter of nullity of marriage, is that of the Roman Rota, which can supply for the law in the case of a *lacuna* and was instrumental in this regard in the period just prior to the 1983 Code in identifying *capita nullitatis* not stated in the 1917 Code.[33] Among the tribunals of the Church, this solely applies to the Tribunal of the Roman Rota in regard to causes of nullity of marriage, as was taught by Pope St. John Paul II in his 1992 discourse to the Roman Rota.[34]

---

32. Si certa de re desit expressum legis sive universalis sive particularis praescriptum aut consuetudo, causa, nisi sit poenalis, dirimenda est attentis legibus latis in similibus, generalibus iuris principiis cum aequitate canonica servatis, iurisprudentia et praxi Curiae Romanae, communi constantique doctorum sententia.

33. Cf. Baura, "Riflessioni sul valore canonico della giurisprudenza," 1392–1399; Ewers, "De quibusdam quaestionibus," 639–643; Finocchiaro, "La giurisprudenza nell'ordinamento canonico," 995–1000, nn. 3–4; Llobell, "Perfettibilità e sicurezza," 1231–1258; Mariano López Alarcón, "La posición de la jurisprudencia en el sistema de fuentes del Derecho Canónico," in *La norma en el derecho canonico*, 1105–1112; Gian Paolo Montini, "La giurisprudenza dei Tribunali Apostolici e dei Tribunali delle Chiese particolari," in *Il diritto della Chiesa. Interpretazione e prassi*, Studi Giuridici 41 (Vatican City: Libreria Editrice Vaticana, 1996) 122–126; Varalta, "De iurisprudentiae conceptu," 49, no. 11.

With regard to the development of matrimonial norms, especially in the period preceding the promulgation of the 1983 code, see, e.g., Paolo Moneta, "Giurisprudenza e diritto matrimoniale nell'ordinamento canonico," in *La norma en el derecho canonico*, 1045–1069; Mario F. Pompedda, "La giurisprudenza come fonte di diritto nell'ordinamento canonico matrimoniale," *Quaderno Studio Rotale* 1 (1987) 47–72, English translation in *Marriage Studies. Reflections in Canon Law and Theology*, ed. John A. Alesandro (Washington, D.C.: CLSA, 1990) 105–131; Sebastiano Villeggiante and Celestino Gnazi, "Crisi della norma e della giurisprudenza canonica nella prospettiva di un nuovo diritto della Chiesa," in *La norma en el derecho canonico*, 1125–1133. This point has also been recognized *passim* in the pontifical Magisterium; see, e.g., John Paul II, Allocutio ad Sacrae Romanae Rotae Tribunalis Praelatos Auditores, Officiales et Advocatos coram admissos, February 26, 1983: *AAS* 75 (1983) 558, no. 4.

34. John Paul II, Allocutio ad Romanae Rotae Iudices coram admissos, January 23, 1992: *AAS* 85 (1993) 142, no. 4: "Ancora e proprio nell'ambito della interpretazione della legge canonica, particolarmente ove si presentano o sembrano esservi 'lacunae legis', il nuovo Codice—esplicando nel canone 19 ciò che poteva essere desumibile anche dall'omologo canone 20 del precedente testo legislativo—pone con chiarezza il principio per cui, fra le altre fonti suppletorie, sta la giurisprudenza e prassi della Curia Romana. Se poi restringiamo il significato di tale espressione alle cause di nullità di matrimonio, appare evidente che, sul piano del diritto sostantivo e cioè di merito, per giurisprudenza deve intendersi, nel caso, esclusivamente quella emanante dal Tribunale della Rota Romana. In questo quadro e quindi da intendere anche quanto afferma la Costituzione *Pastor bonus*, ove attribuisce alla stessa

Notwithstanding the developments of the 1983 Code in the matter of matrimonial law, whereby the *lacunae* filled by Rotal jurisprudence resulted in new general legislation, this remains a phenomenon that is ever operative within Rotal jurisprudence. In his 1984 discourse to the Roman Rota, Pope St. John Paul II underscored this in these terms:

> In the new Code, especially in the matter of matrimonial consent, not a few explicit statements of natural law have been codified, thanks to the contribution of Rotal jurisprudence. But there are still canons of noticeable importance in matrimonial law which have necessarily been formulated in a generic manner and which await further clarification, to which the qualified Rotal jurisprudence could above all make a valid contribution.

And he gave as examples the further explanation of what a grave defect of discretion of judgment is (CIC c. 1095, 2°; CCEO c. 818, 2°), what is included in the concept of "the essential obligations of marriage" (CIC c. 1095, 3°; CCEO c. 818, 3°), as well as what is involved in the deceit of canon 1098 (CCEO c. 821).[35] It is also illuminating in regard to questions of procedural law that merit further precision, such as with regard to what particular events cause a definitive sentence to be null in the sense of canons 1620 and 1622 (CCEO cc. 1303 §1 and 1304 §1).[36]

Rota compiti tali per cui essa 'unitati iurisprudentiae consulit et, per proprias sententias, tribunalibus inferioribus auxilio est'."

35. "Nel nuovo Codice, specialmente in materia di consenso matrimoniale, sono state codificate non poche esplicitazioni del diritto naturale, apportate dalla giurisprudenza rotale. Ma rimangono ancora canoni, di rilevante importanza nel diritto matrimoniale, che sono stati necessariamente formulati in modo generico e che attendono una ulteriore determinazione, alla quale potrebbe validamente contribuire innanzitutto la qualificata giurisprudenza rotale. Penso, ad esempio, alla determinazione del *'defectus gravis discretionis iudicii,'* agli *'officia matrimonialia essentialia,'* alle *'obligationes matrimonii essentiales'* di cui al can. 1095, come pure alla ulteriore precisazione del can. 1098 sull'errore doloso, per citare solo due canoni" (Allocutio, January 26, 1984: 648, no. 7).

36. Cf. Llobell, "Perfettibilità e sicurezza," 1255–1257. In this regard, Gian Paolo Montini observed that the Rota helps lower tribunals not only by its sentences but by all its decisions, including its decrees pertaining to procedural questions ("La Rota Romana e i tribunali locali," 54, note 43). For an illustration of the contribution of Rotal jurisprudence on the particular question of the nullity of the sentence, see William L. Daniel, "The Nullity of the Definitive Sentence in the Jurisprudence of the Tribunal of the Roman Rota," *Studia canonica* 48 (2014) 5–100.

IV. The Unity of Jurisprudence

During the discussions of the *Coetus studiorum de processibus* entrusted with preparing what is now Book VII of the Latin Code, the treatment of the canons on the hierarchical structure of tribunals gave an occasion for highlighting the importance of jurisprudence. There was a proposal to establish regional third instance tribunals whose jurisdiction would not impede the right to appeal to the Roman Rota. However, this proposal was not accepted, however, since it would compromise the unity of jurisprudence in the Church, which was described as "a good of no little importance" that was entrusted to the same Rota.[37] Finally, about 10 years after that discussion, the responsibility of the Roman Rota for a unity of jurisprudence was declared in the general legislation. This section analyzes the Rota's role in fostering the unity of jurisprudence and then identifies some specific means for promoting such unity in the Church.

A) The Roman Rota's Influence on the Unity of Jurisprudence

In art. 126 §1 of the Apostolic Constitution *Pastor bonus*,[38] it is declared that the Tribunal of the Roman Rota is entrusted with, among other things, providing for a unity of jurisprudence in the Church: "This Tribunal of higher instance . . . provides for a unity of jurisprudence and, by means of its sentences, assists lower tribunals" (*"Hoc Tribunal instantiae superioris . . . unitati iurisprudentiae consulit et, per proprias sententias, tribunalibus inferioribus auxilio est"*). It would seem that providing for the unity of jurisprudence and giving assistance to lower level tribunals by means of its sentences are not purely distinct titles of competence but are complimentary. How this is so will be made evident in the forthcoming discussion.

It the first place, this norm of *Pastor bonus* imparts the concept that the juridical principles flowing from the decisions of the Roman Rota are what form the jurisprudence of the canonical system, especially in the area of

---

37. *Communicationes* 10 (1978) 243: "Consultoribus non placet, quia hoc modo evacuaretur tribunal Apostolicum, per quod assequitur bonum non parvi momenti scilicet uniformitas iurisprudentiae pro tota Ecclesia."

38. John Paul II, apostolic constitution *Pastor bonus*, June 28, 1988: *AAS* 80 (1988) 892, taken together with Benedict XVI, motu proprio *Quaerit semper*, August 30, 2011: *AAS* 103 (2011) 569–571.

marriage.[39] This is because of the particular dignity with which Rotal jurisprudence is endowed. Such dignity, especially in causes of nullity of marriage, becomes evident if one considers the matter on four planes, namely, the constitutional, the technical, the pastoral, and the juridical planes.

On the constitutional plane, Rotal jurisprudence is endowed with apostolic dignity inasmuch as it emanates from the ordinary (usually appellate) tribunal of the Apostolic See, that is, the judicial organ that exercises the vicarious power of the Successor of St. Peter for the causes that are legitimately deferred to it. In this regard, one commentator stresses "the primacy and directive character of Rotal jurisprudence before diocesan and regional tribunals, as a procedural manifestation of the marked union existing among the Tribunals of the Apostolic See with the mission of the Roman Pontiff in which they—in their own way—participate profoundly."[40] And this has been recognized by the pontifical Magisterium on several occasions, for example: "The value of Rotal jurisprudence in the Church has always been notable, given . . . the authority that they enjoy as papal judges";[41] "Your sentences, enlightened by this mystery of divine and human love [seen in marriage], acquire great importance, by being a participation—in a vicarious manner—in the ministry of Peter. In fact, you investigate, judge and issue decisions in his name. This is not a matter of simple delegation but of a more profound participation in his mission";[42] "Rotal jurisprudence is seen as an exemplary work of juridical wisdom, fulfilled with the authority of a Tribunal stably constituted by the Successor of Peter for the good of the whole Church."[43]

On the technical plane, this jurisprudence is so valuable, since it emanates from "a tribunal of particular expertise" composed of canonists "of

---

39. Cf. Rodríguez-Ocaña, "El Tribunal de la Rota Romana," 438.

40. See ibid., 433.

41. John Paul II, Allocutio, January 26, 1984: 647, no. 6: "Il valore della giurisprudenza rotale nella Chiesa è stato sempre notevole, data . . . l'autorità di cui godono come giudici papali."

42. John Paul II, Allocutio ad Rotae Romanae praelatos auditores coram admissos, January 30, 1986: *AAS* 78 (1986) 924, no. 5: "Le vostre sentenze, illuminate da questo mistero di amore divino e umano, acquistano una grande importanza, partecipando—in modo vicario—del ministero di Pietro. Infatti, in nome suo voi interrogate, giudicate e sentenziate. Non si tratta di una semplice delega, ma di una partecipazione più profonda alla sua missione."

43. Benedict XVI, Allocutio, January 26, 2008, 87: "La giurisprudenza rotale va vista come esemplare opera di saggezza giuridica, compiuta con l'autorità del Tribunale stabilmente costituito dal Successore di Pietro per il bene di tutta la Chiesa."

a high degree of preparation and of particular abilities of discernment."[44] As Paul VI declared in 1973, "Rotal decisions are a monument of the juridical science and of Christian wisdom."[45] Likewise, Pope St. John Paul II observed in 1984 that "the value of Rotal jurisprudence in the Church has always been notable, given the knowledge and experience of the judges."[46] Indeed, because of the high technical quality of the sentences that contribute to Rotal jurisprudence, it has a distinctively persuasive, instructive and directive value in the whole ecclesiastical judiciary, especially in causes of nullity of marriage.[47] For this reason, the jurisprudence of the apostolic tribunals has justly been hailed by one author as "the monumental sanctuary of canonical jurisprudence."[48]

On the pastoral plane—that is, in the order of the Church's mission for the salvation of souls—there is a grave need for unity in the manner in which the nullity of marriage is judicially examined in the Church. The promotion and protection of marriage and the family are, especially in today's world, central to the Petrine ministry. And since the alleged nullity of marriage and consequent dissolution of family life intimately affect these goods, the guarantee of unity in the treatment of such causes is naturally part of the universal apostolic solicitude.[49] Indeed, since the majority of the causes judged by the Rota and by local tribunals pertain to the

---

44. See Zenon Grocholewski, "Il ruolo specifico della Rota Romana nel Corpo Mistico della Chiesa," *Quaderno Studio Rotale* 8 (1996) 51–52, no. 2.

45. Paul VI, Allocutio ad Praelatos Auditores et Officiales Tribunalis Sacrae Romanae Rotae, a Beatissimo Patre novo litibus iudicandis ineunte anno coram admissos, February 8, 1973: *AAS* 65 (1973) 101: "Le decisioni rotali sono un monumento di scienza giuridica e di saggezza Cristiana."

46. John Paul II, Allocutio, January 26, 1984: 647, no. 6: "Il valore della giurisprudenza rotale nella Chiesa è stato sempre notevole, data la scienza ed esperienza dei giudici."

47. Cf. Montini, "La giurisprudenza dei Tribunali Apostolici," 133. See also Anthony B. Chibuzor Chiegboka, "The Fundamentals of Canonical Jurisprudence," *Apollinaris* 80 (2007) 625–637; Raffaello Funghini, "Tribunale dell Rota Romana," in *Commento alla "Pastor bonus" e alle norme sussidiarie della Curia Romana*, ed. Pio Vito Pinto (Vatican City: Libreria Editrice Vaticana, 2003) 186, *sub* art. 126; José M. González del Valle, "Dottrina, giurisprudenza e prassi nella costruzione del sistema canonico," in *Metodo, fonti e soggetti del diritto canonico. Atti del Convegno Internazionale di Studi "La Scienza Canonistica nella seconda metà del'900. Fondamenti, metodi e prospettive in D'Avack, Lombardía, Gismondi e Corecco."* Roma, *13–16 novembre 1996*, ed. Juan Ignacio Arrieta and Gian Piero Milano (Vatican City: Libreria Editrice Vaticana, 1999) 394.

48. See Varalta, "De iurisprudentiae conceptu," 50, no. 12.

49. This is also the reason that the legislative regulation of the nullity of marriage is reserved to the supreme legislator. Cf. Baura, "Riflessioni sul valore canonico della giurisprudenza," 1399–1401; De Paolis, "La giurisprudenza del Tribunale della Rota Romana," 135–136; Stankiewicz, "The Unity of Jurisprudence," 29.

nullity of marriage, Rotal jurisprudence serves to protect the dignity of marriage: "The function of Rotal jurisprudence in fact is that of leading—also with respect to a healthy pluralism which reflects the universality of the Church—to a more convergent unity and to a substantial uniformity in the protection of the essential contents of canonical marriage."[50] Lacking such unity would contribute (has contributed) to the tragic erosion of the dignity of marriage and the stability of the family in the contemporary world.

And *on the juridical plane*, the unity that can alone be provided by the ordinary pontifical tribunal is necessary in order to promote consistency in the administration of justice in the Church. Indeed, consistency in the manner of judging throughout the whole canonical order is what ensures juridical certitude, lest individual tribunals cast the stability of law into doubt through interpretational and procedural arbitrariness, and gives confidence to the faithful who approach the Church's tribunals that their causes will be decided in accord with the objective truth and the mind of the Church.[51] As Pope Benedict XVI taught in his 2008 discourse to the Roman Rota, being such an example, the jurisprudence of the Roman Rota is meant to announce to the whole Church "what all can expect from tribunals." For the consistent application of "principles and general norms of justice" creates "a climate of confidence in the activity of tribunals" and avoids "the arbitrariness of subjective criteria." The very right of the faithful to call upon the Roman Rota "constitutes in itself an instrument for the unification of jurisprudence."[52]

---

50. John Paul II, Allocutio, February 26, 1983: 559, no. 5: "Funzione della giurisprudenza rotale, infatti, è quella di portare—pur nel rispetto di un sano pluralismo che rifletta l'universalità della Chiesa—ad una più convergente unità e ad una sostanziale uniformità nella tutela dei contenuti essenziali del matrimonio canonico."

51. Cf. Rodríguez-Ocaña, "El Tribunal de la Rota Romana," 439–442. See also Cristian Begus, "Il ruolo della giurisprudenza nell'art. 126 della Costituzione Apostolica *Pastor bonus* e nelle Allocuzioni di Giovanni Paolo II al Tribunale della Rota Romana," *Apollinaris* 76 (2003) 516–517; De Paolis, "La giurisprudenza del Tribunale della Rota Romana," 131–165, *passim*; Montini, "La giurisprudenza dei Tribunali Apostolici," 117; Navarrete, "Independencia de los jueces eclesiásticos," 661–696, *passim*.

52. Benedict XVI, Allocutio, January 26, 2008: 85: "Infatti, [le sentenze rotali] vanno determinando ciò che tutti possono attendersi dai tribunali, il che certamente influisce sull'andamento della vita sociale. Qualsiasi sistema giudiziario deve cercare di offrire soluzioni nelle quali, insieme alla valutazione prudenziale dei casi nella loro irripetibile concretezza, siano applicati i medesimi principi e norme generali di giustizia. Solo in questo modo si crea un clima di fiducia nell'operato dei tribunali, e si evita l'arbitrarietà dei criteri soggettivi."

So it is evident that the Roman Rota is justly attributed the responsibility to promote a unity of jurisprudence through its example and influence as the ordinary apostolic tribunal *de merito*, especially in causes of the nullity of marriage. In what does this "unity" consist? It is not a question merely of the harmonization of diverse jurisprudences but of bringing about conceptual agreement in fundamental questions and essential questions. It is indeed not for the Rota to attempt to find agreement where there is disagreement but to promote a common manner of treating questions pertaining to the nullity of marriage.[53] On the other hand, unity should not be reduced to rigid uniformity but should rather be understood in terms of a concordant unity, according to which the individual judge, who appreciates the solidified juridical principles that generally govern the situation at hand, applies them himself to the concrete case.[54]

Pope St. John Paul II stressed the important contribution that is made to the protection of the family by the attention and openness of diocesan tribunals to, among other things, "the constant Rotal jurisprudence," and he rebuked innovations not in agreement with that jurisprudence: "*Every innovation of law, both substantive and procedural, is in fact reckless which does not find any confirmation in the jurisprudence or praxis of the tribunals and dicasteries of the Holy See.*" For, he observed, the Roman Rota has brought to maturation the doctrine and jurisprudence of the Church on marriage, and proper treatment of matrimonial causes demands conformity to this doctrine and jurisprudence.[55] This is why the judge, while

---

Inoltre, all'interno di ogni organizzazione giudiziaria vi è una gerarchia tra i vari tribunali, di modo che la possibilità stessa di ricorrere ai tribunali superiori costituisce di per sé uno strumento di unificazione della giurisprudenza."

53. Cf. De Paolis, "La giurisprudenza del Tribunale della Rota Romana," 148, 163; Stankiewicz, "The Unity of Jurisprudence," 29–33. It is necessary to insist on this because of the hypothesis of the harmonization of jurisprudence proposed by Manuel Jesús Arroba Conde (e.g., *Diritto processuale canonico*, 5th ed. [Rome: Editiones Institutum Iuridicum Claretianum, 2006] 170) and Cristian Begus (*L'armonia della giurisprudenza canonica* [Rome: Lateran University Press, 2002]).

54. Cf. Arrieta, "Amministrazione della giustizia," 67.

55. John Paul II, Allocutio ad Praelatos Auditores ceterosque Officiales et Administros Tribunalis Sacrae Romanae Rotae: in ferendis sententiis responsis Dicasteriorum et Tribunalium Sedis Apostolicae standum est, January 24, 1981: *AAS* 73 (1981) 232, no. 5: "Alla necessaria tutela della famiglia contribuiscono in misura non piccola l'attenzione e la pronta disponibilità dei tribunali diocesani e regionali a seguire le direttive della Santa Sede, la costante giurisprudenza rotale e l'applicazione fedele delle norme, sia sostanziali sia processuali già codificate, senza ricorrere a presunte o probabili innovazioni, ad interpretazioni che non hanno oggettivo riscontro nella norma canonica e che non sono suffragate da alcuna

he may formulate rational human presumptions, must dismiss presumptions that are contrary to those consolidated by the jurisprudence of the Roman Rota (DC art. 216 §2). Given these emphases in pontifical teaching and the fact that the application of correct jurisprudence is a matter of protecting the dignity of marriage in the ecclesial society, one commentator concludes that lower-level judges acting and deciding in accord with Rotal jurisprudence is a matter of "fidelity to the Magisterium."[56]

The same saintly Pontiff underscored more than once the rule that Rotal jurisprudence must ever be the sure point of reference for local tribunals in carrying out their function.[57] He identified "the specific function of the Roman Rota" as being "the agent of a wise and univocal jurisprudence to which the other ecclesiastical Tribunals must conform themselves, as the authoritative exemplar." And he explained that "Rotal sentences . . . contribute to a correct understanding and deepening of matrimonial law."[58] All of this is what underlies the observation in the preamble to the Instruction *Dignitas connubii*, which declares that, "in order to achieve in the whole Church that fundamental unity of jurisprudence which matrimonial causes demand, it is necessary that all tribunals of a lower level look to . . . the Tribunal of the Roman Rota, whose responsibility it is to

---

qualificata giurisprudenza. *È infatti temeraria ogni innovazione di diritto, sia sostantivo sia processuale, che non trovi alcun riscontro nella giurisprudenza o prassi dei tribunali e dicasteri della Santa Sede.* Dobbiamo essere persuasi che un esame sereno, attento, meditato, completo ed esauriente delle cause matrimoniali esige la piena conformità alla retta dottrina della Chiesa al diritto canonico ed alla sana giurisprudenza canonica, quale si è andata maturando soprattutto mediante l'apporto della Sacra Romana Rota." (emphasis in original)

56. See Rodríguez-Ocaña, "El Tribunal de la Rota Romana," 441.

57. John Paul II, Allocutio, January 30, 1986: 925, no. 7: "Va inoltre valutato l'influsso della Rota Romana sull'attività dei Tribunali ecclesiastici regionali e diocesani. La giurisprudenza rotale, in particolare, è sempre stata e deve continuare ad essere per essi un sicuro punto di riferimento."

58. John Paul II, Allocutio ad Romanae Rotae praelatos auditores, January 17, 1998: *AAS* 90 (1998) 783–784, no. 4: "In esse, l'*officium caritatis et unitatis* a voi confidato si deve esplicare sia sul piano dottrinale sia su quello più propriamente processuale. Precipua appare in questo ambito la funzione specifica della Rota Romana, quale operatrice di una saggia ed univoca giurisprudenza cui debbono, come ad autorevole esemplare, adeguarsi gli altri Tribunali ecclesiastici. [. . .] Le sentenze Rotali, al di là del valore dei giudicati singoli nei confronti delle parti interessate, contribuiscono ad intendere correttamente e ad approfondire il diritto matrimoniale."

provide 'for a unity of jurisprudence and, by means of its sentences, [to] assist lower tribunals' (*Pastor bonus* art. 126)."⁵⁹

B) Means for Promoting a Unity of Jurisprudence

As doctrine has underscored,⁶⁰ the hierarchical structure of ecclesiastical tribunals itself is meant to bring about a unity of jurisprudence in the Church. In particular, the situation of the Tribunal of the Roman Rota over all the tribunals of the Church,⁶¹ to which appeal may be made even in second instance,⁶² fosters the exercise of its grave responsibility to expound upon the proper jurisprudence pertaining to individual causes. The order of things suggests that, from the perspective of ongoing formation, the local and ordinary appellate tribunals follow the course of the cause and attend to the decision issued by the Rota and its motivation. The decision of the Rota ultimately resolves the cause; and the lower level tribunals, especially the one that decided in the minority, are, in principle, instructed as to the correct jurisprudence operative in the case.⁶³

Moreover, to say nothing of the more lofty aim of judging according to right reason, the simple fact that the Roman Rota may one day judge the very same cause should motivate tribunals to issue decisions in accord with the common jurisprudence of the same Rota. For any decisions that do not correspond with this jurisprudence, whether by unbridled innovation or even contradiction, *a priori* stand vulnerable to being reformed by that apostolic tribunal. In addition, parties who make the effort to become educated about the jurisprudence of the Roman Rota, whether themselves or through the guidance of a canonist, can come to appreciate what kind

---

59. Ad obtinendam praeterea in tota Ecclesia illam unitatem fundamentalem iurisprudentiae, quam exigunt causae matrimoniales, necesse est ut omnia tribunalia inferioris gradus . . . prospiciant . . . ad Tribunal Rotae Romanae, cuius est "unitati iurisprudentiae" consulere "et, per proprias sententias, tribunalibus inferioribus auxilio" esse (*Pastor bonus*, art. 126).

60. See, e.g., Arrieta, "Amministrazione della giustizia," 65; Baura, "Riflessioni sul valore canonico della giurisprudenza," 1402; Montini, "La giurisprudenza dei Tribunali Apostolici," 118–122; idem, "La Rota Romana e i tribunali locali," 52–53; Navarrete, "Independencia de los jueces eclesiásticos," 670–671; Stankiewicz, "The Unity of Jurisprudence," 43–44.

61. Cf. Hanna Alwan, "Il Tribunale Apostolico della Rota Romana ed il *Codex Canonum Ecclesiarum Orientalium* (CCEO)," *Iura Orientalia* 6 (2010) 12–47.

62. See CIC c. 1444 §1; *Pastor bonus* art. 128; *DC* art. 257 §2.

63. However, as is discussed below, it is necessary for lower tribunals also to weigh the decision in light of the consistent jurisprudence of the Roman Rota, which may not always be reflected in a particular Rotal sentence. On this point, *vide infra* section VI.

of judgment they can expect in their cause, and may thus appeal to the Roman Rota so that justice may be administered according to the mind of the Church. Here one may think, in particular, of a respondent wishing to vindicate the presumed validity of his or her marriage but whose marriage has been declared null by a local tribunal possibly operating out of a divorce-oriented mentality.

Nevertheless, it is a plain fact that only a small minority of causes actually reach the Tribunal of the Roman Rota during the course of their development, since the local and ordinary appellate tribunals frequently bring the matter to resolution. The hierarchical judicial structure is thus only a limited resource for guaranteeing a unity of ecclesiastical jurisprudence. It is the example of its decisions[64] that is most influential, and so the means for best guaranteeing such unity is the habitual and diligent study of Rotal sentences and decrees by those who can effectively apply this jurisprudence to the daily administration of justice in local tribunals, that is, by the ministers of justice themselves.

This is stressed in art. 35 of the Instruction *Dignitas connubii*, which obliges them ever to deepen their knowledge of matrimonial and procedural law and, in particular, the jurisprudence of the Roman Rota:

> §2. In order to exercise their respective functions properly, judges, defenders of the bond and promoters of justice are to be diligent in continuing to deepen their knowledge of matrimonial and procedural law. §3. It is necessary that they study the particular method of the jurisprudence of the Roman Rota, since it is responsible to promote the unity of jurisprudence and, through its own sentences, to be of assistance to lower tribunals (cf. *Pastor bonus* art. 126).[65]

Evidently, since the administration of justice fundamentally entails the application of the law to the particular controversy pending before the tribunal, knowledge of the law is of primary importance, especially the

---

64. Cf. Urbano Navarrete, "Il concetto di matrimonio nella giurisprudenza della Rota Romana," in *La giurisprudenza della Rota Romana sul matrimonio (1908–2008)*, Studi Giuridici 87 (Vatican City: Libreria Editrice Vaticana, 2010) 18.

65. §2. Ad suum munus recte exercendum, iudices, defensores vinculi et promotores iustitiae solliciti sint ut in dies profundiorem scientiam iuris matrimonialis et processualis acquirant. §3. Peculiari ratione iurisprudentiae Rotae Romanae studeant oportet, cum eius sit unitati iurisprudentiae consulere et, per proprias sententias, tribunalibus inferioribus auxilio esse (cf. *Pastor bonus*, art. 126).

substantive law governing marriage and the procedural norms governing the judicial investigation of its alleged nullity.[66] However, ministers of justice do not operate in a juridical vacuum as if they themselves were the first ever to treat the questions brought before them, or the best equipped. Rather, they operate out of a rich juridical tradition in which many of the same questions, especially in regard to marriage, have been deeply examined and authoritatively addressed with great prudence and skill. This tradition is accessed in the dynamic jurisprudence of the Church and pre-eminently that of the Roman Rota in regard to the nullity of marriage. It is thus critically important for public ministers of justice—that is judges, defenders of the bond, and promoters of justice, together with auditors, instructors, and assessors—as well as advocates to study this jurisprudence frequently, even daily. *Nulla dies sine pagina!*

Here it is a question of resources: how can one study the jurisprudence of the Roman Rota? It must be said that, despite some recent efforts of the Rota itself to publish some of its decisions in modern languages, no profound, serious study of Rotal jurisprudence can be carried out without a proficient reading knowledge of the official juridical language of the Church, Latin. For this is the common tongue of the canonical tradition. The text of the general legislation of the Church is written in Latin, and so it is fitting that the jurisprudence pertaining to that legislation is expressed in the same language. The primary source of jurisprudence is none other than the volumes published by the Roman Rota itself through the Libreria Editrice Vaticana: the *Decisiones seu sententiae* (1909–2009) for its definitive sentences and some interlocutory sentences, and the *Decreta* (1983–2006) for its decrees concerning mostly procedural issues (*de ritu*) but also many substantive matrimonial questions found largely in the decrees *Confirmationis sententiae*. Rotal decisions, even in English translation, can be found

---

66. Deep knowledge of the law should be cultivated not merely to avoid being chastised by the diocesan bishop or the Apostolic Signatura [for an example of which, see the Signatura's January 23, 1996 declaration and decree (prot. no. 26689/96 VAR) in William L. Daniel (ed.), *Ministerium Iustitiae. Jurisprudence of the Supreme Tribunal of the Apostolic Signatura. Official Text with English Translation*, Gratianus Series (Montréal: Wilson & Lafleur Ltée, 2011) 729–730, *sub* 415 (hereafter cited as *Ministerium Iustitiae*): "The judicial vicar is warned on account of his ignorance of the procedural and substantive law of the Church in a matter of such great importance."]. Rather, the continual study of the law and its proper meaning constitutes a service to souls, in order to guarantee that what best promotes their sanctification and salvation is safeguarded through ecclesiastical governance and the administration of justice.

in various canonical journals and can be quite useful for reading more recently issued decisions.

The importance of this jurisprudence has prompted one author to suggest the creation of an office within the Roman Rota whose titular would be responsible for preparing collections of concisely stated jurisprudential maxims, or rules governing substantive and procedural law flowing from the jurisprudence of the Rota.[67] Such an office has not yet been established, but the aim proposed by that author is somewhat accomplished by the publication of the annual report of the activity of the Roman Rota which, however, does not usually report the very text of the decisions contributing to the unity of jurisprudence, nor does it typically offer a full citation of the Rotal *Turnus*, *Ponens*, or date of the decision.[68] Another useful, if not definitive, collection of material is that found in scientific studies on Rotal jurisprudence; those written by Rotal judges are particularly notable. All such studies, though, should be examined with care, always in view of uncovering not merely recent trends or minority views but always the common jurisprudence.

Aside from the efforts that individual canonists can make, there is another ecclesiastical instrument of a largely extrajudicial nature that aids in the promotion of a unity of ecclesiastical jurisprudence, namely, the activities of the Supreme Tribunal of the Apostolic Signatura in carrying out its function of exercising vigilance over the correct administration of justice in the Church.[69] This title of competence was expressed in the previous proper law of the Apostolic Signatura, that is, art. 17 §1 of the

---

67. See Llobell, "Perfettibilità e sicurezza," 1254; idem, *Los procesos matrimoniales en la Iglesia*, 137.

68. See the volumes of *L'attività della Santa Sede* published each year by the Libreria Editrice Vaticana. Some of these have been translated into English by Augustine Mendonça and published in the Indian journal *Studies in Church Law*: see 1 (2005) 359–402 and 2 (2006) 85–124.

69. Cf. Velasio De Paolis, "La funzione di vigilanza della Segnatura sulla retta giurisprudenza," in *La "Lex propria" del S.T. della Segnatura Apostolica*, ed. Piero Antonio Bonnet and Carlo Gullo, Studi Giuridici 89 (Vatican City: Libreria Editrice Vaticana, 2010) 213–238; Montini, "La giurisprudenza dei Tribunali Apostolici," 112–117; idem, "L'unità della giurisprudenza: Segnatura Apostolica e Rota Romana," in *I giudizi nella Chiesa. Il processo contenzioso e il processo matrimoniale*, Quaderni della Mendola 6, ed. Gruppo italiano docenti di diritto canonico (Milan: Glossa, 1998) 235–242; Navarrete, "Independencia de los jueces eclesiásticos," 675–680; Rodríguez-Ocaña, "El Tribunal de la Rota Romana," 442–448; Stankiewicz, "The Unity of Jurisprudence," 41–42; Varalta, "De iurisprudentiae conceptu," 50–57.

Normae speciales, in these terms: "It is for the first section of the Supreme Tribunal to have the responsibility to be vigilant over the administration of justice according to the norm of the Sacred Canons and therefore to safeguard a correct jurisprudence."[70] In the current *Lex propria* of the Apostolic Signatura, it is likewise stated that included in its function of exercising vigilance over the correct administration of justice is the faculty to "give precepts to a tribunal in order to safeguard a correct jurisprudence" (art. III §1).[71] This may be done on various occasions, such as upon receipt of the annual report concerning the state and activity of a tribunal that gives indications of an immoderate use of a particular ground or the use of a fabricated or illegitimate ground; the denunciation of a tribunal's jurisprudence by a spouse who is party to a cause, the defender of the bond or promoter of justice, or another interested party; or the deferral of a matter to the Supreme Tribunal by the Bishop Moderator of the tribunal when he is in doubt about his tribunal's jurisprudence.

In a particular case, in which is raised an unsettled or grave question that would have an impact on the jurisprudence of the Church, the Apostolic Signatura, which is absolutely incompetent *a iure* to carry out an ordinary trial concerning the nullity of marriage, can request the faculty from the Supreme Pontiff to adjudicate a cause of nullity of marriage so as to safeguard or direct the jurisprudence on the matter (art. III §3).[72] On the other hand, the publication of its own jurisprudence in matters within its competence (cf. art. II §4) can also safeguard a correct jurisprudence, especially when it is a matter of possibly correcting a pattern of decisions within the Roman Rota itself, as can happen when it grants a

---

70. "Sectionis primae Supremi Tribunalis est invigilare pro munere suo iustitiae ad normam SS. Canonum administrandae, ideoque rectae iurisprudentiae tuendae" (Supreme Tribunal of the Apostolic Signatura, Normae speciales in Supremo Tribunali Signaturae Apostolicae ad experimentum servandae, March 23, 1968: in *Documenta recentiora circa rem matrimonialem et processualem cum notis bibliographicis et indicibus*, ed. Ignacio Gordon and Zenon Grocholewski (Rome: Pontificia Universitas Gregoriana, 1977) 1: 377.

71. Benedict XVI, motu proprio *Antiqua ordinatione*, June 21, 2008: AAS 100 (2008) 513–538, at 535–536: "Caput I. De rectae administrationis iustitiae invigilantia [. . .] Art. III. § 1. De praeceptis tribunali dandis ad rectam iurisprudentiam tuendam . . . in Congressu decernitur, si quidem graves irregularitates detectae fuerint." Latin text and English translation in *The Jurist* 75 (2015) 619–657.

72. "Art. III. [. . .] § 3. Quoties ad rectam iurisprudentiam tuendam necessarium videatur, Signatura Apostolica a Summo Pontifice petere potest potestatem iudicandi etiam de merito" (ibid., 536).

new proposition of a cause denied by the Roman Rota.[73] That type of intervention, however, is exceptional, since the constant jurisprudence of the Roman Rota itself is fundamentally the correct jurisprudence to which the Supreme Tribunal directs tribunals. As the previous prefect of the Supreme Tribunal declared: "As must be clear, it is the jurisprudence of the Rota which is necessarily and happily one of the principal points of reference for the vigilance that the Apostolic Signatura exercised in the name of the Roman Pontiff."[74] It is well known to tribunals that the Signatura habitually refers tribunals to the jurisprudence of the Roman Rota when intervening in particular cases, such as when granting an extension of competence to a local tribunal or responding to an annual report.[75]

In light of all of this, it is evident that, in addition to the Roman Rota, all the tribunals of the Church are to have also the Apostolic Signatura as an important point of reference for employing a correct jurisprudence. This was highlighted in the preamble to the Instruction *Dignitas connubii*, which we quote again now in full:

> In addition, in order to achieve in the whole Church that fundamental unity of jurisprudence which matrimonial causes demand, it is necessary that all tribunals of a lower level look to the Apostolic Tribunals, that is, to the Tribunal of the Roman Rota, whose responsibility it is to provide 'for a unity of jurisprudence and, by means of its sentences, [to] assist lower tribunals' (*Pastor bonus* art. 126) and to the Supreme Tribunal of the Apostolic Signatura to which it pertains, 'apart from the function of Supreme Tribunal which it exercises,' to provide 'that justice be correctly administered in the Church' (*Pastor bonus* art. 121).[76]

---

73. A well known example of this was its intervention in 2005 in a cause originating in the Archdiocese of San Francisco decided before the Rota on the erroneously formulated ground of "defective convalidation." For an unofficial English translation of all of the major decisions issued in the *iter* of the cause, see *Studies in Church Law* 5 (2009) 363–477.

74. See Raymond Leo Burke, "La collaborazione tra Segnatura Apostolica e Rota Romana per la retta amministrazione della giustizia nella Chiesa, con particolare attenzione alla simulazione del consenso matrimoniale," *Quaderni dello Studio Rotale* 21 (2011) 19.

75. See, e.g., *Ministerium Iustitiae*, 644 (no. 2), 671, 741.

76. Ad obtinendam praeterea in tota Ecclesia illam unitatem fundamentalem iurisprudentiae, quam exigunt causae matrimoniales, necesse est ut omnia tribunalia inferioris gradus ad Tribunalia Apostolica prospiciant, scilicet ad Tribunal Rotae Romanae, cuius est "unitati iurisprudentiae" consulere "et, per proprias sententias, tribunalibus inferioribus auxilio" esse (*Pastor bonus*, art. 126), atque ad Supremum Tribunal Signaturae Apostolicae, ad quod spectat "praeter munus, quod exercet, Supremi Tribunalis," consulere "ut iustitia in Ecclesia recte administretur" (*Pastor bonus*, art. 121).

Another instrument of great importance related to the promotion of a unity of jurisprudence is the practice of the Supreme Pontiff delivering an annual discourse (*allocutio*) to the Tribunal of the Roman Rota at the beginning of its judicial year. Such discourses are part of the ordinary Magisterium of the Church, especially in regard to marriage and its nullity, the marriage nullity process, the judicial function of the Church, and the nature and purpose of canon law. As such they are valuable to the whole Church, especially to canonists and all engaged in the administration of justice. In relation to jurisprudence in particular, they have "a doctrinal-directive function."[77] They are therefore often quoted in the decisions of the Roman Rota and taken as an impetus for addressing particular questions and thus must be assiduously attended to by local tribunals.[78]

V. The Question of Local Jurisprudence

The reference in Varalta's definition quoted above[79] to *the tribunals* that issue the complex of uniform decisions raises the question of the jurisprudence of an individual tribunal. It is true that an individual tribunal may bring about its own jurisprudence. This naturally flows from the fact that particular elements of the local culture enter into the juridical facts of a particular case. Thus, an individual tribunal should strive to be consistent in the manner in which it examines proofs and arrives at decisions, thus respecting the rights of the faithful to an objective and equal treatment of causes before them.[80] Above all, the jurisprudence of local tribunals is presumed to lack any evolutionary potential in itself in relation with the unity of the jurisprudence of the whole canonical order, given the limits of its jurisdiction.[81] On the other hand, if a cause pending before a local tribunal should give rise to a novel question or a more astute way of addressing a

---

77. See Navarrete, "Independencia de los jueces eclesiásticos," 680–694, esp. 683. See also Arrieta, "Amministrazione della giustizia," 67.
78. One decree of the Signatura expressed concern that "[t]he jurisprudence of the [local] Tribunal seems to be hardly in conformity with the teaching proposed on this question by the Supreme Pontiff (cf. Allocution to the Roman Rota, 5 February 1987 . . . , and also that of 25 January 1988 . . .)" (*Ministerium Iustitiae*, 687, *sub* 383; in the same sense, see also ibid. 712–713, *sub* 401 and 739–740, *sub* 422).
79. Vide supra I.A.
80. Cf. Baura, "Riflessioni sul valore canonico della giurisprudenza," 1401.
81. See Arias, "Jurisprudencia eclesiástica," 1020.

particular problem—always in accord with the norm of law—it is conceivable that the local tribunal could have an influence on a new jurisprudential direction, even within the Rota if the cause reached that level, and thus contribute to ecclesiastical jurisprudence.[82]

Nevertheless, especially given the fact that most tribunals of the Universal Church treat the same subject matter which is regulated also by the divine law (viz., the indissolubility of marriage), local jurisprudence becomes juridically unreasonable (cf. CIC c. 24) if it is contrary to or strives to be autonomous from the universal ecclesiastical jurisprudence. This matter was addressed in a 1975 Rotal sentence *coram* Raad, where we read:

> The jurisprudence of lower tribunals is not rejected, especially where it concerns entirely new situations, but without prejudice to the right of the Tribunals of the Holy See to reform it, if the case warrants. Lower level judges imprudently and rashly act if they judge contrary to Rotal jurisprudence. Moreover, it is necessary that jurisprudence in matrimonial matters be uniform, which can only be verified except by the highest jurisdiction by the Apostolic Signatura and the Rota.[83]

This is the teaching of the pontifical Magisterium itself. Paul VI declared the following in his 1978 discourse to the Roman Rota: "Likewise, it is necessary to rebuke the tendency to create a jurisprudence not in conformity with correct doctrine, which is proposed by the ecclesiastical Magisterium and is illustrated by canonical Jurisprudence."[84] And as Pope Benedict XVI taught, "it would be improper to recognize an opposition between Rotal jurisprudence and the decisions of local tribunals." It is critical that the development of local forms of jurisprudence be avoided, especially by the more effective dispersion of Rotal jurisprudence, which is to

---

82. Cf. Baura, "Riflessioni sul valore canonico della giurisprudenza," 1401.

83. "Iurisprudentia tribunalium inferiorum non recusatur, potissimum ubi agitur de conditionibus prorsus novis, salvo tamen iure Tribunalium Sanctae Sedis eam reformandi, si casus ferat. Inferiores iudices imprudenter ac temere agunt si contra Rotalem iurisprudentiam ius dicunt. Ceteroquin, necesse est iurisprudentiam in re matrimoniali uniformem esse, quod verificari nequit nisi a summa iurisdictione per Signaturam Apostolicam et Rotam" (Sentence c. Raad, *Marianopolitana, Nullitatis matrimonii*, April 14, 1975: SRR Dec 77: 264, no. 23).

84. Paul VI, Allocutio, January 28, 1978: 183: "Parimenti, è da riprovare la tendenza a creare una giurisprudenza non conforme alla retta dottrina, quale è proposta dal Magistero ecclesiastico ed è illustrata dalla Giurisprudenza canonica."

be given a more "uniform application in all the tribunals of the Church."[85] Particularly serious are local jurisprudential tendencies that violate the norm of the natural law according to which every human person is presumed to be capable of marriage, which is verified, for example, in the unjust broadening of the notion of grave defect of discretion of judgment. Such tendencies fracture ecclesiastical jurisprudence and are to be replaced with a correct jurisprudence.[86]

VI. The Impact of Recent Developments on the Consolidated Rotal Jurisprudence

The foregoing general treatise on jurisprudence touches upon themes of enduring importance, given the dynamic nature of the ecclesial society and the activity of her judiciary. And as was suggested in the introduction, it is a topic of contemporary importance as well, especially in the wake of the reforms to the marriage nullity process enacted by Pope Francis on August 15, 2015. This is due to the possible jurisprudential implications of the well known normative prescription of art. 14 §1 of the *Ratio procedendi* attached to the motu proprios, as well as some related remarks in a general document issued by the Roman Rota (the *"Subsidium"*).[87] Some other indications also suggest trends that could introduce new challenges into arriving at an appreciation of a correct jurisprudence.

---

85. Benedict XVI, Allocutio, January 26, 2008: 86, 87: "Pertanto, sarebbe improprio ravvisare una contrapposizione fra la giurisprudenza rotale e le decisioni dei tribunali locali . . . [. . .] Nella Chiesa, proprio per la sua universalità e per la diversità delle culture giuridiche in cui è chiamata ad operare, c'è sempre il rischio che si formino, *sensim sine sensu*, 'giurisprudenze locali' sempre più distanti dall'interpretazione comune delle leggi positive e persino dalla dottrina della Chiesa sul matrimonio. Auspico che si studino i mezzi opportuni per rendere la giurisprudenza rotale sempre più manifestamente unitaria, nonché effettivamente accessibile a tutti gli operatori della giustizia, in modo da trovare uniforme applicazione in tutti i tribunali della Chiesa."

On the problem of "so many national jurisprudences," making reference to "northern European and, above all, North American" tribunals, see Piero Antonio Bonnet, "La competenza del Tribunale Apostolico della Rota Romana e del Supremo Tribunale della Segnatura Apostolica," *Ius Ecclesiae* 7 (1995) 21.

86. Cf. Arrieta, "Amministrazione della giustizia," 66; De Paolis, "La giurisprudenza del Tribunale della Rota Romana," 136.

87. Apostolic Tribunal of the Roman Rota, *Subsidium* for the application of the M.p. *Mitis iudex Dominus Iesus* (Vatican City: 2016).

(1) The aforementioned art. 14 §1 lists several "circumstances of events and persons" which could in a given case justify use of the abbreviated matrimonial process before the bishop, that is, which may give rise to supposedly "manifest nullity."[88] There is no doubt that this list by no means establishes any new defects of matrimonial consent; it therefore should not lead to the use of any novel grounds in marriage nullity trials. Since the list contains examples that are not in the codes, however, it would not be illegitimate for an ecclesiastical judge to cite an item on that list as support of some observed factual indication of nullity in a cause before him. At the same time, however, the examples in that list are also treated already in Rotal jurisprudence. It would therefore be incumbent upon such a judge to study the common jurisprudence in order to obtain a proper understanding of how such an indication contributes to the probative edifice in the case before him.

(2) The release in January 2016 of the above-cited *Subsidium* issued in the name of the Apostolic Tribunal of the Roman Rota may have some bearing on the grave task of deciphering the constant jurisprudence of the Roman Rota on a given question. For in the third section of the second major part of the *Subsidium*, in the context of treating the abbreviated matrimonial process before the bishop, an explanation of the aforementioned art. 14 §1 is given. After recognizing that that norm does not establish any new grounds of nullity, it declares: "We are dealing here simply with situations that the jurisprudence has long enucleated as *symptomatic elements of the invalidity of matrimonial consent* . . ."[89] The invocation of "jurisprudence" here may seem natural enough, being a document of the Roman Rota; however, one may question the legitimacy of this subtle use of that passing word in such an irregular document.

---

88. "Art. 14 §1. Inter rerum et personarum adiuncta quae sinunt causam nullitatis matrimonii ad tramitem processus brevioris iuxta cann. 1683–1687 pertractari, recensentur exempli gratia: is fidei defectus qui gignere potest simulationem consensus vel errorem voluntatem determinantem, brevitas convictus coniugalis, abortus procuratus ad vitandam procreationem, permanentia pervicax in relatione extraconiugali tempore nuptiarum vel immediate subsequenti, celatio dolosa sterilitatis vel gravis infirmitatis contagiosae vel filiorum ex relatione praecedenti vel detrusionis in carcerem, causa contrahendi vitae coniugali omnino extranea vel haud praevisa praegnantia mulieris, violentia physica ad extorquendum consensum illata, defectus usus rationis documentis medicis comprobatus, etc."

89. *Subsidium*, 3.1.b), 32, emphasis in original.

The *Subsidium* appears to be a "general document" of a dicastery of the Roman Curia,[90] but such an act emanating from the Tribunal of the Roman Rota would be one approved by and likely attributed to the College of Prelate Auditors of the Roman Rota.[91] However, nowhere is the approval or even the involvement of the College indicated, nor is that of the Supreme Pontiff; there is not even any signature on it.[92] In fact, it is not a juridical document, properly speaking—that is, it not a juridical act or a normative source and, what is important in the context of this discussion, not an authoritative interpretation of the law (cf. CIC c. 16, CCEO c. 1498). As such, it does not contribute to or in any way alter the consolidated jurisprudence of the Roman Rota, and it is out of place for such a document to propose to do so. This is particularly unsettling in view of the fact that several points may seem to be in tension if not contradiction with the consistent jurisprudence of the Rota.[93]

(3) Without at all minimizing the institutional role of the Roman Rota to provide for a unity of jurisprudence and to help lower tribunals by its sentences—which role has been quite celebrated in this article—one may have reason to doubt the jurisprudential value of particular, more recently issued decisions of the Rota. For in our time, a certain mentality subversive to the indissolubility of the matrimonial bond seems to have taken root—*proh dolor!*—within the Rota itself. For on different occasions it has been suggested that more affirmative decisions ought to be issued and that decisions that declare nullity of marriage not to have been established are somehow a thing to be avoided.[94] This mentality fails to appreciate

---

90. Cf. John Paul II, apostolic constitution *Pastor bonus*, 859 and 864, artt. 2 §1 and 17.

91. Cf. Tribunal of the Roman Rota, norms *Quammaxime decet*, April 18, 1994: AAS 86 (1994) 509 and 514, artt. 1, 16 §§1–2; Mario F. Pompedda, "Il Tribunale della Rota Romana," in *Le "Normae" del Tribunale della Rota Romana*, Studi Giuridici 42 (Vatican City: Libreria Editrice Vaticana, 1997) 12–13; Vincenzo Fagiolo, "La figura e i poteri del Decano della Rota Romana," in ibid., 98–100 *et passim*; Luigi de Luca, "La figura del Collegio dei Prelati Uditori ed i rapporti con il Decano," in ibid., 103–112.

92. See Secretary of State, Regolamento generale della Curia Romana, April 30, 1999: AAS 91 (1999) 681–682, artt. 131–132, esp. art. 131 §6: "Il testo del documento sarà sottoposto all'esame dei Membri del Dicastero e, dopo la sua approvazione, presentato al Sommo Pontefice"; in §7 of the same article, the customary need for signatures on the document is prescribed.

93. Cf. Ronny Jenkins, "Applying Article 14 of *Mitis iudex Dominus Iesus* to the *Processus Brevior* in Light of the Church's Constant and Common Jurisprudence on Nullity of Consent," *The Jurist* 76 (2016) 231–265 and this volume, 305–339.

94. For example: "Decisiva in tal senso [viz., "abbattendo l'imponente mole di procedimenti pendenti"] è stata l'esperienza delle *videntibus septem*, vero antidoto non solo

that the whole canonical system and the Church herself stand ever firm in the *favor matrimonii* and the *favor veritatis*. For this reason, just decisions *pro nullitate* and *pro vinculo* alike promote an urgently needed "culture of indissolubility in the Church and in the world."[95] Nor is it understood how such a mentality can be reconciled with the impartiality so essential and foundational to the judicial function.

Because of this troubling dynamic, it is necessary for ministers of justice and scholars, even while recognizing the juridical value of a Rotal decision and its presumed jurisprudential value inasmuch as it emanates from the ordinary appellate tribunal of the Apostolic See, to be cautious in attributing any particular recently issued decision the ability to redirect Rotal jurisprudence as regards a well-established maxim of jurisprudence, being especially vigilant about a possible divorce-oriented mentality that could be operative in the case. One may even begin to see evidence of more pronounced conflicts among Rotal judges as regards a correct jurisprudence.[96] Let it be clear that the constant jurisprudence on the Roman Rota pertaining to all the grounds of nullity and the elements of their proof stands and cannot be reversed by a contemporary, possibly passing trend.

VII. Conclusion

A just concern for the more expeditious treatment of causes of nullity of marriage, lest the faithful be left in doubt for an excessive period of time while their cause is pending before a tribunal, need always be harmonized in the Church with the primary principle of the judicial protection of the indissolubility of marriage. The perennial source for the proclamation and safeguarding of that principle has been the jurisprudence of the Tribunal

---

contro la citata *diuturnitas causarum*, ma anche contro *l'ingiusto prevalere di decisioni negative sulle affirmative*, unicamente ancorati alla Verità fattuale illuminata e guidata dallo Spirito, attraverso l'apporto di diverse sensibilità umane e giuridiche, altre rispetto a *quelle talvolta rigide dell'automatismo del Turno a tre*" ["Indirizzo di omaggio del Decano S.E. Mons. Pio Vito Pinto a Sua Santità Francesco," January 24, 2014: *Quaderni dello Studio Rotale* 22 (2015) 14, emphases added].

95. See John Paul II, Allocutio ad Romanae Rotae Tribunal, January 28, 2002: *AAS* 94 (2002) 344, no. 7.

96. Regarding conflicts in jurisprudence, cf. Ombretta Fumagalli Carulli, "Le allocuzioni di Benedetto XVI alla Rota Romana," in *"Iustitia et iudicium." Studi di diritto matrimoniale e processuale canonico in onore di Antoni Stankiewicz*, ed. Janusz Kowal and Joaquín Llobell, Studi Giuridici 90 (Vatican City: Libreria Editrice Vaticana, 2010) 3: 1366. Up to now, there have been "few points of disunity in the field of substantive matrimonial law, aside from small jurisprudential points in the minority" (Stankiewicz, "The Unity of Jurisprudence," 43).

of the Roman Rota. For such jurisprudence has consistently exemplified for ecclesiastical ministers of justice the detailed examination of facts and careful application of sound juridical principles to a concrete case.

In the daily labor of justice carried out by the tribunals of the Church, it is critically important that their ministers of justice devote themselves to the regular study of the unified, common matrimonial jurisprudence of the Church. For only in so doing can they be sure that their weighing of proofs and issuance of decisions correspond with the objective truth of the matter of the alleged nullity of marriage.

Pope Francis' August 15, 2015 reform of the norms governing causes of nullity of marriage make no explicit reference to the common jurisprudence of the Roman Rota, and it does not seem to have intended any alteration of it, being a revision of procedural norms. Nevertheless, it seems to have become an occasion for certain doubts about the Roman Rota's jurisprudential continuity to arise. While this, if true, is not a little disturbing, in no way can such a phenomenon eliminate the rich patrimony of Rotal jurisprudence and its enduring force in the Church's judiciary. Each minister of justice should continue carefully to study the common jurisprudence, with confidence in its value and with the knowledge that the indissolubility of marriage will thus be better promoted and protected in the Church and in the world.

ABSTRACT

Canonical jurisprudence, in the strict sense, is what arises from an ensemble of concordant judicial decisions on a particular matter. Typically, therefore, neither an individual decision nor the decisions of an individual judge nor the most recent decision(s) create jurisprudence. Rather, this happens over the course of time through the activity of diverse judges operating according to consistent principles of juridical logic. In the Church, as regards the matter of the nullity of marriage, the jurisprudential authority is the Tribunal of the Roman Rota, whose rich patrimony promotes a unity of jurisprudence. The ordinary pontifical Magisterium directs this jurisprudence, and the vigilance of the Apostolic Signatura promotes it. Local jurisprudence in this area may not justly diverge from Rotal jurisprudence but receives and applies it to local situations.

RONNY E. JENKINS*

Applying Article 14 of Mitis Iudex Dominus Iesus to the *Processus Brevior* in Light of the Church's Constant and Common Jurisprudence on Nullity of Consent

When rendering judicial decisions regarding marriage nullity, ecclesiastical judges are to follow the constant and common jurisprudence of the Church. Pope John Paul II stated this emphatically in an early address to the Roman Rota: "We must be convinced that a serene, attentive, thought-out, complete, and exhaustive examination of marriage cases demands full conformity to the correct doctrine of the Church, to canon law, and to sound canonical jurisprudence, which has come to maturity above all through the contribution of the Sacred Roman Rota."[1] The pope then added, with his own emphasis, "*Indeed, any innovation of law, substantive or procedural, that does not correspond to the jurisprudence or practice of the tribunals and dicasteries of the Holy See, is reckless.*"[2]

---

* Associate Professor, School of Canon Law, The Catholic University of America, Washington, DC.

1. John Paul II, Allocution to the Roman Rota 5, January 24, 1981: *AAS* 73 (1981) 232. English available in William H. Woestman, ed., *Papal Allocutions to the Roman Rota 1939–1994* (Ottawa: Faculty of Canon Law, 1994) 165–170.

2. Ibid., with the emphasis in the original text. In a later address to the same apostolic tribunal, Pope John Paul II refined the notion of what source of jurisprudence is most applicable to cases of marriage nullity: "Again, precisely in the context of interpreting canon law, particularly where there are, or seem to be, *lacunæ legis*, the new Code—explaining in c. 19 what could be inferred also from the corresponding c. 20 of the preceding legislative text—clearly

The obligation to follow common jurisprudence binds all ecclesiastical judges. This includes bishops who make use of the *processus brevior*, or briefer process [BP], authorized by Pope Francis by the Apostolic Letter, *Mitis Iudex Dominus Iesus* [MI].[3] In fact, close adherence to accepted jurisprudence is even more critical to justice when the briefer process is used since, as Pope Francis remarks in the *motu proprio*, "We are not unaware of the extent to which the principle of the indissolubility of marriage might be endangered by the briefer process." Accordingly, by following closely the Church's common jurisprudence, most especially that of the Roman Rota, bishops (and those who assist them) will more assuredly render correct decisions without harm to the doctrine of the indissolubility of the marriage bond.

---

lays down the principle according to which the jurisprudence and praxis of the Roman Curia take their place among the other supplementary sources. If then we limit the significance of this expression to cases of marriage nullity, it seems evident that, on the level of substantive law, i.e., in deciding the merit of the cases presented, jurisprudence must be understood exclusively as that which emanates from the Tribunal of the Roman Rota. This context, therefore, explains what the constitution *Pastor bonus* states in attributing to the Rota the responsibility of fostering 'unity of jurisprudence, and by virtue of its own decisions provides assistance to lower tribunals' (art. 126)." Allocution to the Roman Rota 4, January 23, 1992: *AAS* 85 (1993) 140–143. English available in Woestman, 219–222.

3. Francis, Apostolic Letter issued motu proprio, *Misericors Iudex Dominus Iesus*, August 15, 2015. The document has not yet been published in *AAS*. An English translation can be found in *Origins* 45 (2015) 418–422. Citations of MI in this article will follow the edition found in *Origins* since the English addition available on the website of the Holy See does not contain pagination. When a canon or article of MI is cited, only the canon or article number will be given. One the same day that MI was published, Pope Francis also issued another Apostolic Letter motu proprio, *Mitis et Misericors Iesus*, also not yet contained in *AAS*, that applied to the Code of Canons of the Eastern Catholic Churches. Both documents are almost entirely similar in content and contain the same Art. 14, with the same wording of the text. Therefore, for the sake of simplicity I will refer in this article only to *Misericors Iudex Dominus Iesus*, with the understanding that the content of the article applies to both legislative texts.

For treatments of the legal elements that lay at the foundation of the text, see: Marco Antonio Hernández, "Los criterios que han guiado la reforma del proceso declarativo de nulidad matrimonial," *Revista Mexicana de Derecho Canónico* 21 (2015) 261–296 and Carmen Peña García, "Agilización de los procesos canónicos de nulidad matrimonial: de las propuestas presinodales al motu proprio *Mitis Iudex Dominus Iesus* y retos pendientes tras la reforma," *Ius Canonicum* 56 (2016) 41–64. A general presentation of the briefer process can be found in Guillermo Rodríguez, "Del proceso de nulidad matrimonial más breve ante el Obispo. Elementos estructurales," *Revista Mexicana de Derecho Canónico* 21 (2015) 339–348; Gerardo Nuñez, "El proceso *brevior*: exigensias y estructura," *Ius Canonicum* 56 (2016) 135–155); and, with a more detailed analysis, in William L. Daniel, "The Abbreviated Matrimonial Process before the Bishop in Cases of 'Manifest Nullity' of Marriage," *The Jurist* 75 (2015) 539–592 and Erasmo Napolitano, "Il *processus brevior* nella Lettera Apostolica motu proprio datae *Mitis Iudex Dominus Iesus*," *Monitor Ecclesiasticus* 130 (2015) 549–566.

Mitis Iudex Dominus Iesus stipulates that the briefer process can be used only when the nullity of marriage is already manifest in the petition for nullity at the time of its presentation. The manifest character of nullity must arise from recurring circumstances of things and persons that are supported by both testimonies and records that cannot demand a more accurate inquiry or investigation.[4] This petition—with its manifestation of nullity—forms the substantial basis for the decision of the bishop with regard to the question of whether nullity of consent has, in fact, been established to the standard of moral certitude. It is this decision that must be guided and formed by the constant and common jurisprudence of the Church.

Article 14 §1 of MI presents several examples of what might constitute circumstances of things and persons that can manifest nullity. Each of them is taken from situations found in Rotal jurisprudence. And each of them, if taken as a basis for use of the BP, will need to be evaluated based on the principles of the same body of jurisprudence. This article will consider how the examples of Art. 14 §1 are to be read in light of the Church's common jurisprudence as found in the Tribunal of the Roman Rota. The first part will discuss the juridic character of the Procedural Rules found at the conclusion of MI and of Art. 14 as one of those rules. The second part will consider each of the circumstances included in the first paragraph of Art. 14. And the third and final part will offer some practical observations on how those officials engaged in the briefer process might take account of the Church's jurisprudence when fulfilling their tasks. Always foremost in mind will be the question of how Art. 14 might contribute to the manifestation of the nullity of marriage without harm to the teaching on the indissolubility of the bond, something greatly desired by Pope Francis.

1. The Nature and Purpose of the Procedural Rules and Article 14

Mitis Iudex Dominus Iesus is divided into three sections. It begins with an untitled section of seven introductory paragraphs, in which the Roman Pontiff lays out the rationale for the modifications to the marriage nullity

---

4. The BP is to be used only when the "circumstances of things and persons recur, with substantiating testimonies and records, which do not demand a more accurate inquiry or investigation, and which render the nullity manifest." MI, c. 1683, 2°, 421.

process. The changes to the law are meant to promote the speed and simplicity of the process, "so that the heart of the faithful who await clarification of their status is not long oppressed by the darkness of doubt. . ."[5] The first section then presents eight "fundamental criteria" that governed the reform of the law. Two of the eight are of note for the purpose of this article and will be discussed later. The first is the criterion that "the bishop himself is judge (III)" and the second is "the briefer process (IV)" in which the bishop carries out that role of judge in cases where, "the alleged nullity of marriage is supported by particularly clear arguments."[6]

The second section of MI provides a set of 21 canons, with sub sections, meant to replace canons currently in the Latin code or provide entirely new norms. Five of these canons govern directly the briefer process and one regards it indirectly. The final section of MI then presents a set of 21 Articles, referred to as *procedural rules* [PR], which correspond more or less to the 21 canons in the previous section. The third section of MI, consisting of these PR, follows after the signature of the Holy Father that comes immediately after the second section. The PR are not meant to be incorporated into the existing codified law.

Article 14, the particular subject of this article, is one of the 21 articles that comprise the PR. They are first referred to at the end of the second section of MI, just prior to the signature of Pope Francis. The Holy Father states: "Attached and made part hereof are the procedural rules that I considered necessary for the proper and accurate implementation of this new law, which must be observed diligently to foster the good of the faithful."[7] The third section of the *motu proprio* is then entitled "Procedural rules for dealing with causes of nullity of marriage."[8]

Given that the 21 articles follow the conclusion of the main body of the *motu proprio*, and the signature of the Holy Father that concludes it, it is reasonable to ask what status the articles have. Are they an integral part of the *motu proprio* standing as obligatory procedural norms promulgated by the Legislator? Or are they more of an appendix that is meant to provide helpful examples, some of which can be used and others ignored if not helpful? The *motu proprio* itself does not provide a direct answer. Pope

5. MI, 419.
6. Ibid.
7. MI, 422.
8. Ibid.

Francis says the PR are "necessary for the proper and accurate implementation" of the canons of MI. However, the introductory paragraph to the articles characterizes the PR as "some tools" or *instrumenta quaedam* to help implement the changes to the law. Article 6, in turn, states that the PR are meant specifically, "to illustrate the main legislative innovations and, where appropriate, to complete it." None of these phrases offers a clear notion of the PR's juridic status. Nor is a reading of the 21 articles entirely helpful since they vary in nature from exhortatory, to explanatory and merely suggestive.[9]

In an address delivered two months after the promulgation of the text, one member of the papal commission charged with drafting the text commented: "Although this second section [the *ratio procedendi*] is an integral part of the document, it nevertheless comes after the signature of the Pope. It could, in a way, be considered to serve as a complement to *Dignitas connubii*. No matter what the legal significance of this part of the document may be, there is no doubt that it is to be observed."[10]

Although the large majority of commentators on the PR will concur that the articles are to be observed as binding, not all will agree that the PR might form a type of instruction as provided for in canon 34 §1. Among those who do hold the PR could perhaps serve as an instruction are included, for instance, Massimo del Pozzo who writes that the PR "should represent a sort of instruction,"[11] even if they do not clearly do so due to the "unusual legislative technic" used by MI to present the articles.[12] Bernard du Puy-Montbrun holds that the procedural rules are "in the guise

---

9. In fact, the precise status of the PR is but one of numerous aspects of the *motu proprio* that would benefit from clarification. As Mario Giuseppe Ferrante has put it: "Come tutte le grandi riorme, però, anche quella in oggetto non è immune da problem interpretative ed applicative che sembrano, anzi, acuiti da un testo normativo non sempre chiaro bensì pervaso da incertezze ermeneutiche." *Newsletter* of Osservatorio delle libertà ed istituzioni religiose (10/2015) 2.

10. Francis G. Morrisey, "The *Motu Proprio Mitis Iudex Dominus Iesus*," *The Canon Law Society of Great Britain and Ireland Newsletter* 184 (2015) 23.

11. Massimo del Pozzo, "L'organizzazione giudiziaria ecclesiastica alla luce del m. p. Mitis iudex," *Stato, Chiese e Pluralismo Confessionale* 36 (2015) 5, n. 16.

12. Ibid., 5: "L'inconsueta tecnica legislativa, può destare qualche perplessità sul valore normativa del disposto."

of a new instruction"¹³ and then proceeds to refer to them as "the new instruction."¹⁴

Others argue the PR do not serve as an instruction, but do constitute legally binding provisions. Joaquín Llobell posits that the articles enjoy a legislative nature *strictu sensu*, and so bind all those subject to them.¹⁵ To Llobell, it is of no consequence that the articles come after the signature of the pope since by signing the final document he made the post-signature articles his own. Moreover, they are referenced in the first part of the *motu proprio*. This indicates clearly the pontiff wished them to be part of the legislative text itself. Llobell concludes by remarking that the articles would appear to fit better into the category of a general executory decree (c. 32) rather than an instruction (c. 34 §1). But they are, in fact, of neither type. They are laws properly understood (c. 29).

Rafael Rodríguez Chacón admits that the placement of the PR and the characterization given to them by use of the title "procedural rules" can give the impression that they are juridically subordinate to the canons found in the second section of MI.¹⁶ However, he then asserts that the fact that there is no indication of another author of them than the Supreme Legislator and the fact that the same legislator references the procedural norms in the second section of MI leads to the conclusion that the PR are laws as strictly understood under canon 29, even if the drafting of the legislation should have brought greater clarity to their status. This would seem to be the position as well of the Pontifical Council for the Interpretation of Legislative Texts. In a private response dated April 8, 2016, the Council implied that the binding force of the PR comes from the fact that they are attached to the *motu proprio* and so promulgated by the legislator with it. The Council does so by merely quoting the content of MI regarding the

---

13. ". . . en guise de nouvelle Instruction." Bernard du Puy-Montbrun, "Analyse canonique du Motu proprio Mitis Iudex Dominus Iesus," *Liberté Politique* (October, 2015) 5.

14. "L'article 12 de la nouvelle Instruction ajoute . . ." Ibid., 6.

15. "In effetti, dette regole hanno natura legislativa *strictu sensu*, sono cioè vere leggi in quanto prodotte e promulgate dal Legislatore ed innovatrici dei codici." Joaquín Llobell, "Alcune Questioni Comuni ai Tre Processi per La Dichiarazione di Nullità del Matrimonio Previsti dal M.P. 'Mitis Iudex'," *Ius Ecclesiae* 28 (2016) 15.

16. Rafael Rodríguez Chacón, "Antecedentes, estructura y valor jurídico en el sistema normative canónico de los dos *motu proprio* de 15 agosto de 2015 y sus normas añejas," in *Proceso de Nulidad Matrimonial tras la Reforma del Papa Francisco*, ed. Maria Elena Olmos Ortega (Madrid: Editorial Dykinson, 2016) 40.

PR. It otherwise does not qualify the legal title that might be given to the rules.[17]

Geraldina Boni also recognizes the difficulties with determining the legal nature of the PR due to the uncommon legal technique used by MI of appending the PR at the end of the document.[18] She acknowledges as well that the conclusion can be drawn from both the title given to the RP and to their placement in the document itself that the PR serve as an instruction.[19] However, Boni then takes a common sense approach by suggesting that the fact that the PR were promulgated as part of the *motu proprio* leads us to conclude they do carry binding force and so should be taken as normative (no matter what the intended legal form is ultimately determined to be).

Javier Ferrer Ortiz, writing more recently, recognizes that the briefer process is governed not only by the new canons presented in the second section of MI (before the Pope's signature), but also by the PR.[20] However, he subsequently writes that the PR were, "published at the same time of the motu proprio *Mitis Iudex Dominus Iesus*, but do not form part of it and do not modify nor can they modify the Code of Canon Law, including most especially the norms relative to causes of nullity."[21] At the same time,

---

17. The text of the response reads: "Riguardo alla questione sulle Regole procedurali, la risposta alla prima domanda è data dal m.p. MIDI nella parte finale, dove viene precisato che le Regole procedurali sono unite allo stesso motu proprio perché ritenute "necessarie per la corretta e accurata applicazione della legge rinnovata, da osservarsi diligentemente a tutela del bene dei fedeli' e nello stesso testo delle Regole procedurali nella parte introduttiva, dove si legge che 'unitamente con le norme dettagliate per l'applicazione del processo matrimoniale, è sembrato opportuno . . . offrire alcuni strumenti affinché l'operato dei tribunali possa rispondere alle esigenze dei fedeli, che richiedono l'accertamento della verità sull'esistenza o no del vincolo del loro matrimonio fallito'." The Pontifical Council did not publish the original question to which this response is given. The response of the Council can be found at: http://www.delegumtextibus.va/content/dam/testilegislativi/risposte-particolari/Procedure%20per%20la%20Dichiarazione%20della%20Nullit%C3%A0%20matrimoniale/Due%20questioni%20sulle%20Regole%20procedurali%20e%20sul%20can.%201676%20%C2%A71%20del%20m.p.%20Mitis%20Iudex%20Dominus%20Iesus.pdf.

18. Geraldina Boni, "La recente riforma del processo di nullità matrimoniale. Problemi, criticità, dubbi, Parte Prima," *Stato, Chiese e Pluralismo Confessionale* 9 (2016) 8.

19. Boni, Parte Prima, 8–9.

20. Javier Ferrer Ortiz, "Valoración de las circunstancias que pueden dar lugar al proceso abreviado," *Ius Canonicum* 56 (2016) 160.

21. Ibid., 165: ". . . se trata de unas *Reglas de procedimiento*, publicadas al mismo tiempo que el motu proprio *Mitis Iudex Dominus Iesus*, pero que no forman parte de él y no modifican ni pueden modificar el Código de Derecho canónico, incluidas muy especialmente las normas relativas a las causas de nulidad."

Ferrer Ortiz offers a compelling observation, if only indirectly. The second section of MI modifies the Church's universal legislative text. New canons are introduced. The PR do not claim to do so, but present themselves as tools for implementation of those modifications. In light of this, MI would benefit from further discussion of how the PR differ from the new legislation. If both the new canons and the PR are taken to be laws strictly speaking, then how do they relate given the distinctive form, placement and appellations given to them by the legislation itself.

In summary, the consensus among those who have considered the question of the legal status of the PR appears to hold that the 21 articles are part of the substance of the legislative text—with most arguing they hold the same strictly legal character—have the juridic character of legislation, and possibly serve in a similar way as an instruction, although this last point has not found a majority opinion. What cannot help but be noted, however, is how much discussion among experts the legal nature of the PR has engendered. This witnesses primarily to the lack of clarity the legislative text itself presents at times. It also forces authors to resign themselves to this less than ideal situation. Paolo Moneta provides one example when he states, "Therefore [the PR] have the same binding juridic value as the [canons] inserted in the text of the *motu proprio*, even if their content is supplementary or explanatory."[22]

Once it is agreed that the PR constitute legally binding provisions, a question follows concerning the juridic character in particular of Art. 14 of the PR. We noted that two essential conditions for the use of the briefer process are the presence in the *libellus* of recurring circumstances of things and persons that must then be supported by testimonies and records. Paragraph one of Art. 14 offers eight examples in a non-exhaustive list of circumstances of things and persons that might manifest nullity of consent and paragraph two provides one example of what is meant by supporting records. Given that the motu proprio offers no indication as to the legal weight or character of the examples in Art. 14, questions arose early as to whether they might constitute new grounds of nullity, presumptions of

---

22. "Esse hanno quindi lo stesso valore giuridicamente vincolante di quelle inserite nel test del *Motu proprio*, anche se nel contenuto risultano integrative od esplicative di quest'ultime." Paolo Moneta, "La dinamica processuale nel m.p. '*Mitis Iudex*'," *Ius Ecclesiae* 28 (2016) 48.

law in favor of nullity of consent or some other figure that could impact the traditional substantive law regarding grounds of nullity.[23]

The publication by the Tribunal of the Roman Rota of a *Subsidium* for the application of the motu proprio one month after the effective date of MI offered a clarification.[24] The *Subsidium* repeats the list of circumstances and adds brief, if uneven, explanations of what is meant by each circumstance, what grounds of nullity might relate to many, and, regarding a minority of the circumstances, what document might suffice to support the manifest nullity of consent. With regard to the legal character of Art. 14, the *Subsidium* states: "It is necessary to clear away any equivocation in this area: *these circumstances are not, in fact, new grounds of nullity.*"[25] The text continues: "We are dealing here simply with situations that the jurisprudence has long enucleated as symptomatic elements of the invalidity of matrimonial consent, which can easily be proved by testimonies or documents that can be readily procured."[26]

From the standpoint of the *Subsidium*, then, it is clear that the grounds of nullity provided for in the universal law remain and, significantly, it follows that the common jurisprudence of the Church with regard to those grounds plays a central role in the *processus brevior*. The examples provided for in Art. 14 §1 are intended to serve merely as illustrative examples of

---

23. For discussion of this from various standpoints, see Daniel, 568–569; Geraldina Boni, "La recente riforma del processo di nullità matrimoniale. Problemi, criticità, dubbi, Parte Seconda," *Stato, Chiese e Pluralismo Confessionale* 10 (2016) 16–20, and Klaus Lüdicke, under 1683/6, in *Münsterischer Kommentar zum Codex Iuris Canonici,* (loose-leaf edition November 2015), ed. Klaus Lüdicke et al. (Essen: Legerus Verlag, 1984–).

24. Apostolic Tribunal of the Roman Rota, *Subsidium for the application of the M.p. Mitis Iudex Dominus Iesus* (Vatican City State, 2016). Available at: http://www.rotaromana.va/content/dam/rotaromana/documenti/Sussidio/Subsidium%2c%20english.pdf. The *Subsidium* lacks any indication of its juridic character. No author or publisher is given and no authorization for its publication appears in the document. It is safe to conclude it at least shows the mind of the Roman Rota (or its dean) on aspects of the *motu proprio* in hopes that this will be helpful to its implementation. Even this conclusion, however, is not supported by any attestation in the text of the *Subsidium*. When the *Subsidium* was sent to the Church's bishops, a letter from the Dean of the Roman Rota accompanied it. That letter claimed the *Subsidium* expressed the mind of the Legislator with regard to MI. This is clearly not the usual means by which the mind of the Legislator is conveyed, most certainly not in an authoritative sense. Nor is the letter to be found attached to any of the editions of the *Subsidium* found at the website of the Tribunal of the Roman Rota. Given this, the *Subsidium* remains a helpful document for implementation of MI, but not one of binding authority.

25. *Subsidium*, 32. Emphasis in the original.

26. Ibid.

some circumstances of things and persons that, together with other required elements, lead to the manifestation of nullity and so the use of the BP. What remains confusing, however, is that some of the examples of Art. 14 are current legal grounds of nullity while others are not. Moreover, some of the examples appear to be mere presumptions that up to this point would not qualify as manifesting nullity even if documents were shown to support that. For these reasons, among others, Javier Ferrer Ortiz concludes that it might have been more helpful if both MI and the *Subsidium* had refrained from presenting the illustrative list of Art. 14.[27]

At any rate, what is clear is that the mere fact that one or even more of the circumstances of Art. 14 is present in the petition does not of itself allow use of the BP since the circumstances do not serve as presumption of manifest nullity.[28] Additional elements will be necessary; most importantly, documents or records needing no further investigation. Indeed, as we have noted Pope Francis places the protection of the indissolubility of the marriage bond at the heart of the new legislation. Article 14 must be interpreted in light of this.[29]

The term *circumstances* as used by both the motu proprio and the *Subsidium* could also benefit from some comment. The circumstances regard either persons or facts. They must be evident, recurring and greatly probative of nullity or the "manifest" standard cannot be met. Accordingly, as Carlos Morán Bustos remarks, the term *circumstances* cannot refer to "mere estimations, conjectures, suspicions, or presumptions."[30] Moreover, he continues, the circumstances must be corroborated by additional *indicia* if they are to be fully probative; that is, "by other concrete, certain facts that can indicate, demonstrate, reveal and allow knowledge of this other fact which is the subject of proof."[31] In other words, the examples of Art.

---

27. Javier Ferrer Ortiz, "Valoración de las circunstancias que pueden dar lugar al proceso abreviado," *Ius Canonicum* 56 (2016) 136: "A mi juicio, y moviéndome todavía en el plano de las generalidades del artículo 14, diría qu es un precepto desafortunado y que puede crear más problemas que los que trata de resolver; y lo mismo cabe decire del *Sussidio applicativo*."
28. See Moneta, 11.
29. A point well made by Massimo del Pozzo, "L'organizzazione giudiziaria ecclesiastica all luce del m.p. 'Mitis iudex'," *Stato, Chiese e pluralismo confessionale* 36 (2015) 3 and n. 10.
30. Carlos M. Morán Bustos, "El proceso 'Brevior' ante el Obispo Diocesano," in Maria Elena Olmos Ortega, ed., *Proceso de Nulidad Matrimonial tras la Reforma del Papa Francisco* (Madrid: Editorial Dykinson, 2016) 144: "Es decir, deben ser circunstancias referidas a personas y hechos, no meras valoraciones, ni conjeturas, ni sospechas, ni presunciones."
31. Ibid.

14 carry probative weight as does all circumstantial proof. But they can never be taken in themselves as legally relevant for the invalidation of matrimonial consent. Full proof of nullity arises from all sources of proof, weighed in light of substantive jurisprudence, and not merely from the fact that the presence of a recurring circumstance of things or persons has been established.[32]

Regarding these circumstances, the *Subsidium* states, "These can present, in some cases, [with] such a factual weight as to suggest evidence of the nullity of marriage."[33] However, MI states clearly that the circumstances must make the nullity "evident and manifest," and not simply suggestive.[34] For this reason, the motu proprio mandates that the circumstances of things and persons contained in the *libellus* be supported by testimonies and documents which are to be attached to the petition and which themselves do not require further investigation or inquiry.[35] It is only when the circumstances are supported by documents and records of this high quality of proof (needing no further inquiry) that the manifest nullity of consent can arise. The call of the *Subsidium* for a "more attentive and realistic reading of the global condition of the faithful in today's world,"[36] and the cultural context that accompanies that, does not remove

---

32. Carmen Peña García, "El nuevo proceso *breviore coram episcopo* para la declaración de la nulidad matrimonial," *Monitor Ecclesiasticus* 130 (2015) 580: "Por otro lado, respecto a las concretas circumstancias recogidas en este elenco, no cabe negar su voloridad y su diverso valor probatorio en orden a una possibile nulidad matrimonial, al incluirse en este elenco tanto hechos y circumstancias que—uan vez comprobados todos los requisites legalmente exigidos—constituiríran evidentes supuestos fácticos de nulidad matrimonial, como otros hechos o circumstancias que, aun pudiendo se jurídicamente relaventes, no tienen *per se* fuerza invalidante del consentimiento, por lo que deberán ser cuidadosamente valoradas conforme a los criterios jurisprudencialies y al mismo derecho sustantivo vigente, sin apriorismos injustificados."

33. *Subsidium*, 33.

34. As Roch Pagé has noted all abuse of the use of the examples of Art. 14 must be avoided. He writes: "If we were to do otherwise, we would have to seriously consider if we are passing from the presumption of validity of marriage of canon 1060 to the presumption of its invalidity in virtue of a number of different types of presumption of fact. The proper use of the briefer process would seem to be urgent consideration of this question." Roch Pagé, "Questions Regarding the Motu Proprio Mitis Iudex Dominus Iesus," *The Jurist* 75 (2015) 612 and this volume, 360.

35. This is another indication that the Supreme Legislator wishes to avoid any harm to the teaching on the indissolubility of marriage when the briefer process is used. In my view, the bar has been set very high for use of the new process.

36. *Subsidium*, 33.

the need for production of documents and records in order to manifest nullity in the petition.

Ideally, testimony will be provided by qualified witnesses to assure this high level of evidentiary weight. This would exclude, for instance, medical or psychological experts who attended to one or both of the petitioners during a non-suspect time. Other qualified witnesses, such as pastors, would count here as well.[37] The documents should also have a qualified character to them; that is, they should be expert reports, also from a non-suspect time, or public records. As we will see, the second paragraph of Art. 14 implies as much. Private documents, such as correspondence, diaries or emails, would not qualify since private documents by nature require further substantiation to assign them probative weight.[38] Private documents can still be included in an eventual use of the BP, of course, but not for the purpose of establishing manifest nullity of consent.

Finally, if the circumstances contained in the petition cannot require further inquiry or investigation, then we can ask what is the purpose for the petition to indicate what proofs can be readily collected and of the session held by the instructor in which he or she is to collect "the proofs in a single session." Bustos considers this to be "an internal contradiction" of norms, but one that can be overcome.[39] Both the collecting of readily available proofs and the investigator's session must concern the *indicia* that regard the circumstances alleged and which are—without need for further investigation—able to manifest nullity of consent at the time the judicial vicar determines the briefer process will be used. If this were not so—if the circumstances and supporting proofs themselves needed further inquiry—then the briefer process would not be available from the start.

In summary, then, we have seen that the two conditions for use of the briefer process are the existence in the petition of circumstances that are supported by testimonies and documents and that do not need further investigation. These must make manifest the nullity of consent, partly so

---

37. With the understanding, of course, that all legal safeguards regarding confidentiality are maintained, including the impermissibility of the use of information in a judicial process that was gained from sacramental confession (c. 1550 §2, 2°).

38. See Bustos, Retos de la reforma, 24–25, who rightly excludes as well documents such as reports of private investigators, and Moneta, 13, who notes that such documents (or instruments) can, however, serve to corroborate the statements of the parties or witnesses.

39. Bustos, El Proceso, 146–147.

that an accepted ground of nullity can form the basis of the accusation of the marriage. The constant and common jurisprudence of the Church—and especially of the Roman Rota—must inform and guide the decision making process, from the time the petition is prepared to the moment the bishop comes to a decision.

2. The Circumstances of Things and Persons of Article 14

We will now turn to Art. 14 to ask how these general principles apply to each of the circumstances listed there. In other words, what might common jurisprudence require in order for the circumstance to manifest nullity of consent and what testimonies and documents might provide support for it.

a. Defect of the Use of Reason

We will begin with the last concrete circumstance mentioned in Art. 14, the defect of the use of reason which is proved by medical documents, because I believe it is the most likely candidate for use in the briefer process given the likelier availability of documentary, medical proof of serious conditions. It is also the circumstance that is related most directly to the second paragraph of Art. 14.

As Ferrer Ortiz observes, the wording of Art. 14 implies that the circumstance of a defect of the use of reason relates only to c. 1095, 1°.[40] However, the *Subsidium* for its part states that under this circumstance falls "consensual incapacity due to psychic reasons,"[41] which would encompass all three sections of c. 1095. This, he concludes, could open a canonical "pandora's box" if the briefer process is used to adjudicate what jurisprudence considers to be some of the most difficult grounds of nullity to use.[42] This is so even with regard to c. 1095, 1° in cases where the lack of

---

40. This is the understanding of Lüdicke, for instance, in comments offered before the *Subsidium* appeared. See Lüdicke, 1683/6.
41. *Subsidium*, 35.
42. See Ferrer Ortiz, 186–187. He observes that the *Subsidium* cannot change the law of MI; so the wording of the *motu proprio* should stand to include only the first section of c. 1095. This might be so strictly speaking. However, Art. 14 §1, by including the word "etcetera" allows for additional circumstances to be taken into account. This could, then, include the

sufficient use of reason is due to a transitory cause before consent or one that was not present at all before consent.

We have seen that MI retains the requirement of the use of experts in marriage cases involving mental illness, "unless it is clear from the circumstances that it would be useless to do so."[43] In the ordinary nullity process, fuller sources of proof are used and an instruction of the cause is necessary. That is the moment when the judge determines whether the *evidenter* standard has been met that removes the obligation to use experts. Georg Bier, by way of example, has tried to lay out criteria for meeting the standard. These include cases where expert witnesses have already presented evidence, when a diagnosis is clearly discernable or when an extraordinary impact on the marriage is seen.[44] But none of these are applicable to the briefer process.

Paragraph two of Art. 14 indicates what type of document is able to establish the manifest nature of nullity under this ground (and possibly others) in the briefer process: "Among the documents which support this petition are included all medical records which can evidently render useless the requirement for an *ex officio* expert." In other words, if upon examining the petition, it is determined that an expert witness must be used, the briefer process cannot be used. And we should note that Art. 14 speaks of medical records, not private expert reports that the parties have requested in a suspect time.

The *Subsidium* speaks further to the nature of these medical reports. It first repeats strongly the need for "an in depth scientific investigation by an expert" in the ordinary process. Then, with regard to the briefer process, it lays out four criteria. First, it is a question of, "instances of the gravest pathologies." These must then be "duly documented," so that they allow for a judgment made "according to well-established jurisprudence" and that is rendered "without any shadow of positive doubt" concerning the nullity of the marriage.[45] The examples given are clinical records of

---

two other sections of c. 1095, even if, as Ferrer Ortiz prudently warns, abuses could easily arise from doing so.

43. C. 1678 §3 of MI.

44. See Georg Bier, "Urteilsfindung ohne Gutachten? Die Beiziehung von Sachverständigen in Fällen von psychischer Eheunfähigkeit," *De Processibus Matrimonialibus* 6 (1999) 145–170, especially 154–163.

45. *Subsidium*, 35–36.

treatment or psychiatric reports that were admitted in civil courts. The documents should ideally have originated in a non-suspect time. And so they would not include reports of private experts prepared at the request of the petitioners. Of course, the assessor who participates in the briefer process might be a medical expert who assists in the interpretation of the admitted medical evidence.

We can ask, next, what might serve as "gravest pathologies" according to Rotal jurisprudence. Based on this author's reading of the jurisprudence, a non-comprehensive list of those pathologies more readily open to proof by medical or psychiatric reports include chronic, manifest schizophrenia, bipolar disorder, manifest anti-social personality disorder, central nervous system conditions, and other serious psychiatric or medical conditions that require extensive in patient treatment prior to or at the time of consent. What I believe would not be open to such proof (but not excluded outright either) are affective immaturity, depression that does not require clinical treatment, some instances of drug and alcohol addiction, obsessive-compulsive disorders, neuroses, and certainly not non-specific disorders.

In all instances the presence of symptoms or behaviors in testimonies, together with mere reference to the DSM manual, or other diagnostic resources, will not suffice for use of the briefer process. Medical and psychiatric records will need to be attached to the petition and they will need to establish the manifest nullity of consent due condition admitted by jurisprudence on canon 1095. What we should not see going forward is the large number of cases judged to date in the ordinary process on a ground of canon 1095 (at least in the majority of tribunals in the United States) simply transfer to the briefer process when the petition shows that troubling behaviors took place prior to consent or even if discernable, negative psychic conditions were present. In fact, given the high standard of documentary proof required to manifest nullity, it seems likely that use of the BP would be limited to circumstances involving canon 1095, 1° since it is a lack of sufficient use of reason that would lend itself most clearly to proof through medical records.[46]

46. A point emphasized by Bunge (19): "Sin duda, la prueba mediante documentos médicos, sobre todo pericias psicológicas o psiquiátricas, no es fácilmente incontrovertible, y por esta razón parece más applicable este ejemplo a causas de nulidad por falta de suficiente uso de razón (canon 1095 1°), que a causas por defecto de discreció de juicio (canon 1095 2°) o por

A final word under this circumstance that can apply to the others as well. The manifest nullity of consent present in a petition does not guarantee the ability of the bishop to reach moral certitude regarding the nullity of the marriage. The standard of manifest nullity in the petition is one that allows a type of process to be used. That process, in turn, must now lead to moral certitude regarding nullity of consent. There is no guarantee that the mere attachment of documents, including compelling medical reports, to the petition will result in a finding of nullity. That conclusion can only be drawn once the petition, documents and witnesses (together with all the facts and circumstances) are weighed by the bishop. In this sense, the BP may require less time to complete than the ordinary process, but it cannot receive less attentiveness and consideration than is due the formal process. This also helps to assure that the circumstances of Art. 14 do not devolve into informal grounds of nullity or illegitimately used presumptions.[47]

B. The Defect of Faith Which Can Generate Simulation of Consent or Error That Determines the Will

The first circumstance mentioned in Art. 14 §1 is, "The defect of faith which can generate simulation of consent or error that determines the will." This is the initial of several circumstances that regard the grounds of either total simulation of consent or partial simulation of an essential element or property of marriage.

It is important to begin by noting that this particular circumstance does not concern a lack of faith among the baptized that, simply due to the lack of faith, results in an invalid marriage. Magisterial teaching, and Rotal jurisprudence following on it, consistently hold that all that is required of the baptized who marry is an intention to enter marriage as naturally instituted by God. It is Christ the Lord who then raises that marriage to the dignity of a sacrament. Accordingly, if a lack of faith is to

---

incapacidad para asumir las obligaciones esenciales del matrimonio (canon 1095 3°), en las que la valoración de la prueba pericial puede ser a veces muy compleja."

47. A concern Geraldina Boni, among others, clearly holds. See Boni, Seconda Parte, 17–18.

impact the validity of consent it must do so by means of a positive will to exclude sacramental dignity rather than by a mere lack of faith.[48]

We see this in a later address to the Roman Rota given by Pope John Paul II, who says: "An attitude on the part of those getting married that does not take into account the supernatural dimension of marriage can render it null and void only if it undermines its validity on the natural level on which the sacramental sign itself takes place."[49] And Pope Benedict in his final address to the same Apostolic Tribunal states: "The indissoluble pact between a man and a woman does not, for the purposes of the sacrament, require of those engaged to be married, their personal faith."[50] Finally, Pope Francis in his most recent address to the Rota affirms: "It is worth clearly reiterating that the essential component of marital consent is not the quality of one's faith, which according to unchanging doctrine can be undermined only on the plane of the natural."[51]

The jurisprudence of the Roman Rota has emphasized this teaching as well. To cite only two of many available examples, a decision heard before the Dean of the Roman Rota pronounced: "Faith is not necessary in order to contract marriage validly; only consent is. For those who wish to marry wish something instituted by God through the natural law."[52] And a decision issued two years earlier *coram* Turnaturi stated: "Adhering to the magisterium, our jurisprudence has constantly and frequently declared and

---

48. See, Danilo Marinelli, "La mancanza di fede che può generare la simulazione del consenso secondo la giurisprudenza rotale più recente," *Monitor Ecclesiasticus* 130 (2015) 439–476; and Cormac Burke, *The Theology of Marriage* (Washington, DC: The Catholic University of America Press, 2015) 1–29. Marinelli (451) summarizes the traditional position on the role of faith in consent: "In conclusione è possibile asserire che l'assenza di fede non costituisce motive di nullità, perché ciò che rivela è solo la presenza di un valido patto nuziale, ma può diventarne una causa indiretta qualora provochi nel nubente un errore determinante della volontà oppure una simulazione del consenso coniugale, ossia quando determine un'alterazione della minima intenzionalità richiesta, rivolta, cioè, all'unione matrimoniale naturale."

49. John Paul II, Address to the Roman Rota 8, January 30, 2003: *AAS* 95 (2003) 397. An English available in *Canon Law Society of Great Britain and Ireland Newsletter* 133 (2003) 6–10.

50. Benedict XVI, Address to the Roman Rota 1, January 26, 2013: *AAS* 105 (2013) 168. English available in *Origins* 42 (2013) 597–599.

51. Francis, Address to the Roman Rota, January 22, 2016. As of this time the discourse has not yet been published in *AAS*. It is a brief, one-page speech. The text does not include paragraph or section numbers. An English version can be found in *Origins* 45 (2016) 624.

52. *Coram* Stankiewicz, November 28, 2007, *RRDec* 99: 331: "Ad validum contrahendum matrimonium fides necessaria non est, sed unus consensus. Nam, qui vult matrimonium, vult aliquid a Deo, ope legis naturae, institutum."

established that for the valid contracting of marriage consent is sufficient; faith is not required."[53]

At the same time, even if a lack of faith has no presumed, direct impact on the validity of consent, a lack of faith can serve as a circumstance or quality of character that motivates a person to exclude the sacramental dignity of marriage (canon 1101) or that indicates the presence of error that determined the person's will in such an impact results (canon 1099). As the *Subsidium* mentions, the current loss of Christian culture and the worldly mentality that comes with it, one that can lead to a faith "imprisoned in subjectivism" creates a climate for such simulation or error to arise. The situation is aggravated when the lack of faith is joined by a "psychological and moral fragility, particularly if they are young or at least immature."[54]

We find in the jurisprudence some examples of specific situations that can suggest a person was at least remotely predisposed to simulation or error of this type. These include adherence to an atheistic organization, radical ideological error combined with lack of faith, membership in political parties that expressly exclude sacramental dignity of marriage, lack of faith together with morally depraved character, public repudiation of the faith and a choice to wed without a religious ceremony precisely because of previous rejection of faith. All of these, when strongly present, can serve as indicators of the nullity of consent (especially as possible motives for exclusion). However, rotal jurisprudence consistently rejects the notion that such memberships or mentalities are themselves sufficient proof of a nullifying exclusion.[55]

---

53. *Coram* Turnaturi, July 21, 2005, *RRDec* 97: 403: "Magisterio adhaerens constanter vel haud semel nostra iurisprudentia edixit statuitque ad valide contrahendum matrimonium sufficere consensum non require fidem." Geraldina Boni offers an interesting perspective on the very inclusion of this circumstance in the MI given the ongoing debate that surrounds the question of the impact a lack of faith might have on the validity of consent. She concludes with a cautionary note: "Diviene quindi non remota l'eventualità che alcuni tribunal ecclesiastici, in specie 'immersi' nelle società secolarizzate occidentali, si spingano a interpretare la norma nel senso che la mancanza di fede di per sé provochi l'invalidità del vincolo, con l'esito di quella che è stata argutamente definita un 'amnistia matrimoniale'."Boni, Parte Seconda, 21–26

54. *Subsidium*, 34.

55. Marinelli (469) remarks: "Dalla ricerca svolta emerge che la mancanza di fede, le idee averse all Chiesa cattolica, la mentalità pervasa di ateismo, l'adesione ad un Partito politico sotenitore di principi contraria a quelli cristiani, non sono stati considerati indizi sufficienti a provare l'esclusione della sacramentalità del matrimonio qualora il nubente, contestualmente,

It is likewise a heavy burden to demonstrate that lack of faith caused a radical error to influence the will to choose marriage not as God intended it. Simple or general error does not qualify. Instead, it must be shown that the error radically influenced the person's will such that exclusion by implicit simulation takes place or the will is circumscribed by the error such that it cannot choose otherwise than marriage deformed of its sacramental essence or other essential property or element. In either case (and the debate on the nature of the ground of error continues) we again face the need to demonstrate a positive movement of the will that results in marriage devoid of an essential element or property.

We can say this as well with regard to lack of faith that is alleged to have led to nullity not based on an exclusion of sacramental dignity or radical error regarding it, but based on the exclusion of marriage itself, exclusion of another essential property or element of marriage, or relevant error regarding them.[56] This possibility is raised by the *Subsidium*, which states:

> The text [of Art. 14 §1] refers to a lack of faith that leads to a *false understanding* of marriage or to an induced simulation, not devoid of consequences for the maturing nuptial will. In other words, one is facing an error that determines the will (cfr. Can. 1099), or a defect of a valid intention through the exclusion of the marriage itself, or of one of its essential elements or properties (cfr. Can. 1101 §2).

In these cases as well, and even arguably more so than with the exclusion of sacramental dignity, a mere lack of faith is not sufficient to prove that exclusion occurred by a positive act of the will or even to manifest nullity in an introductory petition. Instead, the lack of faith becomes a circumstance that, together with other required proofs, including the demonstration of a motive, together allow moral certitude to be reached. As Ferrer Ortiz succinctly puts it with regard to simulation: "That which must be proven in any case is not the lack of faith so much as the simulation of consent, the positive act of the will to exclude marriage itself or an essential

---

ha desiderato e volute un vero matrimonio." See also footnote 156 where Marinelli provides numerous citations from rotal decisions to support his conclusion.

56. A common example encountered in jurisprudence is the indirect exclusion of the indissolubility of marriage based on a motivation related to a deeply rooted lack of faith.

element of property." To which he adds, "And, as the doctrine teaches and jurisprudence shows, this is not easy to demonstrate."[57]

Since use of the briefer process requires the attachment of documents or records to the petition that manifest nullity of consent, we can ask what type of documents would suffice to establish this if simulation or error due to a lack of faith are the grounds proposed? Given the difficulty of proof required to establish simulation or error, the quality of documents would seem to be all the more important here.

In general, I find it difficult to imagine many cases where the high standard of documents or records required by MI would be available. With regard to the circumstance of a lack of faith, the *Subsidium* offers no examples (as it does with other circumstances). We might think of an official document that records a formal defection from the faith.[58] Others could include membership rolls in atheistic societies or publications or videos that witness to strongly held errors contrary to the nature of marriage. Even if we stipulate that the latter documents meet the standard of MI, we still have to demonstrate the motive that led the person to apply these errors or beliefs to the consent being challenged. Who are the witnesses that might be able to assist with that? And will a brief session to gather proofs suffice to assure the quality necessary to reach moral certitude? Admittedly, questions such as these will be answered in large part as the practice of the use of the briefer process unfolds. The answers, however, should always be arrived at in light of the jurisprudential doctrine.

C. A Brief Conjugal Cohabitation

The next circumstance of Art. 14 regards a brief conjugal cohabitation. The *Subsidium* lists several possible grounds related to this circumstance, including exclusion of the *bonum fidei*, condition, error (presumably error of person here), deceit, and the inability to assume the essential obligations of marriage.[59] What we should note with regard to a brief conjugal life considered under any of these grounds is that the question of brevity

---

57. Ferrer Ortiz, 174: "En todo caso, lo que debe probarse no es tanto la falta de fe cuanto la simulación del consentimiento, el acto positive de voluntad de excluir el matrimonio mismo o un element o propieded esencial. Y, como enseña la doctrina y demuestra la jursprudencia, esto no es tan fácil de demostrar."

58. As suggested by Lüdicke, 1683/4.

59. *Subsidium*, 34.

serves as an indication of possibly nullity and not in itself as a ground of nullity or a presumption in its favor. In fact, jurisprudence holds that the short length of cohabitation is not itself a manifest indication of nullity, just as a lengthy cohabitation is not always positive proof against nullity.

A notably brief term to conjugal life could, however, serve as a strong *indicium* of invalid consent.[60] For instance, a person who marries only to obtain legal residency in another country might end common life immediately or shortly after achieving the new legal status. Or marriage might take place to give legitimacy to a child. Once the birth occurs, the marriage ends. In any event, the question also arises as to what is meant by a brief conjugal cohabitation. At what point in the length of its life does the brevity of common life manifest nullity?[61] Because there is no clear standard possible, the additional elements of proof will be critical to establishing nullity. Whether the briefer process lends itself to achieving this remains to be seen.

What documents would suffice to manifest nullity under these situations? This depends, of course, on which ground is being proposed with this circumstance. It is easy enough to present a document that demonstrates a short time of cohabitation, such as some type of official change of residence form.[62] What is not so easy is finding documents that support the cause behind it. Still, let us imagine the ground of condition. A woman marries a man with the present condition that he does not suffer from a hereditary illness that would threaten children born of the marriage. He says he does not, but she doubts it, resolving the doubt by the condition: I marry you provided you are free of this genetic condition. Shortly after consent she discovers a medical report from before the wedding that establishes he does have the illness. She separates immediately. Although this scenario also requires additional proof—especially the establishment

---

60. See Alejandro W. Bunge, "Presentación del Nuevo Proceso Matrimonial," delivered at the 110th Plenary Assembly of the Episcopal Conference of Argentina in November 2015 (accessible at: http://www.awbunge.com.ar/Nuevo-Proceso-Matrimonial.pdf.), 18.

61. See Pagé, 611: "Once again, what does this [the brevity of conjugal life] mean? One month? Six months? Four years? Ten years? How brief should a conjugal life last to be considered as a circumstance which can allow the use of the briefer process? Would this not be the return to a presumption of fact which was used in the past and forbidden later by the Apostolic Signatura?"

62. See Lüdicke, at 1683/4. Of course, the simple fact that there was a sudden change of residence following consent does not establish manifest nullity of consent (which Lüdicke does not suggest).

of the intention to place the condition prior to consent—it at least allows us to conceive of a type of document that might assist in manifesting nullity at the time of the introduction of the petition. We can perhaps see how this would play out with some of the other grounds mentioned in the *Subsidium*, such as deceit and error of quality of person. Here, too, we would have some type of official document or weighty records that demonstrates the presence or lack of a quality that when discovered creates aversion and so departure. But again, the document itself does not establish nullity. All proofs together must do so.

D. An Abortion Procured To Avoid Procreation

Article 14 §1 next mentions the circumstance of an abortion procured to avoid procreation as one that can manifest nullity. If the abortion was procured precisely to exclude the good of children, then this circumstance obviously relates to the ground of simulation *contra bonum prolis*. This is what the *Subsidium* indicates when it states: "This [circumstance] constitutes a vehement indication of a simulated will, typically contrary to the good of children."[63]

However, here, too, the context of common jurisprudence is helpful. It first provides that not every intention to procure an abortion is necessarily indicative—even remotely—of an intention against the *bonum prolis*. There may be reasons the abortion was procured that were, in a contorted form of reasoning, intended to advance future life. For instance, a woman might have procured the abortion during a pregnancy troubled for health reasons so that health could be restored to assure future pregnancies would more likely succeed. The gravely objective wrong of directly procuring an abortion, which is never permitted, has been committed; but it was not done to exclude children from the marriage.[64]

A recent decision before the Dean of the Rota indicates what three elements must be established to prove nullity due to simulation against the good of children. These apply as well to cases involving a procured abortion. There must be an express (not implicit, much less tacit) intention not

---

63. *Subsidium*, 34.
64. Ferrer Ortiz (178), offers two more possible scenarios where a procured abortion would not serve as a vehement indication of an exclusionary will: where the abortion relates to a moral disorder of one or both of the spouses or where the woman wishes to conceal a pregnancy that resulted *ab alio*.

to exchange right to acts per se apt for the procreation of children so that, in fact, no children will be born. Evidence must exist of an actual plan to impede sexual relations from openness to life. And then the intention to interrupt life already conceived, especially through direct abortion, has to be proven.[65]

What these three elements indicate is that it is not sufficient to establish nullity of consent by merely proving that an abortion did, in fact, take place. This is so even if the abortion was procured freely and willingly by the woman and with the concurrence of the man. Rotal jurisprudence has consistently held that full proof can arise from the mere fact of an abortion taking place only if clear and compelling circumstances are present that establish to the standard of moral certitude that the abortion was undergone based on a compelling exclusionary motive.[66]

Given the above, we would expect to see when the briefer process is used medical records (or related documents from a clinic) that demonstrate an abortion was procured. Proof that this was concomitant with the intention not to exchange the right to acts per se apt for the procreation of children and so part of a plan to impede fruitful relations cannot be established by medical records alone. Testimony from qualified witnesses will be necessary, such as medical experts or counselors.[67] These should corroborate the statements of the parties. The principle that *facta sunt validiora quam verba* can also open an important source of proof. Behaviors of the parties around the time of the abortion can reveal a great deal regarding the intention that motivated the act. This might include means of birth control used throughout the common life, means used to avoid

---

65. See *coram* Pinto, June 15, 2007: *RRDec* 99: 216.
66. *Coram* de Lanversin, June 26, 1991: *RRDec* 83: 424–425: "Patet reapse hoc scelus tunc in usu positum praesumptiones inducere posse, quae attamen per se non sufficient ad provocandam necessariam certitudinem morale circa adsertam exclusionem iuris in corpus, nisi certis ac univocis roborentur circumstantiis."
67. Bunge, 18: "Se deberá verificar, a partir de las declaraciones de las partes, que el aborto procurado haya sido movido por la firma voluntad e excluir la prole. La declaración jurada de quien haya procurado el aborto, los indicios como por ejemplo los métodos anticonceptivos aplicados en forma habitual, y adminículos como las constancias médicas, pueden llevar a la certeza moral que las partes, o al menos una de ellas, celebraron el matrimonio con la firme intención de excluir la prole en modo perpetuo, recurriendo al aborto cada vez que se ha producido un embarazo no querido."

procreation, the refusal to engage in sexual relations and the reaction of one or both of the spouses to the conception of a child.[68]

E. An Obstinate Persistence in an Extra Conjugal Relationship at Time of or Immediately After Consent

Article 14 moves on to present "an obstinate persistence in an extra conjugal relationship at time of or immediately after consent" as the next circumstance that might demonstrate manifest nullity of consent. This circumstance falls under the ground of simulation *contra bonum fidei*. It is also a qualified circumstance. The infidelity must be obstinately persistent (*permanentia pervicax*). The *Subsidium* adds that the circumstance is especially strong if it is accompanied by a refusal to engage in sexual relations with the spouse.[69]

Rotal jurisprudence speaks much more to the invalidating impact of infidelity that takes place prior to consent rather than only after consent is exchanged. As a general rule, the existence of unfaithful relations after consent—with none having occurred beforehand—is a much more difficult case to prove.[70] Even when it is a question of infidelity prior to consent, the fact that such behavior took place repeatedly is not sufficient to prove nullity of consent, or even to manifest it.[71] It is surprising, then, that the possibility now exists for infidelity that occurs only following consent and never before the exchange of consent to manifest the invalidity of the marriage and so open the way to use of the BP. In other words, what Rotal jurisprudence has long considered to be the more difficult case to prove (infidelity only after consent) can now give rise to manifest nullity at the time of the submission of the petition.

As for what documents would be relevant to this circumstance, the *Subsidium* mentions private detective reports, letters, transcripts of telephone

---

68. See Hector Franceschi, "L'esclusione della prole," in *La Giurisprudenza della Rota Romana sul Consenso Matrimoniale: 1908–2008* (Vatican City: Libreria Editrice Vaticana, 2009) 175–208, especially 205–206 where Franceschi provides a seven-point summary of decades of Rotal jurisprudence on the elements of proof for simulation *contra bonum prolis*.

69. *Subsidium*, 34.

70. As Lüdicke (1683/4) notes: "Hier [in Art. 14] geht es um ein Verhalten, das den behaupteten Ausschluss der ehelichen Treuepflicht schon nach herkömmlicher Rechtsprechung stützt. Allerdings wurde bisher nur die Fortsetzung eines vor der Heirat bestehenden ehewidrigen Verhältnisses in Betracht gezogen, nicht die Untreue unmittelbar nach her Heirat."

71. See, for instance, *coram* Pinto, March 21, 1986: *RRDec* 86: 300–308.

conversations, and emails.[72] Presumably the *Subsidium* means by this documents from a non-suspect time. It is worth asking, in any case, if any of these are sufficient to establish the manifest nullity of consent. If we hold to the norm of MI for use of the briefer process—that the documents cannot need further inquiry or investigation—then it is uncertain how private letters or emails, which must be authenticated, do not require further inquiry. Similarly, if not more so, the report of a private investigator would need to be examined in light of many factors that the report itself may not contain. For instance, were there findings that the investigator left out? Did the investigator use legitimate means *quoad modum et substantiam* to obtain the information? With regard to transcripts of telephone conversations, a judge should accept transcripts with a clear knowledge of whether they are authentic and are complete or edited. Determining the probative weight of these type of documentary sources requires further investigation in most every case, which is not permitted by MI.

Perhaps another example of a document that does more readily fit the requirements of MI would be the official report of a psychologist, counselor or social worker who had one or both of the spouses as a client during a non-suspect time and during which admissions to "obstinate" infidelity were recorded by the professional care giver. It is arguably more likely, however, as Klaus Lüdicke observes, that "proof of this ground of nullity will be possible only through witnesses."[73] If so, that proof would be raised in the ordinary process rather than through use of the BP.

F. The Deceitful Concealment of Sterility, Grave Contagious Illness, Children from a Previous Relationship, Incarcerations

The next circumstance suggested by Art. 14 §1 involves the ground of deceit or imposed error as provided for in c. 1098. Specifically, although not exhaustively, the article mentions the deceitful concealment of sterility, grave contagious illness, children from a previous relationship, and incarcerations. All of these situations have been the subject of Rotal jurisprudence. So, too, have others, such as concealment of severe drug or

---

72. *Subsidium*, 34.
73. Lüdicke, 1683/5: "Der Beleg dieses Nichtigkeitsgrundes wird nur durch Zeugnisse möglich sein."

alcohol addictions and falsification of one's religious, social, educational or professional status.

In more recent years, Rotal jurisprudence has reached a broad consensus on the manner in which deceit can lead to invalidity of consent; the elements follow closely the wording of c. 1098. Whereas the *Subsidium* mentions only one of these elements, it is critical to keep all of them in mind.[74] One of the parties is led into an antecedent error caused by an act of deceit that was placed in order to gain consent from the one deceived. The content of the deceitful act must be a quality of the other party that can either objectively or subjectively gravely disturb conjugal life.[75] It is not sufficient to establish simply that deceit took place concerning one of the situations mentioned in Art. 14. No matter how gravely disturbing an act of deceit might have been, if it was not perpetrated to gain marital consent, it does not invalidate under the heading of c. 1098.[76]

How much of this can be established to the standard of manifest nullity through documents and witnesses? It depends once more, I believe, on the nature of the quality that was the subject of deception. Incarcerations, grave illness, the existence of children, these situations are all open to proof by documents needing no further investigation. What is not so readily available, especially by documents, is proof that the intent of the deceiver was to gain consent and the impact the deceit had on conjugal life, especially if the impact was subjective in nature. It would seem in this case that corroboration of the statements of the *deceptus* would be necessary to show how the will to marry was undermined by the deceit perpetrated to obtain consent.

---

74. As Ferrer Ortiz (180) puts it: "Por su parte, el *Sussidio applicativo* no resulta concluyente, pues describe parcialmente los elementos del *caput nullitatis* e incluye algunos exemplos de posibles pruebas incontrovertibles."

75. An excellent updated presentation of the jurisprudence on the ground of deceit is found in Maria Teresa Romano, "Il dolo (can. 1098)," in VV.AA., *La Giurisprudenza della Rota Romana sul Consenso Matrimoniale (1908–2008)* (Vatican City: Libreria Editrice Vaticana, 2009) 85–104, especially 102–103.

76. If the error in question was substantial in nature, rather than accidental as happens with the ground of deceit, invalidity might arise based on the ground of error as provided for in c. 1097.

G. A Cause of Marriage Completely Extraneous To Married Life, or Consisting of the Unexpected Pregnancy of the Woman

Article 14 §1 now passes to a circumstance that falls under the ground of total simulation of marriage, even if that phrase is not used by MI. The phrasing used in the text is a bit awkward inasmuch as one possible motive for total simulation—the unexpected pregnancy of the woman—is mentioned separately from the general notion of total simulation, the choice of marriage for a reason entirely extraneous to its purpose. In fact, the discovery of an unexpected pregnancy can often be better judged under the ground of force and fear or even the psychological ground of lack of due discretion.[77] In any case, the *Subsidium* offers additional examples, such as exchanging consent for the sole reason of acquiring citizenship or exclusively for the legitimation of children. These examples would seem to further indicate that total simulation is the prevalent ground intended by this circumstance.

The *Subsidium* also states that with total simulation cases there are often additional circumstances that appear, including shortness of conjugal life and the initiation of civil divorce proceedings.[78] Once again, witness testimony will be important to demonstrate that such a serious act as total simulation took place. Depending on what is the motive for simulation, official records might be available as well. It is difficult to envision what they might be outside of concrete cases. I am not sure what official or even heavily probative documents would be readily available in other cases, such as the unexpected pregnancy, but they would again be necessary at the time the petition is submitted in order to move forward with the briefer process.

In any event, unlike with partial simulation, where at least a marriage is intended—albeit one devoid of an essential aspect—total simulation is commonly, but not exclusively, understood to be born of an entirely fraudulent will. In every case, no marriage whatsoever is intended. Proof of such a striking contradiction between what is said and what is intended is not as easy as might be thought since it is never presumed that a person

---

77. See Lüdicke, 1683/5.
78. *Subsidium*, 35.

engaged fictitiously in the exchange of consent.[79] Testimonies and documents used to establish the manifest nullity of such a circumstance would need to take account of this.

Given the difficulty that arises with proof of total simulation, it is not easy to envision what types of documents needing no further investigation or inquiry will be available here to manifest the nullity of consent in the introductory petition. The medical reports regarding birth of an unexpected child would not include the unexpected nature of the pregnancy although they might offer some indication of the state of mind of the mother if this rose to the level of a health concern. Likewise, if it is a case of marriage for the sole reason of obtaining citizenship then we would not expect this to be noted in an official document since this could likely constitute a type of fraudulent activity. In other words, with regard to total simulation of consent the testimony of the parties and witnesses is critical since the radical nature of this act of exclusion is normally not evidenced in official records or documents. If so, this would preclude in many instances the ability of documents to manifest the nullity of consent at the time of the submission of the petition.

H. Physical Violence Inflicted To Extort Consent

This final circumstance mentioned in Art. 14 §1, physical violence inflicted to extort consent, appears to relate to the ground of force or grave fear inflicted from without (c. 1103). The *Subsidium* remarks that this circumstance involves "actual acts of violence and harm."[80]

Javier Ferrer Ortiz raises compelling questions as to why this circumstance was included in Art. 14 and what ground it actually relates to.[81] He notes that there are only two cases to be found in published rotal jurisprudence that involve marriages entered into due to external violence inflicted on one of the spouses (force); in these two cases both victims were women. The first case regarded a marriage contracted in 1929 in China[82] and the second concerned a marriage contracted in 1913 in Egypt.[83] Fer-

---

79. *Coram* Pena, May 6, 2005: *RRDec* 97: 226: "Hic totalis voluntatis nuptialis defectus certo certius quid abnorme constituit ideoque non est facile affirmandus."
80. *Subsidium*, 35.
81. See Ferrer Ortiz, 183–184.
82. *Coram* Quattrocolo, December 9, 1930: *RRDec* 22: 653–662.
83. *Coram* Jullien, May 11, 1935: *RRDec* 27: 299–306.

rer Ortiz argues that the rarity of these type cases contradicts the *Subsidium*'s claim that the circumstances are, "situations that the jurisprudence has long enucleated as *symptomatic elements of the invalidity of matrimonial consent.*"[84] So it must not be that the circumstance regards the ground of force. He resolves the contradiction by appropriately presuming the circumstance actually regards induced fear rather than the imposition of external physical violence (force). The external violence might give rise to fear of greater harms that then results in a choice of marriage in order to flee those greater harms.[85] Ferrer Ortiz concludes, a greater clarity between the ground of force and of fear would be beneficial to Art. 14 and the *Subsidium*'s comments regarding it since as things stand a confusion can arise between the objective cause of nullity arising out of external force and the subjective cause originating from imposed fear.

In fact, once we read this circumstance in light of Ferrer Ortiz' analysis, we see that it more easily fits the essential elements needed for fear to have a nullifying effect: the fear must be grave and brought on by an extrinsic cause. And the person suffering from the fear must conclude there is no means to escape it except to consent to marriage. Where these elements are present in a petition for nullity, the manifest nature of nullity can be supported by documents such as medical and police reports. This would once more arguably exclude private experts or private documents. Still, as has been noted already on several occasions, the simple existence of a cause of fear and related documents to establish a cause for it is not sufficient to establish nullity. The principles of jurisprudence must be applied as well if full proof is to be achieved. This includes the need to establish the grave and extrinsic nature of the fear, its essential role in causing consent, and the aversion to the marriage that arises in the one subject to the fear. Documents that need no further investigation will be able to establish only the first element.

---

84. *Subsidium*, 32. Emphasis in the original.
85. Ferrer Ortiz, 184: "Sin embargo, la descripción de este comportamiento permite concluir que enrealidad se trat de la figura del miedo y que la violencia fí va acompañada de amenazas de males mayors, y que debería reunir los requisites de éste para ser causa de nulidad: antecendente, externo e indeclinable (c. 1103)."

I. Etcetera . . .

Article 14 ends with the uncommon legislative use of the word, "etcetera" to indicate that the list of circumstances presented in MI is not complete. A petition might be presented that contains other circumstances that manifest nullity of sentence. If this is the case, these, too, would have to be judged against the standard of rotal jurisprudence. Caution is called for if the circumstance is not commonly treated by the Rota as able to manifest nullity. In all cases, the same standard of supporting proof is required and the documents and records cannot require further inquiry or investigation.

3. Practical Observations on the Use of Jurisprudence and the *Processus Brevior*

Given the important role jurisprudence plays in the *processus brevior*, it might be helpful to conclude with a brief consideration of some particular moments in the process where the jurisprudential doctrine will need special attention by officials engaged in it.

a. The Preparation of the Petition

An initial, critical moment will be the preparation of the *libellus*, most especially if the petitioners wish to request use of the briefer process. The circumstances of things and persons must manifest nullity and be supported by the weighty proofs we have discussed above. Since all this must be in the petition—and not require further investigation or inquiry (but be immediately accessible)—a failure to produce a suitable petition will mean no access to the briefer process.

Accordingly, those charged with assisting in the preparation of the petition should be well informed, trained personnel. They should be familiar with the standard that has to be met to use the briefer process and with the jurisprudence related to the circumstances proposed. MI and the *Subsidium* refer to a "pastoral investigation" that takes place prior to the submission of the petition. The text of the *motu proprio* states: "This same investigation is entrusted to persons deemed suitable by the local ordinary, with the appropriate expertise, though not exclusively juridical-canonical."[86]

---

86. MI, Art. 4.

And the purpose of this pastoral investigation is evidently to prepare the petition itself since, as we read, "All elements having been collected, the investigation culminates in the *libellus*."[87]

It is not clear if the same persons engaged in the pastoral investigation are then to assist with the drafting of the petition. If they do, and if they are not well trained in the law and jurisprudence of marriage nullity, then I believe the briefer process will be rarely open to use due to under prepared petitions. Although the briefer process is meant to bring swifter decisions it also requires greater attention to the early stages of the process for that goal to be reached in a just manner. At the same time, the petition is not meant to serve as a collection of proofs sufficient for determination of nullity. The Instructor will be responsible for assembling the proofs. Perhaps preparation of the *vademecum* mentioned in Art. 3 of MI will assist in this regard.[88]

b. The Role of the Judicial Vicar, Defender of the Bond, Instructor, and Assessor

It belongs to the judicial vicar to make the determination of whether the manifest nature of nullity exists in the petition submitted following the pastoral investigation.[89] This is obviously the essential moment for moving forward with the process. The judicial vicar is to make the decision on whether the BP is to be used based on the petition—with attached documents—presented to him. He is not permitted to conduct an investigation or inquiry into the petition. If the circumstances presented, and the supporting proofs, do not manifest nullity then the ordinary process must ensue. And here, too, the judicial vicar is bound to make his decision with due consideration of the common jurisprudence of the Church. Although

---

87. MI, Art. 5. For more on the interplay of the legal and pastoral elements of this moment in the process, see: "Pedro A. Moreno García, "El servicio de indagación prejudicial: aspectos jurídicos-pastorales," *Ius Canonicum* 56 (2016) 65–85 and Manuel Jesús Arroba Conde, "La pastoral judicial y la preparación de la causa en el *motu proprio Mitis Iudex Dominus Iesus*," in *Proceso de Nulidad Matrimonial tras la Reforma del Papa Francisco*, ed. Maria Elena Olmos Ortega (Madrid: Editorial Dykinson, 2016) 63–82.

88. See Arroba Conde (76) for more on the distinction between what is contained in the petitioner and what will constitute proofs used in the BP.

89. See c. 1676 §2 of MI. The role of the judicial vicar under the BP is notable. As Geraldina Boni, Parte Seconda, 33, remarks: "È communqie il vicario giudiziale il fulcro attorno al quale tutto ruota (e questo si viverbererà sull'equilibrio della 'gestione' dell'intera attività processuale del tribunale)."

the judicial vicar is not required to reach moral certitude regarding the nullity of consent—that will be the standard for the judge—he would prudently consider whether the bishop, with the minimal collecting of proofs that will occur under the instructor, would likely be able to do so. Otherwise, the BP might result in a delay in resolving the question of nullity of consent since, if the bishop cannot reach moral certitude, the case will be returned for adjudication according to the ordinary process.[90]

Once the judicial vicar determines the BP is to issue a decree indicating as much. The same decree is to determine the formulation of the doubt according to which the marriage will be accused of nullity.[91] Here, too, the judicial vicar will need to pay close attention to the Church's jurisprudence. The doubt chosen should relate directly to the manifest character of nullity in the petition.

The judicial vicar is also to appoint an instructor and assessor to assist with the briefer process. These officials also should be well informed about the common jurisprudence. The instructor should use the session for collecting proofs to ascertain whether the required elements of proof are present in the petition and whether those attending the session can further support this. And the assessor, for his or her part, needs to at least have a general knowledge of jurisprudence so that the expertise the person brings will be useful to the bishop, most especially if he is not a canon lawyer or otherwise not familiar with the Church's common jurisprudence.[92]

The defender of the bond plays a crucial role in the briefer process given the possibilities of abuse that might arise from its use. For instance, the defender should ascertain whether the use of the BP is warranted due to a lack of manifest nullity or a failure to follow the procedures set out for the process. I believe an indispensable contribution the defender will make in the briefer process is to examine carefully whether jurisprudential

---

90. Canon 1687 §1 of MI. Erasmo Napolitano (578–579) observes regarding the decision of whether to use the BP: "Se trata de una deció delicada, que debe evitar tanto el peligro de prejuzgar la causa como el de admitir sin base suficiente un proceso extraordinario, que tiene predefinido por el legislador unos requisitos concretos y exigentes para su utilización, entre cuales se encuentra que las circunstancias concurrentes y prueba protada con la demanda patente la nulidad, sin necesidad de una profusa instrucción."

91. Canon 1685 of MI.

92. For more on these phases of the BP, see: Paolo Bianchi, "Lo svolgimento del processo breve: la fase istruttoria e di discussion della causa," in *La riforma dei processi matrimoniali di Papa Francesco* (Milan: Àncora Editrice, 2016) 67–90.

elements of proof are present and weighty enough to establish the nullity of the marriage. The bishop, for his part, will like any judge take serious account of the observations of the defender when coming to a decision.

c. The Role of the Diocesan Bishop

The conclusion of the briefer process comes with the decision of the diocesan bishop, either for nullity or for use of the ordinary process. As we noted, Pope Francis considers the briefer process to be open to abuse. It is largely for this reason that he authorizes the diocesan bishop alone to conduct the process since he, "is with Peter the greatest guarantor of Catholic unity in faith and in discipline."[93]

Accordingly, the bishop is bound to reach the standard of moral certitude when declaring nullity of consent. Article 12 of the PR emphasizes this, albeit with some lack of precision.[94] The bishop is to reach this standard personally, based on a thorough evaluation of the acts presented to him, and not by adopting the opinions of the assessor and the investigator.[95] And to arrive at moral certitude, the bishop should take close account of the common jurisprudence of the Church. Otherwise, his

---

93. MI, Art. IV. For a discussion of the role of the diocesan bishop in the BP, see: Massimo Mingardi, "Il ruolo del vescovo diocesano," in *La riforma dei processi matrimoniali di Papa Francesco* (Milan: Àncora Editrice, 2016) 91–106. Alessandro Giraudo, among others, questions how most diocesan bishops will be able to take the time to become sufficiently familiar with the jurisprudence of the Church in order to give nullity cases under the BP a suitable hearing. Additionally, he will need to devote sufficient time to studying the acts, the opinions of the defender of the bond, the instructor and the assessor in order to reach a just decision. See: "Snellimento della prassi canonica in ordine alla dichiarazione di nullità del vincolo matrimoniale?," *Quaderni di Diritto Ecclesiale* 28 (2015) 324–325. For a discussion of the use of the BP offered from the standpoint of a diocesan bishop, see: Thomas John Paprocki, "Implementation of *Mitis Iudex Dominus Iesus* in the Diocese of Springfield in Illinois," *The Jurist* 75 (2015) 593–605 and this volume, 341–353.

94. Art. 12 reads: "To achieve the moral certainty required by law, a preponderance of proofs and indications is not sufficient, but it is required that any prudent doubt of making an error, in law or in fact, is excluded, even if the mere possibility of the contrary is not removed." As Bernard du Puy-Montbrun (6) notes, it is not simply the law that mandates the standard of moral certitude, but legal doctrine does as well. Additionally, the text of Art. 12 makes a distinction between "proofs" and "indications," whereas indications are, in fact, a type of proof.

95. Bustos, El proceso, 164, offers appropriate caution in this regard: "En mi opinion, estamos ante un dato que es muy importante, pues ya de inicio despeja cualquier duda sobre la necesidad de que sea el Obispo quien materialmente maneje las pruebas, las confronte, las etudie y las valore, no pudiendo caer en la tentació de qu 'le den' la solución-decisión materialmente tomada, limitándose él al formalism de la firma."

decision can easily take on the character of a personal decision rather than an official pronouncement of the Church. As Art. 12 of MI reads: "Any prudent doubt of making an error, in law or in fact, is excluded."

Finally, if the bishop concludes in favor of nullity, his sentence should at least minimally refer to the law and jurisprudence that allowed him to reach that decision. It is essential not only for his sentence to be just, it must also and always appear just. In this way, we can best avoid any sense of "Catholic divorce" when using the briefer process.

4. Concluding Comments

By establishing the briefer process for determination of marriage nullity, Pope Francis seeks to promote the good of the faithful who are "oppressed by the darkness of doubt due to the lengthy wait for a conclusion"[96] to the clarification of their status. At the same time, the Holy Father also insists strongly that no harm come to the Church's teaching on the indissolubility of marriage. If we are to avoid harm to the Church's teaching, then use of the briefer process should conform strictly to the conditions set in the law. This means the petition should contain circumstances that manifest nullity, be supported by weighty testimonies and documents—none of which require further investigation or inquiry—and indicate a standing ground of nullity regarding which jurisprudence will guide the process to the end.

In the end, however, it remains to be seen whether conscientious adherence to the requirements of law for use of the briefer process might result in the rarity of its use. As Bustos concludes: "I believe that the option of the briefer process should be an extraordinary and exceptional option that should not be justified by agility or speed, but by the evidence of nullity."[97] Klaus Lüdicke recently observed that if we understand the list of circumstances as truly requiring proof under specific nullity grounds, following common jurisprudence, and needing allowing for no possibility of an *accuratior disquisitio aut investigatio* (can. 1683, 2°), "then false

---

96. MI, 419.

97. Carlos Morán Bustos, "Retos de la reforma procesal de la nulidad del matrimonio," *Ius Canonicum* 56 (2016) 28: "Por todo ello, creo que la opción del proceso *brevior* debería ser una opción extraordinaria y exceptional, y debería venir justificada, no por la agilidad y la cereridad, sino por la evidencia de la nulidad."

expectations will be raised" about the use of the process.⁹⁸ This is an arguably sound conclusion since, in most cases, the verification of simple facts related to the proposed circumstance will not suffice for establishing with moral certainty marriage nullity that is founded on the constant and common jurisprudence of the Church. At the same time, full efforts should continue to make use of the briefer process in a just and sound way so that whenever possible the goals set out by the Supreme Legislator will be achieved for the sake of the faithful and the salvation of souls.

ABSTRACT

Mitis Iudex Dominus Iesus *stipulates that the use of the* processus brevior *for adjudicating causes of nullity of consent may be used only when the introductory petition includes recurring circumstances of things and persons, supported by testimonies and documents that require no further investigation, which together manifest the nullity of consent. Article 14 of the Procedural Rules included with the legislative text presents several examples of circumstances of things and persons that might manifest nullity. Each of them is taken from situations found in Rotal jurisprudence and all of them need to be evaluated based on the principles of the same body of jurisprudence. This article considers how the examples of Article 14 are to be read in light of the Church's common jurisprudence on marriage nullity. The first part discusses the juridic character of the Procedural Rules in general and of Art. 14 in particular. The second part considers each of the circumstances included in the first paragraph of Art. 14. And the third and final part offers some practical observations on how those officials engaged in the briefer process might take account of the Church's jurisprudence when fulfilling their tasks.*

---

98. "Liest man ihn hingegen so, dass in den genannten Fallgestaltungen der Beweis des eigentlichen Nichtigkeitsgrundes, der den geltenden Maßstäben folgen muss, in einfacher, keine *accuratior disquisitio aut investigatio* (1683 2°) erfordernden Weise möglich sei, dann warden falsche Erwartungen geweckt. Denn in den meisten Fällen reicht die Verifizierung des einfachen Faktums, des angeführten Umstandes nicht aus, um den Tatbestand des betreffenden Nichtigkeitsgrundes sicherzustellen." Lüdicke, 1683/6.

THOMAS JOHN PAPROCKI*

Implementation of *Mitis Iudex Dominus Iesus* in the Diocese of Springfield in Illinois

Introduction

The promulgation of the motu proprio *Mitis iudex Dominus Iesus*, issued by the Supreme Pontiff Francis on August 15, 2015, has put into place a major reform of the canonical process for the declaration of the nullity of marriage in the Code of Canon Law effective December 8, 2015. This reform replaced, in their entirety, canons 1671–1691 in Book VII of the Code of Canon Law, Part III, Title I, Chapter I, Cases to Declare the Nullity of Marriage. The purpose of this article is to describe the interpretation and implementation of this reform in the Diocese of Springfield, Illinois, in the hope that it may be of assistance to other bishops and canonists as they interpret and implement this reform in their dioceses and tribunals.

At the outset, the motivation for this reform is expressed by Pope Francis in his own words in the introductory paragraphs of the motu proprio where he says, "The zeal to reform has been fueled by the enormous number of faithful who, while wishing to act according to their consciences, are too often separated from the legal structures of the Church due to physical or moral distance." Those who are "separated from the legal structures of the Church due to physical or moral distance" would seem to be referring more to dioceses without functioning tribunals, rather than

---

* Bishop of Springfield in Illinois and Adjunct Professor of Law, Loyola University Chicago School of Law.

to dioceses such as Springfield, where we have a fully functioning tribunal, adequately staffed with credentialed canonists. Nevertheless, while though the revision may have been motivated by concern for those parts of the world without functioning tribunals, it does appear that the new norms for the expedited process do indeed apply everywhere.

It also appears that this remains somewhat of a work in progress with many as of yet unanswered questions. As Cardinal Francesco Coccopalmerio, President of the Pontifical Council for Legislative Texts, said in his remarks at the press conference presenting the motu proprio on the Reform of the Process for Declaring Nullity of a Marriage, published in *America Magazine*, "We should remember too that since the church is extended in all continents, the experiences of the different surroundings will bring better understanding and eventual normative precisions."[1]

The new canons are themselves accompanied by twenty-one "Procedural rules for dealing with causes of nullity of marriage" that further specify the implementation of the revised processes. Nevertheless, the new canons and accompanying procedural rules themselves contain provisions that require some decisions for their proper implementation.

Role of the Diocesan Bishop

One of the key points of emphasis noted by Pope Francis in various parts of the document is the role of the diocesan bishop. Two of the six "fundamental criteria which have governed the work of reform" as mentioned in the introduction to the motu proprio call for greater involvement of the diocesan bishop, specifically:

> II.—*A single judge acts under the responsibility of the bishop.*—The constitution of a single judge, who nevertheless is to be a cleric, is in the first instance committed to the responsibility of the bishop, who in the pastoral exercise of his judicial power is to take care that no laxism whatever is indulged.
>
> III.—*The bishop himself is judge.*—In order that the teaching of the Second Vatican Council may finally be put into practice in an area of great importance, it was decided to make it clear that the bishop himself, in his church

---

1. See Gerald O'Connell, "Cardinal Coccopalmerio on the Reform of the Process for Declaring Nullity of a Marriage," September 8, 2015, http://americamagazine.org/content/dispatches/cardinal-coccopalmerio-reform-process-declaring-nullity-marriage.

of which he is constituted shepherd and head, is by that reason himself a judge among the Christian faithful entrusted to him. It is greatly hoped that in large as well as in small dioceses the bishop becomes a sign of the conversion of ecclesiastical structures and does not leave the judicial function in matrimonial matters completely delegated to the offices of his curia. This is especially true in the briefer process which will be established to resolve the most evident cases of nullity.

Pope Francis is frankly addressing the reality that in many dioceses (if not most) it has been the practice of the diocesan bishop to "leave the judicial function in matrimonial matters completely delegated to the offices of his curia." The Holy Father is, in a sense, reminding bishops of their responsibility to exercise judicial power as well as legislative and executive power of governance, as provided by canon 391. Even when this judicial power is exercised vicariously through his judicial vicar, the diocesan bishop should remain involved in some way, as he does with the vicarious exercise of his executive power of governance through his vicar general, episcopal vicars and delegates. Of course, this will depend to a great extent on the bishop's familiarity with canon law, and especially with the canons dealing with the nullity of marriage. In my case, my involvement in marriage nullity cases will be greatly assisted by the fact that I have a doctorate in canon law (J.C.D.) and experience serving for several years as a judge on the Court of Appeals for the Province of Chicago. Yet even in those circumstances where the diocesan bishop does not have a degree in canon law or any tribunal experience, he is still ultimately responsible both canonically and pastorally for the exercise of judicial power in his diocese. In such cases, the diocesan bishop will need to decide, in consultation with his judicial vicar and tribunal staff, the best way for him to be involved in such cases.

Collegiate Tribunal of Three Judges vs. Single Clerical Judge

A key issue that the diocesan bishop must decide procedurally is raised in new canon 1673 §3, which says, "Cases of nullity of marriage are reserved to a college of three judges. A clerical judge must preside; the remaining judges can even be laypersons." There is an exception in §4: "The bishop moderator, if a collegial tribunal cannot be constituted in the diocese or in a nearby tribunal chosen according to the norm of §2, is to entrust cases to a single clerical judge who, where possible, is to employ two assessors of upright life, experts in juridical or human sciences, approved by the bishop for this task."

This requirement for a three-judge collegiate tribunal is in keeping with canon 1425 §1, which states, "Every contrary custom being reprobated, the following cases are reserved to a collegiate tribunal of three judges: (1) contentious cases: (a) concerning the bond of sacred ordination; (b) concerning the bond of marriage." However, an exception to this requirement of a collegiate tribunal of three judges was given in canon 1425 §4, which states, "If it happens that a collegiate tribunal cannot be established for a trial of first instance, the conference of bishops can permit the bishop to entrust cases to a single clerical judge as long as the impossibility of establishing a college perdures; he is to be a cleric and is to employ an assessor and an auditor where possible." At its General Meeting in November 1983, following the promulgation of the 1983 Code of Canon Law, the National Conference of Catholic Bishops (as the United States Conference of Catholic Bishops was then called) approved the following complementary norm: "In accord with the prescriptions of canon 1425 §4, the National Conference of Catholic Bishops authorizes diocesan bishops to entrust a trial of first instance to a single clerical judge."

It appears that the complementary norm of the United States Conference of Catholic Bishops (USCCB) for canon 1425 §4, has now been rendered obsolete. The new canon 1673 §4 now permits the bishop moderator to make the determination to entrust cases to a single clerical judge, without reference to any prior favorable vote of the episcopal conference.

Using language similar to canon 1425 §4, the new canon 1673 §4 speaks of being "unable" (*nequeat*) to constitute a collegial tribunal ("*Episcopus Moderator, si tribunal collegiale constitui nequeat in dioecesi vel in viciniore tribunali ad normam §2 electo, causas unico iudici clerico committat . . .*"). Addressing this in his commentary published in *America Magazine*, Cardinal Coccopalmerio said: "If it's possible, the tribunal should be collegial and formed of three members who are clerics; if it's not possible that all the members are clerics, it's permitted that one only need be a cleric and be the president of the tribunal, while the others can be lay people; if, moreover, it's not possible that the tribunal can be collegial, it's permitted that it be formed of one judge only, but he should be a cleric."[2]

2. Ibid.

Thus, the criterion for establishing a tribunal consisting of a single judge is *impossibility* to form a collegiate tribunal of three judges in the diocese or in a neighboring tribunal. This would seem to be contradictory to the second fundamental criterion mentioned by Pope Francis in the introduction to the Motu proprio, namely, *"A single judge acts under the responsibility of the bishop."* Since this is only introductory language, however, the language of the canon is normative. The introductory language is helpful in the interpretation of the canons, and in this regard the introductory comments may be understood as referring to the exception and not to the normative principle of the three-judge collegiate tribunal.

In determining the *impossibility* of establishing a three-judge collegiate tribunal, the question of *impossibility* must be distinguished from *inconvenience*. In a diocese that has at least three credentialed clerical judges, it may be geographically inconvenient for them to function as a collegiate tribunal if they are also assigned to parishes in parts of the diocese that are distant from each other or the seat of the tribunal, but that would not necessarily amount to impossibility in an age when documents can be photocopied and sent by postal mail or scanned and sent by electronic mail. It may also be burdensome for them if they have other pastoral responsibilities, but such burdens do not necessarily constitute moral impossibility to perform the task.

The new canons themselves make it easier to constitute a collegiate panel using one cleric and two lay judges. Previously, in marriage nullity cases, canon 1421 §2 allowed the conference of bishops to "permit lay persons to be appointed judges" and "when it is necessary, one of them can be employed to form a collegiate tribunal." This was also adopted as a complementary norm for the United States in 1983. New canon 1673 §3, now provides that in a collegiate tribunal of three judges in marriage nullity cases a "clerical judge must preside," but "the remaining judges can even be laypersons." In a small diocese with only one priest-canonist, it may be a financial burden to hire additional credentialed lay canonists to serve as judges, but that does not necessarily make it impossible. Moreover, even when it is impossible to constitute a three-judge collegiate tribunal, new canon 1673 §4 says that the single clerical judge, "where possible, is to employ two assessors of upright life, experts in juridical or human sciences, approved by the bishop for this task." Although these assessors do not need to have canon law degrees, they must be "experts in juridical or human sciences," such as a civil lawyer or psychologist. So, either way, three people need to be employed, whether as a collegiate tribunal of three judges or a single clerical judge with two assessors who are experts in juridical or human sciences.

In the Tribunal of the Diocese of Springfield, Illinois, in addition to a religious brother with a canon law degree who serves as Defender of the Bond, we currently have four priests along with me who have canon law degrees to serve as judges and a fifth priest who will be completing his canon law studies at the end of the current academic year. So with five priests and myself having canon law credentials, and a caseload of about 120 cases per year in our diocese, it would not seem to be impossible to form a collegiate tribunal of three judges for our marriage cases.

Moreover, new canon 1673 §4 adds a new requirement not found in the prior requirements for the collegiate tribunal in marriage cases according to canon 1421 §4, namely, if a collegiate tribunal of three judges cannot be constituted in the diocese, then it must be determined if that can be done "in a nearby tribunal." Thus, before determining that a single clerical judge is warranted due to the impossibility of establishing a collegiate tribunal of three clerics (bishop, priests and/or deacons), or two clerics and a lay judge, or one cleric and two lay judges, the option must first be explored of constituting a three-judge collegiate tribunal in the tribunal of a nearby diocese or perhaps by sharing credentialed personnel with a nearby diocese.

Quality Control

There is an additional reason for using a collegiate tribunal of three judges rather than a single clerical judge: since the mandatory appeal is being abolished, a three-judge panel will help provide some "quality control" at least by peer review. Previously, the single clerical judge would be aware that there would be a mandatory appeal in which an appellate tribunal consisting of three judges with credentials in canon law would review his sentence. Even if this appellate review rarely resulted in a negative decision, the dynamic of the first instance decision being automatically reviewed undoubtedly provided a good measure of quality control motivating the judge to make sure that he did a good job. Without the review of the three appellate judges in the mandatory appeal, a three-judge tribunal in first instance provides for the two other credentialed canon lawyers serving as judges to review the work of the *ponens* and for all three of them to serve as resources for each other in reviewing the facts of the case and coming to the right conclusion with moral certitude.

A further measure of "quality control" is the involvement of the diocesan bishop himself. In his motu proprio, the Holy Father expressed his hope "that in large as well as in small dioceses the bishop becomes a sign of the conversion of ecclesiastical structures and does not leave the judicial function in matrimonial matters completely delegated to the offices of his curia." Since I have a doctorate in canon law and experience with our Interdiocesan Court of Appeals, I plan to serve as *praeses* for all cases of nullity of marriage in the ordinary process in accord with canon 1673 §1 ("*In unaquaque dioecesi iudex primae instantiae pro causis nullitatis matrimonii iure expresse non exceptis est Episcopus dioecesanus, qui iudicialem potestatem exercere potest per se ipse vel per alios, ad normam iuris*"). One of the other judges will be assigned as *ponens* or relator, who reports on the case at the meeting of the judges and puts the sentence into writing (canon 1429). With an average of 120 cases per year, we should be able with a monthly meeting to handle a reasonable caseload of reviewing ten cases per month.

The Briefer Matrimonial Process before the Bishop

For "The Briefer Matrimonial Process before the Bishop," canon 1685 and article 15 provide that the Judicial Vicar is to identify cases for the Briefer Matrimonial Process and refer them to the diocesan bishop after he has appointed an assessor and instructor for the case. After the diocesan bishop has received the acts, consulted with the instructor and the assessor, and considered the observations of the defender of the bond and, if there are any, the defense briefs of the parties, the diocesan bishop would then decide per canon 1687 whether to issue the sentence if he has reached moral certitude about the nullity of marriage or refer the case to the ordinary method if he has not reached the requisite moral certitude about nullity. It should be noted that the diocesan bishop does not render a negative decision if it appears to him that nullity cannot be established based on the evidence presented to him. In that case, he is to remand the case to the ordinary process for further investigation and full review of the case.

It must be said, however, with regard to the Briefer Matrimonial Process, that it is not altogether clear what circumstances "render the nullity manifest" as per canon 1683. The provisions of article 14 §1 of the procedural rules for dealing with causes of nullity of marriage do not establish new grounds for nullity, but only indicate "the circumstances of things and persons which can allow a case for nullity of marriage to be handled by means of the briefer process according to cann. 1683–1687." Examples given for such circumstances of things and persons are: "the defect of faith which can generate simulation of consent or error that determines the will; a brief conjugal cohabitation; an abortion procured to avoid procreation; an obstinate persistence in an extraconjugal relationship at the time of the wedding or immediately following it; the deceitful concealment of sterility, or grave contagious illness, or children from a previous relationship, or incarcerations; a cause of marriage completely extraneous to married life, or consisting of the unexpected pregnancy of the woman, physical violence inflicted to extort consent, the defect of the use of reason which is proved by medical documents, etc."

In particular, with regard to "the defect of faith which can generate simulation of consent or error that determines the will," this area is quite unclear. While Pope Benedict XVI addressed this issue in his allocution to the Roman Rota in 2013, he cautioned, "I certainly do not intend to suggest any facile automatism between the lack of faith and the invalidity of the matrimonial union, but rather to highlight how such a lack may, although not necessarily, also damage the goods of the marriage, since the reference to the natural order desired by God is inherent in the conjugal pact (cf. Gen 2:24)."[3]

Pope Benedict noted that Pope John Paul II had addressed this in his talk to the Roman Rota ten years previously, pointing out that "an attitude on the part of those getting married that does not take into account the supernatural dimension of marriage can render it null and void only if it undermines its validity on the natural level on which the sacramental sign itself takes place."[4] Accordingly, Pope Benedict called for additional study

---

3. Benedict XVI, Address to the Tribunal of the Roman Rota, January 26, 2013: *AAS* 105 (2013) 169. English translation from *Origins* 42/37 (February 21, 2013) 598.

4. John Paul II, Address to the Tribunal of the Roman Rota, January 30, 2003: *AAS* 95 (2003) 397. English translation from *Papal Allocutions to the Roman Rota. 1939–2011*, ed. William H. Woestman (Ottawa: Faculty of Canon Law Saint Paul University, 2011) 277.

of this question, saying, "With regard to this problem it will be necessary, especially in today's context, to promote further reflection."[5]

Pope Francis offered further reflection on this topic in his allocution to the Roman Rota on January 23, 2015, saying that

> the judge, in pondering the validity of the consent expressed, must keep in mind the context of values and of faith—or the absence or lack thereof—in which the intention to marry is formed. Indeed, ignorance of the contents of the faith could lead to what the code calls an error conditioning the will (cf. canon 1099). This circumstance can no longer be considered exceptional as in the past, precisely because worldly thinking often prevails over the magisterium of the church. Such an error threatens not only the stability of marriage, its exclusivity and fruitfulness, but also the ordering of marriage to the good of the other.[6]

Nevertheless, judges must also keep in mind that they are required from time to time to review marriages between the non-baptized and even atheists, who are quite capable of entering into a valid marriage by exchanging consent to the proper ends of marriage and are capable of assuming the essential obligations of matrimony per canons 1095–1107.

The Relationship between Law and Pastoral Care

There may be a temptation on the part of some to treat the whole question of judicial processes for the determining the nullity of marriage as being opposed to genuine pastoral care for those who find themselves in the unfortunate situation of a broken marriage. This is not a new misunderstanding. Following the Second Vatican Council, a debate over canon law ensued in which law and pastoral care were posed in opposition to each other. Pope John Paul II addressed this false dichotomy directly in his allocution to the Roman Rota on January 18, 1990, when he said "it is not true that to be more pastoral the law must make itself less juridical. The

---

5. Benedict XVI, Address to the Tribunal of the Roman Rota, January 26, 2013: *AAS* 105 (2013) 169. English translation from *Origins* 42/37 (February 21, 2013) 598.
6. Francis, Address to the Officials of the Roman Rota, January 23, 2015: *AAS* 107 (2015) 183. English translation from *Origins* 44/36 (February 12, 2015) 596.

juridical dimension and the pastoral dimension are inseparably united in the pilgrim Church on this earth."[7]

Pope Benedict XVI took up this topic with the judges of the Roman Rota in 2006, explaining that "that love of the truth links the institution of canonical causes of the nullity of marriage with the authentic pastoral sense that must motivate these processes."[8] He returned to this theme in his address to the Rota in 2011, saying that he wanted "to consider the juridical dimension that is inherent in the pastoral activity of preparation and admission to marriage, to try to shed light on the connection between such activity and the judicial matrimonial processes." The Holy Father noted that the relationship between the law and pastoral ministry

> is often the object of misunderstandings to the detriment of law but also of pastoral care. Instead, it is necessary to encourage in all sectors, and in a particular way in the field of marriage and of the family, a positive dynamic, a sign of profound harmony between the pastoral and the juridical that will certainly prove fruitful in the service rendered to those who are approaching marriage.[9]

Pope Francis has also weighed in on the topic of the relationship between law and pastoral care in his address to the judges of the Roman Rota on January 24, 2014, saying:

> The juridical dimension and the pastoral dimension of the Church's ministry do not stand in opposition, for they both contribute to realizing the Church's purpose and unity of action. In fact the judicial work of the Church, which represents a service to truth in justice, has a deeply pastoral connotation, because it aims both to pursue the good of the faithful and to build up the Christian community.[10]

It would be good for diocesan bishops and tribunal officials to keep these papal reflections in mind when implementing the new norms for marriage nullity cases, since the judicial function of the diocesan bishop

---

7. John Paul II, Address to the Tribunal of the Roman Rota, January 18, 1990: *AAS* 82 (1990) 874. English translation from *Papal Allocutions to the Roman Rota. 1939–2011*, ed. William H. Woestman (Ottawa: Faculty of Canon Law Saint Paul University, 2011) 211.

8. Benedict XVI, Address to the Tribunal of the Roman Rota, January 28, 2006: *AAS* 98 (2006) 138. English translation from *Origins* 35/36 (February 23, 2006) 601.

9. Benedict XVI, Address to the Tribunal of the Roman Rota, January 22, 2011: *AAS* 103 (2011) 113. English translation from *Origins* 40/36 (February 17, 2011) 599.

10. Francis, Address to the Officials of the Roman Rota for the Inauguration of the Judicial Year, January 24, 2014: *AAS* 106 (2014) 89. English translation from *Origins* 43/36 (February 13, 2014) 588.

is a true exercise of his pastoral care as the shepherd of souls of his spiritual flock.

Conclusion

The diocesan bishop should promulgate his decisions regarding the implementation of the Apostolic Letter *Mitis iudex Dominus Iesus* by issuing a general executory decree, which according to canon 31 serves "to determine more precisely the methods to be observed in applying the law." In his the revision of the canonical process for the declaration of the nullity of marriage in the Code of Canon Law, Pope Francis has not only taken steps to make these processes more readily available to those in need of the judicial function of the Church, but has also called for diocesan bishops themselves to be more personally involved in the exercise of their judicial power of governance as described in canon 391. In this way, diocesan bishops more fully exercise their threefold *munera* to teach, govern and sanctify the People of God entrusted to them as successors of the apostles by divine institution.

ABSTRACT

The diocesan bishop should promulgate his decisions regarding the implementation of the motu proprio Mitis iudex Dominus Iesus *by issuing a general executory decree, which according to canon 31 serves "to determine more precisely the methods to be observed in applying the law." In his the revision of the canonical process for the declaration of the nullity of marriage in the Code of Canon Law, Pope Francis has not only taken steps to make these processes more readily available to those in need of the judicial function of the Church, but has also called for diocesan bishops themselves to be more personally involved in the exercise of their judicial power of governance as described in canon 391. In this way, diocesan bishops more fully exercise their threefold* munera *to teach, govern and sanctify the People of God entrusted to them as successors of the apostles by divine institution. Bishop Paprocki of the Diocese of Springfield in Illinois explains how he implements* Mitis iudex *in his diocese.*

Appendix—General Executory Decree issued for the Diocese of Springfield in Illinois

GENERAL EXECUTORY DECREE

Implementing the Apostolic Letter Issued *Motu Proprio* by
His Holiness, Pope Francis,
Mitis Iudex Dominus Iesus

In the Name of the Most Holy Trinity. Amen.

Whereas on September 8, 2015, His Holiness the Supreme Pontiff, Pope Francis, promulgated his Apostolic Letter issued *motu proprio, Mitis Iudex Dominus Iesus,* by which the canons of the *Code of Canon Law* pertaining to cases regarding the nullity of marriage were reformed, with an effective date of December 8, 2015;

Whereas in the introduction to his Apostolic Letter the Holy Father stated, "It is greatly hoped that in large as well as in small dioceses the bishop becomes a sign of the conversion of ecclesiastical structures and does not leave the judicial function in matrimonial matters completely delegated to the offices of his curia";

Whereas canon 1425, §4 states, "If it happens that a collegiate tribunal cannot be established for a trial of first instance, the conference of bishops can permit the bishop to entrust cases to a single clerical judge as long as the impossibility of establishing a college perdures; he is to be a cleric and is to employ an assessor and an auditor where possible";

Whereas, at its General Meeting in November 1983, following the promulgation of the 1983 *Code of Canon Law*, the National Conference of Catholic Bishops (as the United States Conference of Catholic Bishops was then called) approved the following complementary norm: "In accord with the prescriptions of canon 1425, §4, the National Conference of Catholic Bishops authorizes diocesan bishops to entrust a trial of first instance to a single clerical judge";

Whereas the new procedural law for marriage-nullity processes states that "cases of nullity of marriage are reserved to a college of three judges" (new canon 1673 §3), but allows for a single clerical judge only "if a collegial tribunal cannot be constituted in the diocese or in a nearby tribunal" (new canon 1673 §4);

Whereas the diocesan bishop is therefore to assess whether collegiate tribunals of three judges can be constituted, in which case recourse to a single ordained judge is not to be had; and

Whereas in the Tribunal of the Diocese of Springfield in Illinois, in addition to a religious brother with a canon law degree who serves as Defender of the Bond, we currently have four priests along with me who have canon law degrees to serve as judges and a fifth priest who will be completing his canon law studies at the end of the current academic year;

Now therefore, I, the Most Reverend Thomas John Paprocki, by the grace of God and the Apostolic See Bishop of Springfield in Illinois, in accord with the revision of the canons of the *Code of Canon Law* pertaining to cases regarding the nullity of marriage mandated by the Apostolic Letter issued *motu proprio* by Pope Francis, *Mitis Iudex Dominus Iesus*, hereby issue this General Executory Decree in accord with canon 31, to determine more precisely the methods to be observed in applying the law, as follows:

1. I find that our diocesan tribunal is in a position to judge marriage-nullity cases through our own colleges of three judges, including me.
2. With the coming into force of the new procedural law on December 8, 2015, marriage-nullity cases will be assigned to colleges of three judges in our diocese.
3. I choose to exercise my judicial power personally per canon 1419 §1 and new canon 1673, §1 by serving as the presiding judge (*praeses*) in all such cases, while assigning one of the other judges to serve as the *ponens* or *relator* who reports on the case at the meeting of the judges and puts the sentence into writing per canon 1429.
4. These arrangements will be subject to evaluation after they have been in place for one year.

Given at the Chancery of the Diocese of Springfield in Illinois, on November 10, 2015, the Memorial of Saint Leo the Great, Pope and Doctor of the Church.

✠ Most Reverend Thomas John Paprocki
Bishop of Springfield in Illinois

Reverend Christopher A. House
Chancellor / Ecclesiastical Notary

ROCH PAGÉ*

Questions Regarding the Motu Proprio *Mitis Iudex Dominus Iesus*

Introduction

The motu proprio *Mitis iudex Dominus Iesus*[1] of Pope Francis "on the Reform of the Canonical Process for Declaration of Nullity of Marriage in the Code of Canon Law" was received with surprise by many bishops, including, most probably, many of the delegates to the Synod of Bishops, to say nothing of the canon lawyers of the world. Especially so since the issue was still on the agenda of the ordinary assembly of the Synod of Bishops in October 2015. Unlike the ongoing project for the revision of Book VI of the Code of Canon Law on Penal Law, there was no draft offered for discussion by Conferences of Bishops or by specialists in canon law from around the world. The Special Commission established by Pope Francis on August 27, 2014 to study the question,[2] worked with no trans-

---

* Judicial Vicar Canadian Appeal Tribunal, Ottawa; Guest Professor, School of Canon Law, The Catholic University of America, Washington, DC; former Dean, Faculty of Canon Law, St. Paul University, Ottawa, Canada.

1. Francis, motu proprio *Mitis iudex Dominus Iesus*, August 15, 2015.

2. "Istituita dal Pontefice una commissione speciale di studio per la riforma del processo matrimoniale canonico," *L'Osservatore Romano. Daily Italian edition* 154/215 (September 21, 2014) 1: "Il 27 agosto 2014, Papa Francesco ha deciso l'istituzione di una commissione speciale di studio per la riforma del processo matrimoniale canonico. Lo ha reso noto sabato 20 settembre un comunicato della Sala stampa della Santa Sede, nel quale si specifica che la commissione sarà presieduta da sua eccellenza monsignor Pio Vito Pinto, decano del tribunale della Rota romana, e sarà composta dai seguenti membri: il cardinale Francesco Coccopalmerio, presidente del Pontificio Consiglio per i testi legislativi; l'arcivescovo Luis Francisco Ladaria Ferrer, gesuita, segretario della Congregazione per la dottrina della fede; il vescovo Dimitrios Salachas, esarca apostolico per i cattolici greci di rito bizantino; i monsignori Maurice Monier, Leo Xavier Michael Arokiaraj e Alejandro W. Bunge, prelati uditori del tribunale della Rota

parency over the few months it took to prepare the substance of the motu proprio.

A. Juridical Solution to a Doctrinal Problem

During an in-flight press conference at the end of his papal trip to America on September 27, Pope Francis was asked about his decision to streamline the process for declaring the nullity of marriages. He replied that the change is strictly juridical and not doctrinal, adding that it is not a move towards "Catholic divorce." This was his intention. Moreover, he said, it responded to a request made by the majority of bishops at the extraordinary assembly of the Synod of Bishops on the family in October 2014.[3]

First of all, the 2014 Synod of Bishops consisted mostly of the gathering of presidents of episcopal conferences of the world; that is to say about two hundred bishops, including some bishops of the Roman Curia. The Synod of 2015 consisted of a larger number of bishops of the world delegated by their colleagues or mandated by the Holy Father. Pope Francis has not expanded on why he did not wait for so important a decision to be discussed by a greater gathering of bishops rather than by a few canonists, members, and consultants of a Special Commission he established to study the question. It would have been a much better expression of the collegiality to which he so often refers. Moreover, there was an obvious lack of transparency in the process. Hopefully, some bishops will have dared to raise that question during the Synod in a way or another.

---

romana; padre Nikolaus Schöch, francescano, promotore di giustizia sostituto del Supremo tribunale della Segnatura apostolica; padre Konštanc Miroslav Adam, domenicano, rettore della Pontificia università San Tommaso d'Aquino (Angelicum); padre Jorge Horta Espinoza, francescano, decano della Facoltà di diritto canonico della Pontificia università Antonianum; e il professor Paolo Moneta, già docente di diritto canonico presso l'università di Pisa. I lavori della commissione speciale nominata dal Papa inizieranno quanto prima e avranno come scopo di preparare una proposta di riforma del processo matrimoniale, cercando di semplificarne la procedura, rendendola più snella e salvaguardando il principio di indissolubilità del matrimonio."

3. Synod of Bishops, "Final Report of the Extraordinary Synod of Bishops on the Family," *Origins* 44/24 (November 13, 2014) 401: "Some synod fathers, however, were opposed to this proposal because they felt that it would not guarantee a reliable judgment. In all these cases, the synod fathers emphasized the primary character of ascertaining the truth about the validity of the marriage bond."

On the other hand, how many bishops knew that, being first judges of first instance in their dioceses (see c. 1419 §1), they would eventually have to put this role into practice in a shortened procedure? If they had been asked their opinion only on this issue, would they have been eager to agree with the papal proposal? This is, by far, the most serious question raised by his decision.

In the same press conference, the Pope mentioned that the reform of the marriage nullity process is not to be perceived as granting Catholic divorce, the change being strictly juridical and not doctrinal. However, although this may be his intention, one knows that there are very few laws in the Church which do not refer to, or are not founded on, the doctrine; even more so in the domain of sacramental law. This is especially true in matrimonial law when indissolubility of marriage is directly concerned.

In fact, for all intents and purposes, Pope Francis brought a juridical solution to a doctrinal problem. And this could be considered by some pastors and canonists as the beginning of a solution to the situation of Catholics who are divorced and civilly remarried. What happens to those few remaining couples whose marriage cannot be declared null even after the reform takes effect? Some Orthodox Churches have a solution: in virtue of the principle of οἰκονομία, understanding, forgiveness, charity, the bishop can grant a *constat* of divorce, allowing a new union which is not sacramental, since the first marriage was and remains indissoluble. Such a solution is not strictly juridical but doctrinal, since it is made in virtue of the capacity of mercy granted to the Church by its founder. The doctrine of the indissolubility of marriage is not nearly so tested in those Churches as it now seems to be in the Catholic Church following *Mitis Iudex*, even if, in principle, the marriage nullity process does not dissolve a marriage but rather investigates whether or not a valid marriage was present from the beginning, as the Pope said. Now, it will be much easier to find a ground, given the recourse to spurious presumptions of fact and the widened scope for arbitrary, unappealable decisions.

Presumptions of Fact and Arbitrary Decisions
An apostolic letter in the form of motu proprio is a legislative text which, by its very nature is the object of interpretation, as is any law. Usually,

a motu proprio consists of an introduction which is doctrinal, exposing some principles on which the second part, which is normative, will rest. The present motu proprio is one of a kind, with a doctrinal introduction, together with some "fundamental criteria which have governed the work of reform" followed, as usual, by the normative part derogating or abrogating some canons of the Code of Canon Law and introducing some brand new ones. This corresponds to the usual format of a legislative text. What is unusual in this motu proprio is the addition, after the signature of the Pope, of a third part entitled: *Procedural rules for dealing with causes of nullity of marriage*. Given the content of the normative part, why was there such a need for clarification, and if there is a need, what is the force of this third, papally unsigned, section? It sounds rather like an instruction.

But, since it is an integral part of the motu proprio, it is also, necessarily, the object of interpretation as is any legislative text. Its twenty-one articles are potentially useful, though with some clear difficulties. Article 14 §1 of Title V—*The Briefer Matrimonial Process before the Bishop*—raises some serious questions. As far as we know, it is the first time that a legislative document gives examples to illustrate a procedure, in this case the briefer one. Moreover, it ends with the term "etc", which is not a very juridical one. It means that the door is opened to other examples, depending on "the circumstances of things and persons". The first two examples deserve to be commented on.

> a) The first one is "the defect of faith which can generate simulation of consent or error that determines the will." What does a "defect of faith" mean? Is it the same as a lack of faith? Or is it rather an imperfect faith? If so, what elements should be lacking to constitute a defect of faith? A defect of canonical form, like a lack of form, can be easily proven. But a defect of faith? Are there degrees in faith? If so, what degree will support or cause a ground of nullity? And since marriage is the only sacrament which needs two faithful who wish to do what the Church wants to do, it probably suffices that only one of the two parties showed a defect of faith at the moment of sharing their consent for their marriage to be declared null. Can there be merely illicit defects of faith, or are they all invalidating?
>
> We do not currently have a "fideo-meter" to assess the degree of faith needed to perform a sacramentally valid marriage. By

the very fact of petitioning for the nullity of his or her marriage, a Christian faithful is presumed to have a certain degree of faith; at least in the Church. Is such a degree of faith sufficient to have performed a sacramental marriage when he or she married in the Church? Moreover, according to the motu proprio, the "defect of faith" should generate simulation of consent or error that determines the will. One knows how difficult it is to prove a simulation of any essential aspect of marriage, especially its sacramentality. How many cases will come to rest on an invented presumption and inevitably lead to arbitrary decisions?

If it is difficult to determine the defect of faith of one of the Catholic faithful, what about the application of this criterion to Christian non Catholics, whose marriages are presumed valid and sacramental, who apply for a declaration of nullity when "it is necessary to establish the free state of at least one party before the Catholic Church"[4]? What object of their faith will have to be investigated? Or are they excluded from this criterion for the briefer process?

b) The second example concerns "a brief conjugal cohabitation." Once again, what does this mean? One month? Six months? Four years? Ten years? How brief should a conjugal life last to be considered as a circumstance which can allow the use of the briefer process? Would this not be the return to a presumption of fact which was used in the past and forbidden later by the Apostolic Signatura?

The other "circumstances of things and persons" mentioned in the same article 14 §1, together with the "etc" at the end of it, can be considered as the basis for presumptions of fact of different kinds and lead to accordingly arbitrary decisions. This second example cannot but remind us of the forty four so-called "El Paso Presumptions" of the nineteen-nineties, the use of which was forbidden by a decree of the Apostolic Signatura of December 13, 1995.[5] *Mitis Iudex* being, clearly, an object of interpretation like any

---

4. *Dignitas connubii*, art. 3, § 2

5. For the decree of December 13, 1995 of the Supreme Tribunal of the Apostolic Signatura, see *Roman Replies and CLSA Advisory Opinions 1996*, ed. Kevin W. Vann and James I. Donlon (Washington: CLSA, 1996) 34–39, and *Forum* 7 (1996) 15–20. The text is published in Latin

other legislative document, and intended to fit within the canonical tradition of the Church and not to strike out in a totally new legislative and jurisprudential direction, we can, and indeed must, reject the resurrection of these "presumptions" which have already been determined by jurisprudence to be against the interests of justice. Therefore, when implementing the briefer process, the El Paso Presumptions of fact must be avoided, as must any similar abuse of the "examples" of article 14 §1, and "etc".

If we were to do otherwise, we would have to seriously consider if we are passing from the presumption of validity of marriage of canon 1060 to the presumption of its invalidity in virtue of a number of different types of presumption of fact? The proper use of the briefer process would seems to beg urgent consideration of this question.

The *Processus Brevior*

Together with the elimination of the mandatory appeal of an affirmative sentence of first instance, the creation of a briefer process is undoubtedly the most significant change found in this motu proprio. It raises questions with regard to the safeguarding of the principle of the indissolubility of marriage and the seriousness of the process to reach an informed decision concerning the nullity of a marriage.

It is to be noted that a few weeks before the end of the *vacatio legis*, six questions of "clarification"—not of interpretation—were addressed by the Pontifical Council for Legislative Texts, the majority about the *processus brevior*. Presumably private, even if they "can be made known among other canonists", the responses to those questions were issued incredibly quickly after being received by the Council, and without the papal approval as is usual when there is an authentic interpretation. We can compare this to the first response to a question asked to the Council on the whole revised Code which was issued on June 26, 1984, that is about one year and a half after its promulgation and about seven months after it came into force. Needless to say that those questions and others to come

---

with an English translation. For a commentary, see Charles J. Scicluna, "The Use of 'Lists of Presumptions of Fact' in Marriage Nullity Cases," *Forum* 7 (1996) 45–67.

would have probably not been raised had a previous draft been sent to conferences of bishops and institutes of canon law, as happened with the project to review Book VI of the Code on Penal Law, and of which we are still expecting a second draft. *Mitis Iudex* looks like an improvised document.

Two of the six questions of clarification concern the necessary participation of the respondent as a preliminary condition to initiate the brief process.[6] In the response of the Council, the consent of both parties to initiate this procedure is even presented as a condition *sine qua non* to hear a case with the briefer process. Moreover, the letter of the Council says: "This explicit consent is foremost necessary because the brief process is an exception to the general norm." Logically, the second response of the Council mentions that "If the whereabouts of a respondent are unknown the case cannot be accepted for the *processus brevior*."

One must not forget that the consent of the respondent is not the only condition for a bishop to apply the briefer procedure. The second condition *sine qua non* is: "whenever circumstances of things and persons recur, with substantiating testimonies and records, which do not demand a more accurate inquiry or investigation, and which render the nullity manifest" (c. 1683, 2°).

The major problem here is: since the process has not begun yet, where do the "substantiating testimonies and records" come from? From the petition? This would surely be problematic, to say the least, since they are the most interested in the declaration of nullity of their marriage. We also read: "In issuing the citation in accordance with canon 1685, the parties are informed that, if possible, they are to make available, at least three days prior to the session for the instruction of the case, those specific points of the matter upon which the parties or the witnesses are to be questioned, unless they are attached to the *libellus*." (art. 17). What if this is not possible? It would seem, then, that the judicial vicar would be tempted to construct some kind of presumption from the examples mentioned in article 14 §1 to still use the briefer process.

---

6. Pontifical Council for Legislative Texts, Letter on the Conversion of a Formal Canonical Proces into a *processus brevior* and Consent of the Petitioner and the Respondent for the Use of the *processus brevior*, October 1, 2015 (Prot. N. 15138/2015): *The Jurist* 75 (2015) 663–664 and this volume, 367–368, and Pontifical Council for Legislative Text, Letter on the Consent of the Petitioner and the Respondent for the Use of the *processus brevior*, October 1, 2015 (Prot. N. 15139/2015): *The Jurist* 75 (2015) 665 and this volume, 369.

The instruction has not begun yet when the judicial vicar, after determining that "circumstances of things and persons recur," as in the presumptions of article 14 §1, decides that "the case may be treated with the briefer process" (art. 15). *Causa audita est?* As a matter of fact, one can rather say that some marriages will be presumed invalid and so, the presumption of canon 1060 will be overturned and it is its validity that will have to be proven. Following this inversion of justice and doctrine, one understands why there would be no need for a judge nor even a canonist to be named as an instructor nor as an assessor. It now gives the appearance of a truly administrative procedure until the bishop receives the acts to issue the sentence after consulting "with the instructor and the assessor, and having considered the observations of the defender of the bond and, if there are any, the defense briefs of the parties" (can. 1687 §1).

"The diocesan bishop himself is competent to judge the cases of the nullity of marriage with the briefer process" (can. 1683) when the conditions exposed above are present. As in the 1917 Code (see can. 1572), the 1983 Code states that "in each diocese and for all cases which are not expressly excepted in law, the judge of first instance is the diocesan Bishop" (can. 1419 §1). The newness of canon 1683 is that now, the diocesan bishop is to exercise what he is in virtue of his episcopal consecration when he received "together with the office of sanctifying, the offices also of teaching and of ruling" (can. 375 §2), the last one consisting of the threefold power: legislative, executive and judicial. As for his competence in canon law, before being elected as a bishop, he is presumed "to hold a doctorate or at least a licenciate in Sacred Scripture, theology or canon law [. . .] or at least be well versed in these disciplines" (can. 378 §1, 5°).

It is to be expected that the diocesan bishop will have to rely on the instructor and the assessor, who will not necessarily be canonists as mentioned above, or on the judicial vicar, who will not have necessarily been present during the instruction of the case as in most cases presently. It is also to be expected that even bishops who have a degree in canon law will not write the sentences themselves, even if art. 20 §1 makes it relatively easy in giving him the faculty to "determine the way in which to pronounce the sentence." Does this mean that he will not be obliged to follow the provisions of canon 1611 among others? We can presume that the means of notifying the parties is left to him as well. So, to what extent will the diocesan bishop of a large diocese with a huge number of cases not be simply rubber-stamping decisions presumed from the beginning? In any case, he will be responsible for the decisions made in his name. Could he delegate someone else to sign the sentence? According to the letter of the law, "the diocesan bishop himself is competent to judge" (can. 1683); and according to the spirit of the law, the diocesan bishop cannot grant a special mandate to the judicial vicar as he can grant a special mandate to his vicar general or his episcopal vicar in the context of executive power (see can. 134 §3).

Conclusion

One of the intents of Pope Francis in reforming the procedural law was not only to shorten the process, but that "the Church, as a mother, makes herself closer to her children who consider themselves separated" (introduction to the motu proprio). In virtue of the "principle of proximity between the parties and the judge" of artt. 7 §1 and 19, Pope Francis wishes the diocesan bishop to constitute for his diocese a tribunal for the cases of nullity of marriage (see can. 1673 §2). As a matter of fact, this is not really new, since the basic structure of the administration of justice in the Code is on the diocesan level. The Pope just wants to reestablish the traditional structure but "without prejudice to the faculty of the same bishop to approach another nearby diocesan or interdiocesan tribunal" (ibid).

Pope Francis knows that in many countries, "with the approval of the Apostolic See, several diocesan bishops" have taken advantage of the exception provided by can. 1423 "to establish for their dioceses a single tribunal of first instance in place of the diocesan tribunals mentioned in cann. 1419–1421." Now, the motu proprio advises the bishop to "withdraw from an interdiocesan tribunal constituted in accordance with can. 1423" (art. 8 §2). If a bishop decides to apply this article, he will have, in accord with the response of the Pontifical Council for Legislative Texts to the fourth question of clarification,[7] to observe the same procedure as the one he observed when he joined the interdiocesan tribunal and therefore request the approval of the Signatura.

7. Pontifical Council for Legislative Texts, Letter on the motu proprio *Qua cura* and Regional Tribunals in Italy, October 13, 2015 (Prot. N. 15157/2015): *The Jurist* 75 (2015) 667–668 and this volume, 371–372.

However, considering the availability of competent personnel and financial means in some dioceses, the reestablishment of a tribunal on the diocesan level could be problematic for many dioceses, at least on a short term period or by the end of the *vacatio legis* on December 8, 2015. To see the truth of this, we need only think of the appointment of a Judicial Vicar who must be a priest (see can. 1420 §4) or a sole judge who must be a cleric (see can. 1673 §4). At least, the motu proprio allows for more than one lay judge to be members of a collegiate tribunal (see can. 1673 §3).

The reorganization of tribunals will, most probably, need much more time in some dioceses which have been members of an interdiocesan tribunal for decades. In Canada, certain dioceses, members of such tribunals, undertake the instruction of the case and then send the file to the see of the interdiocesan tribunal for the decision. That work is usually done by the chancellor who may, or may not, be a canonist, or a layman or woman who does not, and cannot, act as a sole judge. Some other dioceses function like branches of the interdiocesan tribunal; that is to say, they have the necessary competent personnel to deal with a case from the reception of the petition until the sentence inclusively. As a matter of fact, those tribunals are already functioning as if they were proper to the diocese. The head of the branch is Assistant-Judicial Vicar of the Judicial Vicar of the interdiocesan tribunal.

Finally, the question raised at the beginning of this short study will most probably remain unanswered: why did Pope Francis make such an important decision without a formal consultation of those immediately interested—bishops as active judges and canonists as ministers of tribunals—beyond the members of a special and relatively small committee with little or no recent experience of first instance practice? What was the benefit of such haste? Moreover, why did he make those changes before the ordinary assembly of the Synod of Bishops while the topic was still in the *Instrumentum laboris* of this gathering?

ABSTRACT

The promulgation of the motu proprio Mitis iudex *has not only changed the procedural laws to process matrimonial nullity cases, but has left canon lawyers with a number of unanswered questions. In this article, Msgr. Roch*

Pagé reflects on some of the aspects of Mitis iudex *and offers very helpful insights. He also touches upon the now famous article 14 of the procedural norms and argues that it cannot resurrect the so-called El Paso Presumptions, explicitly forbidden by decree of the Apostolic Signatura.*

PONTIFICAL COUNCIL
FOR LEGISLATIVE TEXTS

Letters Clarifying Some Unclear Points of the motu proprio *Mitis Iudex Dominus Iesus**

1. Conversion of a Formal Canonical Proces into a *processor brevior* and Consent of the Petitioner and the Respondent for the Use of the *processus brevior*

Prot. N. 15138/2015

1st October 2015

Dear Msgr.,

responding to your letter of 8th September with which you asked for two clarifications regarding the Motu Proprio *Mitis Iudex*, we observe the following:

The question about the conversion of a formal canonical process regarding the declaration of nullity of a marriage to the *processus brevior* introduced by the aforementioned Motu Proprio: If a process has begun in a formal way, there is—in a similar way as the passage from a formal process to the request of a dispensation *super rato* (cf. new canon 1678 §4)—the

---

* The letters were published with the permission of the Pontifical Council for Legislative Texts. The letters that were not in English but in Italian were translated into English; this English translation was subsequently reviewed and approved by the Pontifical Council for Legislative Texts.

possibility to suspend the formal process and ask the parties for their consent to continue the instruction under the rules of the brief process.

The new canon 1683 and Art. 15 of the procedural norms make clear that the consent of the petitioner and the respondent (whether given by a joint signature of the parties or by other means) is a preliminary condition to initiate the brief process. The consent of both parties required to initiate this procedure is a condition *sine qua non*. This explicit consent is foremost necessary because the brief process is an exception to the general norm.

If the whereabouts of a respondent are unknown, the case cannot be accepted for the *processus brevior*. While the legislator formulated a presumption regarding the disposition of the respondent in art. 11 §2 of the procedural norms, this presumption applies only to the ordinary process and not to the brief process. Though the consent of the respondent can be given by several means, those means must however guarantee publicly and unequivocally his or her will, also for the protection of the judge and the parties. Otherwise, the brief process cannot be introduced.

Hoping that this answer, which can be made known among other canonists will be helpful for your important work in the tribunal, I am

Yours sincerely *in Domino*,
✠ Francesco Card. Coccopalmerio
President

✠ Juan Ignacio Arrieta
Secretary

2. Consent of the Petitioner and the Respondent for the Use of the *processus brevior*

Prot. N. 15139/2015

1st October 2015

Dear Msgr.,

responding to your letter of 13th September regarding a clarification of the presuppositions of the shorter process, introduced by the Motu Proprio *Mitis Iudex* we observe the following: The brief process cannot be used, if the respondent remains silent, does not sign the petition or declare his consent.

The new canon 1683 and Art. 15 of the procedural norms make clear that the consent of the petitioner and the respondent (whether given by a joint signature of the parties or by other means) is a preliminary condition to initiate the brief process. The consent of both parties required to initiate this procedure is a condition *sine qua non*. This explicit consent is foremost necessary because the brief process is an exception to the general norm.

While the legislator formulated a presumption regarding the disposition of the respondent in art. 11 §2 of the procedural norms, this presumption applies only to the ordinary process and not to the brief process. Though the consent of the respondent can be given by several means, those means must however guarantee publicly and unequivocally his or her will, also for the protection of the judge and the parties. Otherwise, the brief process cannot be introduced.

Hoping that this answer, which can be made known among other canonists will be helpful for your important work in the tribunal, I am

Yours sincerely *in Domino*,
✠ Francesco Card. Coccopalmerio
President

✠ Juan Ignacio Arrieta
Secretary

3. Meaning of Senior Suffragan Bishop

Prot. N. 15155/2015[1]

13 October 2015

Your Eminence,

by letter of 17 September, which arrived here on the 12 of this month, you asked this Pontifical Council for an opinion about the new wording of can. 1687 §3, contained in the Motu Proprio *Mitis Iudex* on the reform of the procedure for the causes for the declaration of nullity of marriage. More precisely, you asked if the appeal against a sentence of the Metropolitan Bishop which—according to said canon—"*datur ad antiquiorem suffraganeum*" must be made to the oldest bishop of the metropolitan province or to the bishop who is most senior in episcopal promotion.

The CIC mentions the *suffraganeus antiquior* also in canons 421 §2, 425 §3 and 501 §3, referring to the additional duties he has to carry out in determined and more rare cases, however always adding that it is the Bishop *promotione antiquior*. This reference to promotion, namely to the appointment of the Bishop, is missing in the *motu proprio* of 8 September.

On the other hand, given that the appeal against the sentence of the Metropolitan ex can. 1687 §3 could occur with a certain regularity, legal security when conducting processes requires that the recipient of the appeal be stable and not subject to continuous changes. The stability of the judge of second instance is, in fact, a principle guaranteed by the general norms on processes (cf. can. 1438 CIC, in particular §2). Therefore, it must be deduced that the suffragan Bishop to whom the appeal is directed is not the oldest in age or promotion, but rather the Bishop of the oldest see of the province.

Hoping to have given a response that could be useful for the correct application of the motu proprio *Mitis Iudex*, I take gratefully advantage of

---

1. The text was translated from Italian into English by Prof. Kurt Martens. The English translation was subsequently reviewed and approved by the Pontifical Council for Legislative Texts.

the circumstances to express my feelings of profound esteem, and I am of Your Eminence most devoted *in Domino*,

☖ Francesco Card. Coccopalmerio
President

☖ Juan Ignacio Arrieta
Secretary

4. Motu proprio *Qua cura* and Regional Tribunals in Italy

Prot. N. 15157/2015[2]

Vatican City 13 October 2015

Dear Monsignor,

because of the office you hold, you have asked the Pontifical Council for Legislative Texts clarification about the application of art. 8 §2 of the "Procedural norms for dealing with causes of matrimonial nullity" (RP), promulgated by the motu proprio *Mitis Iudex Dominus Iesus*, of 8 September 2015, in relation to what was established by Pope Pius XI with the motu proprio *Qua cura*, of 8 December 1938, AAS 30 (1938) 410–413.

As you know, with the motu proprio *Qua cura*, Pope Pius XI, for each of the so-called conciliar or ecclesiastical Regions in which the Italian territory had previously been divided, established: *"circumscriptionem unicam unumque habebit regionale tribunal quoad tractationem et decisionem causarum de nullitate matrimoniorum"* (n. I, p. 412), and added other norms concerning the related instances for appeal and the forms to integrate the composition of such tribunals. The norm represented a special papal

---

2. The text was translated from Italian into English by Prof. Kurt Martens. The English translation was subsequently reviewed and approved by the Pontifical Council for Legislative Texts.

arrangement given for Italy because of its peculiar diocesan structure and following the organization previously established for the celebration of regional Councils provided for by can. 283 of the 1917 *Codex* (cfr. *Sacra Congregatio Consistorialis, Decretum Pro celebratione conciliorum et appellationibus in regionibus Italiae*, of 15 February 1919, *AAS* 9 [1919] 72–74; Idem, *Lettera circolare all'episcopato italiano in esecuzione del decreto "Pro conciliorum celebratione in regionibus Italiae del 15 febbraio 1919"*, of 22 March 1919, *AAS* 9 [1919] 175–177). Said organization has then taken the form of the current ecclesiastical Regions provided by the Code, to which the Congregation for Bishops gave canonical juridic personality in the sense of can. 433 §2 CIC, by Decree of 4 November 1994, *AAS* 87 (1995) 369–391.

With regard to the legal sources to be considered in the present situation, can. 20 CIC, substantially following can. 22 *Codex* 1917, establishes that *"lex universalis minime derogat iuri particulari aut speciali, nisi aliud in iure express caveatur"*. Consequently, the aforementioned art. 8 §2 RP, which is a universal norm, would derogate from the motu proprio *Qua cura*, which is a particular pontifical norm for Italy, only if an explicit derogation would have been given by the Supreme Legislator, something that did not happen.

Therefore, the provisions of the motu proprio *Qua cura* in force so far, on the basis of which the Italian episcopate adopted other norms, including of an economic nature, must retain their full force. Thus, their Excellencies the Bishops who eventually thought of having to withdraw from the regional Tribunals must obtain the relative "dispensation" from the general norm from the Holy See, which is, according to art. 124 of the apostolic constitution *Pastor Bonus* of 28 June 1988, *AAS* 80 (1988) 841–930, the competence of the Tribunal of the Apostolic Signatura. It pertains to the same Supreme Tribunal to approve in such cases the tribunal of second instance chosen by the Bishop (can. 1438, 2° CIC).

Wishing that this present answer could be of use for the correct application of the motu proprio *Mitis Iudex Dominus Iesus*, I greet you with vivid cordiality.

✠ Francesco Card. Coccopalmerio
President

✠ Juan Ignacio Arrieta
Secretary

5. Force of the Authentic Interpretation of Canon 1686

Prot. N. 15182/2015[3]

Vatican City 18 November 2015

Your Excellency,

with the present letter I reply to your letter with Prot. N. 2774/8/15 of 28 October of this year, with which you have asked this Pontifical Council to interpret can. 1688 of the m.p. *Mitis Iudex Dominus Iesus* and to clarify if the authentic interpretation of can. 1686 by the Pontifical Council for Legislative Texts [*AAS* LXXVI (1984) 746–747] and the answer of the Apostolic Signatura of 3 January 2007 [*Periodica* 97 (2008) 45–46] still remain in force.

After careful consideration of the abovementioned questions, I hasten to give you the following opinion.

The discipline of the new can. 1688 of the m.p. *Mitis Iudex Dominus Iesus* does not make significant changes to what was stated in the former can. 1686 CIC, therefore, it does not seem necessary to make any interpretation.

As a result, the elements upon which the authentic interpretation of can. 1686 by the Pontifical Council for Legislative Texts and the subsequent answer of the Apostolic Signatura that had said interpretation as source were based, seem not to have been changed.

Hoping to have given a useful response, I take this opportunity to confirm my feelings of kind regard,

and I am of Your Excellency most devoted *in Domino*,

✠ Francesco Card. Coccopalmerio
President

✠ Juan Ignacio Arrieta
Secretary

---

3. The text was translated from Italian into English by Prof. Kurt Martens. The English translation was subsequently reviewed and approved by the Pontifical Council for Legislative Texts.

6. About the Application of the Motu proprio *Mitis Iudex Dominus Iesus*

Prot. N. 15201/2015[4]

Vatican City 18 November 2015

Your Excellency,

I refer to your recent question Prot. 30/PO/2015, about the application of the motu proprio *Mitis Iudex Dominus Iesus* in your diocese.

With regard to your question, even if the diocesan Bishop has no intention to withdraw from the Regional Tribunal, in the case of Italy, he will still have to work, in a prescriptive way, to be able to accept in the diocese the causes for which is established the shorter procedure according to the new cann. 1683–1687 CIC. There is, in this regard however, no need to establish his own "tribunal" only for the causes to be handled according to the shorter procedure, because it will be himself, the diocesan Bishop, to be in such a case the "single judge" of the same causes.

He must, however, make use of two offices that must give the diocesan Bishop the help he needs to be able to judge: the judicial vicar, whose appointment in a stable way is also prescriptive (can. 1420 §1 CIC) and who will have to accept the petition which introduces the cause (art. 15–16 Procedural Norms), and the defender of the bond (cann. 1435–1436 CIC), who must necessarily act in the process. In addition, he must be able to have at his disposal the instructors and assessors, mentioned in the new can. 1685 CIC, which, however, must not necessarily be set up as stable offices.

In other words, if the choice of the diocesan Bishop is the one you mentioned, it is not necessary to establish your own "tribunal", since there will be no college to judge, but only the Bishop on the basis of the work prepared by his collaborators.

In this new situation, the diocesan Bishop must refer to the Regional Tribunal for the causes that follow the ordinary process, as has been done

---

4. The text was translated from Italian into English by Prof. Kurt Martens. The English translation was subsequently reviewed and approved by the Pontifical Council for Legislative Texts.

thus far, and to himself and his proper collaborators in the diocese (judicial vicar, defender of the bond, etc.) when instead the new shorter procedure is to be followed.

From the point of view of the faithful, they can turn to the judicial vicar of the diocese, if they believe their case can follow the shorter process, or directly address the President of the Regional Tribunal, if the case is more complex or lacks the concordance of the two wills as required by the new can. 1683, 1° CIC. Both the judicial vicar of the diocese and the President of the Regional Tribunal must assess, on the basis of the petition and in accordance with the norms given in the recent motu proprio, whether to accept the request or to direct the parties, in the first case, to the ordinary process or, in the second hypothesis, to the shorter procedure, in conformity with what is indicated in art. 15 of the Procedural Norms.

Hoping that I have been of assistance for the application in your diocese of the recent norms, I take gratefully advantage of the circumstances to express me of Your Excellency most devoted

In Domino,

✠ Francesco Card. Coccopalmerio
President

✠ Juan Ignacio Arrieta
Secretary

7. Two Questions about the Application of the Motu Proprio *Mitis et misericors Iesus*

Prot. N. 15170/2015

Vatican City, 25 November 2015

Reverend Father,

with the present I respond to your letter of 20 October of this year, with which you asked for the opinion of this Pontifical Council on two questions about the new motu proprio *Mitis et misericors Iesus*.

Paragraph 2 of can. 1372 CCEO, hitherto in force, establishes that the premarital inquiry mentioned in can. 748 is sufficient to demonstrate the free state of the person who was to observe the form of celebrating matrimony prescribed by the law, but who had attempted marriage before a civil official or a non-Catholic minister.

The new can. 1374 of the motu proprio *Mitis et misericors Iesus*, instead, makes no reference to the content of said paragraph 2 of can. 1372 and mentions the cited case among the causes that constitute a defect of the legitimate form, requiring for all a declaration of nullity of the marriage by judgment in the documentary process.

As a consequence, with the entry into force of the motu proprio *Mitis et misericors Iesus*, the premarital inquiry will no longer be sufficient to demonstrate the free state of those who have attempted marriage in the aforementioned circumstances, but the nullity of the previous marriage must be declared while observing the norms of the new can. 1374 on the documentary process.

The second question you presented emerges from a conflict between can. 1087 §2 CCEO and the new can. 1359 §3. Can. 1087 §2 is a norm concerning judgments in general, while the new can. 1359 §3 of the motu proprio *Mitis et misericors Iesus* is incorporated in the part on the special processes, and regards only matrimonial processes.

Although the text of paragraph 3 of the new can. 1359 is not explicit in indicating whether, for the appointment as judges *alii christifideles*, the permission mentioned in can. 1087 §2 CCEO is needed, the overall logic of the provisions of the motu proprio on the broad power that is given to the eparchial Bishop, one must conclude that in the processes of marriage nullity the eparchial Bishop can appoint judges that are other Christian faithful without the previous permission of the authority indicated in can. 1087 §2 CCEO.

In the hope to have given you a useful opinion, I take this opportunity to confirm me,

yours sincerely in the Lord

✠ Francesco Card. Coccopalmerio
President

✠ Juan Ignacio Arrieta
Secretary

8. Further Appeal to the Third Instance Tribunal

Prot. N. 15264/2015

12 January 2016

Your Eminence,

by letter of 17 December 2015, you have asked this Pontifical Council for an opinion on the question if, in a cause of the declaration of the nullity of a marriage, the petitioner after an affirmative decision in first instance and a negative decision in second instance can appeal to the tribunal of third instance, namely to the Roman Rota. The matter has been examined by the Dicastery with the assistance of its own experts.

The motu proprio *Mitis iudex* on the reform of the process for the causes of declaration of the nullity of a marriage has confirmed the prior discipline (cf. can. 1683 §3 CIC) according to which the Roman Rota remains the tribunal of third instance for the entire Church (cf. also can. 1444 §1, 2, CIC). When it is deemed appropriate, however, there is the possibility for the Bishop to ask the Apostolic Signatura for the so-called Pontifical

Commission, that is the entrustment of the case in third instance to a tribunal other than the Roman Rota for a just and reasonable cause (cf. art. 124 a.c. *Pastor bonus* and art. 115 *Lex propria* if the Apostolic Signatura). This possibility is now supported by the criteria that inspire the reform in question of the matrimonial process in favor of the proximity of the tribunals and the greater involvement of the Bishop in judicial activities.

Hoping to have given an answer which will be useful for the correct application of the motu proprio *Mitis iudex*, I gladly take this opportunity to express the sentiments of my highest esteem,

Yours sincerely *in Domino*,

Francesco Card. Coccopalmerio
President

✠ Juan Ignacio Arrieta

9. Some Questions about the Constitution of the Diocesan Tribunal

Prot. N. 15291/2016

Vatican City, 12 February 2016

Reverend Lord,

with the present I respond to your mail of 16 January of this year, with which you have asked the opinion of this Pontifical Council about a few questions on the constitution of the diocesan tribunal.

After a careful examination of the abovementioned questions, I hasten to inform you as follows.

With regard to the first question about how to proceed to erect a diocesan tribunal, the motu proprio *Mitis Iudes Dominus Iesus* establishes in art. 8 §2 the right of the diocesan Bishop to withdraw freely from an interdiocesan tribunal constituted according to the norm of can. 1423 CIC and in can. 1673 §2 the right/duty of the diocesan Bishop to establish, if possible, his own diocesan tribunal for cases of nullity of marriage, without the need for any approval by the Apostolic Signatura.

With regard to the second question about the appointment of the judicial vicar, can. 1420 §1 CIC allows for the possibility for the diocesan Bishop to appoint the same vicar general as judicial vicar in cases where "the small size of the diocese or the small number of cases suggests otherwise."

Relative to the third question about the personnel of the tribunal, the law establishes that the following must be appointed: the judicial vicar, who must be a priest of at least 30 years, of unimpaired reputation, doctor or at least licentiate in canon law (cf. can; 1420 §§1 and 4 CIC); judges, who are clerics or laity, of unimpaired reputation and doctors or at least licentiates in canon law (cf. can. 1421 CIC); the promotor of justice, who is a cleric or lay person, of unimpaired reputation, doctor or at least licentiate in canon law, and proven in prudence and zeal for justice (cf. cann. 1432 and 1435 CIC); the notary, who must be a person of unimpaired reputation and above all suspicion (cf. cann; 483 and 1437 CIC); stable legal representatives, who will assume the office of advocates or procurators, who must have attained the age of majority and be of good reputation (cf. cann. 1483 and 1490 CIC), moreover, the advocate must be a Catholic and a doctor in canon law or otherwise truly expert.

In case one of the employees of the tribunal does not have the academic degrees required by law, it is possible to ask the Apostolic Signatura for a dispensation from the titles (cf. Ap. Const. *Pastor Bonus*, art. 124, 2° and *Lex propria* of the Apostolic Signatura, art. 35, 2°).

In the hope to have given you a useful opinion, I take this opportunity to confirm me,

yours sincerely in the Lord

✠ Francesco Card. Coccopalmerio
President

✠ Juan Ignacio Arrieta
Secretary

10. Two Questions about the Procedural Norms and About Can. 1676 § of the Motu Proprio *Mitis Iudex Dominus Iesus*

Prot. N. 15363/2016

Vatican City, 8 April 2016

Illustrious Sir,

with the present I respond to your letter of 4 March of this year, with which you have asked for the opinion of this Pontifical Council on two questions about the motu proprio *Mitis Iudex Dominus Iesus (MIDI)*.

After a careful examination of the two questions, I hasten to inform you of the following opinion.

With regard to the question about the Procedural Norms, the answer to the first question is given by the motu proprio *MIDI* in the final part, where it is stated that the Procedural Norms are united with the same motu proprio because they are considered "necessary for the proper and accurate implementation of this new law, which must be observed diligently to foster the good of the faithful" and in the same text of the Procedural Norms in the introductive part, where one reads that "together with the detailed norms for the application of the matrimonial process, it has seemed opportune ... to offer some tools for the work of the tribunals to respond to the needs of the faithful who seek that the truth about the existence or non-existence of the bond of their failed marriage."

With regard to the second question about the *mémoire introductive d'instance*, the answer is given by the provision of the new can. 1676 §1, which does not provide for the notification of the respondent of the *mémoire introductive d'instance* with the libellus.

In the hope to have given you a useful opinion, I take this opportunity to confirm me,

yours sincerely in the Lord

✠ Francesco Card. Coccopalmerio
President

✠ Juan Ignacio Arrieta
Secretary

www.ingramcontent.com/pod-product-compliance
Lightning Source LLC
Chambersburg PA
CBHW032024290426
44110CB00012B/663